BRAND NFL

Brand NFL

MAKING AND SELLING AMERICA'S FAVORITE SPORT

MICHAEL ORIARD

WITH A NEW AFTERWORD
BY THE AUTHOR

THE UNIVERSITY OF
NORTH CAROLINA PRESS
Chapel Hill

This book was published with the assistance of the Thornton H. Brooks Fund of the University of North Carolina Press.

Set in Scala and Franklin Gothic types by Keystone Typesetting, Inc.
Manufactured in the United States of America

The paper in this book meets the guidelines for permanence and durability of the Committee on Production Guidelines for Book Longevity of the Council on Library Resources.

The University of North Carolina Press has been a member of the Green Press Initiative since 2003.

The Library of Congress has cataloged the original edition of this book as follows:
Oriard, Michael, 1948–
Brand NFL : making and selling America's favorite sport / Michael Oriard.
    p. cm.
Includes bibliographical references and index.
1. Football—United States—Marketing. 2. Football—United States—Management. 3. National Football League. I. Title.
GV954.3.O75 2007
796.332'64—dc22   2007008867

ISBN 978-0-8078-7156-0 (pbk.: alk. paper)
ISBN 978-0-8078-3142-7 (cloth: alk. paper)(2007)

14 13 12 11 10   5 4 3 2 1

For Julie, Colin, and Alan

CONTENTS

Introduction 1

1 The Creation of the Modern NFL in the 1960s 10

2 No Freedom, No Football 55

3 The End of the Rozelle Era 95

4 The New NFL 140

5 Football as Product 175

6 Football in Black and White 210

Conclusion 250

Afterword 258

Notes 265

Acknowledgments 315

Index 317

TABLES

1. Franchise Values and Revenues, 1991–2006 154

2. Television Contracts, 1987–2006 169

BRAND NFL

INTRODUCTION

> Pro football is a continuation of war by other means.
> —Thomas B. Morgan, *Esquire*, October 1965 (after Von Clausewitz)

> It ain't even war, it's just show business.
> But show business is a kind of war.
> —Peter Gent, *Esquire*, September 1980

Before it became a "brand," the National Football League had an image. In fact, for most of its first half-century, the NFL had a serious image problem. Football in the United States developed over the final third of the nineteenth century as an intercollegiate game, and colleges created the standard against which other forms of football would be measured into the 1950s. The professional version developed haphazardly in midwestern mill towns for two decades before it was organized in 1920 into what became the National Football League, with franchises in places like Akron and Dayton, Ohio; Hammond, Indiana; and Rock Island, Illinois, as well as Chicago and later New York City. After several years of small successes and many failures, with the number of teams fluctuating between 8 and 22, the NFL was reorganized in 1933 into its modern form, a league with a fixed number of franchises (initially ten), all located in major metropolitan areas (with the sole exception of Green Bay, Wisconsin).

From the beginning, professional football struggled against the perception that it lacked the college game's pageantry and spectacle, and that professional football players were at once bloodthirsty and bloodless, brutal on the field but lacking in "die-for-dear-old-Rutgers" spirit. Improvement in play, more attention from the national media, increasing appeal for working-class men with no relationship to any college, and the circumstance that major college teams tended to be located in smaller towns—leaving major cities for the professionals—led to slow but steady growth in the NFL's popularity over the 1930s and 1940s. But for most sports fans, pro football still seemed a ragtag affair closer to the grunt-and-groan pro wrestling circuit than to big-time college football, an employment opportunity for ex-collegians with no better prospects in the legitimate job market.

Professional football's image changed in the 1950s. Writers in popular magazines stopped apologizing for the pros' failings and began celebrating those same qualities as virtues. Lacking a collegiate aura, pro football belonged to everyone, not just those with college ties. Lacking pageantry and spectacle, pro football was a highly skilled game for savvy fans without the distractions of bands and cheerleaders. Lacking rah-rah spirit, the pros were true professionals, who played the game at the highest level of technical and physical skill. And being brutal, but in a manner governed by rules, pro football provided an antidote to a civilization grown soft through prosperity and threatened by a Soviet enemy ready to exploit every American weakness. Football's "sanctioned savagery," as one particularly insightful commentator put it, offered "an escape from or a substitute for the boredom of work, the dullness of reality."[1]

These ideas, and most significantly that last point, emerged from a number of remarkable articles about pro football in magazines such as *Life*, *Look*, *Time*, *Esquire*, and the *Saturday Evening Post* throughout the 1950s and into the 1960s, and from TV specials such as Walter Cronkite's 1960 documentary for CBS, *The Violent World of Sam Huff*, and William Friedkin's *Mayhem on a Sunday Afternoon* for ABC in 1965.[2] Violent defense became exciting. The heroes of the moment were not glamorous quarterbacks and graceful receivers but crushing linebackers like Sam Huff, Joe Schmidt, and Ray Nitschke. Even the quarterbacks of the late 1950s and early 1960s were mostly hard-hat guys: Johnny Unitas, with his sandlot background and high-top shoes; paunchy, hard-drinking Bobby Layne; and Y. A. Tittle, kneeling on the turf with blood trickling from a gash in his bald head in a famous photograph.

In this climate the modern NFL was born. On December 28, 1958, the Baltimore Colts beat the New York Giants in sudden-death overtime in the NFL championship game, as 30 million Americans watched, enthralled, on television. TV was the key. College football had thrived before television, because every state and region had its own teams to follow. As the new medium fully arrived over the 1950s (fewer than 10 million TV sets were in American homes in 1950, more than 67 million by 1959), the National Collegiate Athletic Association fought it to protect gate receipts, but pro football embraced it to expand its fan base. (The NFL protected gate receipts by "blacking out"—making TV broadcasts unavailable to a team's local stations—home games that had not been sold out.) Commissioner Bert Bell understood the power and economic potential of television, but during his tenure individual NFL clubs signed their own TV contracts and created their own regional networks. The 1958 championship was the first NFL game televised to a national audience. Bell's successor, Pete Rozelle, understood television's promise even better. Rozelle is commonly recognized as the architect of the modern NFL, his defining act being the first national TV contract that he negotiated on behalf of all NFL clubs in 1962. The marriage of the National Football League to the television networks has been the most intimate and mutually enriching in American sports (and governed by the most ruthlessly negotiated prenuptial agreements that lawyers can devise).

Television, and the media more broadly, have an important place in the story that I tell in this book—not a chronicle of NFL seasons but an attempt to understand what pro football means to us today and how its meaning has changed or stayed the same since the 1960s. For this story I would choose a symbolic beginning several months after that overtime championship game in December 1958. On October 1, 1959, NFL Enterprises was created as a division of Roy Rogers Enterprises, the merchandising business of TV's "King of the Cowboys," with Rogers taking half of the royalties and the 12 NFL owners sharing the rest. The NFL's first product marketed under the new arrangement was team logo glassware, sold to Standard Oil Company to give away with gas fill-ups. Within a year, 45 manufacturers were producing 300 NFL items. Rogers's general manager, Larry Kent, came up with the original idea for the partnership with the NFL, but Rogers himself made the telling statement when a reporter asked how a TV cowboy got into the football marketing business: "Merchandising is merchandising," Rogers answered. "There's no difference, whether a store is selling a Roy Rogers revolver or a junior St. Louis Cardinal football outfit just like the pros wear."[3]

Double-R Bar brand or NFL brand, it did not matter to Rogers—or to Kent, who left Rogers for the NFL when Rozelle brought NFL Enterprises in-house and renamed it NFL Properties (NFLP) in 1963. NFLP would not produce significant profits until the late 1980s (its birth date in 1959 is only symbolically important), but in the 1990s it would become something like a nerve center for a "new NFL" broadly embracing the Roy Rogers principle that pro football was a product in the entertainment business, competing against not just baseball and basketball but also MTV, blockbuster movies, video games, and everything else vying for Americans' leisure time and loose dollars. How that happened and what that reorientation has meant for the place of NFL football in American life lie at the heart of the story I tell here.

This story is necessarily about money, lots of money. Professional football has always been about money—that is what made it "professional"—but in its early years the NFL was starved for money, and for its first half-century its fans had no reason to think very much about it. For those who scorned the NFL, money tainted the pros, making them mercenaries instead of loyal sons of their alma mater. This legacy haunted the NFL even after Americans embraced professional football as their favorite sport in the 1960s. Joe Namath's signing with the New York Jets for $427,000 right out of college marked him as someone special, but also as someone grotesquely overpaid. Over the following years, fans did not mind players quietly improving their salaries, but when they went on strike—as they did in 1974, 1982, and 1987—fans were outraged by their "greed." Exactly how much the owners made in profits was never very clear, and when they cried poor and worried publicly about rising costs and soaring salaries, fans did not have enough information to know whether to take their complaints seriously.

Only in recent times has the NFL been swimming in dollars, with salary caps and signing bonuses, club seats and luxury boxes, corporate branding and the cost of a commercial minute during the broadcast of the Super Bowl becoming part of our collective understanding of pro football's place in our world. The romanticizing of NFL players from the 1950s in recent years must derive in part from a sense that they were our neighbors, more like the rest of us than not, trudging off to football practice instead of the factory or office, but sharing the same worries about the mortgage and braces for the kids.[4] Today's stars belong to an alternate universe of wealth and celebrity, inhabited also by rock stars and Hollywood actors, where they are more dazzling but also more remote. All players now who survive four years in the NFL earn the right to be mercenaries, to play for the highest bidder instead of sticking with the team. Teams are not just local treasures but also municipal investments. Stadiums have become expensive theme parks as well as football arenas. On Sundays, they no longer accommodate the democratic masses but are divided into neighborhoods with escalating property values: the end zones and upper decks (already out of the price range of most fans), the club seats, and the "gated community" of luxury suites.

In 1964 *Fortune* magazine addressed a "breathtaking rise" in pro football revenues. That season, 14 NFL teams would collectively gross $18 million at the gate, on top of $16 million from television. (Then, as now, *Fortune* had to estimate many of its figures, because neither the owners nor the league wanted the public to know their bottom line. Later reporting put the TV contract at $14 million.) At $75,000 per minute, the NFL charged the highest advertising rates in daytime television. The average ticket price was about $4.50, and the average annual club payroll, about $1,115,000. A head coach and six assistants accounted for $125,000 of the payroll. Due to competition from the rival American Football League, total player salaries had soared to about $750,000 per club (around $18,000 per player), with a star quarterback earning $25,000 and Jim Brown and John Unitas reputed to make more than $50,000. Franchise profits of about $800,000 left $415,000 after taxes (except that owners could depreciate their players' contracts and write off what they owed the government). Some in the football business predicted that clubs could earn as much as $5 million in ten years. The Baltimore Colts franchise was worth around $9 million, and the New York Giants well over $10 million. Each week, more than 15 million homes tuned in to NFL football on television.[5]

For 2003 *Forbes* calculated gross revenue of $5.3 billion for 32 franchises. Over $2.5 billion of that came from television, or $80 million per club. The average head coach made $2.5 million; the average player made $1.2 million, with top stars making several times that much. A salary cap set total player salaries at $75 million per club. Ticket prices averaging $52.95 seemed almost an afterthought, pocket change from the premiums for club seats and luxury boxes leasing for tens, even hundreds of thousands of dollars. Nearly 140 million Americans watched some part of the Super Bowl that year, for which a thirty-second ad cost $2.1 million. The average franchise was worth $733 million, with the Washington Redskins topping $1 billion.[6]

With a dollar in 1964 equivalent to roughly six 2003 dollars, inflation does not quite account for the growth. What happened? And the more interesting question: how has all of that money affected the game and its meaning for those it touches? This book tries to answer those questions, particularly the more elusive second one.

The Watergate scandal taught us to "follow the money" in order to uncover the workings of influence and power. For the NFL, the sources are in plain sight: television, sponsorships, merchandise, stadium deals. The sums overwhelm comprehension, however. How many fans can truly grasp the consequences of the latest TV contracts for more than $3.7 billion a year, or the league's gross revenues in 2005 of $6.2 billion? These numbers are widely published but remain practically unreal. Moreover, the published figures on financial matters are constantly shifting, as reporters depend on whatever information is available to them.[a]

a. Jerry Jones, for example, was usually said to have bought the Dallas Cowboys for $140 million in 1989, but sometimes the figure cited was $170 million. Even on the occasions when the NFL was forced to "open its books" in court, the numbers did not always add up. During one of Al Davis's lawsuits, in 2001, NFL officials released figures showing that the Buffalo Bills had $7.8 million in annual stadium expenses, despite a lease that shifted all of the cost to the county; that the Dallas Cowboys earned $11.7 million

ESPN, the broadcast networks, *Sports Illustrated*, and the sports sections of daily newspapers provide most of our information about teams and players, but to understand the NFL over the past 15 years, the financial sections, along with publications such as *Financial World*, *Forbes*, and *Street & Smith's Sports-Business Journal*, have become essential reading. Even in the financial press, while the sheer magnitude of NFL billions has become central to its public image, the owners' actual profits remain a closely guarded secret. Owners and NFL executives still prefer to operate behind closed curtains like wizards of a football Oz, letting fans see only the games and personalities, not the financial dealing behind the scenes. My hope is not to expose the wizard but to understand the consequences of his wizardry. Following the money is what the NFL has been doing since the 1960s. My task, too, is to follow that money, not to see where it leads but to ponder how it might have changed the sport. And when the subject is the NFL's public image, what actually happens is less important than what the media reports as happening. Image and brand are about perception—what we think when we think about football. For understanding that, one must look to what we collectively have been watching and reading about football over the years.

My story, then, is about pro football's image and meaning, and about how money has affected them. Along the way, I attempt to lay out a fairly comprehensive history of the NFL's past half-century, taking into account its merger with the American Football League and the evolution of the Super Bowl, the development of NFL Films and ESPN, the roles of iconic figures from Vince Lombardi and Joe Namath in the 1960s to Deion Sanders in the 1990s, the eruption of drug scandals in the 1980s and domestic-violence scandals in the 1990s, the shifts in labor relations and racial attitudes throughout the entire period—always to weigh their impact on what football means to us, individually and collectively.

Finally, this economic and cultural history is also a personal story. I begin it in the 1960s, the decade when the modern NFL took shape and when pro

---

from 380 luxury suites in 1999 (when *Forbes* magazine calculated $31.9 million); that the Miami Dolphins earned just $1.9 million from 183 suites, which the club leased for between $55,000 and $155,000 in 1999 (at the lowest figure the total would exceed $10 million). Nonetheless, the available sources are adequate for the story I want to tell—not a certified accounting of football finances but a teasing out of the ways that financial growth has affected NFL football. Whether the Patriots sold for $80 million or $90 million in 1988 is not crucial to this story. What matters is the scale of difference between either figure and the franchise's estimated value of more than $500 million in 2000.

football's reign as the United States' number-one spectator sport commenced. In October 1965, the Louis Harris polling agency reported that, for the first time ever, professional football was more popular than Major League Baseball.[7] But this was also the era in which I myself played, after an almost fairytale experience at Notre Dame as a walk-on who became a starter and offensive captain, then was drafted by the Kansas City Chiefs in 1970. The 1960s for my purpose are the "long sixties" that ended with Richard Nixon's resignation on August 8, 1974—coincidentally, three days before the end of the first major NFL players' strike, which *not* coincidentally ended my own brief NFL career a month later.

An obvious personal interest meets a crucial event in NFL history in the 1974 strike and its long aftermath. My own football experience has also made me impatient with both mindless boosterism and the blanket judgments routinely passed on sports in general and football in particular. My Kansas City teammates were neither saints nor thugs but as richly varied representatives of humanity as any with whom I have worked before or since. For all the media scrutiny of players' lives in recent decades, we know less about them today than we did in the 1960s, when journalists still regarded their private lives as private. We know less because we think we know more. I do not presume to know what today's players are "really" like, but I do know that there are always human beings behind the media's images.

As I have followed football over the years since I played, I have also tended to be put off by celebrations of coaching "genius," as if the players were interchangeable and disposable parts to be manipulated by a masterful coach. I have marveled at films like Oliver Stone's *Any Given Sunday*, written and directed by Hollywood's most notorious antiestablishmentarian, who made his hero not the players ruining their bodies on the field but their old-school coach. As I followed the strikes in the 1980s from afar, I always understood that players drew the fans who made the owners rich; that the players, not the owners, risked crippling injury on every play only to become crippled in middle age anyway, even if they managed to avoid major injuries. Readers may occasionally find a former player's bias in the chapters that follow.

This is a book, then, about the image and meaning of NFL football, and about how money and marketing transformed the "modern NFL" of the 1960s into the "new NFL" of the 1990s, told partly from the perspective of a 1960s-era player. I entered the NFL in 1970, more or less on the cusp of Pete Rozelle's power as commissioner, and left at the end of the league's period of consolidation and the beginning of its period of internal fracturing. Following the strikes of 1974, 1982, and 1987, labor peace was not finally achieved until 1993. Al Davis won a major lawsuit against the NFL in 1982 and moved the Raiders from Oakland to Los Angeles, unleashing an upheaval among NFL franchises whose owners now could exploit their own free agency while still denying it to players. By 1989, when Rozelle retired, the NFL was hugely popular and making millions for its owners yet also appeared on the verge of implosion due to franchise instability, labor conflict, and a steady stream of player arrests for abusing drugs. Out of this chaos, instead, emerged a "new NFL," more profitable than ever, rooted in labor peace, league expansion, lucrative stadium deals, and marketing the "product" and "brand" of NFL football on an unprecedented scale. Rozelle, a PR man, was replaced by a corporate lawyer, Paul Tagliabue, who presided over what became the envy of every other professional sports organization.

It so happened that I was finishing a draft of this manuscript in March 2006 when Tagliabue announced his retirement, effective in July. Instantly and unexpectedly, my book now covered the two complete terms of the NFL's commissioners since 1960 (with the advantage of considerably more hindsight for assessing Rozelle's). Perhaps the book, too, can offer a vantage point from which to look toward the NFL's future under Tagliabue's successor, Roger Goodell.

As a player, I was neither particularly savvy about the workings of the NFL nor particularly enlightened about its past; but for 30-odd seasons since then I have been an interested observer, and for the past 15 years or so I have been writing about the meaning of American football and its history. I also tell this story, then, as a serious student of the game. As a cultural historian but also a former player, I have repeatedly wondered about the impact of the changes I observed in the present. Having played at a time when All-Pro linemen did not make much more than backups like myself, I have wondered what it felt like to be a left guard making $300,000 and playing alongside a left tackle making $6 million. Having grown up during the era of "The Game of the Week," I have pondered how football fandom has been altered by having sports on television 24/7, and NFL games televised not just throughout the day on Sunday but on Sunday nights, Monday nights, and occasional Thursday or Saturday nights, as well.

Having participated in the first major players' strike, I closely followed the subsequent strikes in 1982 and 1987, marveling as working-class fans again sided with plutocrat owners, watching with dismay each time another generation of NFL players failed to pull together. I watched Al Davis take the Oakland Raiders to Los Angeles and back to Oakland, the Colts move to Indianapolis, the Rams to St. Louis, the Oilers to Nashville; I watched city after city cough up public dollars to build gaudy stadiums to keep their teams from leaving, for owners to fill with luxury boxes and sell naming rights for millions of dollars; and I wondered, what does all of this mean for what players, coaches, league executives, owners, sportswriters, and sometimes even ordinary fans reverently invoke as "the game"?

Over the years I have learned a great deal about Americans' fascination with football since the 1880s. I now cannot help but wonder if football's hold over us has changed, or how it has changed, as money has washed over it. When the NFL becomes a "product" and "brand," is it different as a sport? This book is my attempt, if not to find definitive answers, at least to tease out what is at stake in that question.

THE CREATION OF THE MODERN NFL IN THE 1960S

Professional football became Americans' favorite spectator sport in the 1960s. It was a decade of great players (as is every decade): Johnny Unitas and Sonny Jurgensen, Lenny Moore and Gayle Sayers, Deacon Jones and Dick Butkus, John Mackey and Raymond Berry. Nearly the entire starting lineup of the Green Bay Packers—Bart Starr, Paul Hornung, Jim Taylor, Boyd Dowler, Max McGee, Jerry Kramer, Fuzzy Thurston, Jim Ringo, Forrest Gregg, Ron Kramer, Willie Davis, Henry Jordan, Ray Nitschke, Herb Adderley, Willie Wood—became household names. Without question, the greatest of them all was Jim Brown, one of the NFL's few truly transcendent players from any era. In just nine seasons Brown rushed for 12,312 yards, averaging 5.2 yards per carry and leading the league eight times. He was Rookie of the Year, then league MVP four times; he played in nine Pro Bowls and missed not a single game—then walked away after the 1965 season, at age 30, still in his prime but with nothing left to prove. Few stars in any sport have been so unfettered by their own stardom. Among other interests, Brown embraced his role as a black man in a barely integrated sport, as few African American professional athletes of his generation did, at a time when such actions provoked more anger and resentment than respect. On the field, Brown was an astonishing fusion of speed, power, and agility, but no one player, no matter how good, can guarantee championships in pro football. Brown and Cleveland were perennial runners-up,[a] winning just one title, in 1964, an interruption in the run of the Green Bay Packers through the 1960s.

a. In Brown's other eight seasons, Cleveland won two conference titles but lost the

Starr and Hornung notwithstanding, the Packers above all meant Vince Lombardi. No coach in NFL history so impressed his own personality on his team as did Lombardi with the Packers. In December 1962, when Lombardi appeared on the cover of *Time* magazine, he also became the first noncollegiate coach to transcend the narrow world of football's X's and O's to become a truly national figure. Over the 1960s, Lombardi emerged as the face and the spirit not just of the National Football League but also of a vanishing America under assault from civil rights and antiwar protestors, and a counterculture that celebrated everything "traditional" football feared and despised.

The counterculture prevailed, of course, absorbed into the middle-class mainstream, but the NFL did more than just survive the upheaval. It thrived, in part by absorbing its own countercultural force in the person of Joe Namath— as potent an icon of the NFL as it headed into the 1970s as Lombardi had been in the 1960s. Lombardi and Namath were the polar icons of the NFL's cultural transformation, but the master architect of the modern NFL, the man who laid the foundations on which all of this played out, was Pete Rozelle.

Pete

Alvin "Pete" Rozelle, as the press invariably identified him (with his actual middle name, Ray, sometimes inserted as well), was no one's first choice in early 1960 to succeed Bert Bell as commissioner after Bell died suddenly of a heart attack the previous October. On January 26 Rozelle was elected on the twenty-third ballot, breaking an impasse between an old guard of owners who wanted Austin Gunsel, the compliant interim commissioner, and the new blood who wanted Marshall Leahy, an attorney for the San Francisco 49ers. Gunsel and Leahy became footnotes in NFL history; Rozelle became the most influential commissioner in pro sports since baseball's Kennesaw Mountain Landis banned eight Chicago "Black Sox" in 1921. Rozelle had been the general manager of the Los Angeles Rams and, before that, the club's director of public relations. Early in his tenure as commissioner, he established the league's first PR department, and he hired as his top executives men with backgrounds in public relations or the newspaper business. Rozelle remained essentially a PR guy for nearly 30 years as commissioner, though with much steel and shrewdness beneath the "affable" demeanor repeatedly mentioned by sportswriters.[1]

---

championship, finished second four times, and third twice. In the "old days," of course, only conference champions had a shot at the title. "Wild cards" were for unserious poker players.

Rozelle's first official act—moving league offices the short distance from Philadelphia to Rockefeller Center in New York—had both actual and symbolic consequences. Through its alliances with Madison Avenue, Wall Street, and the TV networks in its new neighborhood, the NFL fully escaped its low-rent roots to become a Fifth Avenue sort of operation and the model for every major professional sports organization. The foundation for that model—what journalist David Harris has termed "League Think," the principle that clubs' individual interests were best served by sharing, not competing, financially—began with the first leaguewide network television contract negotiated by Rozelle. When the new commissioner was elected in 1960, the league's 14 clubs had individual television deals ranging from $75,000 for Green Bay to $175,000 for the New York Giants. In 1961 Rozelle persuaded the most powerful major-market owners—the Mara family in New York, George Halas in Chicago, and Dan Reeves in Los Angeles—that short-term sacrifice would pay long-term dividends. Sharing television revenue meant rough parity and financial stability throughout the league. More important, the new commissioner (following the example of the rival American Football League) understood that, because the NFL could never have franchises everywhere, viewers willing to turn on pro football every week in much of the country would have to be fans of the league, not just of the New York Giants or Los Angeles Rams. More than any other single factor, that first national TV contract made the NFL what it has become.[2]

There was only one hitch in this initial agreement: a cooperative television contract violated antitrust law. Rozelle's lobbying won congressional approval of the Sports Broadcasting Act in 1961 and secured the future of the NFL. This episode exemplifies two of the key ingredients in the spectacular success of the National Football League over the next several decades: the sealing of its marriage to television and the importance of the government (federal in this case but often local) as a powerful enabling, but non-profit-sharing, partner.

As the TV audience for NFL football grew over the 1960s, rights fees rose from $4.65 million a year in 1962–63 under the initial contract, to $14.1 million in 1964–65, $18.1 million in 1966–69, and $46.25 million in 1970—the first season of the now-combined NFL and American Football League. The sums now look paltry, compared to the multi-billion-dollar deals in recent years, but the $330,000 per club under the initial contract nearly doubled the Giants' $175,000 in 1960, and each new contract seemed at the time an extraordinary windfall that confirmed Rozelle's genius.[3]

Television was the cornerstone but also part of the broader foundation that Rozelle laid in the 1960s, which included NFL Films along with NFL Properties, merger with the rival American Football League, and creation of the Super Bowl. Rozelle established his reputation with the public and his power with the owners who paid his salary when he suspended Paul Hornung and Alex Karras for the 1963 season for betting on their own teams. Karras was just a cantankerous defensive tackle for the Detroit Lions, albeit an All-Pro, but the Green Bay Packers' Hornung was the NFL's Golden Boy, its leading scorer in 1960 and 1961 (his 176 points in 1960 in just 12 games remained an NFL record until 2006), league MVP in 1962, and the heart of its most glamorous team. Rozelle's action provoked controversy at the time—it was criticized for being either too harsh or too soft—and it has been second-guessed ever since. (Why suspend two players while ignoring the high-stakes betting of Baltimore Colts owner Carroll Rosenbloom?) But *Sports Illustrated*'s Tex Maule summed up the general response when he applauded Rozelle for taking a stand as a "strong commissioner" among the more typical "glorified secretaries" who supposedly ruled pro sports but were really just puppets of the owners. Following that 1963 season, chiefly on the basis of his "wise severity" in dealing with Hornung and Karras, *Sports Illustrated* named Rozelle its "Sportsman of the Year," the first nonathlete to receive the honor (and still the only nonathlete or noncoach).[4]

Though guilty, Karras and Hornung were also scapegoats for a larger problem among the Lions (Rozelle also fined five of Karras's teammates for betting on other games but not their own) and around the league.[b] By suspending them, Rozelle sent all NFL players a message.[5] He also sent a message to NFL fans that they could trust him to safeguard "the integrity of the game." Both potent and meaningless, that term is something like "love of

b. That players in the 1950s and 1960s routinely bet on games is widely acknowledged. That they shaved points is a more controversial claim, made most fully in a 1989 book, *Interference: How Organized Crime Influences Professional Football*, by a crime reporter named Dan Moldea. Moldea made allegations about point-shaving, based on dubious claims by a Detroit bookmaker. Most of *Interference* develops more sensationalistic (and even less credible) claims about NFL owners' relations with organized crime figures. As for Rosenbloom, the 1958 championship game was periodically haunted by a suspicion that the Colts went for a touchdown on third down in overtime, instead of kicking a chip-shot field goal, in order to cover the spread and save their owner's large bet—against the counterargument that the Colts had a certifiably lousy placekicker. Moldea claims that Rosenbloom won $1 million on that game (and lost $1 million on Super Bowl III). On the persistent rumor that Rosenbloom's drowning in 1979 was really a murder by underworld figures, Moldea concludes that his death was indeed accidental. There is too much information in *Interference* for none of it to be true, but also too much unsubstantiated conjecture that undermines the more credible assertions.

country" or "peace and justice." Who could oppose it? But what does it actually mean? For Rozelle, it seems to have meant a genuine desire that NFL football remain uncorrupted in reality but also a greater concern that it appear uncorrupted to the public. Ultimately for Rozelle, the quintessential PR man, reality and image were indistinguishable. In notes written on the occasion of his retirement in 1989, Rozelle remembered a lesson from a childhood church camp that had guided him as commissioner: "Character is what you are as a person and reputation is what people think of you. If you have a bad reputation you might as well have a bad character."[6] By the same reasoning, the game's actual integrity was its appearance of integrity. This was the creed of a PR man.

During this period, sociologists were writing about the decline of "character" into "personality," and of "inner-directed" individuals into "other-directed" ones. Rozelle's views about "character" and "reputation" might be taken as a case in point. My point, however, is not that Rozelle was superficial, but that he was right. Unlike other forms of popular entertainment, NFL football is *real*—the players actually do what they appear to be doing—yet at the same time it is a creation of the media, and it generates some of the most powerful fantasies in our culture. The actuality of football is the source of its cultural power, but media-made images of that reality are all that most fans know. Pete Rozelle understood this about football long before "spin" became the official language of the realm.

NFL Films and the Epic of Pro Football

In 1963, the same year that he suspended Hornung and Karras, Rozelle incorporated NFL Properties, and in 1964 he brought NFL Films in-house as "a promotional vehicle to glamorize the game and present it in its best light."[7] In relation to the later marketing of NFL football, Rozelle's initial steps seem small, and they were always predicated on the assumption that pro football itself, the game on the field, was the NFL's own best advertisement. But Rozelle's actions in 1963–64 laid the foundation on which the later more highly commercialized, less football-centered NFL would be grounded. NFL Properties remained a relatively small-scale enterprise until the 1980s, with profits so modest the league gave them to charity for the public relations benefit. (I will return to NFL Properties in Chapter 5.) NFL Films had a more immediate and enduring impact as pro football's troubadour and epic poet.

NFL Films' own story, more fairy tale than epic, is nearly as well known as its highlight reels. Once upon a time, an overcoat salesman named Ed Sabol received a 16-millimeter Bell & Howell movie camera for a wedding present and began shooting everything in sight, eventually including his son's prep-school football games. After many years of this, Sabol retired from the cloth-ing business because work felt like going to the dentist every day, and he began looking for ways to make money from his hobby. "Big Ed" was passion-ate about two things, sports and movies, and after watching the highlight film of the NFL's 1961 championship game, he decided that he could do better. Learning that the NFL had received $1,500 for the filming rights in 1961, Sabol submitted a bid to Pete Rozelle for twice that amount for the 1962 contest between Green Bay and New York. (As befits a creation myth, there are variants and apocrypha. *Sports Illustrated* in 1967 put the price at $12,500, and a $5,000 figure appeared in some later retellings, but $3,000 has be-come the more or less official version.) Despite his lack of experience (not to mention staff and equipment), and perhaps aided by Rozelle's four martinis at lunch, Sabol convinced the commissioner by telling him that he would shoot the game with eight cameras instead of four, from ground level as well as high in the stadium, and in slow motion as well as normal speed. In due course the game was played, in freezing temperatures in Green Bay that left cinematographers, cameras, and film frostbitten or frozen, but Sabol and his crew salvaged enough footage for a 28-minute film that Rozelle proclaimed the finest football movie he had ever seen. Sabol repeated his performance under better conditions the following year, making a few extra bucks by renting his films to Kiwanis Clubs and Boy Scout troops. He then persuaded Rozelle and the 14 NFL owners to purchase his company, Blair Productions (named after his daughter), for $20,000 per club ($12,000 in one version of the tale) and bring it in-house. NFL Films was born.[8]

Unlike some modern fairy tales, this one actually happened. And it has a long sequel. Ed Sabol conceived the basic idea to shoot football games like Hollywood movies. His son Steve transformed that vision into the distinctive look and sound of NFL Films. Steve grew up like his father, loving football and movies, then went to Colorado College, where he majored in art and was "a pretty average fullback" according to his roommate (*Sports Illustrated* elevated him retroactively to All-Conference). The next part of the story is always the same: father Ed calls son Steve and tells him, "I can see by your grades that all you've been doing for the past four years is playing football and going to the movies. So that makes you uniquely qualified for this assignment."[9] Steve comes home to work for his father, bringing with him an artist's sensibility and an athlete's passion for football.

In interviews over the years, the younger Sabol has consistently invoked the same handful of painters, filmmakers, and classic film moments that shaped his own crafting of the NFL Films style. For tight close-ups: the impressionist Paul Cézanne taught him that "all art is selected detail," and in the 1946 film *Duel in the Sun*, shots of hands digging into rock and sweat pouring from faces captured the struggle of Gregory Peck and Jennifer Jones as they claw their way up a hill. For multiple camera angles: Picasso painted a woman's figure from several angles simultaneously. For use of light and shadow: Renaissance painters used chiaroscuro "to heighten certain dramatic effects." For low-angle shots, with sky and clouds in the background: Leni Riefenstahl, in her classic film of the 1936 Olympics, "used the sky in a way that increased the grandeur and epic sense of the competition." A relatively obscure eighteenth-century painter, Giacomo Di Chirico, framed his subjects in a manner that taught Steve how to shoot stadiums. Claude Lelouche's 1966 film, *A Man and a Woman*, demonstrated how a moving camera could tell a story without words. The rousing musical scores for film classics *Gone with the Wind*, *Victory at Sea*, *High Noon*, *El Cid*, and *The Magnificent Seven* showed how music could tell the same story that the actors played out on the screen.[10]

NFL Films always emphasized telling stories: from the beginning, the Sabols did not merely record football highlights but told stories about pro football in a self-consciously epic mode. The NFL Films style was fully developed by 1966 in the company's first feature film, *They Call It Pro Football*, which Steve Sabol likes to call "the *Citizen Kane* of sports films."[11] The instantly recognizable style begins with the use of film itself, whose textures are warmer and deeper (and much more expensive) than videotape. The key elements of the style are familiar to virtually any sports fan who has watched pro football on television sometime in the past 40 years:

- Images: slow motion and tight close-ups, shot with telephoto and zoom lenses by cameras located at various positions throughout the stadium
- Sound: equally important elements of symphonic music punctuated by grunts, collisions, and shouts caught by wireless microphones on players and coaches
- Narration: lean and weighty (Sabol calls it "Hemingwayesque"),[12] sometimes poetic, always melodramatic, and in the major productions from NFL Films' classic period intoned by John Facenda
- Editing: montages with distinct segments (collisions, followed by graceful receptions, screaming coaches, crazy fumbles, snowflakes floating downward in super slow motion, and so on)
- Story: romantic, melodramatic, epic, mythic, usually with playful and humorous interludes

Ed Sabol used slow motion in his very first highlight film, and he invented the shooting of football by what he called "Trees," "Moles," and "Weasels." The Tree had the fixed camera high on the 50-yard line, from which all football games had been shot since the early newsreels. Sabol's great innovations were the Moles and Weasels. The Mole had a handheld camera at field level for shooting close-ups of faces, hands, and tight-spiraling footballs (NFL Films' signature image). The Weasel also carried a handheld camera but "burrowed" through the stadium, high and low, looking for anything striking or bizarre. Beginning in 1964, NFL Films covered every regular-season game with at least two and usually three cameras, one of them shooting only in slow motion, adding more cameras for the playoffs and eventually as many as 18 for the Super Bowl. For his very first film, Ed also abandoned Sousa marches for music modeled after Henry Mancini's jazzy score for the hit TV series *Peter Gunn*. He set out from the beginning to make *movies* about football, not just document the games.[13]

Steve turned his father's original innovations into the full-blown NFL Films style. Steve himself wrote the scripts, looking to Rudyard Kipling and Grantland Rice for inspiration. To read them, he hired John Facenda, whose resonant baritone, "the voice of God," rumbled over most of NFL Films' major productions—features and Super Bowl films but not the routine weekly highlights—from 1966 to 1984. Steve hired Sam Spence to write original music recorded in Munich with a 64-piece orchestra from 1966 to 1990. Something like symphonies for bassoon, French horns, and tympani, Spence's music was percusssive, soaring, pounding, jaunty (with moments of tinkling counterpoint). Listen to the early music without the images and you think you are hearing the soundtrack from a widescreen Western of the 1950s or early 1960s (with the theme from *The Magnificent Seven* most explicitly echoed). The unsung hero of NFL Films was Yoshio Kishi, a Japanese film editor who had never seen a football game before he joined the company. Without understanding the game, Kishi immediately understood that highlights need not show the entire play, only "the apex of action." Kishi's montages, which first appeared in *They Call It Pro Football* (along with the first microphone on a coach, the first original score, and the first narration from Facenda), immediately changed the standards for editing highlight films.[14]

Major trade journals such as *American Cinematographer* and *Film Score Monthly* have saluted NFL Films for its technical innovations and artistic achievements. A writer for the *New York Times* has gone so far as to call Steve Sabol "perhaps the most underrated filmmaker working today." With its distinctive style, NFL Films has been likened to the Hollywood studios of the

1930s. I would add that the alternating segments of percussive violence, balletic grace, and slapstick humor also resemble the acts in a vaudeville or burlesque show—only they are done in high dramatic style, with colliding male bodies substituting for female ones. NFL Films has no equal when it comes to capturing the varied moods and rhythms of football.[15]

The technical innovations of NFL Films, adopted by ABC for *Monday Night Football* and eventually by all the networks for routine telecasts of games, made football more comprehensible to television viewers. The artistry of NFL Films has done more: in an era of debunking, it has not just sustained but increased football's cultural power. NFL Films is one of the all-time great masters of illusion. A highlight reel or feature from NFL Films is no less artificial than one of the NFL's marketing campaigns of the 1990s. Yet the effect of the technical virtuosity is a hyperrealism that is at once larger than ordinary life and more "true" than the football we watch with our own eyes. An NFL Films cinematographer has described the goal as portraying "reality as we wish it was."[16] Through the montages of violent collisions and the close-ups of bloodied fists and contorted faces spraying sweat drops in super slow motion, NFL Films lets the viewer see and feel more intensely the thrill and power and struggle of professional football.

The presence of NFL Films' cameras and microphones sometimes turns players into conscious performers, mugging for the viewers or screaming at teammates and opponents in the adopted role of team leader.[17] But against this manufactured drama, NFL Films also captures subtle dimensions of football that elevate it. For several years after freezing weather nearly sabotaged them in Green Bay, the company's cinematographers dreaded rain, snow, and fog. In time, however, they started praying for bad weather,[18] for the stunning shots of snowflakes floating gently down on embattled armies, of muddied warriors trudging to the line like Napoleon's forces before the gates of Moscow, of players appearing then disappearing into eerie fog, of footballs and feet bouncing and sliding crazily on ice. In these otherworldly moments pro football seems like a mighty struggle governed by the forces of nature, like Odysseus blown by fair winds or foul as the meddling gods dictate. The alternating segments of endlessly drawn-out, slow-motion images followed by rapidly cut collisions likewise create a sense of football time unbound from the ticking of mechanical clocks. A season can be compressed into 30 seconds; a long pass can seem to float forever before descending into outstretched hands. With "the voice of God" intoning martial poetry and "gladiator music"[19] thundering in the background, NFL Films has sustained a sense of mythic grandeur in our decidedly antimythic times.

Merger

While Pete Rozelle was laying the foundation for the National Football League with NFL Films, NFL Properties, and the national TV contract, competition from the rival American Football League was threatening to undermine it. In August 1959, five months before Rozelle became commissioner, 27-year-old Dallas oilman Lamar Hunt, son of the legendary billionaire wildcatter H. L. Hunt, announced plans for a new league with teams in Dallas, Houston, Denver, Los Angeles, Minneapolis, and New York. Buffalo and Boston were soon added. Hunt, along with Houston's Bud Adams (a fellow Texan and oilman) and their other partners, did not want war with the NFL. Hunt came up with the idea for a rival league only after failing to acquire an NFL franchise, then discovering that he was not alone in his frustration. Hunt even naively approached Bert Bell to be commissioner of both leagues, à la Major League Baseball with its American and National Leagues. For his part, Bell had his own worries, as a Senate subcommittee was investigating the NFL's seemingly monopolistic behavior. With Hunt's approval, Bell in his testimony before the subcommittee actually made the public announcement about the new AFL and assured the senators that he was "all for the league and would help nurture it."[20]

How far Bell would have gone to back up his word can never be known, because he died suddenly in October 1959, leaving key NFL owners to begin behaving suspiciously like monopolists. The NFL with supposedly no interest in expansion now offered franchises to Hunt and Adams, who turned them down out of loyalty to their partners. Not all of their partners were so loyal in return. On January 27, 1960 (the day after Rozelle became commissioner), the group representing Minneapolis withdrew from the AFL and accepted an NFL franchise a day later—the same day that Dallas also received a franchise. Hunt now had a crosstown rival as well as a hole in his new league, which Oakland filled two days later. In June the AFL filed a $10 million antitrust lawsuit over the expansion franchises for Dallas and Minneapolis. The same month, the AFL's prospects became instantly promising when the league signed a five-year, $8.5 million TV contract with ABC, the weakest of the networks and the only one willing to take a chance on the upstart league. Television, along with the deep pockets of Lamar Hunt and Bud Adams, assured at least short-term survival. When informed that his son lost close to a half-million dollars in the AFL's first season, H. L. Hunt, either the richest or the second-richest man in the world according to journalists, and the source of Lamar's trust fund, commented, "At that rate, he can't last much past the year 2135 A.D."[21]

In May 1962 the AFL lost its antitrust case in district court, then lost its appeal in November 1963, but despite these setbacks it would not go away. The turning point came with a new five-year, $36 million television contract with NBC, signed in January 1964 to begin with the 1965 season, paying about $900,000 per year to each team—just under the $1 million per team negotiated by the NFL for 1964–65. (Unable to match NBC's offer, ABC sold its rival the final year of its initial AFL contract.) Gate receipts were still the major source of revenue in pro football, and the NFL's average attendance roughly doubled the AFL's,[c] but $900,000 was $100,000 more than clubs' average annual expenses. The contract with NBC guaranteed the AFL's survival. The NFL had to win the war; the AFL only had to keep hanging around.[22]

And winning was becoming expensive. After the owner of the New York Jets, David "Sonny" Werblin, shocked the football world by signing rookie Joe Namath for $427,000 in January 1965, salaries quickly spiraled out of control. In the most-publicized signings, Green Bay coughed up $1 million for Donny Anderson and Jim Grabowski, and Tommy Nobis leveraged $600,000 from the new NFL franchise in Atlanta. Facing a ruinous bidding war for rookies, Rozelle authorized Dallas general manager Tex Schramm to meet secretly with Lamar Hunt through the spring of 1966 to work out a merger. On June 8, Rozelle announced a peace settlement, over the objections of Al Davis, who had recently replaced Joe Foss as the AFL's commissioner and wanted a fight to the finish. The two leagues agreed to form a single National Football League by 1970, with a single draft of college players in the meantime and a championship game between the leagues (later conferences) beginning with the 1966 season. Rozelle would be commissioner of the combined leagues, a decision that left Davis embittered and his personal war with Rozelle and the NFL only postponed.

As with the national television contract, one more hurdle remained: the merger violated antitrust law at the expense of the players, who would no longer be able to pit one league against the other in bidding for their services. Rozelle succeeded in Congress again, this time by promising Senator Russell Long and House Majority Leader Hale Boggs, both from Louisiana, to place a franchise in New Orleans. Boggs circumvented the antagonistic House Judiciary Committee by attaching the antitrust exemption to a budget bill with unshakable support in both houses. Congress passed the bill on October 21,

c. AFL average attendance increased slowly but steadily—from 16,538 in 1960 to 17,905 in 1961, 20,486 in 1962, 21,584 in 1963, 25,855 in 1964, and 31,828 in 1965—while the NFL's rose from 40,106 to 47,286 over that same period.

1966. New Orleans received an NFL franchise on November 1. NFL rookies again had to take whatever their drafting teams offered them.[23]

The merger in 1966 completed the creation of the modern NFL. The 14-team league of 1960 now had 26 teams, acquiring an entire extended family in something like a second marriage. AFL coaches were more freewheeling and innovative, and by the 1970s the old NFL clubs would have to adjust. The AFL also had "fan-friendly" rules, such as the two-point conversion and players' names on their jerseys, which the combined league adopted.[24] In Davis, Rozelle acquired an evil stepbrother, and in Namath the entire league acquired the wayward son who proceeded not only to break all the rules but to get the other kids acting out. Rather than continue an expensive war, the NFL had grudgingly accepted the lesser league as a full partner, only to be remade in the AFL's image.

Football in Red, White, and Blue

Among other consequences, the NFL-AFL merger begat the Super Bowl—destined to become the country's number-one sports attraction, TV attraction, and showcase for advertisers, though only its number-two day for eating (behind Thanksgiving). But not right away; the first two Super Bowls did not yet have that official title, let alone a Roman numeral after it. They were the NFL-AFL World Championship Games, in which the established league demonstrated its indisputable superiority. Kansas City stayed close to Green Bay for the first half of the first contest, in January 1967, before being swamped 35–10. Oakland never threatened the Packers in 1968, falling 33–14. Both games drew large television audiences: 41.1 percent of all TV sets in 1967 (split between CBS and NBC because each owned the rights to one of the two leagues), just under 37 percent in 1968 for CBS alone.[25] But there were 31,000 empty seats in the Los Angeles Coliseum in 1967, and neither game was anything more than football's version of a pro championship.

The victories of Joe Namath and the New York Jets over the Baltimore Colts in the 1969 championship (the first to be officially named the Super Bowl, becoming Super Bowl III in the retrospective counting) and of Kansas City over Minnesota in 1970 were more momentous because they established parity between the two leagues as they became one. But in 1969 and 1970, the Super Bowl was still several years away from becoming an unofficial civic holiday and orgy of consumerism. For all its historical importance, Super Bowl III had the lowest TV rating in the game's history, as the public expected another NFL blowout despite Namath's shocking "guarantee" of a Jets' victory. For Super Bowl IV, the rating improved from 36.0 to 39.4, still almost 10 rating points below the eventual peak in 1982.

It seems clear, however, that Pete Rozelle early on envisioned something like what the Super Bowl would become; and his vision, as always, concerned the NFL's image. The fact that Rozelle decided from the beginning on a neutral site for the contest meant that he expected it to stand alone without needing home team partisanship. In this sense, the Super Bowl extended the philosophy behind the national TV contract, which marketed the entire league, not individual teams. What kind of event Rozelle envisioned, though, is most evident in what he later called "a conscious effort on our part to bring the element of patriotism into the Super Bowl."[26] "Superpatriotism" would be more accurate. After the unspectacular staging of the inaugural game, the second one included what would become a Super Bowl signature: a pregame flyover by Air Force jets following the national anthem. The halftime show for Super Bowl III was the first to have a theme, "America Thanks," which struck the patriotic note that would become embedded in the event. The pregame show that year (and again in 1970 and 1973) featured astronauts leading the Pledge of Allegiance, inaugurating the NFL's special tie to NASA. The New Christy Minstrels, who provided the pregame entertainment in 1970, were introduced as "young Americans who demonstrate—with guitars." The halftime show featured a reenactment of the Battle of New Orleans.[27]

All of this, of course, resonated more deeply in 1968, 1969, and 1970 than it would have even a couple of years earlier. Those years marked the height of everything that the term "the sixties" has come to mean, and the NFL positioned itself clearly on one side of the era's political and generational divide. (As a college football player during these years, I knew that one could play football and oppose the war in Vietnam, but I also understood that many people regarded football as a kind of war, whether heroic or imperialistic.)

Pete Rozelle and the NFL were not the first to make this move; they learned how to play the superpatriot game from Earnie Seiler, the impresario of college football's Orange Bowl from 1935 through 1974, where he reigned as the entire football world's king of pious and patriotic kitsch. The NFL first hired Seiler to stage the second Super Bowl, played in Miami, then again in 1969 and 1971 when the game returned there. (New Orleans was the site in 1970.) Whether or not Rozelle and the NFL might have followed a similar course independently, Seiler brought the spectacle and superpatriotism of the Orange Bowl to the Super Bowl. To some degree, the Orange Bowl simply exported Bible Belt piety and Dade County politics to a national TV audience. For Rozelle, the Super Bowl was chiefly an advertisement for NFL football, investing the game with "traditional American values."

Compared to the Orange Bowl, the Super Bowl was actually a restrained affair in its early years, though of course that changed. To get ahead of the story for a moment, the intensity of the patriotic display at the Super Bowl slackened with the fall of Saigon and the resignation of Richard Nixon—the end of "the sixties"—but routine celebrations of patriotism became as predictable as dousing the winning coach with Gatorade. By the 1990s, when the United States was actually at war—in 1991 in the Persian Gulf, then in 2002 in Afghanistan in the aftermath of the September 11 terrorist attacks, then again after 2004 in Iraq—an element of self-conscious calculation was unmistakable. Rozelle's successor, Paul Tagliabue, shared Rozelle's view that the Super Bowl, as Tagliabue put it, is "the winter version of the Fourth of July celebration."[28] For the 1991 game, played just a few days into the Persian Gulf War, that meant American flag decals on the players' helmets, images of soldiers in the desert throughout the pregame show, and a halftime address from President George Bush, who described the Gulf War as *his* Super Bowl.

The highest PQ (Patriotism Quotient) thus far belongs to Super Bowl XXXVI in 2002, telecast by Fox, the network more generally known for excess. To have the *Patriots* of New England pitted against the St. Louis Rams was a marketer's dream, as American troops pursued Al-Qaida and the Taliban in Afghanistan. Tagliabue spoke before the game of the NFL's responsibility as "a keeper of the nation's mood" and of the league's objective "to strike a balance between reflecting the risks that our society faces on the one hand and being positive, self-confident, resilient, and inspirational on the other." The NFL had by this time become hyperconscious of not alienating any part of its audience.[d] In contrast to the more militaristic displays during the Vietnam era, NFL vice president Roger Goodell disavowed "making any political statements" this time, because "it's not our place." The telecast would focus on "everyday heroes" and "American ideals." "Fewer F-111s, more founding fathers," as a reporter for *SportsBusiness Journal* put it.[29]

Fox's three-hour pregame show, "Heroes, Hope, and Homeland," opened with actor Michael Douglas's voice-over declaring this Sunday "a special day where Americans come together to share a common vision." "Postcards" from American soldiers in Afghanistan preceded commercial breaks, and the feature stories included one on the firefighter brothers of Patriot guard Joe Andruzzi (one of whom nearly died in the World Trade Center) and another on Bob Kalsu, the only NFL player to lose his life in Vietnam. For the climactic

d. The muting of patriotic display in 2006 and 2007, when the public had turned decisively against the younger President Bush's war in Iraq, illustrates the NFL's desire to connect with the popular mood, not promote any political agenda.

"Tribute to America," former NFL stars read from the Declaration of Independence, and former presidents recited Abraham Lincoln's speeches from an earlier national crisis, as the Boston Pops played Aaron Copeland's *Lincoln Portrait* in the background. After this, the halftime show—a musical performance by rock band U2, whose lead singer Bono flashed the American-flag lining of his leather jacket at the finale as a list of those who died on September 11 scrolled up the TV screen—seemed relatively subdued.

It is impossible to know how many viewers were moved by these highly choreographed expressions of spontaneous feeling, or how many believed that such sentiments had any relationship to the football game at hand.[30] One member of the Andruzzi family conspicuously declined to be interviewed for the pregame show: Jimmy, the brother who nearly died at Ground Zero. Whatever his reasons, Jimmy Andruzzi's silence invited the thought that the bombastic production of the Super Bowl might not be the proper venue for honoring "true heroes."

Likewise, the profile of Bob Kalsu might have reminded older viewers not just of an earlier war that divided rather than unified the country, but also of how few NFL players actually fought in it, or in any war since. Kalsu had long been forgotten, until *Sports Illustrated* did a cover story on him in July 2001. Rocky Bleier, my old Notre Dame teammate, was the NFL's most famous Vietnam veteran, a man of limited physical gifts but great heart who recovered from serious leg wounds to create with Franco Harris the league's best running game in the late 1970s. A total of 638 NFL players served during World War II, 19 of them dying. Besides Bleier and Kalsu, just four other pro football players served in Vietnam.[31] To protect their economic interests, several NFL clubs in the 1960s had special ties to local reserve or National Guard units for sheltering their players from the draft (at a time when these units had long waiting lists). This was no secret. *Life* magazine in 1966 described such arrangements for the Dallas Cowboys, Boston Patriots, Washington Redskins, Green Bay Packers, Philadelphia Eagles, and Baltimore Colts. That year, when 27 percent of young men between 18 and 35 classified 1-A by the Selective Service were drafted, just two NFL players failed to avoid the draft.[32]

The NFL's "warrior culture"[e] has always been about image.[33]

e. The outpouring of tributes in April 2004 when Arizona Cardinal safety Pat Tillman died in an ambush in Afghanistan, after leaving behind a $3.6 million contract (and a new wife) to enlist in the war on terrorism, was another collision of image and reality. With Army Rangers standing grimly behind him, Tagliabue at the 2004 NFL draft saluted Tillman as a man who "personified the best values of America and of the National Football League." Tillman, however, became a hero by *abandoning* the NFL.

Football in Prime Time

To return to Pete Rozelle and the foundation he laid in the 1960s, we have one more cornerstone to consider. All of Rozelle's promotional efforts derived from a bedrock belief in the marketing power of pro football itself. Rozelle's challenge as commissioner was to bring NFL games to an ever-wider audience and to satisfy the desires of an audience that already existed. Televising games in prime time was yet another of Rozelle's early ideas, a plan for reaching beyond the serious fans who tuned in on Sunday afternoons. Between 1966 and 1969, CBS indulged Rozelle by broadcasting five games on Monday nights, but always "to mediocre ratings." At the networks, only Roone Arledge believed that football could compete for a general audience with sit-coms and serial dramas, but Arledge could not persuade his bosses at ABC. When Rozelle in 1970, however, threatened to sell a Monday night package to the independent network owned by Howard Hughes, executives at ABC suddenly foresaw their third-ranked network dropping to fourth. Rozelle's shrewdness as a negotiator won Monday night for the NFL, but when *Monday Night Football* debuted in 1970, Roone Arledge at ABC did much more than Pete Rozelle at the NFL to make the first decisive shift from treating football as a sport to treating it as an entertainment product.[34]

Arledge brought to televised football the idea that the show, not the game, was what mattered. In a famous memo, written in 1960 to his bosses at ABC before he had filmed his first football game, Arledge described applying the techniques used for televising variety shows, political conventions, and travel or adventure shows in order to target women as well as men by appealing to their interest in the pageantry and "the feeling of the game." Instead of the standard three stationary cameras, which missed much of the action and all of the color and surrounding excitement, Arledge would use six cameras that would shoot anything of interest in the stadium when not focused on the play. He would mount cameras on jeeps, on risers, in helicopters, on mike booms. And he would use a "creepy-peepy" (handheld) camera

> to get the impact shots that we cannot get from a fixed camera—a coach's face as a man drops a pass in the clear—a pretty cheerleader after her hero has scored a touchdown—a coed who brings her infant baby to the game—the referee as he calls a particularly difficult play—two romantic students sharing a blanket late in the game on a cold day—the beaming face of a

---

Also, it turned out that Tillman was killed by friendly fire, and that the army deliberately lied to his parents as well as the public in order to have a "poster boy" for the war.

substitute halfback as he comes off the field after running 70 yards for a touchdown, on his first play for the varsity—all the excitement, wonder, jubilation, and despair that make this America's number-one sports spectacle, and a human drama to match bullfights and heavyweight championships in intensity.

In short—we are going to add show business to sports![35]

Here lay the future of televised football, before any part of it had yet arrived (and before Ed Sabol sold his similar vision to Pete Rozelle).

Historians Randy Roberts and James Olson call Arledge "probably the most important single individual in modern sports."[36] Behind his revolution in televising football lay an understanding that the game itself provided "a supply of human drama that would make the producer of a dramatic show drool." Or to put the matter more simply, that football by its very nature tells powerful stories. Arledge worked out his ideas initially with ABC's college football telecasts, then for one season (1963) of broadcasting the AFL, which provided "a veritable production laboratory on the field and the freedom to experiment." The upstart AFL allowed ABC latitude in its game coverage that the NFL would not give CBS. While CBS (and NBC) still shot games from the 50-yard line, Arledge (like Sabol) placed cameras and microphones throughout the stadium and along the sidelines. NFL Films built on Arledge's innovations, and Arledge in turn learned from NFL Films how to achieve a "cinematic look" with low angles and tight close-ups, along with driving music and powerful narration. He personalized the players after they made key plays, with on-screen graphics and videotapes of previous highlights. He even tried miking a quarterback (for an episode of *Wide World of Sports*), until the device picked up a lineman yelling "Shee-it!" after a missed call by an official. Arledge's work with AFL games laid the groundwork for *Monday Night Football* and became the standard for the industry soon after.[37]

Adding show business to football broadcasting initially meant enhancing the game's storytelling ability, not reducing but amplifying football's epic or mythic power. More cameras, including the use of close-ups, slow motion, and replays, meant an ability to capture the raw human emotions of joy, agony, disappointment, and rage. With *Monday Night Football*, Arledge would add another element: his broadcasters went beyond describing and analyzing plays to establishing "storylines," with plots as simple as the raw emotions. Any football fan could name several off the top of his or her head—the traditional-rivals story, the bitter-enemies story, the wounded-hero story, the Cinderella or Ugly Ducking story, the son-challenging-the-father story (former assistant versus wily mentor), and so on. These stories, unsurprisingly, are versions of the oldest and most-repeated narratives in the Western world. Football itself tapped into them, and from the moment that newspapers began extensively covering the games in the 1880s, the media elaborated on them. Beginning in the 1960s, however, sportswriters and broadcasters became increasingly self-conscious and intentional about doing this, and Arledge led television in this direction. By the 1990s, showmanship itself would increasingly become the story, at the expense of the elemental stories inherent in the game. Arledge enhanced football's cultural power, but the forces he put in motion would later threaten to undermine it.

Monday Night Football introduced "the new paradigm of sportscasting," replacing "the game-in-a-cathedral model of CBS and NBC" with "up-close, camera-rich, three-in-the-booth entertainment."[38] With Chet Forte as his director, Arledge had a prime-time arena for televising football games with new camera angles and more cameras than the other networks used, as well as more graphics, more men in the broadcast booth (where irreverence and controversy replaced solemnity and deference), and "storylines" to guide the commentary—all of this, as Arledge put it in that early memo, "to gain and hold the interest of women and others who are not fanatic followers of the sport we happen to be televising."[39] By the late 1980s, *Monday Night Football* would become just another football game on TV, but in the 1970s it was a cultural phenomenon. It altered domestic relations, leisure habits, and workplace gossip; and it was indeed more about Howard Cosell trading jibes with "Dandy" Don Meredith in the broadcast booth than about the Redskins and Cowboys or Rams and 49ers fighting it out on the field. As Roberts and Olson put it, while Arledge's technical innovations gave every game "an epic quality," the announcers "made the show."[40] Cosell played the key role here. Even more than Roone Arledge, Howard Cosell believed that *he* was the show on Monday nights, the football game just his stage. To some degree he was right. Cosell instantly became both the most admired and most despised broadcaster in sports, and in both roles he drew viewers to *Monday Night Football*, which just as quickly became one of the top-rated shows in all of prime time.

I was among those who despised Cosell for his ignorance about football despite his constant *ex cathedra* pronouncements.[f] Above all, I resented Co-

f. I would not appreciate Cosell's politics—his championing of Muhammad Ali when the sporting establishment reviled and feared him—until many years later. I viewed Cosell as Ali's creation without giving Cosell himself sufficient credit. And I would not realize that Cosell was a passionate defender of striking NFL players in 1987 until I researched this book.

sell's belief that he was, in his own words, "bigger than the game." Cosell was great at getting the "inside" story from coaches and players before the game. He was lousy at analysis, and he too often insisted that the "storylines" he announced at the beginning of the game were playing out on the field even when they did not. Cosell railed against the "jockocracy" of ex-athletes allowed into the broadcast booth without professional training for the job, including his own partners Frank Gifford and Don Meredith. The fact is, the ex-jocks, for all their limitations as broadcasters in some cases, understood football.[41]

Where Cosell had no peer was in the drama he brought to the halftime highlights of Sunday's games, which became a weekly TV event in themselves. NFL Films provided the footage; Cosell added the hyped-up narration. Here was born the highlight film that ESPN's *SportsCenter* would eventually make the very center of our sporting universe.

As a show-biz phenomenon, *Monday Night Football* could not be sustained. The ratings slide from their 1981 peak began before Cosell left in 1984, and subsequent personnel changes in the booth had little impact. As Sunday night football and Thursday night football made Monday just another football night, whether the games themselves were thrilling or boring determined the quality of the broadcast. But Arledge and Forte had by then created a new technical standard for all of the networks by putting a premium on production values and storytelling. In the 1990s, when the NFL itself authorized "Ump Cams," miked players, halftime interviews with coaches, and sideline interviews with players, it was embracing and extending the vision of Roone Arledge.[42]

Before the 1977 Super Bowl, the sportswriter Roger Kahn asked Pete Rozelle "if the National Football League was show business." "Sure," Rozelle told Kahn, "but we prefer the word entertainment. What we do object to is constant psychoanalysis. Football is warlike. Football is violent. . . . The game has nothing to do with war. Our league provides action entertainment, nothing less and nothing more."[43] Rozelle shared Arledge's vision, but whether he spoke for the fans is not so obvious.

St. Vince and Broadway Joe

As Vince Lombardi lay dying of colon cancer in the summer of 1970, his wife Marie heard him bark in a troubled sleep: "Joe Namath! You're not bigger than football. Remember that." Describing the scene for *Esquire* in 1997, David Maraniss explained that for the three years before his death the coach "had been giving speeches lamenting what he considered the deceit of modern times. . . . In the rebellious sixties, freedom had become idealized against order, he said. The new against the old, genius against discipline. Everything was aimed at strengthening the rights of the individual and weakening the state, the church, and all authority. Now he feared that the battle had been too completely won and that society was reeling from the superficial excesses of freedom." Muttering in his sleep "Joe Namath" gave a specific name to the changes he feared were already accomplished, while Lombardi himself, of course, represented everything that had been cast aside. As Maraniss wrote in 1997, "It was as though, in his dying vision, [Lombardi] saw Michael Irvin and Brian Bosworth and Deion Sanders coming along behind Broadway Joe."[44] The dying icon of a vanishing football world might have been even more shocked to know that the rights of the individual against authority and "the state"—the NFL, that is—would be invoked by profit-minded owners such as Al Davis, Jerry Jones, and Art Modell over the coming decades, not just by high-stepping cornerbacks and strutting receivers.

Lombardi was right about the battle already having been "too completely won." Namath was the NFL in 1970, as Vince Lombardi had been the NFL in the 1960s. Several later coaches and innumerable players would have a greater impact on how professional football is played, but not on what it means. And despite the tremendous expansion of the engines of celebrity making since the 1960s, none would come close to their impact on the larger culture. As symbols, "Lombardi" and "Namath" could represent opposed values at the heart of football itself since its beginnings—violence and discipline on the one hand, artistry and self-expression on the other. Football exerts its unique power in the tension between the two. Lombardi and Namath also harken back to older and more universal archetypes: to the Apollonian and Dionysian principles that seemed to show up everywhere in my literature classes in college in the 1960s; to work and play, control and abandon, pain and pleasure, deferred and instant gratification. But Lombardi and Namath embodied those ideas in distinctive ways for their own time. By the end of the 1960s, Lombardi was football's past, Namath its present and future. "Lombardi" is still with us, and not just on the trophy awarded each season to the Super Bowl champion. In Super Bowl pregame shows and elsewhere, Lombardi's name and image are repeatedly invoked to conjure up the world of pro football when it was more elemental, less glitzy. Less Namath-like. Joe Namath made football safe for the counterculture, the Me Generation, and the Gen-Xers and Gen-Yers of the future, for all of those who would want their football with a bit of style.

The Lombardi Sixties

Although Lombardi came to symbolize a kind of "traditional" football, he by no means created the tradition, nor was it a tradition already associated with professional football. In one sense Lombardi simply brought to the NFL a coaching style with a long history in the colleges. Impassioned tyrants could be found throughout the college football world in the early 1960s—several of them would face rebellion from their black players by the decade's end—and their lineage could be traced back through coaches like Red Blaik (Lombardi's own mentor), Frank Cavanaugh (the "Iron Major"), Biff Jones, and Jock Sutherland, all the way to Doc Spears and Bill Roper in the 1920s. The iron-fisted style supposedly would not work with professionals, who were adults, not children. Many old-time pros were barely housebroken, if the stories told about them had any truth. The 1997 issue of *Esquire* in which Maraniss recounted Lombardi's dying words carried a companion piece by Charles Pierce, "Does Football Matter?," about the "authentic barbarians" of the early NFL, men like Green Bay's Johnny Blood, who trained in brothels and honky-tonks and played football with a kind of joyful recklessness that supposedly had disappeared from the game. "By comparison," declared Pierce, "Namath's entire career as a public sybarite probably didn't add up to a good weekend for Johnny Blood."[45] Coaches of old-time players, by necessity, would have had to be closer to harried zookeepers than all-powerful leaders like Lombardi, or sideline "geniuses" like Paul Brown and later Bill Walsh.

Pierce lamented the sterility of the modern game and its personalities, the disappearance of football as unleashed Id. As legendary Bad Boy, Joe Namath served as a measure of how far the NFL had fallen away from being an entire league of true Bad Boys, "authentic barbarians." Pierce's lament fit into a long tradition of nostalgic complaints: the game is always declining from some Golden Age. (There is also, of course, a competing narrative, in which today's football is always better than the past's.) In mourning that NFL football might no longer matter, Pierce failed to mention that in Johnny Blood's time almost nobody cared.

As a self-proclaimed bible of masculinity ("The Magazine for Men" or "Man at His Best" in different eras), *Esquire* has published a number of perceptive essays about football over the years, including Thomas Morgan's "The American War Game" in October 1965. The memorable cover had a New York Giant kneeling on the field, hands clasped and head bowed in prayer, with the caption, "Heaven help him—he's going to play 60 minutes of pro ball." With the war in Vietnam just beginning to escalate, Morgan saw "an eerie parallel in the recent histories of U.S. politics and pro football," as the NFL's "sluggardly, ground-oriented game" gave way to aerial attacks ("Throw the bomb!") that mirrored the Pentagon's shift toward a doctrine of "massive retaliation."[46]

"The American War Game" did not glibly celebrate football's violence but challenged the tendency to emphasize its cerebral and technological aspects in accounting for its appeal. Basically, Morgan argued that football expressed, in a controlled way, something profoundly primitive that held a special appeal in over-civilized times, though he insisted on football's "lethal difference" from actual war. Contrary to the idea, prominent during both World Wars, that football was an ideal training ground for combat, Morgan endorsed what became known as the catharsis theory of violent sports. Football's "purgative purpose," Morgan wrote, was to provide a vicarious outlet for the human instinct for war. Writing before the massive buildup in Vietnam, Morgan could contemplate football's warlike nature more positively than would soon be possible.

Morgan did not mention Vince Lombardi, but Lombardi was in fact becoming the dominant symbol of a 1960s football world defined by violence, discipline, and stoicism. Lombardi had been what would now be called the offensive coordinator for the New York Giants teams of the late 1950s that were celebrated for their "sanctioned savagery," but journalists heaped most of their praise on the architect of the defense, Tom Landry. Had the cerebral, bloodless Landry gone to Green Bay in 1959 instead of Dallas in 1960 and been as successful as Lombardi became, the popular image of pro football in the 1960s might have looked very different. But Landry and the Cowboys won no championships until the 1970s; the 1960s belonged to Vince Lombardi and the Packers.

Green Bay in 1959 was one of the NFL's most-storied, most-sentimentalized, and in recent years least-successful franchises. In 1958, the year before Lombardi arrived, the Packers won just 1 of 12 games and had not had a winning season since 1947. In Lombardi's first season as coach, the team went 7–5. In his second season, the Packers topped the Western Conference but lost the title game to the Philadelphia Eagles. Green Bay then won NFL championships in 1961, 1962, 1965, 1966, and 1967, along with the first two Super Bowls, after which Lombardi retired briefly, then was lured back to the sidelines by the Washington Redskins for the 1969 season. Again he turned a loser into a winner (the team went 7-5-2), though whether he would have repeated the rest of his Green Bay magic can never be known. He died the following September.

Lombardi's life has been chronicled in a first-rate biography by David

Maraniss, but to appreciate his impact on his time it is useful to go back to the magazine profiles of the 1960s.[47] The Lombardi known to football fans—like the public image of Namath—was the one created in the media. The sporting press responded immediately to Lombardi's success in Green Bay, and in his second season, when he won his first conference championship, the news weeklies and general-interest magazines also began paying serious attention. The outlines of the Lombardi Legend that would be full-blown by 1967 emerged in these earliest pieces.[48] The "stocky, swarthy" Italian American from Brooklyn had been an undersized but overachieving guard on Fordham's famous Seven Blocks of Granite in the 1930s. After graduation he began law school at Fordham but left in 1939 to coach at St. Cecilia High School in Englewood, New Jersey, where he also taught chemistry, physics, and Latin. (*Sports Illustrated* awarded Lombardi a law degree, but in reality he left law school after one semester with poor grades. Successful coaches in this era did not have to pad their résumés; sportswriters did it for them.) After eight years at St. Cecilia's, including a stretch of 36 straight victories, Lombardi coached two seasons as an assistant at Fordham, five seasons under the coach who most influenced him, Col. Red Blaik at Army, and five more under Jim Lee Howell of the New York Giants before his call to the Packers.

Mythological heroes always have obscure, unpromising backgrounds. Then come the successes and setbacks and the ultimate triumph over the forces of darkness. In Green Bay, the "Siberia" to which opposing coaches threatened to trade their unruly players, Lombardi inherited a team of losers and underachievers, acquired some castoffs through trades and a few shrewdly selected draft choices, and then transformed all of them through the force of his will. To the self-effacing quarterback, Bart Starr, Lombardi gave self-confidence; to the confused All-American washout, Paul Hornung, he gave a clear role; to the entire team he gave "backbone." "To play in this league," *Time* magazine quoted him as saying, "you've got to be tough— physically tough and mentally tough."

Lombardi football was a violent game, to be played violently without apology; it was "rugged" and "old-fashioned." He had no use for fancy formations and tricks on offense. Every defense that took the field against Green Bay knew the Packers' sweep was coming—Hornung around end, with a fullback, tight end, two guards, and even a tackle in front of him—but no defense could stop it. "Football," Lombardi liked to say, "is two things. It's blocking and tackling." In 1961, in only Lombardi's third season and before he had won his first NFL title, the sports editor of *Look* magazine Tim Cohane (a friend and admirer since their time together at Fordham in the 1930s) already predicted that Lombardi would "become one of the greatest coaches of all times, if, indeed, he is not that already."

Initially, the story was as much about the resurrection of the Green Bay community as the personality of Vince Lombardi. Later, the emphasis would shift more and more to Lombardi's handling of his players. *Sports Illustrated*'s "New Day in Green Bay" in 1960 told a story whose details would be repeated by other sportswriters and journalists, the kind of romanticized hardship tale of the old days told by grandfathers to wide-eyed tykes. Green Bay was "the last of the 'town teams' " from the original NFL, the sole remaining link to "the romantic yesterdays when the game was the product and the possession of Canton and Massillon, of Muncie and Hammond, of Decatur and Rock Island."

Curly Lambeau started the team in 1919 with $500 for uniforms from the Indian Packing Company and divided the profits at the end of the season, $16.75 per man. After several more years of shaky finances, the Packers won NFL titles in 1929, 1930, and 1931, then three more in 1936, 1939, and 1944; yet bankruptcy always loomed. Once, in the 1920s, Lambeau saved the team by persuading a friend to sell his Marmon roadster and loan him the proceeds. The final crisis was repeatedly postponed until after the 1949 season, when the franchise was salvaged by a sale of stock to local citizens, with most of the 1,699 stockholders buying just one $25 share, and no one allowed more than 200. The town owned the team, not for profit (there would be no dividends), but for pride. Frank Capra could have made the movie.[49]

The reborn Packers survived without thriving. Home attendance in the mid-1950s averaged about 22,000, but paid attendance was half that, and NFL rivals hated to travel to Green Bay. Then came Lombardi. In his first year the club set financial records with a million-dollar gross and more than $100,000 in profit. More important, success restored pride in the community. "You can't realize how much joy there is in this team," a local druggist told *Sports Illustrated*, "until you know the heartaches and despair of the last few years."[50]

This was a feel-good 1950s story: small-town America with old-fashioned values whipping Chicago, New York, and the rest of the big-city bullies.[51] The way the Packers did it became the 1960s story of Vince Lombardi. Although Lombardi employed brutal and uncompromising methods from the beginning, the early accounts only hinted at this. *Sports Illustrated*'s first notice of Lombardi emphasized his "combination of steely football acumen and arrant sentimentalism." *Time* reported that "Lombardi yelled so long and loud" during the first week of practice "that he lost his voice." He also required injured players to run during practice and warned that anyone who crossed him would be run all the way out of town. Cohane called Lombardi a "driver" but insisted that he was "above all a teacher," with a "penetrating, logical mind." Herbert Warren Wind wrote in the *New Yorker* in 1962 that, though very emotional, Lombardi's "chief characteristics are a really formidable intelligence, thoroughness, pride, and a quiet but relentless drive." That "quiet" is what most surprises. Wind clearly formed his impressions in Lombardi's office, where the coach appeared "cogitative, analytical, and almost scholarly" in talking about football, not at Packer practices.[52]

With a long cover story in *Time* magazine in 1962, Lombardi fully arrived as a national figure, with a full-blown legend now rather than a mere story. "Lombardi hit Green Bay so hard the grass is still quivering," *Time* reported. He drove the slackers out of the training room, complainers out of town. He instituted fines for breaking curfew, and players who missed a block or dropped a pass "instantly felt the sting of his acid tongue." Lombardi fired up his players with locker room talks "like something out of *The Spirit of Notre Dame*" (later stories would add that he also choked up and often cried when his players came through for him). With this mix of brutality and sentimentalism, Lombardi took "a gang of has-beens" and "romantically molded" them into "superstars" by making them believe in themselves and in him.[53]

Over the next few years, a small body of anecdotes and quotations became Lombardi lore: his first encounter with his new team, when he routed a couple dozen players with minor hurts from the training room; the words he used to instill confidence in Starr, Hornung, Willie Wood, and Willie Davis; the price his wife Marie paid for his preoccupation with the week's opponent (he didn't talk to her on Mondays, Tuesdays, or Wednesdays, said "hello" on Thursdays, became "civil" on Fridays and "downright pleasant" on Saturdays); and the most-quoted line of all, Henry Jordan's remark that Lombardi treated all of his players the same: "like dogs." Football fans became familiar with Lombardi's "grass drills" and "nutcracker drill" and the endless wind sprints that hardened his players while nearly killing them, with his contempt for malingerers nursing minor injuries, with "Lombardi Time" (arrival 15 minutes before the bus was to leave or practice to start). Lombardi would not allow his players to drink water during practice. He preached the importance of God, family, and Packer football, supposedly in that order. He also preached that second place was for losers, that a team that *will* not be beaten *cannot* be beaten. He called football a "game for madmen" that required hate but was also somehow a higher calling.[54]

Lombardi's football world was the one in which I played as a kid growing up in Spokane, Washington, far from Packerland. The Lombardian virtues—

mental toughness, physical conditioning, stress on the fundamentals, play-ing with pain—were the air I breathed. My high school coach did not believe in injuries, either ("Rub a little dirt on it!" he'd growl), nor in drinking water during practice. He did not learn this approach from reading about Lom-bardi; both men absorbed it from a common source, the world of football in which they played in the 1930s, coached in the 1940s and 1950s, and carried into the 1960s.

But I was a kid, taught to trust and obey my elders; Lombardi's Packers were grown men, many with children of their own. Lombardi motivated his players by fear—fear of his wrath, fear of losing their jobs. He tore down their egos, making them hunger for his approval, then doled out that approval in just the right way at just the right time. From our vantage point today this sounds like psychological terrorism, the pathology of the concentration camp. Packer right guard Jerry Kramer described himself to a reporter as "brainwashed" by Lombardi to never be satisfied with his performance. In 1968 that word conjured up *The Manchurian Candidate* and stories of North Vietnamese POW camps. Kramer recalled the 1962 season, when Lombardi "had me all screwed up. He would call me an old cow and say I looked like homemade horseshit. I really believed I was the worst football player in America. Then when the polls came out I was voted all-pro by the A.P., all-pro by the U.P.I, and then All-Star. I couldn't believe it. I thought they were all crazy."[55]

Kramer more than forgave Lombardi every cruelty. "I loved Vince," Kramer wrote (with Dick Schaap) in his "diary" of the 1967 season, published first in *Look* magazine in the fall of 1968, then as *Instant Replay*, pro football's first best seller. With this book, along with the photograph of Kramer rooting out Jethro Pugh at the goal line so that Bart Starr could score to beat the Dallas Cowboys for the conference title in 1967's "Ice Bowl," Kramer became the most famous offensive lineman in America. Yet the book mostly focused on Lombardi. "Sure I had hated him at times during the season," Kramer summed up his feelings in one of the excerpts in *Look*, "but I knew how much he had done for us, and I knew how much he cared about us. He is a beautiful man; and the proof is that no one who ever played for him speaks of him afterward with anything but respect and admiration and affection. His whippings, his cussings, and his driving all fade; his good qualities endure."[56]

Instant Replay appeared just after Lombardi retired. He went out on top, winning his second straight Super Bowl and fifth NFL championship in nine seasons. (After Lombardi's first two years in Green Bay, the Packers failed to win the NFL title only in 1963, when Hornung was suspended for gambling and Starr and Nitschke were injured; and in 1964, when Kramer missed the season due to injury and Hornung had not yet regained his kicking accuracy. Key Packer players obviously mattered as much as their coach.) Lombardi had perfect timing, not just because the aging Packers would have declined in 1968 with or without him (they finished 6–7–1), but also because signs of a blacklash to the Lombardi Legend were already beginning to appear. Kramer's comments about brainwashing appeared in a 1968 profile of Lombardi as "The Toughest Man in Pro Football," written by Leonard Shecter for *Esquire*. By this time a distinct formula marked the profiles of Lombardi: "he is a raging tyrant, but . . ." Anecdotes of his bellowing and bullying were followed by stories about his sentimentalism or his kindness, or by testimonies from his players to the debt they owed their coach for their own success and the achievements of the team. Shecter followed this formula, too, but he shifted the emphasis—more on Lombardi's abusiveness, less on its compensation—and he implicitly questioned whether the ends justified the means. Admirers and detractors shared a common understanding of Lombardi's complexity and his players' conflicted feelings about him. Jerry Kramer wrote that he hated Lombardi, *but* he loved him. Leonard Shecter wrote that the Packer players respected Lombardi, *but* they despised him. Whether respect trumped hate or hate trumped love was a personal matter for the players and a matter of journalistic priorities for sportswriters.

Shecter, along with Larry Merchant of the *New York Post* and Robert Lipsyte of the *New York Times*, belonged to a new breed of iconoclastic sportswriters in the 1960s beginning to question old verities. For *Esquire*, Shecter largely maintained his journalistic detachment, allowing the details to speak for themselves. Free to express his own opinion in his 1969 book *The Jocks*, Shecter acknowledged that "it takes toughness to be a successful coach," but there is "a high price" to pay; "this toughness is paid for in humanity." In *And Every Day You Take Another Bite* (1971), Merchant wrote that "Vince Lombardi was a hard man coaching a hard game with a hard code, and he coated it in moral rectitude, in terms of God, family, and team, duty, responsibility and discipline, and respect for authority. Not a bad list but all too often used by coaches as more of those animal biscuits to get athletes to sit up on their hind legs and follow by blind unreasoning obedience." Merchant saw less danger in the man he called "St. Vince" than in the appropriation of his "tough slogans" by "every little high school despot with a whistle and a ball." In *SportsWorld* (1975), Lipsyte looked back on Lombardi as a "decent man" with a dangerous legacy, "the subordination of self to group, of group to authority, of authority to goal. All to win a football game."[57]

The psychoanalytically inclined among both Lombardi's fans and his critics saw in his relationship to his players an all-powerful "Father" dealing with unruly or needy "Sons." Jerry Kramer described how he once played a full game with two broken ribs. After a doctor finally diagnosed the injury the following week, Kramer went to Lombardi, expecting a "pat . . . on the head" or a "nice going." Lombardi only muttered, "I guess they don't hurt any more." Kramer followed this story with another, about Lombardi visiting him in the hospital after he had "nearly died" from a variety of ailments in 1964, telling him "that the Packers would pay my salary in 1964 and 1965 even if I couldn't play, and would pay all my hospital bills." Kramer's comment: "He really cares about his players. They're his children, and he nurses them when they're sick and scolds them when they're bad and rewards them when they're good." In a review of *Instant Replay*, Richard Schickel described Lombardi as "the pater familias, demanding that his respect—his love—be earned and re-earned constantly." Under the title "Proud Father, Proud Sons," *Time* magazine's obituary summed up Lombardi's career this way: "Football's proudest father died of cancer last week at the age of 57, and the rugged sons who loved, hated, feared, and—most of all—obeyed him will never forget how he took them to heights that they never knew they could reach."[58]

The same idea sounds more problematic coming from Larry Merchant or Robert Lipsyte. Merchant called Lombardi a "stern patriarch" who "became the big daddy and the players his children whose only desire was to please him." Lipsyte wrote that Lombardi "believed that athletes, like children, re-spond best to absolute power used responsibly and fairly."[59] In the saga of Lombardi and the Green Bay Packers in the 1960s, Bart Starr was the "de-pendable son," Paul Hornung the "prodigal son," and Lombardi's own child Vincent "the conflicted son."[60] The crux of the matter was how one felt about grown men, who happened to play professional football, being treated like children. What sort of character did football build if it locked players in childhood?

Back in 1961, in a profile of Hornung for *Sport* magazine written by Dick Schaap, Lombardi appeared briefly as a thoughtful and modest man, and Schaap wrote that his players "kid about Lombardi and accuse him of distinct martinet tendencies. But every single one of them respects what he has done for them." Many years later, describing this same visit to Green Bay, Schaap admitted "being frightened" of Lombardi when he interviewed him, and he described Hornung and several other Packers listening to a tape recording of a Lombardi tirade at practice, into which they had edited their own com-ments: "Yeah, sure. Yeah. Go — yourself, Vince!" and the like. Schaap described the players laughing as they listened to the tape, "with hilarity and glee and terror," finding "private release from the pressure Lombardi imposed."[61] It is a funny scene, but a painful one, too, and none of it appeared in the 1961 article. These were men reduced to little boys, mocking Big Daddy behind his back, fearful that he would catch them but enjoying their private revenge before returning to the field for more abuse.

In 1961 the image of professional football players as rambunctious boys, lovable but irresponsible, had a fairly long history. By the end of the 1960s, a younger generation had rejected its elders, and "boys" playing college football, particularly black ones, demanded treatment as men. Lombardi was remarkably free from racism and generous to his black players, but in a paternalistic way that might not have worked with a new generation of young black men entering the NFL at the end of the decade. In the 1970s, NFL players would begin demanding their rights as workers, striking briefly in 1970 and much longer in 1974. Boys don't strike.

Vince Lombardi ultimately was a paradox as a man and an anomaly among coaches. He went to daily Mass. His sentimentalism was as real as his brutality. He failed his family, knew it, and regretted it. He struggled with his temper. He believed in fair play but not in good losing. He was obsessed with football yet ambivalent about his obsession over what was, after all, a game.[62] But he won championships. He had to win, of course. One of his great players, Willie Davis, admitted almost 30 years later in a tribute to Lombardi before the 1998 Super Bowl, "It was only in victory that you could tolerate what Lombardi put you through."[63]

Lombardi won with carefully selected and self-selecting players. He won with men who were willing to be his boys. The ones whom Lombardi ran off mostly left no record of their feelings. At least one of them did, a tough little player named Billy Butler, who played just one season in Green Bay. Butler considered Lombardi "the biggest asshole I ever met in my life."[64] Lombardi had initial success with the Washington Redskins before he was stricken with cancer, but had he repeated the same methods and not quickly produced a champion, he might have faced rebellion. On the other hand, to the consternation of his admirers he might have succeeded by adjusting to the changing times. Either possibility would have been hard on the Lombardi myth.

The Coming of Broadway Joe

The idea that Vince Lombardi and Joe Namath were yoked in some kind of fearful symmetry emerged after Namath's Jets upset the Baltimore Colts in Super Bowl III to displace Lombardi's Packers atop the world of pro football.

Lombardi recognized this in those dying words in 1970. Namath did, too. It so happened that Namath occupied the same hotel suite before Super Bowl III in which Lombardi had stayed the previous year. As Namath coyly put it in his autobiography, "I'm not sure he would have approved of everything I did in his old room the week before the Super Bowl."[65] Larry Merchant offered readers of his 1971 book back-to-back chapters on "St. Vince" and "The Sensuous Quarterback." Robert Lipsyte described Lombardi and Namath as "the two most important culture heroes that football imposed upon us in the sixties." Lipsyte noted that Lombardi and Namath were "both sons of immigrants, both hard-working, loyal, talented products of Americanization, and both willfully misunderstood." But the two were radically different cultural icons. Lombardi was the father, Namath the son, in a football "psychodrama." Lombardi stood for football "as a sadomasochistic adventure show." Namath was "Flash. Zap. Pizzazz."[66]

Writing shortly after Super Bowl III, Merchant called Namath "one of the most important athletes this country has ever spawned." Writing just a few years later, Lipsyte was already debunking Namath, who no longer seemed a "threat to the moral order of the universe."[67] Namath did not change; the NFL and the country changed by absorbing him.

As with Lombardi, it is useful to reconstruct Namath's impact on NFL football from contemporary accounts. Before he emerged as the anti-Lombardi, Namath was repeatedly set against other representatives of Establishment values. Upon signing with the New York Jets immediately after playing brilliantly for Alabama in a narrow loss to Texas in the 1965 Orange Bowl, Namath was initially contrasted to John Huarte, the quarterback from Notre Dame signed by the Jets for $200,000 as insurance on their $400,000 investment in Namath. Unlike the "easygoing" Namath, Huarte was "ramrod-straight," "precise and analytical," and a conservative dresser. Huarte intended to work on his MBA while in New York. Namath had not quite graduated from Alabama, where he carried a "C" average in industrial arts with a minor in P.E. (This was before the Buckley Amendment of 1974 made student information confidential.)[68]

Once Namath became the Jets' starting quarterback, he was set against Fran Tarkenton, rival quarterback for the crosstown Giants. Here, Namath represented the razzle-dazzle, upstart AFL; Tarkenton, the established and buttoned-down NFL. (Ironically, due to bad knees Namath was a classic dropback passer, while Tarkenton was a scrambler who threatened to turn every play into a circus. Tradition and improvisation cut both ways.) The more important contrast was moral and cultural, and faintly political. Tarkenton was a neatly groomed preacher's kid and active member of the Fellowship of Christian Athletes. He stood for marriage, home, and smart conservative investments for his family's economic future. Namath was the scruffy son of a western Pennsylvania millworker, and a hyperactive member of the Jet Set. He stood for promiscuous sex, bachelor pads, and cashing in on his celebrity. As Merchant put it in the short-lived *Jock New York* magazine, Namath "lives out his fantasies Monday through Saturday as gadfly–enfant terrible–single swinger–pop hero," while Tarkenton is "as orthodox as the law allows." (For the visual joke, a scruffy Tarkenton adorned the front cover, with a neatly groomed Namath on the back.)[69]

The Namath/Tarkenton split chiefly interested New Yorkers. Super Bowl III set Namath against Baltimore's Johnny Unitas for the entire football world. Unitas had missed most of the 1968 season with tendonitis in his elbow, but he was still football's most famous quarterback, and he entered the game in relief of Earl Morrall to rally the Colts' to what little offense they could muster. As the reigning NFL quarterback, Unitas had an image out of the 1950s: crew cut, high-topped black shoes, workmanlike demeanor, and flawless execution (with a similar crew cut, Morrall was a lesser Unitas). Unitas's story was out of Horatio Alger: cut by the Steelers after being drafted in the ninth round, he toiled on the sandlots in western Pennsylvania for $6 a game until the Colts signed him; he then led Baltimore to an NFL championship in his third season and became the dominant quarterback of his generation. Namath's long hair, white shoes, playboy lifestyle, and erratically brilliant or dreadful performances made him Unitas's antithesis in every way. There was no slow, determined rags-to-riches rise for Namath but something closer to the luck of the novice who hits the jackpot the first time out in Las Vegas: an initial contract guaranteeing him more than $400,000 (at a time when NFL stars made $25,000), "just enough to pay the annual salaries of 75 postal clerks," as John Underwood put it in *Sports Illustrated*.[70]

Sportswriters defined Namath as much by what he was not as by what he was: the anti-Lombardi, anti-Huarte, anti-Tarkenton, anti-Unitas. He also played under circumstances that were a gift from the gods. Drafted by both the NFL's St. Louis Cardinals and the AFL's New York Jets, when the war between the two leagues for college players doubled or tripled their market value, Namath nearly chose the Cardinals (who would apparently have traded him to the Giants). Either way, he was destined for New York. Main Street Joe in St. Louis or Kansas City would not have been the cultural icon that Broadway Joe became in New York.[71]

Had Joe Namath ended up in New York but with the Giants instead of the

Jets, he would likely have been smacked down from the outset and crammed into the image of a proper NFL quarterback. The NFL had a commissioner and ownership group obsessed with maintaining a conservative image for the league. The AFL had an overriding need to attract fans. It was an accident that came to seem foreordained that the managing partner of the Jets happened to be Sonny Werblin, who had worked for 30 years at the Music Corporation of America, the largest talent agency in show business, before retiring as vice president to join four partners in paying $1 million to salvage the AFL's pitiful New York Titans in 1963. The Maras, who owned the Giants, were as old-school as they come. Werblin regarded pro football as show business and was looking for a marquee star.

"I believe in the star system," Werblin told *Sports Illustrated*. "It's the only thing that sells tickets. It's what you put on the stage or playing field that draws people." In Namath, Werblin saw a young man who walked into a room and "you know he's there."[72] Namath's $427,000 contract was itself a star maker, instantly transforming a rookie quarterback into a celebrity. A month after Namath signed, not only *Sports Illustrated* but also *Time* gave the surgery performed on his "$400,000 knee" the sort of coverage, complete with anatomical illustrations, usually reserved for the separation of conjoined twins or the first experimental heart transplants.[73] As Namath's career unfolded over the next few years, Werblin always insisted that Namath deserved special treatment. When Jet assistant coaches suggested at one point that Namath ought to move from midtown Manhattan closer to the Jets' practice facilities in Queens, Werblin objected, "Oh, no, not Joe. He's a Park Avenue guy."[74] Werblin never fit in with other NFL and AFL owners, and he lasted a short time as the Jets' president (forced out by his partners in 1968, partly over a dispute concerning Namath's new long-term contract), but the NFL's future would ironically prove Werblin to have been a visionary, the first owner to believe he ran an entertainment business.

Joe Namath was neither pro football's first playboy nor its first Bad Boy, merely the first Playboy/Bad Boy to play in New York for an owner who understood and exploited his marketing value on those terms. Johnny Blood had played in Green Bay, Wisconsin, in the 1930s when an indifferent public viewed pro football players as semisavage. As a quarterback for the Detroit Lions in the 1950s, Bobby Layne was known to enjoy a drink and a party, but he looked like an overweight steelworker who punched the clock every Sunday afternoon to do a tough job. Paul Hornung, handsome lady-killer and brilliantly efficient running back for the Packers, could have claimed Namath's role, except that he played a few years too soon, in Green Bay, and for

Vince Lombardi. Sonny Jurgensen, Billy Kilmer, and Hornung's bar mate Max McGee also maintained an NFL tradition of partying, but mostly outside the public view. According to Hornung, many of the sportswriters and broadcasters of that generation were themselves hard drinkers, not likely to spill the secrets of the players' private lives or to report on the times they showed up for a game drunk or with a hangover.[75] And for all of these players, the playboy image ended where the football began.

Namath was the first to blur the boundary and get away with it. As the literary critic Leslie Fiedler pointed out around this time, Americans had a long love affair with what he called "Good Bad Boys," rascals with good hearts, like Tom Sawyer or the hipsters in Jack Kerouac's saga for the Beat Generation, *On the Road*. Fiedler offered no comments on the world of sports, but he could have mentioned Babe Ruth and Dizzy Dean, or Bobby Layne and Paul Horning, as adult versions of this cherished figure: wild men off the field who always came through for the coach, their teammates, and their fans. (Only whites could play this role. At 6′7″ and 295 pounds, Eugene "Big Daddy" Lipscomb, with an appetite for women and drink as prodigious as his strength and speed on the football field, was also known for his gentleness with children; but in the racial climate of the 1950s and early 1960s, Lipscomb, as a black man, was too frightening to be lovable.) Just before Namath arrived on the scene, *Life* magazine and the *Saturday Evening Post* cast a hugely talented but troubled running back named Joe Don Looney for the role as "football's marvelous misfit" and the "bad boy of the pros," but Looney finally could not adapt to the NFL's demands, or the NFL to his needs. Namath thus initially seemed a familiar figure, but whether he was another Good Bad Boy or just a bad one—maybe a complete jerk—was the question for sportswriters and football fans to ponder over his first four years with the Jets.[76]

After the initial gasps over the $427,000 contract and the knee surgery to salvage it, Namath's career fell into two distinct phases: Before the Super Bowl and After the Super Bowl. BSB Namath polarized sportswriters, teammates, and fans. He became known to the football world as "Broadway Joe" the summer before his rookie season, when teammate Sherman Plunkett christened him after seeing the *Sports Illustrated* cover of Namath in his football uniform in Times Square. Inside, Robert Boyle described Namath as "a real ring-ding-a-ding finger-snapper, a girl ogler, a swingin' cat with dark good looks who sleeps till noon" and whose "major interests are 'girls and golf, girls and golf.' "[77]

But Namath still needed a truly inspired Virgil to properly sing his exploits.

Such a bard arrived in the person of Dan Jenkins, in his account of "The Sweet Life of Swinging Joe" for *Sports Illustrated* a year later. Jenkins's opening paragraph captured Namath for the moment and the ages:

Stoop-shouldered and sinisterly handsome, he slouches against the wall of the saloon, a filter cigarette in his teeth, collar open, perfectly happy and self-assured, gazing through the uneven darkness to sort out the winners from the losers. As the girls come by wearing their miniskirts, net stockings, big false eyelashes, long pressed hair and soulless expressions, he grins approvingly and says, "Hey, hold it, man—foxes." It is Joe Willie Namath at play. Relaxing. Nighttiming. The boss mover studying the defensive tendencies of New York's off-duty secretaries, stewardesses, dancers, nurses, bunnies, actresses, shopgirls—all of the people who make life stimulating for a bachelor who can throw one of the best passes in pro football. He poses a question for us all: Would you rather be young, single, rich, famous, talented, energetic and happy—or President?[78]

The answer in 1966, as they would now say, was a no-brainer. Joe Namath had everything that Youth could want—Youth not marching for civil rights or against the war, that is. Namath's hedonism belonged more to an older era than the 1960s—booze and broads, not dope and hippie chicks—but set against the ascetic and violent image of professional football, it seemed not just rebellious but revolutionary.[79]

Jenkins wrote self-consciously as an "ancient" contemplating the unprecedented celebrity of a precocious 23-year-old. Compared to Babe Ruth, Joe DiMaggio, and Sugar Ray Robinson—also New Yorkers but "grown men" when they achieved their fame—Namath represented the supremacy of resplendent Youth. He was also decidedly not what an American hero should be. When Namath's draft board the previous December classified him 4-F for his damaged knee, the public outcry prompted a review by the surgeon general and forced the Pentagon to justify the decision with a fact sheet for members of Congress. The *New York Times* editorialized at the time that Namath should have been approved for limited duty, so as not to demoralize the troops abroad and anger their families at home. Instead of keeping quiet, Namath offended the country's "superpatriots" when he cracked, "I'd rather go to Vietnam than get married." (He was commenting on marriage, not the war.)[80]

Jenkins reported that Namath did indeed shine shoes as a kid, but unlike the honest bootblack in a Horatio Alger story, he also earned spending money by hustling pool and delivering messages for bookies. Now he lived in an apartment on the Upper East Side with a llama-skin rug, Italian marble bar, and large oval bed nearly as famous as he. He drove a Lincoln Continental convertible with the radio blaring, wore "tailor-made suits with tight pants and loud print linings, grabbing checks, laughing, enjoying life, spending maybe $25,000 a year ('On nuthin', man') and wondering why anyone should be offended." He lived by a simple philosophy: "I believe in letting a guy live the way he wants to if he doesn't hurt anyone."[81]

Jenkins also more soberly retraced Namath's rise from Beaver Falls, Pennsylvania, to Alabama with Bear Bryant, then to the New York Jets, whose 5–8–1 record Namath's rookie year did not quite meet the rookie's dazzling promise. And the usually tough-minded Jenkins could not resist a sentimental conclusion to his tale, the glimpse of the "genuine, considerate, sincere, wonderfully friendly and likeable young man" behind the "gaudy surface." Bad Boys must be Good, finally, to be eligible as heroes. But the Namath who came alive in these pages was the casual hedonist with the magical right arm who only wanted to "live and let live."[82]

Accounts of Namath's pre–Super Bowl life were always the same, even to the specific details.[83] The llama-skin rug, along with his full-length mink coat and Fu Manchu mustache a bit later (which he shaved off for $10,000 in a TV commercial during the 1968 season), became familiar symbols of the Namath style and lifestyle. Namath was not the first star to party late and play well the next day, but even more than Paul Hornung, Namath shattered the myth that sex before a game would sap the athlete's strength. And then there were his white shoes. It is difficult to conceive today what it meant when Namath took the field in white football shoes in 1965. Imagine an ambassador wearing sneakers to a state dinner, or a debutante showing up in work boots for the cotillion. The real problem was not that no pro football player had ever worn anything but black, but that Namath's white shoes *looked good*. What business did a football player have in looking good rather than unselfconsciously doing his tough job? Football fans might not read all of the stories about the penthouse apartment and the late nights at the Copa and the Pussy Cat, but when the Jets played on TV, they could not miss the white shoes. Of all the Namath totems, the white shoes most clearly defined his live-and-let-live philosophy in defiance of tradition and The Establishment.

Namath was despised as well as idolized from the beginning. Football had long been a working-class game, but Namath reeked of privilege despite his own working-class roots. Football was a *team* game, but Namath seemed to believe he was a solo act. The first rumors of dissension on the Jets came just a month after he signed with Werblin, when *Sports Illustrated* reported that "other Jets resented Namath's fat contract." Midway through his celebration of Namath's "sweet life," Jenkins quoted teammate Gerry Philbin, who admitted that the previous year "there was an undercurrent of resentment . . . about Joe's money and his publicity," but it "disappeared when everybody found out what a great guy he was."[84] Positive stories referred to resentment in the past; negative or ambivalent stories said that it continued. Due to his sore knees, Namath missed preseason practices and games that teammates had to play. He ignored curfews. He criticized Jets head coach Weeb Ewbank, and Werblin always backed his star against his coach. He went AWOL from training camp in August 1967 and ended up in a scuffle with the sports editor of Time. The team split over Namath, first between veterans and young players, then between offense and defense. (Larry Merchant later reported that at least one teammate on the offense, running back Matt Snell, "made no secret of his contempt for what he saw as a double standard in the organization's indulgence of Namath.") In his first three seasons with the Jets, Namath's teammates did not even vote him their MVP (he finished sixth in 1967).[85]

While Sports Illustrated (with the exception of its chief pro football writer, Tex Maule) celebrated Namath, writers for its sister publications, Time and Life, loathed him. Time described him arriving at his first Jets training camp in his green Continental and with unlimited self-regard, reporting the line that became another of Namath's totems, as well as the title of his autobiography: "Ah cain't wait 'til tomorrow," Namath said as he gazed at himself in a mirror, "'cause ah get better lookin' every day." Namath also regaled "barflies" at a local tavern with tales of his football exploits, then left them with a farewell, "Ah'm glad y'all had a chance to meet me." Tone and context are everything, but Time offered no hint that Namath might have been poking fun at his own celebrity. Life was appalled by Namath's initial contract, then ignored him until the end of the 1968 season, just weeks before the Jets took on the Colts and the NFL in the Super Bowl. On the occasion of Namath shaving his mustache for a commercial, Life's John McDermott opened his story this way: " 'Ain't he neat?' snarled one of Joe Namath's teammates, as if what he really wanted to do was rip off that mandarin hairlip with his bare hands." More barbed paragraphs followed, with comments about the "moody quarterback," his "magnanimous disdain" for booing fans, and the tolerance of teammates for a guy who "sometimes acts like Superjerk" so long as he helps them win. McDermott eventually got around to the "tremendous courage" with which Namath played on his injured knees, but not before he made it clear that the Jets succeeded for all the wrong reasons.[86]

The 1968 season determined what Namath would ultimately mean for professional football. After a miserable rookie season in 1965, he had improved, along with the Jets, but not nearly to the level expected of one of the game's highest-paid players. Famous for a rifle arm and the quickest release anyone had ever seen, Namath also had a bad habit of throwing to covered receivers instead of taking a loss. Following their 5–8–1 record in 1965, the Jets finished 6–6–2 in 1966, as Namath threw 19 touchdown passes but 27 interceptions. In 1967, he became the first pro quarterback to throw for more than 4,000 yards but also had another 28 interceptions (to go with 26 touchdowns), as the team went 8–5–1 and finished second in its division. At the beginning of the 1968 season, *Esquire* magazine published a fawning tribute to Namath from a friend and teammate, Bill Mathis, intercut by debunking comments by the journalist Al Hirshberg.[87] Two radically different views of Namath were up for grabs. The Jets won 11 and lost 3 in 1968, as Namath threw for fewer yards and fewer touchdowns (17), but also fewer interceptions (19), than the year before. The Super Bowl in January would determine whether or not Joe Namath finally mattered.

In Super Bowl III, Namath did what a rule-breaking athlete must do: he delivered on the field. Just as Lombardi's players would not have tolerated his treatment had they not quickly won NFL titles, many of Namath's teammates would not have accepted his behavior had he not taken them to the championship. And to old-fashioned fans he would have been just an overpaid loudmouth, rather than a brilliant quarterback who preferred the truth to Frank Merriwell platitudes. The Packers' easy victories in the first two Super Bowls had confirmed the NFL's overwhelming superiority. For the third test, *Sports Illustrated*'s Tex Maule, the epitome of NFL traditionalism, was fairly typical in giving the Jets no chance to win (he picked Baltimore, 43–0), but he went further in finding "unfathomable" most experts conceding an edge to the Jets at quarterback.[88] With the outcome seemingly inevitable, Namath provided the only drama. In the week before the game, he absolutely shattered the Merriwellian code. First, he predicted the Jets would beat the Colts (nearly 20-point favorites with the bookies). Then he told reporters that five or six quarterbacks in the AFL were better than Earl Morrall, who had recently been named the NFL's Most Valuable Player as Johnny Unitas's replacement (Namath won that honor in the AFL).

As the Colts played surprisingly badly, Namath coolly picked apart their secondary in the face of their supposedly unnerving pass rush, then trotted off the field waving his right index finger to signal that he and the Jets were "Number 1"—yet another insult to football tradition that within a few years would become as routine as mouthing "Hi, Mom," to the TV cameras. The white shoes of the rinky-dink AFL walked away with a 16–7 triumph over the black shoes of the not-so-mighty NFL, with Unitas himself on the field at the end. Even Maule now conceded that "the folk hero of the new generation" was also "a superb quarterback." And that professional football had forever changed: "So the era of John Unitas ended and the day of Broadway Joe and the mod quarterback began. John is crew cut and quiet and Joe has long hair and a big mouth, but haircuts and gab obviously have nothing to do with the efficiency of quarterbacks."[89] A bitter pill, but Maule swallowed it.

Super Bowl III was the first NFL championship officially named the Super Bowl, and, thanks to Namath, it established the title game as truly super. Not everyone embraced him afterward, but Namath could no longer be dismissed as a minor irritant that would fade away. The sports columnist for the *Oregon Statesman* likely spoke for many in the provinces when he wrote after the game that the guy he had considered "little more than a spoiled, mouthy jerk who needed a lesson" had proven himself "one of the best, mechanically, if not the very best" among NFL quarterbacks. "Too bad in a way," he added, "for now that he's established himself to such extent, everything he says or does will be noted more and more. And many of the things he says and does aren't what you'd like your kids to become interested in."[90]

While Namath had proven that first-rate football was compatible with the hedonistic lifestyle of Youth and the counterculture, his significance was still mostly limited to the world of sports. Then, in June, Namath inadvertently became a hero and victim of a vaguely political sort, when NFL commissioner Pete Rozelle ordered him to sell his interest in a Manhattan saloon called Bachelors III because it was frequented by gamblers and mobsters. Rozelle did not question Namath's integrity but, as always, he worried about the NFL's image. All of the news organizations covered Namath's press conference, during which he tearfully refused Rozelle's ultimatum and retired from football "on principle." Ever ready to dump on Namath, *Life* magazine did a cover story complete with mug shots of five Cosa Nostra wiseguys known to frequent Bachelors III. *Life*'s Sandy Smith acknowledged the appearance of a double standard, by which Rozelle seemed unconcerned that the Jets' new president, Philip Iselin, owned a race track, and that the Colts' owner, Carroll Rosenbloom, had bet heavily on his team in the Super Bowl. But Smith also reminded readers that players had more power to affect the outcome of games. He marveled that "Namath seems to be absolutely charmed by wrongos and has made a practice of talking, drinking, and chumming around with an appalling lot of larcenous slobs, as if totally oblivious to the fact that the most casual word from a quarterback before a game could affect the point spread." Even William F. Buckley Jr.'s conservative *National Review*, no fan of countercultural rebels, weighed in—on Namath's side!—not against Rozelle's ruling but against the unrestrained FBI wiretapping that had turned up the evidence about Bachelor III's unsavory clientele.[91]

Magazine accounts of men with names like Tea Balls, Harry the Hawk, Snake, and Johnny Echo gave off a whiff of Damon Runyon, but Rozelle saw nothing lovable in such characters. Rozelle had secured his credibility and power as commissioner by suspending Paul Hornung and Alex Karras for merely betting on NFL games. Bachelors III offered another ready-made opportunity to stand up for "the integrity of the game." In 1969, however, the issue took on larger significance, with Namath standing for individual rights and personal freedom against the power of The Establishment. As *Newsweek* put it, "in an age of youthful independence and rebellion inside and out of sports," the conflict between "the most vibrant young star" and "the strongest commissioner in sports . . . could hardly be more dramatically symbolized." *Life* less evenhandedly attributed to Namath "that same delight in anarchy which motivates the more typical 'revolutionists' of his age group." Three of Namath's teammates vowed to quit if Joe did; another saluted their star's stand on "principle" and called his retirement a "tragedy." Namath remained "retired" for a little over a month, until he and Rozelle announced an agreement that he would sell his share in Bachelors III and return to the Jets.[92]

The Bachelors III incident left Namath permanently embittered against certain sportswriters and publications,[93] but otherwise everyone could be happy. Joe Namath was the best thing to happen to the NFL since television, and the PR-minded Rozelle undoubtedly knew that, but Rozelle also had to know that Namath needed the NFL more than the NFL needed Namath. The incident strangely benefited both parties, as Namath's capitulation was generally satisfying. Retiring was foolish—not enough was at stake. The dispute mirrored the conflict tearing American society apart, but it concerned a game, not war in Vietnam or war in the streets. The stakes were more symbolic than real. Those outraged by Namath's rebelliousness could take pleasure in Rozelle's having put him in his place, but those who took Namath's side could be satisfied, too. They had the pleasure of despising Rozelle and The Establishment, and of seeing Namath as a victim of tyranny, while also agreeing that Namath had made a sensible decision and feeling relieved that he would still play. The games would go on, with the NFL's most glamorous star on the field, where he belonged. Namath emerged as a rebel but no martyr over Bachelors III. He was becoming a safe antihero for a changing mainstream society cautiously exploring its new freedoms.

Restored to the Jets, Namath entered the 1969 season as the most dominating presence in professional football since Red Grange in 1925. The September cover of *True* magazine captured the playboy football hero: Namath in his uniform, sitting on a bench in the locker room, with a miniskirted young woman peaking out of one of the lockers behind him. The introduction to his interview in *Playboy* that December called him a "kind of Belmondo with a jockstrap," a comparison that would puzzle most readers today, for whom Namath's fame has outlived the hunkish actor's. Cover stories in more respectable magazines like *Newsweek* and *Esquire* assessed the quarterback who now transcended sport. *Esquire* cast Namath on its October 1969 cover as King Kong in a Jets uniform under a mink coat, perched atop the Empire State Building with a football cocked to down the strafing aircraft coming at him from all sides. Inside, Jack Richardson, Rex Reed, and William F. Buckley Jr. contemplated "The Higher Truth of Joe Namath," their seriousness laced with irony. *Newsweek*'s Pete Axthelm played it straight. As "a free spirit and a rebel," Namath now clearly exceeded the boundaries of mere sport; but whether he was hero or villain, "a model of youthful independence—or a shaggy symbol of what is wrong with the younger generation," was the question of the moment. His "breakaway from the mold of the clean-cut and modest athletic star that other generations came to know and love" was obvious. "Whether his individual bag is serious politics or sheer style" was not so clear. Namath was more than just a football hero now, but what exactly was he?[94]

History's answer is that Namath's "bag" was more about style than politics, though this was an era in which style, for a brief moment, was political. Namath rocked the National Football League in the 1960s. In the 1970s, the NFL absorbed him and his iconoclasm to attract and hold a new generation of fans. Namath had a solid season in 1969, with his highest quarterback rating as a pro, but the Jets lost the AFL championship to the Kansas City Chiefs (who went on to beat the Minnesota Vikings in the Super Bowl and secure the parity of the AFL with the NFL). He then broke a bone in his passing hand in 1970 and tore another knee ligament in the 1971 preseason, playing a total of nine games over those two years. His status as football's greatest celebrity was in no way diminished, as he continued to make commercials and appear on talk shows and magazine covers, and started what proved to be a brief movie career (*C. C. and Company*, with Ann-Margaret, and *Norwood* both appeared in 1970, *The Last Rebel* in 1971).

Namath separated his shoulder in 1973 and severed two of the three hamstring muscles in his left leg in a waterskiing accident before the 1974 season, the unpublicized injury that rendered him truly immobile.[95] Namath played eight post–Super Bowl seasons with the Jets, sometimes brilliantly, more often not, as the team descended into mediocrity. He was then traded to the Los Angeles Rams in 1977 and retired reluctantly after the season. Namath ended his career with a completion average of barely 50 percent, with 220 interceptions to 173 touchdown passes and with a quarterback rating of just 65.6 (74.3 in his best season)—well below the records of the top quarterbacks.[g] Namath was not efficient but brilliant, and for 13 years he was always the most compelling player in the game. When he walked onto the field, everyone in the stadium knew he was there. Opponents went after him with ferocity, believing the Jets to be overmatched without him; but they spared his legs. They knew that he made money for everyone in the NFL; they also knew what courage it took to play on his damaged knees. "You have to live with yourself," my Chiefs teammate Willie Lanier stated simply in explaining to a reporter why he would never hit Namath below the waist.[96]

Those knees undid Namath, but they also eventually won him the esteem of the entire football world and made him a near-tragic figure. From the beginning, when he signed a contract for $427,000 the day after his final college game, then had surgery a month later, there were always two Namath stories: the one about his golden, god-favored life on and off the field, and the one about the knees that could end his golden football life tomorrow. Journalists made the public as constantly aware of his damaged knees as of his swinging lifestyle, and the added poignancy invested him with a bit of romantic doom. Writing in *Vogue* in 1967, Barbara Long, a writer not typically assigned to interview athletes, called Namath's fragile legs his "Aristotelian tragic flaw."[97] Sportswriters described them more prosaically: they marked his toughness. The pretty boy in white shoes and a fur coat played in constant pain and stood up to the fiercest pass rush, knowing that a single hit could end his career. Over time, the tough competitor increasingly became a wounded god, almost classically tragic, not like the angelic child with a terminal illness in a TV melodrama but something less sentimental, more genuinely haunting. The god-favored was also god-cursed. At the same time, his fragile knees also made Namath merely mortal, despite his fame and celebrity and the available stewardesses on every flight. He was greater than the rest of us but one of us, too. Or, as Murray Kempton put it in *Esquire* in 1972, "He is most immortal in his mortality."[98]

g. Namath's rating is not as low as it seems when compared to those of quarterbacks since the 1980s, when the short-passing game raised efficiency ratings (Joe Montana's lifetime rating was 92.3; Steve Young's, 97.6). Unitas's rating was 78.2; Y. A. Tittle's, 73.6; Terry Bradshaw's, 70.9. (All figures from *Total Football II*.)

Even *Life* magazine came to embrace Namath on these terms. A cover story in 1972 described Namath as "an astonishing combination of talent and vulnerability: the finest passing arm in football mounted on the game's most wretched pair of scarred, misshapen legs." The title of the piece was "Pain Pays the Bills for Joe's Good Life," with a cover photograph of Namath as a smartly dressed young man-about-town, lounging before the fireplace of his antique-furnished apartment. Namath had abandoned his notorious bachelor pad for "a slick Manhattan town house." Instead of flashy mink coats he now wore "$500 Rome-tailored suits." Joe Namath's "good life" had become a model for Park Avenue, not Broadway, let alone Haight-Ashbury. But he paid for it with daily whirlpool treatments and constant pain.[99]

Compared to Muhammad Ali, or to football players Dave Meggysey and Chip Oliver, Namath was finally not much of a rebel, yet he had the greatest impact on his sport. Ali, a genuine revolutionary, didn't change boxing; he changed the country. Oliver, the Oakland Raiders linebacker who left football to join a hippie commune, could be dismissed as a flake. Meggysey was truly radical, his 1970 book, *Out of Their League*, a devastating indictment of football at both the college and the professional levels; but by the time the book appeared Meggysey had left the game, and he had been only a lineman and linebacker, anyway. *Out of Their League* could become gospel to football's radical critics but be ignored or dismissed by the mainstream. Namath, on the other hand, was a star quarterback, a league and Super Bowl MVP, and after Super Bowl III no one could simply dismiss him. But what he stood for came to seem not very daring after all. He was, in political columnist James Reston's pithy phrase, a "long-haired hard-hat." Within the conservative football establishment he was a transformative figure, but in superficial ways. He stood for "hair and hedonism" when they seemed like radical statements, but by the end of the 1960s they were already defining a new middle-class lifestyle.[100]

J. Edgar Hoover once announced, "You won't find long hair or sideburns à la Joe Namath in the F.B.I."[101] Namath even inexplicably showed up on Richard Nixon's notorious "enemies list," the only sports celebrity so distinguished. Yet the "most politically charged words he ever uttered" followed a post–Super Bowl USO tour of military hospitals in Vietnam, that moved Namath to "wonder what the hell we're doing there."[102] That remark was surely offset by comments he made, in early 1973, during a controversy over playing the national anthem at sporting events: "I like it played. Every time I hear it before a game, it reminds me of where we are in the world, in life. I kind of thank God that we're in this country." Namath was fundamentally apolitical, and even as a countercultural rebel at his most flamboyant he barely kept ahead of the middle-class mainstream. On Haight-Ashbury or in Golden Gate Park, Broadway Joe's Beatle-length hair and occasional goatee would have seemed about as radical as the *Smothers Brothers* or *Rowan and Martin's Laugh-In.*[103]

Namath permanently altered the public image of the football hero. By 1974, as one sportswriter put it, Namath's lifestyle was "now standard among most of the country's top athletes."[104] He had this impact because he was actually old-school as much as new-school. His flamboyant style made football more appealing to the rebellious young. His toughness made a new style of football acceptable to traditionalists. But he did not challenge the economics of pro football, or the legal rights of the players, or certainly the political direction of the country. Namath was a safe rebel, the NFL's first football star to become a genuine celebrity in the larger culture, a crossover celebrity between the counterculture and the great American middle class. He even became available as a role model. In 1969 *Senior Scholastic,* the weekly magazine distributed to schoolchildren, ran a two-part profile of Namath as a hero who succeeded by overcoming obstacles, while becoming "a 100 per cent team man." His mother later published a book about her son Joe.[105]

By 1970 or so, to embrace Namath as a football hero was about as daring as letting your sideburns grow to the bottom or your ear lobe or buying a pair of polyester bell-bottoms. Magazines had already begun anointing Namath's heirs apparent, players with good looks and football style like Cincinnati quarterback Greg Cook and San Diego receiver Lance Alworth. Charger quarterback Marty Domres tried self-anointing with an account of the "days and nights of a rookie quarterback" called *Bump and Run.* Over the early 1970s, Namath off the field became a sex symbol firmly committed to a very old-fashioned sexual double standard (he expected his girlfriend of the moment to stay home while he prowled, and when he married, his bride must be a virgin). Following the Jets through the 1973 season, *New York Daily News* reporter Kay Gilman discovered that the club had to post a guard, "sometimes a guard plus a ferocious dog," outside Namath's hotel rooms on the road, to ward off groupies. "Joe Namath is America's sexiest sports personality ever," Gilman concluded. His impact on women lasted for decades.[106]

The safe rebel became as well known for his commercials as his touchdown passes, particularly the ones for Noxema with Farrah Fawcett and for Beautymist pantyhose, in which the camera moved up a pair of shapely nylon-sheathed legs to find Broadway Joe's grinning face at the other end.[107] Namath even became an advertisement for consumerism itself. Perhaps the most revealing image of Joe Namath is the February 1971 cover of *Esquire,* announcing a story about the new style of motorcycles popularized by the film *Easy Rider*. The cover photograph had Namath astride a bike, with a caption: "Which of these two items is a priceless work of art?" The article inside, not an ad but a piece of journalism, did not even mention Namath or football; it described the motorcycles. Namath was simply the icon of the hip male, summoned to validate the hipness of the machine. Football players had been endorsing brand-name products for decades. Namath was the first athlete in any sport to be himself an advertisement for a lifestyle.

Joe Namath transformed American football, but in ways that made it easier for the great American public to continue loving football after the convulsions of the 1960s. In his *Playboy* interview in December 1969, Namath disavowed "being anti-establishment or whatever; it's just that if it's not right for me, then I can't go along with it." What Namath finally stood for is "doing your own thing," a fundamental principle of American life in the 1970s and after. To read today a list of the charges levied against Namath 30-odd years ago, what shocks is how un-shocking they all now seem.[108] That's the point. Joe Namath made the NFL safe for a post-1960s world in which Vince Lombardi had lost relevance. Football still depended on its fundamental tension, but "Lombardi" became the recessive trait, "Namath" the dominant. Broadway Joe helped make NFL football a show that could play in prime time (the first *Monday Night Football* game featured the Jets and Cleveland), turn its Super Bowl into a national holiday, and eventually command billion-dollar television contracts. And as the dying Lombardi seemed to prophesy, Namath made "Prime Time" Deion Sanders and all the lesser Deions possible.

The 1974 players' strike marked the official end of the Lombardi era in the face of the Namath insurgency. Throughout the strike, Prescott Sullivan, a longtime columnist for the *San Francisco Examiner*, repeatedly invoked Lombardi as the one man who could have forced the intransigent players back into line. (Ironically, in 1968, as Bart Starr remained aloof from the NFL's first labor-management confrontation, Lombardi had called his quarterback into his office and told him that he owed his loyalty to the Players Association.)[109] When 49er running back Vic Washington accused his own coach, Dick Nolan, of being a "dictator," Sullivan shot back that the greatest coaches— Knute Rockne, Paul Brown, Bear Bryant, and above all Vince Lombardi—had all been dictators. Yes, but times had changed, and the signs had been visible for some time. Try to imagine Lombardi allowing NFL Films to place a microphone on him for Super Bowl I or II, as Hank Stram did for Super Bowl IV. Namath wore white shoes? In 1972 the entire Kansas City Chiefs team took the field in white shoes—on the road, that is, coordinated with white jerseys and red pants. At home, we wore red shoes, to go with red jerseys and white pants.[h] In 1974 the Baltimore Colts—the team that had "sneered when . . . Namath made white shoes the 'in' thing in pro football"—adopted white shoes, too. And in Atlanta, after the Falcons' old-school dictator, Norm Van Brocklin, abandoned his team's hair code, his middle linebacker, Tommy Nobis, of all people—the epitome of Lombardi-era rock-'em-sock-'em football—reported to camp with a Fu Manchu mustache. Symbolically, this was little less strange than Lombardi himself showing up in Green Bay some summer with a neatly trimmed goatee.[110]

Beneath the visible signs were real changes. With *Monday Night Football*, NFL football now competed in the prime-time TV market. And although the strike itself was widely viewed as an uprising of self-interested players against the traditions of the game, the truly self-interested ones were the veterans who abandoned their teammates on the picket lines. A note of me-first individualism now openly challenged the sanctity of "the team." The reality had never been as simple as it had seemed from the outside. As a product of the old school, I was shocked during my rookie season the first time Kansas City's coaches let several of my star teammates get away with loafing during a special teams drill. Lombardi famously treated all of his players "like dogs." Namath made the case for special treatment for top dogs. Perhaps this had long been the case in professional football. Lombardi, after all, was more an exception among NFL coaches than the standard-bearer of tradition. And perhaps Namath was more a symbol than an agent of change. Over the 1970s, 1980s, and 1990s, labor strife and franchise mobility would profoundly restructure the National Football League; but in the age of television, the reality of professional football for fans more than ever lay in its image, and it was the NFL's image that Joe Namath irreversibly changed.

h. Before our first home game, as I was about to take the field for warm-ups with the kickers, specialists, and other centers, our team clown, George Daney, called out to me, "Let me know if anyone laughs."

NO
FREEDOM,
NO
FOOTBALL

I entered pro football in 1970 at the end of the NFL's second brief work stoppage and exited in 1974 at the conclusion of its first full-blown strike. Between these two events passed four relatively uneventful NFL seasons, marked chiefly by the emergence of the Miami Dolphins as the NFL's newest "dynasty," and of O. J. Simpson as its greatest individual star. On the field, where in 1973 he became the first to rush for more than 2,000 yards, Simpson was a marvel of speed, grace, and control. Off the field, his good looks and nonthreatening charm would soon make him the NFL's first "crossover" black celebrity. In 1971 Kansas City seemed cruising back to the Super Bowl when we slipped up against the Dolphins on Christmas Day, in the first round of the playoffs, with the outcome not decided until the second sudden-death overtime period—an eerie Twilight Zone experience for me and still the longest game in NFL history. Dallas thumped Miami badly in the Super Bowl, but the next year belonged to the Dolphins, with Larry Csonka and Jim Kiick, their No-Name Defense, and what remains the only undefeated season in modern NFL history.

The Super Bowl was still just a championship game with a huge television audience, not yet an unofficial national holiday.[a] The Dolphins repeated in Super Bowl VIII and in 1974 were perhaps on their way to a third straight title

---

a. As a Chief, I was entitled to buy two tickets to the game but did it only once, when a former teammate from Notre Dame called to ask if I could get him seats. The idea that I should buy my allotment every year, because they would be worth a fortune to someone somewhere, never crossed my mind.

when they were derailed, not by Kansas City or Dallas, but by the World Football League (WFL) and their own "legendarily cheap" owner, Joe Robbie. With no rival league since the merger with the AFL in 1966, NFL clubs had no incentive to pay their players what they deserved. After back-to-back Super Bowl championships, Miami was paying $59,000 to Csonka, $58,000 to Kiick, and $70,000 to star receiver Paul Warfield, when Toronto (soon to be Memphis) of the newly announced WFL signed them for a total of $3.5 million for the 1975 season ($1.5 million for Csonka, $1 million each for Kiick and Warfield).[1] As the heart of the reigning Super Bowl champions' offense, Csonka, Kiick, and Warfield were the most visible of many NFL stars to sign future contracts with the new league over the spring and early summer of 1974 (O. J. reportedly turned down $2 million), as the Players Association moved toward a training camp strike.

Football as Work

The 1974 strike was itself a key event in the history of the NFL, the first major battle in a long and bitter labor war that would not end until 1993. But a detailed look at the strike also provides a close-up snapshot of the NFL at the end of the 1960s (the "long sixties" that ended with Richard Nixon's resignation just three days before the strike collapsed), a glimpse of the relations of players, owners, sportswriters, and fans at this moment in the history of the modern NFL.

The labor problems in the summer of 1974 were a long time coming. From 1920, when what became the National Football League was formed, individual players had leverage in negotiating with owners only when a rival league provided competition. In 1926 Red Grange was so powerful as a market draw that he was able to start his own league—the first of four American Football Leagues that would intermittently challenge the NFL. Grange made a fortune through various promotional schemes, but his celebrity was unique and his impact short-lived. The first AFL survived just one year; the second (1936–37) and third (1940–41) lasted just two years each. Into the 1940s, the owners' only real pressure came from the general economy: they had to pay their players well enough to entice them away from jobs in the "real world." Three of the first five Heisman Trophy winners passed up pro football altogether; the other two left after one or two seasons to pursue other careers. Except for top stars, young men who made it to the NFL tended to play not as long as they could but as long as they had to.

Competition from the All-America Football Conference from 1946 through 1949, then from the fourth and final American Football League in the early

1960s, temporarily drove up salaries and forced panicked owners into mergers. In both cases, saving the owners from having to pay market value for their players obviously came at the players' expense. The deal Pete Rozelle struck with Louisiana congressmen Hale Boggs and Russell Long—a franchise in New Orleans in exchange for exemption from antitrust law to allow the merger and end the bidding war for players—epitomizes the relative power of the owners and the "owned."

NFL players first tried to organize in December 1956, during one of the periods of the league's unchallenged monopoly. The owners simply ignored them. The following February, however, when the Supreme Court ruled in *Radovich v. NFL* that the league was subject to antitrust laws, Commissioner Bert Bell recognized the NFL's vulnerability to further lawsuits by players. Without seeking the approval of the owners, who he knew would still balk, Bell in December extended his own recognition to the National Football League Players Association. The owners had already accepted the players' demands for a minimum salary ($5,000), per diem in training camp and on the road during the season, and an injury clause, none of which had existed before, but they fought against recognizing the union. The issue was control. A collective bargaining unit would have the protection of federal labor laws. With a union the owners would have to bargain, not dictate, and power sharing was utterly alien to their view of pro football.[2]

Following *Radovich*, the players actually held the upper hand but failed to realize it or chose not to take advantage of it. Historian Michael Lomax has remarked on the surprising conservatism of Creighton Miller, the players' attorney and union director for the NFLPA's first 11 years. Miller made no attempt to challenge the college draft or the option clause, the two mechanisms by which owners dictated where players could play and ultimately for how much, both of which patently violated antitrust law. Against the desires of more militant players such as NFLPA president Pete Retzlaff and later Bernie Parrish, Miller preferred the association to be a "grievance committee" rather than a collective bargaining unit. Most of the league's stars, who could negotiate their own top salaries, also had little interest in "collective" issues; and without the leadership of the stars, rank-and-file players had no leverage. In 1959, backed by threat of lawsuits, the NFLPA did win the owners' approval of minimal insurance and pension plans, basic benefits for stars and ordinary players alike, but without any guarantee of secure funding. Lomax points out that Congress in these years would have supported much more emphatic rights for players, but the players themselves, behind Miller's leadership, did not push for them.[3]

Over the 1960s, funding the pension plan remained the major issue for the NFLPA, as the players remained divided over whether to become a true union and the owners continued to withhold official recognition. The merger of the NFL and AFL in 1966 left many veterans bitter over missing out on the owners' spending spree and set the stage for conflict.[4] In January 1968, NFL players rejected a proposal from Parrish to ally with the Teamsters (Miller resigned, or was forced out, during the dispute). Instead, they voted to remain an association rather than a full-fledged union, in return for recognition from the owners. The owners then refused to negotiate the players' demands. As the players prepared to strike their training camps in July, the owners locked them out—the first work stoppage in professional sports—and declared their intention to play with rookies if necessary. On July 14, before any exhibition games had been played, the owners and the NFLPA announced the first-ever collective bargaining agreement, largely on the owners' terms. On the key issue, the owners agreed to contribute $3 million over two years to the players' pension fund, slightly more than the current $1.4 million per year and far from the players' initial demand for $5 million annually.[5]

I knew none of this history when, in July 1970, I found myself with the College All-Stars practicing in Evanston, Illinois, for our game against the reigning Super Bowl champion Kansas City Chiefs and listening to representatives from the NFLPA ask for our support in their latest dispute with the owners. The key financial issue remained the pension, but the players also objected to Rozelle's position as a "joint owner," a commissioner hired by the owners with absolute authority to rule on their disputes with players. For the owners the issue was still control, as it would continue to be for the next 23 years. As William Wallace reported in the *New York Times*, the owners "resent the assumption of the management's prerogative by the athletes," and to preserve their "management position" they would cancel the season if necessary.[6] With negotiations stalled, the union leadership on July 9 ordered veterans not to report to camp. As in 1968, the owners responded by locking them out.

We All-Stars felt like bushwhacked bystanders. The College All-Star Game, pitting ex-collegians against the current NFL champions, had become a "summer classic" since its inception in 1934. Sponsored by Chicago Tribune Charities, with proceeds going to worthy causes, it also posed a public relations dilemma for NFL players and owners alike. No one wanted to be known for putting greed before charity. For coaches, the game was actually a nuisance, because it kept their top draft choices out of their own training camps while risking injuries. For us All-Stars, to play in the game was an honor but also a distraction from the more serious business of making our own teams. We were football players but not yet NFL players, asked to strike against owners whose teams we had not yet made.

We ended up boycotting practice for one day "in sympathy" with the striking veterans, then returned to football. In the meantime, coverage of the strike focused on whether Kansas City's veterans would play us. At the last minute, union president John Mackey, the great tight end of the Baltimore Colts, announced that the Chiefs could report to practice and play the game for charity's sake, but they would then leave camp again. It turned out that the Chiefs themselves had already decided on this course and the union was only saving face. Instead of the usual couple of hundred dollars for an exhibition game, the Chiefs would receive a full game check, one-fourteenth of their annual salaries, at a time when the league average was $23,000 and $1,650 meant a lot to most football players. Solidarity with the union would be personally expensive.

Two days before the game, the owners decided to test the resolve of the rest of the veterans by reopening their training camps. When the NFLPA countered by officially declaring a strike, Mike Curtis of the Baltimore Colts announced that he would defy the union and report to camp. Curtis, a fine linebacker, has the unfortunate distinction of being the first in a depressingly long line of NFL players willing to be scabs, though it turned out that he did not have to act on his intentions yet. Over the next few days, a small handful of players joined him in denouncing the strike (a total of 21, including "only three of stature," as Dave Anderson put it in the *New York Times*). The Dallas Cowboys voted unanimously to buck the union—"I'm not pro-owner," quarterback Craig Morton told reporters, "I'm pro-me and pro-team"—then changed their minds.[7]

In the midst of growing uncertainty over the status of the strike, the All-Star Game took place as scheduled on Friday night, July 31 (we lost, 24–3); then on Monday, Pete Rozelle brokered an agreement in a 20-hour negotiating session. (A top union official later claimed that Rozelle's role was minimal, a product "of his own press release," but the resolution of the dispute added luster to Rozelle's aura as a strong commissioner while also haunting him during subsequent strikes when he was unwilling or powerless to resolve them.) The players gained a few modest financial increases and their first-ever disability payments, widows' benefits, and maternity and dental benefits. On the major issue, the owners agreed to contribute $4.535 million annually to the players' pension fund, exactly what they had offered before the strike/lockout. Also, the players withdrew their objections to Rozelle's position as a "joint owner."[8]

The 1968 and 1970 incidents appear insignificant next to the prolonged and bitter strikes of 1974, 1982, and 1987. No regular or even preseason game was cancelled; training camps were barely disrupted in 1970. In light of later events, however, these early skirmishes now look like dress rehearsals for the more serious conflicts to come. Most of the key elements were in place. The owners were more concerned about power than profits. The appearance of union solidarity was misleading, because settlements were reached before individual players had to make any significant sacrifice. The wavering of the Chiefs over the All-Star Game and the first defections led by Curtis gave a preview of the union's future problems. And, of course, the ultimate resolution was on the owners' terms. They were willing to bump up benefits because of their increasing profits from television, not because they had to deal with a strong union.

The one missing element in 1968 and 1970 was public outcry. Deprived of no games, confronted by no picket lines, fans did not have to take sides. But as Leonard Koppett wrote in the *New York Times* after the 1970 settlement, "Labor turmoil in professional sports is here to stay," and the fans would be dragged into the next rounds. Koppett surprisingly judged that the players in 1970 had shown their strength, but he also warned that a "determined enough stand by club owners can, at this stage, probably crush any player union."[9]

1974: The Issues

The NFLPA had a different look in 1974. In January 1971, the National Labor Relations Board certified it as a true union. That same month, executive director Alan Miller was asked to resign, to be replaced in June by Ed Garvey, a young labor lawyer who had been advising the union leadership. In Garvey's first significant move, the NFLPA in 1972 filed a lawsuit in the name of union president John Mackey, challenging the so-called Rozelle Rule, which effectively prevented the movement of players. With three years under Garvey to prepare for contract negotiations in 1974, the prospects for union power seemed much better than in 1968 or 1970. It proved impossible, however, to focus public attention on football players' basic rights as workers and not their "greed." It also proved difficult for the union membership to rise to its rhetoric of solidarity.

Negotiations between the NFLPA and the NFL Management Council began in March 1974 and broke down on June 26, without progress. At issue were

63 demands, reduced from the 90 originally presented by the union on March 16, addressing concerns ranging from minimum salaries and the clubs' arbitrary authority over curfews and fines to a moratorium on new artificial turf fields until completion of an unbiased safety study. Money mattered. The players wanted to increase training camp per diem from $14.15 to $30 a day and raise minimum salaries of $12,000 for rookies and $13,000 for veterans to $20,000 and $25,000. But what immediately became known as the "freedom issues" mattered more. Even sportswriters with some sympathy for Garvey and the union saw a tactical mistake in not reducing the 63 demands to a more negotiable and comprehensible handful.[10] Sixty-three of anything were too many for the public, the owners, and the players themselves to grasp. The long list of demands had actually been intended not for public discussion but as a starting point for negotiations. The Management Council scored its first tactical victory by releasing them to the press.

The players' attack on fines and curfews, their demands to limit practice time and their workday (9 to 5, if you please!) seemed like the petty whining of spoiled brats. Actually, the Players Association wanted to *negotiate* these matters. It wanted to eliminate frivolous, exorbitant, and arbitrary fines, such as the New Orleans Saints' $1,000 penalty under a previous coach for not wearing socks to breakfast, and the Atlanta Falcons' $1,000 "gag rule" fine for publicly saying anything negative about the club. It wanted a say in setting curfews, instead of having an assistant coach telling 30-year-old men with children of their own to turn out the lights at 11:00 P.M. during training camp. Some of the players' specific demands did in fact seem silly, and cumulatively they seemed preposterous, but they were meant to be bargaining chips. They presented owners the reasonable demand to be treated like adults, the specific details to be worked out later. Instead, having to answer for the specific details in the press put union leaders constantly on the defensive. Superior resources and access to the media gave the Management Council control over the flow of information. The owners and their Management Council, for example, circulated figures on the supposed cost of the players' economic demands—a bankrupting $100 million or $130 million or $150 million (against supposed leaguewide revenue in 1973 of $162 million). Most important, league representatives hammered on the point that the "freedom issues" would mean anarchy in the NFL, the destruction of the game as we know it.[11]

The "anarchic" freedoms demanded in 1974 are the basic rights enjoyed by every player in the NFL today, but the strike of 1974 marked the beginning of a slow-motion revolution that took two decades to play out. The modern

NFL was built on two fundamental "anti-freedoms": the players' lack of freedom to move from team to team and the owners' lack of freedom to move from city to city. The Oakland Raiders' Al Davis would win freedom for owners in a three-year legal battle with the NFL in the early 1980s (more on that in later chapters). The players would not win theirs until 1993.

At issue in 1974 was an elaborate system—the draft, the reserve list, the option clause, the waiver system, the Rozelle Rule—that bound players to one club for the duration of their careers, as long as the club still wanted them. All of these mechanisms violated antitrust law but had survived as routine practices. The draft (the only part of the system still mostly intact today) assigned players to specific teams from the beginning of their careers. Any player who refused to sign with the team that drafted him was placed on its reserve list, to prevent him from signing with any other team. Once under contract, a player was bound to his club for the duration of the contract, plus an "option year" at 90 percent of his previous year's salary, if he could not agree with his club on a new one. Theoretically, the player could then negotiate with any team in the league, but there was a catch: if another club signed someone who had played out his option for another team, it owed appropriate compensation in players or draft choices to that team. If the two clubs could not agree on the compensation, the Rozelle Rule kicked in. The commissioner would determine the compensation, and his ruling was absolutely binding on the player's new club.

In theory, players had the option of free agency after four years in the league, the standard three years for which they signed out of college, plus the option year; but in practice the Rozelle Rule made free agency all but impossible for top players. The league adopted it in 1963, after wide receiver R. C. Owens played out his option with San Francisco and signed with the Baltimore Colts. In 1966, as part of the deal to win congressional approval for the NFL-AFL merger at the expense of players' power to negotiate with two leagues, the owners had promised Congress that players would have some freedom of movement. From 1966 through 1970, 42 players indeed became free agents. Twenty-nine received no outside offers. Thirteen signed with new clubs, and Rozelle had to rule in just two of those cases, both in 1968. In the first, he awarded Washington's second- and third-round draft choices to the St. Louis Cardinals after their All-Pro cornerback Pat Fisher signed with Washington. In the second, to compensate the 49ers for the loss of All-Pro tight end Dave Parks to New Orleans, Rozelle gave San Francisco the Saints' recently drafted number-one pick (Kevin Hardy, an All-American defensive tackle from Notre Dame) and a future number-one choice as well.[12] Rozelle's ruling in the Parks case was the chilling one: it instantly made the risk of signing a top free agent exorbitant.

A case involving defensive tackle Phil Olsen in 1971 reaffirmed the risk. As the Boston Patriots' first-round draft choice in 1970, Olsen became a free agent after the season on a technicality, when the Patriots failed to renew his contract by a prescribed date. After Olsen signed with the Los Angeles Rams, the Patriots appealed. Rozelle validated Olsen's contract with Los Angeles but required the Rams to give the Patriots a first-round draft choice *and* the $30,000 Olsen had originally received as a signing bonus from Boston.[13] In both the Parks and the Olsen rulings, Rozelle sent an unambiguous message to clubs contemplating the free-agent market: do not do it. The owners paid Rozelle partly to save them from themselves.

The Rozelle Rule trapped the players through a nifty Catch-22. Less-talented "fringe" players who played out their options had little bargaining power with other clubs. The better the player, the more bargaining power he had, but the more compensation he would also require; and his new club could not know what it would lose until it was too late to reconsider. Free agency remained possible, but no one could take advantage of it. When a federal judge declared the Rozelle Rule illegal in December 1975 (long after the strike collapsed), it had been invoked in just five of 176 possible cases over 12 years, but simply as a threat following the Parks and Olsen signings it had effectively made free agency for top players an illusion.[14]

Likely because it most affected marginal players, the waiver system received less attention during the strike, but it was even less defensible than the Rozelle Rule. When a player was cut, or "waived," by his team, the other 25 clubs had 48 hours to claim him for $100, proceeding in the order of that year's college draft. If a team claimed him, his own club could change its mind and withdraw him from waivers. If no one claimed him (if he "cleared waivers"), the player became a free agent, allowed to negotiate with any club. Most often, the fact that no one claimed him meant no one wanted him, and he disappeared from the NFL. Weaker clubs could sometimes pick up bargains from overstocked more successful teams. The talent-rich clubs, on the other hand, could test the trade market by putting a player on waivers, then withdraw him when another team claimed him, then contact that club to arrange a deal. Why give up the player for the $100 waiver price if you could snag a low draft choice or at least a larger chunk of cash in return?

As I hope this explanation conveys, an NFL player was never more thoroughly a piece of property than in the waiver system, where teams could haggle and barter and discard or keep him without his having any say in the matter, or even any knowledge of what was happening. Clubs handled waivers privately among themselves. Players were waived without their knowing it until after the club had finished whatever wheeling and dealing it wanted to do. A player waived, then recalled from waivers, could not even know which clubs had claimed him to give him a sense of his worth in the marketplace.

The obvious unfairness of the waiver system got lost in the challenge to the Rozelle Rule, which raised the specter of wealthy clubs in attractive locations grabbing all of the best players. Supposedly no player with O. J. Simpson's ability would ever again accept banishment to Buffalo. The NFLPA's attack on the Rozelle Rule was also part of a broader challenge to the commissioner's authority as sole arbiter of disputes between players and management. Girding for the expected strike, the owners in the off-season had extended Rozelle's contract for a reported $200,000 a year, more than all but a small handful of players earned (Joe Namath and Johnny Unitas, and possibly O. J.). The average player's salary in 1974 was about $30,000. How, the union asked, could a commissioner hired and paid by the owners several times that much render impartial judgments? Rozelle managed to maintain an appearance of neutrality. During the strike, Jeff Meyers of the *St. Louis Post-Dispatch* published the results of eight grievances that Rozelle had decided. With four decisions for the player and four for management, Rozelle appeared neutral, but an NFLPA spokesman pointed out that in the cases with systemic implications—challenges to the Standard Player Contract and the compensation for Phil Olsen—Rozelle ruled each time to preserve the status quo.[15]

The reserve list, the option clause, the clubs' and commissioner's authority to levy fines, the commissioner's absolute power to rule on disputes—the core of the NFL's anti-freedoms—were spelled out in a remarkable document known as the Standard Player Contract. Paragraph 4 of the one I signed on April 27, 1970, required me to comply with all the rules and regulations of the league and the club, and declared with thrilling redundancy that the commissioner's decision in disputes "shall be accepted as final, complete, conclusive, binding, and unappealable." Getting rid of the Standard Player Contract, replacing it with "a contract providing for mutuality of rights and obligations,"[16] was the freedom issue most compelling to me both on principle and in my position as a "fringe" player not envisioning potential wealth from free agency.

The one-sidedness of the Standard Player Contract was both philosophically and materially offensive. When a player joined an NFL club, he typically signed for three years. (Coming out of college as a fifth-round draft choice, I signed with the Chiefs for $15,000 in 1970, $16,500 in 1971, and $19,000 in

1972, with a $5,000 signing bonus.) Although the press usually reported such an agreement as a "three-year contract," the player actually signed three one-year contracts. The difference was more than semantic. The most galling inequity in the Standard Player Contract arose in the case of injuries. Paragraph 14 obligated the club, should I be injured, to "continue, during the term of this contract, to pay the Player his salary." "This contract" was for one year; it guaranteed my salary for 1970 if I blew out a knee. Behind it was another identical contract for 1971, and behind that a third for 1972. The club would owe me nothing for 1971 and 1972 if I were injured in 1970. *This* contract protected me under certain circumstances for one year. *These* contracts bound me to the Chiefs for three years, plus an option year (as detailed in paragraph 10). At the end of my third year in Kansas City, I negotiated my "new contract" with head coach Hank Stram: three more one-year contracts (and of course another option year). For a nonstar in particular, signing for another three years was not a matter of choice; the only "option" was the one explained in paragraph 10, and it was the club's, not mine.

Under the provisions of the Standard Player Contract, starters and backups alike who sustained career-ending injuries were routinely dumped at the end of the season or after failing their physicals at the start of the next training camp. Other clubs could take a look at them, but if their injuries were severe, they disappeared from the NFL without an additional penny of compensation. Perhaps there was no obvious injustice in a player's not being paid if he could not perform (although any other worker permanently disabled in a workplace accident would be at least partially compensated for the rest of his expected working life). The greater injustice lay in the one-sided obligation. Add to that inequity the Rozelle Rule, the commissioner's power to decide all disputes, the clubs' and the commissioner's power to levy fines at their own discretion —a thorough system of "owners" and "owned"—and the players' cause that seemed outrageous to their critics in 1974 would now likely appear unimpeachable to everyone.

Even in 1974, the "freedoms" demanded by the players, which meant the "anarchy" decried by the owners, amounted to the rights enjoyed by virtually every worker in the country. But that was the rub. Professional football players earning an average salary of $30,000, when the typical Teamster made $10,000, did not seem like ordinary workers entitled to ordinary workers' rights. Several critics of the striking players pointed out a "double standard" in negotiating collectively for benefits while continuing to negotiate individually for salaries. If the NFLPA were a true union, they argued, it would negotiate a pay scale: so much for quarterbacks, so much for linebackers; this for starters, that for reserves.[17] The current system, of course, was the owners' creation, not the players', and when Ed Garvey proposed a wage scale in 1982, the owners gagged. The "double-standard" in 1974 was theirs: the NFL allowing players to negotiate their own salaries, but with only one team.

NFL players were not workers but well-paid *professionals*, in a profession far more exclusive than the American Medical Association or the American Bar Association. Doctors and lawyers never went on strike. But doctors and lawyers, engineers and professors, enjoyed all of the freedoms that the players demanded. Football players qualified as neither "workers" nor "professionals" in the common understanding of those terms, nor were they yet viewed simply as "entertainers." Despite the contradiction, sports fans in 1974 generally liked to think of pro football players as workers like themselves, but as "heroes," too. As workers, striking players appeared greedy; at the same time, by insisting on their rights as workers they demystified their sport. Heroes might be flawed; Achilles had his heel, after all, not to mention his pigheadedness. But heroes were to be rewarded by the grateful beneficiaries of their exploits, not paid a negotiated salary and permitted a neutral arbitrator in disputes. And heroes certainly did not go on strike (actually Achilles did, but that's another story). Profound ambivalence about the work of professional athletes hung over the 1974 strike.[18]

On the Picket Lines

The players struck in 1974 over freedom and financial issues. The owners cared about those issues, too, but more so about control. Garvey, too, wanted control, and consequently for the owners the strike was also very much about Ed Garvey. In late June, with the strike imminent, Skip Myslenski published an account of the initial bargaining session in March that seems in retrospect to have predicted its failure. NFLP President Bill Curry opened the session on a moderate note, followed by Wellington Mara, who praised Curry and echoed his sentiments. Then Garvey stood up to read his statement: "It is time for change in the NFL. It is time to end the suffocating paternalism and the suppression of constitutional rights in the National Football League." At this point, as Myslenski reconstructed the session, the information director for the Management Council "scribbled in his notebook . . . 'Gloves come off.'"[19]

The players on their own, Myslenski implied, would have pursued an amicable negotiation, but Garvey polarized the two groups. Someone "close to the owners" told Myslenksi, "At the beginning the atmosphere among owners was one willing to make changes. But when they came in with the demands—the phraseology, the tone, the attitude—that turned the owners off. That's where Garvey made his mistake."[20] In other words, the Management Council had been prepared to surrender some of the owners' prerogatives, not concede players' rights. With the exception of Oakland's Al Davis, the owners hated Garvey—for filing the Mackey suit, for his abrasiveness, for his "arrogance."[21] They were also "guided by the domino theory" in opposing the freedom issues, "their fears dominated by the thought that to give a little here will entail giving much more later." Freedom, as Red Smith of the *New York Times* noted, was an absolute. As Smith put it, "the players aren't interested in being a little bit free. . . . A man wearing handcuffs doesn't want them loosened a little to ease the chafing. He wants them off."[22] All of these comments add up to a conclusion that the strike was doomed from the outset. In retrospect, I agree, but the 1974 strike also proved to be a necessary loss to make NFL players' future freedom possible.

Following the collapse of talks with the Management Council in June, the NFLPA—with Houston's Curry as president and an executive committee made up of past president Mackey (retired after a brilliant career with the Colts and Chargers), the Vikings' Alan Page, the Eagles' Kermit Alexander, the Raiders' Willie Brown, the Steelers' Tom Keating, and my Chiefs teammate Ed Podolak—announced that the strike would begin on July 1, two days before the first training camp would open. Because rookies and free agents reported several days before the veterans, the initial skirmishes between management and striking players would be over the opening of the camps to rookies. Once veterans were scheduled to report, the intensity of the strike would escalate, though the financial costs would remain minimal for a time. The veterans would be sacrificing only $14.15 a day in per diems; owners would lose nothing at all until exhibition games began. At that point, the strike would become decidedly consequential for them. The exhibition season accounted for a significant portion of club profits, because the owners paid their players a fraction of their salaries (ranging from $98 to $360 per game, depending on their years in the league) and charged the fans full price for their tickets. Many clubs required tickets for exhibition games as part of the season ticket package. (To maintain its edge in the public relations war, the Management Council would eventually direct clubs to offer refunds for the preseason games played by mostly rookies.)

The initial salvo actually came before players set up their first picket line, when the Colts' Mike Curtis presented an encore of his 1970 performance. This time, he denounced the union for its "greed, greed, greed" and called Garvey "a left-wing opportunist who is trying to make a name for himself at the players' expense." Curtis also admitted to being paid "more than I think

I'm worth" and challenged Garvey's move to eliminate fines and curfews. "When Garvey says mature men should not be under these controls, you have to laugh," Curtis told reporters. "Mature men? Football players? I haven't held a job in my life. I play a game for a living. I'm spoiled and I love it."[23] Picked up by newspapers around the country, Curtis's comments set the tone for the verbal sparring between the union and the owners, and for the commentary in the press. Here was a player, a top player, admitting that he and his teammates had a better deal than any of them deserved. A few days later, one day before picketing was to begin, Miami center Jim Langer accused the Players Association of making "ridiculous demands" and said that 80 percent of his teammates, the defending Super Bowl champions, wanted to play in the College All-Star Game, the next major site for confrontation after the opening of training camps.[24] The players were losing before their strike even started, and their most deadly enemies came from their own ranks.

The San Diego Chargers opened the first training camp, on the campus of U.S. International University under new coach Tommy Prothro. In the days leading up to the July 3 opening date, Garvey and Curry declared the critical importance of keeping rookies and free agents out of camp, a tactical blunder that virtually guaranteed a union defeat in the first skirmish. Each club typically had three or four high draft choices almost certain to make the team. A few others might survive, but they all faced high odds, which would be considerably improved if they received the coaches' full attention while the veterans remained out of camp. Expecting a free-agent rookie or a fourteenth-round draft choice to boycott training camp, to support a union he might never have a chance to join, was a terrible miscalculation. The union should have conceded on the rookie issue and staked its strength elsewhere.

The union planned a public relations coup for San Diego, sending stars from around the league to picket. They arrived in a festive mood, wearing T-shirts with a clenched fist and the slogan, "No Freedom, No Football," and carrying signs that declared, "Monopoly Is Played With Dice, Not People," "Freedom's Not an Issue But a Right," "People Are Players, Not Property," and the like. The symbol and slogans, right out of the Black Power and antiwar movements of just a few years earlier,[b] antagonized several sports-

b. Atlanta coach Norm Van Brocklin fumed that the strikers who harassed his players before one exhibition game "belong at Berkeley or the University of Wisconsin," collegiate hotbeds of the 1960s antiwar movement. In a book on the black revolt of the 1960s, sociologist Douglas Hartmann sees the labor strife in pro sports in the 1970s as the sole athletic arena in which 1960s political activism survived. I suspect that the motives of the majority of football players in 1974 were more personal than consciously political.

writers and likely polarized the public.[25] (After the strike collapsed, a columnist for the *Cincinnati Enquirer* mentioned a "theory" that the freedom issues at the heart of the strike were "substantially black issues," an idea seemingly confirmed by the majority of whites among the big-name stars who eventually turned against the union, though not so clear in relation to the rank-and-file.)[26]

The festive mood lasted one day. On day two, the Chargers denounced Garvey for trespassing on university property and accused one of the picketing players of menacing a club attorney. (After Willie Brown reportedly threatened to "take [the lawyer's] head off," Charger owner Gene Klein solemnly told reporters that this was "a very serious matter" since professional athletes "have lethal weapons in their arms.") In the meantime, all of the Charger rookies and free agents reported to camp, though one free agent, a journeyman receiver named Coleman Zeno, left before the first practice. The union had hoped to lure the team's prize rookies, their two first-round draft choices and quarterback Jesse Freitas, who had emerged as a future star in the recent Coaches' All-America Game. Instead, as *San Diego Union* sports editor Jack Murphy put it when Zeno walked out, "They cast a net for a whale and caught a minnow." On day three, one of the Chargers' top draft picks, linebacker Don Goode from Kansas, did leave camp to join the pickets, but he returned the next day after Klein threatened to rescind his signing bonus.[27] The events in San Diego were a national story, with Round 1 clearly going to the owners, and San Diego set the pattern for the remaining 25 training camps as they opened over the next few weeks.

The threat to rookies' bonuses raised an issue for many veterans as well. By mid-June the World Football League, set to debut on July 10 with franchises in 12 cities, 6 of them with NFL clubs, had signed more than 60 NFL players, most of them to future contracts for 1975 or 1976, after their option year expired. Over the spring and early summer, the Dolphins (after Csonka, Kiick, and Warfield defected), the Cowboys (after losing eight players, the most of any team), and several other NFL teams took preventive measures by signing key veterans to new contracts, often with a hefty signing bonus as a hedge against the strike as well as the WFL. The new contracts typically included a statement about forfeiture for not reporting to training camp on time. Union officials (along with the *New York Times*' Red Smith, the players' most eloquent champion in the press) pointed out that any provision that penalized a player for union activity was an illegal "yellow-dog" contract, but players worried anyway.[28] (The National Labor Relations Board would ultimately rule, but not for two years, that the Chargers and Dolphins could not rescind the signing bonuses of Don Goode in the first case and of Larry Little, Bill Stanfill, and Manny Fernandez in the other.)[29]

The WFL would not even last through a second season, but in the summer of 1974 it seemed a real threat to the NFL and a real godsend to the union, whose leaders believed that the financial pressure from a rival league would force the owners into an early settlement. Instead, the presence of the WFL weakened the players' position. It created free agency for some and a public illusion of free agency for all—why complain about the Rozelle Rule when players were jumping right and left to the WFL for hundreds of thousands of dollars? It also fed a public impression that all NFL players made the huge salaries of the well-publicized few. Most disastrously, the renegotiated contracts created a powerful disincentive for a number of key players, most conspicuously in Miami, Dallas, and Cincinnati, to take a stand with their union. The heady sense of power with which Garvey and other union leaders arrived in San Diego dissipated quickly.

The College All-Star Game scheduled for July 26 became the next key battleground. Unlike in 1970, no agreement by the union permitted the NFL representative, the Miami Dolphins, to play the game then go back on strike. The cancellation, announced on July 10, was another black mark against the union, despite Garvey's immediate announcement that the NFLPA would donate $100,000, half of the anticipated receipts, to Chicago Tribune Charities. Edwin Pope, sports editor of the *Miami Herald* and another of the writers on the side of the union, pointed out that over a 40-year period the All-Star game had raised about $3.2 million for charity, while a banquet sponsored by the NFLPA for just the past eight years had raised $2 million. "This issue isn't quite as one-sided as some of the great humanitarians among the owners would have you think," Pope wrote, but these complicating facts had no discernible impact on public opinion or the media generally.[30]

More damaging to the union than the bad publicity from the cancelled All-Star Game was the bad feeling among the Dolphin players, who would have been paid one-fourteenth of their salaries for playing in the game. As the NFL's best-paid team—thanks to the threat of the WFL, not Joe Robbie's generosity—the Dolphins risked losing the most money in a strike (while also having the most left over after the strike ended, I would add). Angry Dolphins even tried unsuccessfully to have the union tax each member $100 toward making up their personal loss from canceling the All-Star Game. When Miami's training camp opened for veterans on July 17, outspoken Jim Langer and a half-dozen of his teammates (including starters Jim Mandich, Jake Scott, and Mercury Morris) all reported. These four were among 15 Dolphins the club had signed to new contracts, each of the four in the $100,000 range for salary and bonus. Twelve of the 15 ended up reporting before the strike ended—only Little, Stanfill, and Fernandez held out—and were among the 35 out of 49 veterans from the 1973 Super Bowl squad who abandoned the union.[31] (These players today likely prefer to be remembered for their 1972 undefeated season.)

The strike was probably lost in Miami and Cincinnati, if not already in San Diego. Four days before the defections began in Miami, 12 Bengals, led by starting tight end Bob Trumpy and defensive captain Royce Berry, reported on the first day of Paul Brown's camp. Over the off-season, as the *Cincinnati Enquirer* reported, Brown had signed the "solid heart" of the team to multi-year contracts "with substantial raises in salary," a highly effective legal bribe. A rumor that Brown included $5,000 bonuses specifically for reporting to camp circulated widely during the strike.[32] (We heard it on our picket line in Kansas City.) The immediate loss of a dozen veterans put obvious pressure on their striking teammates, and the next several days saw a steady stream of defections in Cincinnati, one or two at a time, including offensive captain Bob Johnson on July 18, All-Pro defensive tackle Mike Reid on July 25, and starting quarterback Ken Anderson on July 28, until 28 of 47 Bengal veterans had given up the strike.[33]

Player reps Pat Matson of the Bengals and Doug Swift of the Dolphins had to stand by and watch the bleeding from their picket lines. At the center of the strike in each NFL city, the team's elected player representative served as the link between his teammates and the union leadership and as chief spokesman with the local media. In most seasons the position entailed little work, and player reps were typically elected in casual ways. (The team has a two-minute meeting at which X is nominated because he went to an Ivy League school or is interested in public affairs. All in favor: aye! All opposed: silence. X is the player rep.) The strike suddenly thrust reps like Matson and Swift into unfamiliar and uncomfortable roles. In addition to feeling betrayed by his teammates while catching hell from the NFLPA leadership for not controlling them, Matson had to weather attacks by Cincinnati fans as the symbol of the whole mess. Other player reps received hate mail and nasty phone calls, but Matson's were particularly personal, including a wish that his off-season business would fail. In one of the strike's many bitter ironies, Matson himself had been picketed several months earlier while building a facility with non-union labor, making him a target even of local labor leaders who supported the striking players.[34]

Swift was the man in the middle of the divided Super Bowl champions. In one of the strike's most widely reported incidents, Swift infuriated his coach, Don Shula, with a comment before the Dolphins' first exhibition game, against Cincinnati no less, that he hoped the Bengals would beat the Dolphins' scabs "like a gong." The son of two doctors and himself an off-season medical student with an undergraduate degree from Amherst, Swift balanced his unwavering commitment to the union's position with an unusually wry and acerbic view of the entire affair. When accused of hypocrisy, since he had made the team as a free-agent rookie in 1970 in the aftermath of the previous brief strike, Swift disarmingly admitted, "I didn't know anything about a union then. I was just a scab like everybody else." Swift's actions and demeanor won the respect of the *Miami Herald*'s Edwin Pope and Bill Braucher. Braucher defended the "gong" remark as "vintage Swift in its traces of exasperation and humor," from a rare football player with a "keen sense of the human comedy." Braucher also reminded readers that Swift happened to be "the most under-rated if not the best" strong-side linebacker in the NFL, one of the key reasons for the team's Super Bowl success. Among the lessons of the strike was how quickly football heroes could become bums in fans' eyes.[35]

Strikers and Strikebreakers

Either Miami or Cincinnati could represent how the strike generally un-folded: a crack in union solidarity kept widening until it became a chasm. But each NFL city also had its own strike experience. Hard-line owners such as Miami's Robbie, San Diego's Klein, Chicago's George Halas, Minnesota's Max Winter, and the New York Giants' Wellington Mara wanted to break the union. (Eulogies on Mara's death in 2005 to the NFL's last Grand Old Man and benevolent patriarch required historical amnesia. The old guard in their day were basically paternalists, benevolent when possible but ruthless when necessary, and in 1974 Mara was among the hardest of the hard-liners.)[36] Pittsburgh's Art Rooney, another member of the old guard but a "players' owner," reacted with more pain than anger.

Likewise, teams revealed varying degrees of solidarity. Besides Miami and Cincinnati, clubs in Dallas, Oakland, Los Angeles, Philadelphia, and Atlanta saw massive defections from the picket lines. In Denver, Washington, Buf-falo, Chicago, Detroit, Kansas City, Minnesota, St. Louis, New Orleans, and New York (Jets), defections were minimal. Between the two extremes, Bal-timore, Boston, Cleveland, Green Bay, Houston, Pittsburgh, San Diego, and San Francisco saw several defections but mostly among "marginal" veterans fearful of losing their jobs. If the local newspaper coverage can be trusted, 10 of the 26 teams (Atlanta, Baltimore, Chicago, Cincinnati, Green Bay, Houston, San Diego, Oakland, Philadelphia, and the New York Giants) experienced serious dissension, either among the players or between the players and management. The other 16 did not all support the strike to the same degree but emerged with fewer scars.

For already dysfunctional franchises, the strike exacerbated problems. The San Diego Chargers were attempting to recover from the NFL's first drug scandal, in 1973, when Commissioner Rozelle fined eight players a total of $40,000. The drugs, amphetamines, had in fact long been handed out by team trainers, and the players were bitter at having been made scapegoats for a leaguewide problem. Most Charger veterans wanted out, and by the end of the strike all eight had been shipped off to other teams. (One of them, Walt Sweeney, won a $1.8 million lawsuit against the club for causing his drug addiction, but not until 1997, long after everyone else had forgotten the incident.)[37] Players wanted out of Chicago, too, where the NFL's once most-respected franchise had become its "most demeaned," and local sportswriters were openly contemptuous. "The Bears are the Siberia of pro football," one Chicago Tribune columnist admitted, the place to which bad boys on other teams were threatened with banishment.[38] (Following the collapse of the strike, one disgruntled St. Louis Cardinal asked to be traded to any team but Chicago and was promptly shipped to the Bears.)[39]

The situations in Baltimore and Houston were worse. In 1972 Carroll Rosenbloom arranged for Robert Irsay to buy the Los Angeles Rams, then swap his Rams for Rosenbloom's Colts. With general manager Joe Thomas as his hatchet man, Irsay immediately began dismantling the Baltimore community's beloved Colts, unloading anyone judged unproductive or disloyal, even the aging but still-revered John Unitas.[40] While many NFL executives were furious at defectors to the World Football League, Thomas went further than the rest, not just dumping the traitors but ripping them in the press afterward. After Ted Hendricks signed with the Jacksonville Sharks, Thomas told reporters that "Hendricks's selection as an All-Pro linebacker the past three years may have been more a result of favorable publicity than consistently strong defensive play." ("Favorable publicity" got Hendricks all the way to the Hall of Fame.) Thomas traded Hendricks to Green Bay and took a similar cheap shot at Tom Drougas after sending him to New Orleans.[41]

Joe Thomas was a pussycat compared to Houston coach Sid Gillman. First with the Los Angeles Rams (1955–59), then with the Los Angeles/San Diego Chargers (1960–71), Gillman had been pro football's most brilliant offensive innovator, the principle architect of the modern passing game. Gillman then moved into the front office of the Houston Oilers as general manager, only to watch the Oilers become the worst team in the league. After they opened the 1973 season with five losses, he fired his coach and took over the team himself (to little effect, as the Oilers finished 1–13 for the second year in a row). Gillman entered the 1974 preseason convinced that his predecessors had been too nice, that the players needed toughening, that a football coach must have total control. Many coaches during the strike subtly pressured their picketing veterans by over-praising some rookie or free agent in camp. Gillman did not bother with subtlety. He publicly called a free-agent rookie tackle "better than anybody I saw last year." He publicly worried that Bill Curry, the Oilers' starting center as well as the NFLPA's president, was not in camp to recover from knee surgery, and he declared a new Oiler claimed from injured waivers (my old roommate from the Chiefs, Sid Smith) to be his starting center for the season. Gillman's contempt for those on strike was shared by linebacker Steve Kiner, who after reporting to camp called Curry "hypocritical" since he owed everything he had to football, and referred to his striking teammates as "those idiots on the hill" (referring to the perch from which they picketed and watched practice). While other teams worried about possible damage to team unity, Gillman declared that players and coaches did not have to love each other in order to win.[42]

There were no happy strikers in 1974, but the teams that stressed unity weathered the strike less painfully. In Denver and Washington, coaches John Ralston and George Allen preferred all of their veterans out of camp, at least initially, rather than some out, some in. Several coaches wanted veterans to report, but the players themselves put solidarity first. (When asked if he preferred that all of his veterans stay out or some report to camp, Pittsburgh coach Chuck Noll answered, "That's like asking if you would rather die by machine gun or fire.")[43] In St. Louis, the strike became an opportunity for a team notoriously divided by "political and racial and intellectual differences" to forge "a feeling of unity that has never existed before," as they stayed out of camp en masse.[44] The Redskins rallied around the union as well as the team. The Buffalo Bills, Boston Patriots, and New Orleans Saints were weak for the union but strong for each other.

In Minneapolis, the Vikings' unity was forged chiefly by Alan Page, not only a union official and the team's player rep, but also the NFL's only defenseman to be named Most Valuable Player. The Vikings were the last team to open training camp and so the team least tested by the draining pressures of a prolonged strike, but it turned out that only Page's dominating personality kept many of his teammates out of camp.[45] Although the Redskins, as a group, were the most militant unionists, the Denver Broncos were the only team whose veterans remained 100 percent on strike to the very end. Player rep Jim Turner and his teammates repeatedly declared their love for coach John Ralston and owner Gerald Phipps, while Ralston and Phipps suppressed their obvious frustration that their unified team stayed out of camp, not in. Despite the antistrike feelings of sports editor Jim Graham, the writers in the *Denver Post* had almost no choice but to subscribe to the party line, constantly reiterating the idea that, by staying together as a team throughout the strike, the Broncos would forge bonds that could carry them into the playoffs.[46]

The experience in most NFL cities fell somewhere between the extremes of Denver and Houston. A supposed commitment to team unity shared by Green Bay coach Dan Devine and Packer players led by Ken Bowman suddenly looked less mutual when the club had 19 pickets arrested outside Lambeau Field before an exhibition scrimmage with the Bears.[47] Atlanta's notoriously hard-line, old-school coach Norm Van Brocklin put the fear of God (or rather, the fear of Van Brocklin) in his less-secure striking veterans when he traded player rep and starting defensive back Ken Reaves on the first day of picketing. (Reaves became the fourth Falcon player rep to be cut or traded in the team's nine-year history.)[48] The fact that 21 Falcon veterans but only 4 starters eventually defected from the strike suggests that Van Brocklin's "fringe" or "marginal" players felt particularly vulnerable.

Either the Philadelphia Eagles were the team most bitterly divided by the strike, or the *Philadelphia Inquirer* simply exposed more bitterness. Leonard Tose was one of the owners, along with the Rams' Carroll Rosenbloom and the Browns' Art Modell, who took the strike as a personal affront. Eagle players expressed "love and respect" for Tose and coach Mike McCormack, but they were also committed to their union, a conflict of allegiances that neither Tose nor McCormack could tolerate.[49] The two of them split the team into bitter factions at a six-hour meeting with their veterans on July 21, the details of which did not come out for several weeks. Tose threatened to sell the team and McCormack threatened to resign; both sides "accused each other of outright lying."[50]

Eagle quarterback Roman Gabriel, "the Messiah" to his teammates, became the focal point of the strikers' anger. From the beginning of the strike, Gabriel remained aloof, "refusing either to join his teammates or cross their picket lines." When he reported to camp four days after the divisive meeting, with his $125,000 contract, several teammates were furious. Many Eagles "hate his guts," one of them told a reporter. When a picketing player cursed him before a practice session at Veterans Stadium, Gabriel flipped him off.

Meanwhile, Eagle management reacted ruthlessly to the strikers, waiving three reserves (Rick Arrington, Al Nelson, and Tom Roussel) while they were still on strike. A personal feud between Tose and player rep Tom Dempsey continued even after the strike ended.[51]

The strike overall was a war of attrition, punctuated by occasional skirmishes, with strikers quietly furious or screaming "Scab!" at strikebreakers in Green Bay, Oakland, and New York (Giants).[52] The most shocking event of the summer had nothing to do with labor conflict: the sudden death on July 28 of the Detroit Lions' 53-year-old coach, Don McCafferty, from a heart attack while working in his yard on a Sunday away from training camp.[53] Suddenly, in Detroit, the strike did not seem like a life-or-death matter, but life goes on, and so did the strike.

Losing in the Press

After the cancellation of the All-Star game, the sites of conflict shifted back to the 26 training camps and to the preseason contests that began with the Hall of Fame game on July 27, matching the Buffalo Bills and St. Louis Cardinals in Canton, Ohio, a city committed equally to football and unions.[54] What should have been a symbolic triumph for the NFLPA, with teamsters and steelworkers picketing alongside football players, became instead another public relations disaster, when the NFLPA's pickets were themselves picketed by NFL old-timers angry that the union refused to seek pension benefits for them. An eloquent statement by Leon Hart on behalf of the NFL Alumni, and an ill-considered retort by the Redskins' John Wilbur that Hart had played too many games in a leather helmet, left a distinct impression—reinforced by numerous columnists—that the current players were selfishly betraying those who had made their privileged lives possible.[55]

Sports editor Jim Graham of the *Denver Post* had reported to his readers weeks earlier that the NFL Alumni had demanded a "full pension or nothing," the cost of which would have "reduced by more than half present-day retirement funds." (A harsh critic of the union during the strike, Graham passed on this information, likely from the Broncos' player rep Jim Turner, "in fairness.") As Graham pointed out, the Players Association had no real choice but to reject the proposal.[56] Like the NFLPA's charity banquet, this bit of information did not make it around the league and was missing from the reports on the confrontation in Canton. Current players always appear somehow diminished from an earlier Golden Age. During the strike, that familiar sentiment played out as greedy players scorning the giants of the past, an image fed by criticism from old-time stars such as Sammy Baugh, Paul

Hornung, Gale Sayers, Steve Van Buren, Dick "Night Train" Lane, and Bill George.[57]

Following the Hall of Fame game, attendance for the first full weekend of exhibitions dropped nearly 50 percent from 1973, a loss of $1.8 million at the gate, but the owners remained adamant that they would take their losses and even cancel the regular season if necessary.[58] The players' apparent victory in hurting attendance was offset by the steady erosion from their picket lines. Each day, the major news services reported the big names among the new defectors, along with an overall tally provided by a spokesman for the Management Council: 104 veterans were in camp by July 20, 183 by July 27 (53 of them "regulars"), 233 by July 29, 251 by July 30, 273 by July 31, 299 by August 1, 310 by August 3.[59] This was news, not propaganda, but it was also the owners' most effective weapon for weakening the resolve of those who remained on strike. (The Management Council directed clubs to include members of the taxi squad as veterans, in order to inflate the numbers.)[60] Union leaders had approached the 1974 strike determined to get their side out to the public more effectively than they had in 1970, but once again they were no match for the league's greater resources and access to both national and local media. On the picket lines in Buffalo or Cleveland or Kansas City, players still on strike felt more vulnerable with each big-name defection and each daily tally. The very day that the press reported the fall-off in attendance, the surrender of three starting quarterbacks—Bob Griese, John Hadl, and Terry Bradshaw—seemed to signal the strikers' doom.

Spokespersons for the Management Council also shaped the public's sense of the stakes by feeding the media selective financial data. In a preemptive strike on June 6, the Management Council released a financial report for the NFL in 1973, claiming total revenue of $162 million, or an average of $6.2 million per club, and average profits of $472,500. A former player, George Burnam, now an economist for the NFLPA, contended that clubs actually averaged $2.3 million in profits, but management's figures were the ones widely circulated. As Edwin Pope noted several weeks later in the *Miami Herald*, "Statisticians can make figures dance to any tune." Among the columnists from the 26 newspapers I surveyed, only Red Smith also challenged management's figures. The owners' after-tax profit of $472,500 (a modest 7.6 percent of revenue) presupposed the same 7.6 percent in taxes, but Smith questioned how much taxes the owners actually paid. Smith hypothesized a franchise worth $16 million, which included $15 million for the value of the players' contracts, depreciated over five years at $3 million a year. An actual profit of $1.5 million for the year would appear as a loss of $1.5 million. Smith also pointed out that clubs counted salaries drawn by the owners and their relatives as "general administrative costs" instead of profits.[61]

With privately owned clubs not required to publish financial statements, Smith and Garvey (whose requests for information on tax payments were ignored) could only challenge the Management Council figures, not produce definitive ones. Moreover, in our information-overloaded, mass-mediated world, some news gains wide currency while other news dies, through processes invisible to outsiders. The day before the union officially declared the strike, the *New York Daily News* compared salaries and benefits in the four major professional sports leagues, showing that football players had the lowest salaries (both average and minimum), shortest careers, and longest wait to receive pension benefits; and that the NFL alone had no impartial arbitrator or grievance board (only football players' insurance benefits matched those in other leagues).[62] This story was not picked up elsewhere, and it did not even influence the *Daily News*'s own Dick Young, one of the striking players' nastiest critics. Also, in the midst of the strike the Brookings Institution released a publication titled *Government and the Sports Business*. Wire service summaries of the government subsidies and tax write-offs that meant huge invisible profits for owners could not clarify the murky economics of NFL football in a way that affected sports page commentary.[63]

The Management Council also had the advantage of representing just 26 voices. While spokespersons for the league and the clubs remained always, as we now say, "on message," the players were more than 1,200 individuals, each with his own ideas and feelings. Players on the picket lines frankly confessed to reporters their desire to be playing football rather than striking, predicted how long the strike would last, in some cases hinted at how long they themselves could hold out. All of these comments sent clear signals to the owners that the players could be outlasted. The owners had not just better access to the media but also more "discipline" in exploiting it.

In its most devious stratagem, the Management Council implemented on July 18, without union assent, a new proposal for preseason pay. Instead of $98 to $360 dollars, depending on years in service, veterans would now receive 10 percent of their salary for the six games, up to a maximum of $10,000. Lost pay for exhibition games suddenly mattered, and mattered more the higher the player's salary. A five-year veteran making $30,000 saw his $360 rise to $500 per game. An All-Pro making $100,000 went from $360 to $1,667. Suddenly, stars could feel they risked more by striking than their "marginal" teammates (who had only their jobs on the line). Jake Scott, one of the strikebreaking Dolphins with a $100,000 salary, had considered returning to the picket line but changed his mind at that point. "When the owners decided to pay 10 per cent of your salary during training camp," Scott told the *Miami Herald*, "it made it awfully difficult for a guy to stay out."[64] (On July 1, 1976, a bit late to affect the strike, the National Labor Relations Board ruled that unilaterally implementing new wage scales for preseason games had been illegal.)[65]

Players on the picket lines received regular updates from player reps, but we also followed the strike through our local newspapers. We read about the mass defections by the Bengals and Dolphins, the steady stream of individual players giving up the strike, the updated overall tallies. We also read our own local columnists and reporters, few of whom took our side. The union's complaint about bias in the press became itself an issue for the press as the strike played out. As Edwin Pope of the *Miami Herald* put it, "The staggering difference in verbal firepower is obvious in the public view of the strike."[66]

Although the claim that the NFLPA had *no* media support in 1974 has been overstated, our backing was meager. It seems likely that newspapers outside NFL cities, with no team to arouse conflicting sympathies, more or less uniformly opposed the strike. In NFL cities, the majority of writers denounced the strike but expressed some sympathy for their own team's striking players. All sportswriters covering the 1974 strike assumed from the beginning that their readers overwhelmingly took the owners' side. A few puzzled over this "unusual occurrence," as Tom Callahan of the *Cincinnati Enquirer* put it, "when steelworkers and clerks find it easier to relate to millionaires like Lamar Hunt and Gene Klein than to men who perspire at their work."[67] Writers opposed to the strike often acknowledged that the union had some "legitimate grievances," though which ones varied among the writers. Some viewed the union's attack on fines and curfews as the reasonable complaint of adults; others saw it as the whining of self-indulgent children. Some endorsed the economic demands but denounced the freedom issues. Others saw unfairness in the Rozelle Rule or the one-sided Standard Player Contract or the arbitrary power of the commissioner to settle grievances but were put off by something else, or by what the *Atlanta Journal*'s Furman Bisher blasted as "the general preposterousness of the whole."[68]

Among 26 newspapers, two for New York (the *Times* and *Daily News*) and one each for the other NFL cities (counting Kansas City's morning *Times* and afternoon *Star* as one), ten utterly opposed the strike, while only the *Miami Herald, Washington Post, Philadelphia Inquirer,* and *Oakland Tribune* consistently sided with the players.[69] Several papers had a pair of columnists with competing views, such as Red Smith and Dave Anderson of the *New York*

Times and Phil Pepe and Dick Young of the *Daily News* (Smith and Pepe for the players, Anderson and Young for the owners).[70] The remaining papers offered a less easily differentiated mix of commentary, on balance opposed to the strike but not wholly one-sided.[71]

The sports department most obviously in the owner's pocket was that of the *Cleveland Plain Dealer*, where Art Modell always had a forum for his views. In the most remarkable piece of strike-related coverage to appear in any of these papers, sports editor Hal Lebovitz and the paper's executive and managing editors conducted an interview with Modell on July 14 that began on page one of the Sunday sports section, took up an entire second page, and concluded on a third. Lebovitz and his colleagues pitched hardball questions at Modell of this sort: "Talking about money, can you give me an idea how much these people who are seeking freedom and so on, are making in the National Football League?" And this: "Aside from the freedom issue, Art, do you and the other owners feel that it would be a deterioration in discipline and in performance if the players' demands are met?"[72] (Given what Modell would do to Cleveland in 1996, when he moved the Browns to Baltimore, the *Plain Dealer*'s deference in 1974 looks even more grotesque in retrospect.)

The players' harshest critics were *Daily News* columnist Dick Young, *Houston Chronicle* sports editor Dick Peebles, and *San Francisco Examiner* columnist Wells Twombly. Twombly repeatedly dreamed up new ways to make the same point about the "denim-wearing Bolsheviks," or "sweaty tycoons," or "underprivileged class" driving to the picket lines "in expensive sports cars," led by "Ed Garvey, the Karl Marx of the shower stall."[73] Garvey presented an easy target, but attacks on the players were always general, never personal; personalities complicated clear-cut issues. John Hall of the *Los Angeles Times*, for example, consistently attacked the union's position but had nothing but admiration for the Rams' player rep, Tom Mack. The *Cincinnati Enquirer*'s Callahan (a supporter of the players) reminded readers that the supposedly selfish and greedy striking Bengals included Pat Matson, who had a reputation for playing hurt, and Neal Craig, who raised money for underprivileged children in the off-season and had founded a Neal Craig House for boys.[74]

The columnists squarely on the players' side were rare but particularly eloquent. Red Smith offered one well-reasoned defense of the players after another.[75] The *Miami Herald*, led by sports editor Edwin Pope and beat writer Bill Braucher, was overall the most supportive newspaper, despite the fact that the home team Dolphins were much less committed to the strike than was the *Herald*'s staff. Pope offered his own explanation: "Full bellies don't make scrap-and-scratch unions." Pope defended Garvey as the hard-nosed negotiator the union needed, and he took on the arrogance of owners such as Joe Robbie and the hypocrisies of players who defied the union while looking forward to the "fat pensions" it gained for them.[76] Braucher's defense of Doug Swift produced some of the most poignant writing about the strike. Of course, there is always more poignancy on the losing side.

Losing with the Public

The opinions of sports columnists could sting or gratify, but the striking players likely felt more sharply the antagonism of fans. Another of the great ironies of the 1974 strike emerged afterward, when a "scientific" Harris poll revealed that more fans sided with the players than the owners (38 percent against 22 percent, leaving 40 percent indifferent).[77] This contradicted everything written during the strike. In mid-July, the results of two not-so-scientific polls appeared in papers everywhere: in one conducted by the *Milwaukee Journal*, 88.7 percent of fans sided with the owners; in the other, a telephone poll by a radio station in Worcester, Massachusetts, found 83 percent supporting management.[78] These polls were informal, but they informed the public debate in the press for the rest of the strike, and they were reinforced by numerous casual "street polls" by local newspapers. Sports columnists in nearly half of the newspapers reported that their mail ran "8-to-1" or "99 percent" or some such figure against the players, or that the fans at exhibition games criticized the strikers, or that the writer's dentist or barber or bartender or insurance agent had heard not a single voice for the players.[79]

Published letters, too, were overwhelmingly against the players (though not necessarily for the owners), often in brutally direct language: the players were a bunch of "spoiled brats" or "heavily muscled behemoths" who should "come out into the everyday work world and punch a time clock every day," because "without football they'd be digging ditches somewhere," and "if you don't like what you have chosen to do, then get the hell out and make room for those ballplayers who do."[80] One letter writer in Green Bay reminded striking players what happened to public schoolteachers in nearby Hortonville the previous spring. (In an event still memorialized by the Wisconsin Education Association, the school board in Hortonville fired 84 striking teachers after they had rejected a minimal salary increase following three years of a pay freeze.)[81] Whether local feelings were stronger in Green Bay or simply reported more fully in the *Press-Gazette*, the town that football fans loved to romanticize as a Norman Rockwell or Frank Capra ideal regarded its football players with unusual contempt. The NFL's only publicly owned team seemed to have hundreds or thousands of imperious owners, not just one.

Sportswriters fed angry fans' belief that the strike did not just inconvenience but *victimized* them, that *they* would have to pay for whatever the players won.[82] Whether genuine or faux populism, this position served the newspapers' own interests in standing up for their subscribers. Fans rightly blamed the striking players for depriving them of "real" NFL football during the exhibition games. But the idea that the players' demands would directly translate into higher ticket prices was one of those distortions that acquired the status of self-evident truth. Thanks to increased TV revenues alone, NFL owners, if they wished, could have absorbed higher personnel costs without touching ticket prices. Ticket pricing was governed by supply and demand, not the cost of doing business.

Another of the strike's more curious ideas was voiced by a fan in Green Bay and echoed loudly by Chuck Heaton, the *Cleveland Plain Dealer*'s beat writer with the Browns: while mercenary strikers walked their picket lines, rookies and free agents in camp were playing for sheer love of the game. In an unintentionally hilarious report on the Browns' rookies flying to Los Angeles for their first exhibition game, Heaton described them as "young, eager, and carefree," a bunch of giddy boys on their first airplane ride to the big city. "Crossing the Rockies in a sleek jet airplane is an adventure," Heaton marveled. "So is stepping on the grass carpet of the Coliseum." (Presumably, they traveled by bus in college and played on sandlots.) Heaton added that, in the absence of the veteran players who would normally appropriate the first-class section, "seating arrangements are democratic." Even Modell "grabs a seat on a catch-as-catch-can basis with all the others." The Browns' owner appears as a jovial daddy off on a lark with his boys. After the strike collapsed and the Browns began cutting their excess rookies, Heaton quoted at length a "love letter" from one of them to his position coach, describing himself as "a romantic, an existentialist, a freak, and a free spirit." The player thanked his coach for the wonderful experience of training camp and ended with a heartfelt farewell: "I'll sign off now and wish you and the rest of the staff a good season, but most of all I wish you my love, for without love this world would be a bitter place." Under other circumstances, a seasoned sportswriter might have mocked the rookie as a harebrained flower child, but in this case Heaton commented: "Not only pro football but the world needs more young men like Michael Puestow."[83]

Public opinion is a curious thing. The "scientific" Harris poll was not simply "true," the informal polls "false." It is quite possible that fans' sympathy shifted to the players after they were whipped by the owners, as the players became "our team" again, while the owners remained just owners. Or perhaps the informal polls were preordained to be skewed, since they surveyed only fans attending the exhibition games instead of honoring the players' picket lines, along with those who felt strongly enough to sound off at the tavern or barber shop, or write a letter to their local paper. Whatever the explanation, the street polls were "true" in the only way that mattered because they and fans' angry letters created the "truth" felt by the striking players on the picket lines and by the owners in their suites waiting for the strike to collapse.

How Not to Win a Strike

The strike began on July 1 in an atmosphere of heady confidence and ended six weeks later in disarray and recriminations. Roughly one-quarter of NFL veterans abandoned the strike at some point over those six weeks. Some teams were held together on the picket lines by extraordinary player reps, like Alan Page in Minnesota, Ken Bowman in Green Bay, Ed Flanagan in Detroit, Del Williams in New Orleans, and Tom Mack in Los Angeles. Bowman and Page—one already a practicing attorney, the other a future Supreme Court justice in Minnesota—were leading militants. Flanagan, Williams, and Mack were eloquent moderates. Having signed with the WFL, Flanagan had nothing to gain for himself, but he held the Lions' veterans steady, even through the trauma of their coach's death. Williams kept all but a handful of Saints' veterans together, ultimately at the cost of his own job. Mack devised the Rams' "no-picket-no-veteran" policy—honor the strike but don't picket the team's practices out of deference to Rosenbloom—until union leaders advised that not picketing would seem a sign of weakness. Mack was an engineer in the off-season, an executive with Bechtel, another bit of irony for the man leading the Rams' defiance of management. When 14-year veteran Joe Scibelli finally gave up the strike, he told reporters that he had "supported the association longer than I ever thought I'd have to" only "because of Tom Mack."[84]

Football teams are surprisingly complex social organisms. Kansas City was one of the teams that stood solidly with the union. Just two starters, defensive end Wilbur Young and free safety Jim Kearney, reported to our training camp in Liberty, Missouri—Young because he risked losing the bonus in his new contract, Kearney because he feared losing the income needed to support his large family (including two nephews as well as his own four children). Three back-ups (quarterback Pete Beathard, offensive tackle

Wayne Walton, and second-year receiver Danny Kratzer, picked up at the end of the previous season) also eventually gave up the strike. With our player rep, Ed Podolak, on the bargaining team and not often in town, Jack Rudnay organized the picketing in Kansas City. I attribute the Chiefs' solidarity also to Len Dawson, Otis Taylor, Willie Lanier, Buck Buchanan, Jim Tyrer—team leaders or leaders of the various position groups within the team. Whatever my own principles or feelings, I could not have reported to camp as long as Clyde Werner, my roommate and best friend on the team, stayed out. I also could not have reported so long as Rudnay, the starting center whom I backed up, stayed out; or so long as Tyrer, Ed Budde, Dave Hill, and George Daney, the other offensive linemen, stayed out. (Wayne Walton was a recent arrival whose defection did not matter in the same way.) Players at other positions had their own personal and group loyalties. We all had Dawson and Lanier, the leaders on the offense and defense. My black teammates probably looked particularly to Lanier, Taylor, and Buchanan. Had any of these players reported, others would surely have followed.

This is not to say that striking or not striking was entirely a personal matter, but that persons mattered. Obviously, the strike also involved principles, but in ways that led as naturally to division as to unity. Each 47-man roster had 22 starters (including a large or small handful of stars), 2 kickers, 16 reserves, and 7 players on the "taxi squad," who practiced but did not play in games and who were paid something in the neighborhood of what I earned for most of my rookie year, $300 a week. (The term originated in the 1940s in Cleveland, where the owner of the Browns, Mickey McBride, owned a taxi company at which he employed extra players he wanted to keep around.) The strike and the 63 issues affected each group differently. Longtime stars felt most comfortable with the status quo. Budding stars stood to benefit most from free agency, but reserves convinced that they were good enough to play for another team could also imagine opportunities if they were only free to pursue them. Younger players who had initially signed as free agents were more conscious of minimum salaries; older players, of pension benefits. The inherent reasons not to strike varied equally by position and status. The aging star risked finding himself expendable. The player from last season's taxi squad did not yet feel that he had made the team. The players with the highest salaries risked the most income; "marginal" or "fringe" veterans risked their entire careers.

While strikebreakers came from all ranks, the stars for obvious reasons received the most attention in the press. Mike Curtis, the Cowboys' Ralph

Neely, and the host of Miami Dolphins made the earliest headlines. Johnny Unitas was the first, and for some time only, San Diego veteran to report. Already an old man displaced from Baltimore to an alien environment—a 1950s beer guy playing with 1970s potheads—Unitas retired just a few days later, sadly not just a crippled has-been but also briefly a "scab" at the end of his extraordinary career. His last act as an NFL quarterback was to zoom past picketing teammates, who screamed at him, "Way to do it to your buddies!," and held a sign that read, "No. 19 You Have Yours! How About Ours?"[85] Neely led a long parade of Cowboy stars—Craig Morton, Walt Garrison, Cornell Green, Roger Staubach, Lee Roy Jordan, Bob Lilly, John Niland, Charlie Waters, Mel Renfro, Cliff Harris, and many others—until 35 veterans, including a majority of the starters, had reported. Jim Otto, Fred Biletnikoff, Kenny Stabler, and George Blanda divided the Oakland Raiders by giving up the strike early.

The defection on the same day of quarterbacks Randy Johnson and Norm Snead, along with All-Pro tight end Bob Tucker, split the New York Giants. The same move several days later by four Los Angeles Rams—John Hadl, Jack Snow, Joe Scibelli, and Lance Rentzel—was less dramatic only because the strike was clearly doomed by this time. Several teams saw a single key player defy the union from the outset: the Patriots' John Hannah, the Falcons' Tommy Nobis, the Packers' Jim Carter, the Cardinals' Larry Stallings, the 49ers' Vic Washington. Compared to the solidarity behind the baseball strike in 1972, this was a dismal record. The NFL's most famous players in 1974, Joe Namath and O. J. Simpson, stayed out with their striking teammates to the end, but many others nearly at their level did not. (Namath honored the strike but did not picket, and he never needed an excuse for missing a few weeks of training camp. Simpson was more outspoken for his striking teammates, despite not even belonging to the union. He had quit after a disagreement with Garvey over the handling of endorsements.)[86]

Starting quarterbacks played a key role. As coaches-on-the-field, they belonged in camp. As leaders of the team, they belonged with their teammates on the picket lines. At least one sportswriter openly questioned whether a strikebreaking quarterback would have the support and respect—and blocking—of teammates he abandoned.[87] Open defiance by the Eagles' Gabriel and the Giants' Johnson was unusual.[88] While most of the established quarterbacks—Namath, Dawson, Fran Tarkenton, Billy Kilmer, Jim Hart, Charley Johnson, Archie Manning—honored the strike to the end, a significant handful (Roger Staubach, John Hadl, Bob Griese) gave up after agonizing over the decision for several days. Younger quarterbacks, less secure in their starting roles, felt more intense pressure. Most resisted the pressure, but several eventually gave in.[c]

The strike played out as a national struggle between competing interests and principles, but with countless local dramas. As numerous sportswriters pointed out, those most affected by the strike were the "marginal" or "fringe" veterans, the guys from the taxi squads and the reserves who played on the special teams. Their jobs were least secure, and in most cases they had not yet put in their five years to qualify for the pension. On strike, they risked their jobs and thus everything for which they were striking. Give up the strike and they risked alienating the teammates they were trying to keep. Sportswriters in many cities designated an unofficial poster boy for the local strike, such as Larry Krause in Green Bay (jeopardizing his fifth season, the one he needed to qualify for his pension) and Merv Krakau in Buffalo (seen by coaches as a possible starter until the strike kept him out of camp).[89] Three players (Don Milan, Dan Medlin, and Kent Gaydos) played this role for the *Oakland Tribune*, as did three (John Bunting, Tom Luken, and Lee Bouggess) for the *Philadelphia Inquirer*.[90] In interviews, these players made clear the personal costs of striking. They spoke of needing to support their families and make payments on a new house, but also of their loyalty or obligation to teammates. In their resolve they seemed quietly heroic, as when Krause explained why he would risk his pension: "It all boils down to what kind of man you are, what kind of person you are." (Krause, Medlin, Bunting, and Luken survived the final cuts; Krakau, Milan, Gaydos, and Bouggess did not.)

As the strike dragged on, coaches, general managers, or owners in virtually every NFL city predicted that a record number of rookies and free agents would make the team that summer. Some overtly threatened those on strike by naming players who should be in camp to protect their jobs, or overly praising the development of some low draft pick or free-agent rookie in camp. Hank Stram one day singled out free-agent rookie center Mike McDaniel as "a great illustration of what the opportunity for concentrated work and instruction can mean." As the only backup center on the Chiefs' roster, I got the point.[91] More often, coaches insisted that they intended no threat but were only predicting the inevitable outcome of the strike: an unusual number of rookies would make the club and a number of marginal or injured veterans

c. Those who stayed out: Mike Phipps, Jim Plunkett, Dan Pastorini, Bob Lee, Bobby Douglass, Marty Domres, Greg Landry, and Steve Spurrier. Those who went in: Terry Bradshaw, Ken Anderson, Dan Fouts, Joe Ferguson, and Jerry Tagge.

would be too far behind to make up for lost time once they reported. (Stram made such comments repeatedly throughout the strike.) It required neither paranoia nor deep insight to recognize that "predictions" and "frank assessments" by the men who controlled team rosters could become self-fulfilling prophecies.

Players who abandoned or defied the strike offered various explanations. Some disliked unions in principle.[92] For others, playing football was simply red meat to a carnivore: I am a football player; football players play football.[93] Some felt comfortable with old-fashioned NFL paternalism, declaring that they "owed everything to football," or were treated well and had no complaints.[94] A small handful claimed divine guidance (this was before the era when every other player invoked the Lord as his captain). Falcon defensive back Ray Easterling "prayed a lot over it" and decided to support the strike. Easterling's teammate Greg Brezina, along with Jet defensive tackle Steve Thompson, Colt running back Joe Orduna, and Lion linebacker John Small, received the opposite message. What Cowboy guard Niland heard from On High defies paraphrasing; here it is as described by the *Dallas Morning News*:

> Niland had decided some time ago to report because of his position "with Christ." Explaining his position he cited verses from the Bible, including Ephesians 6, 5–9; Colossians 3, 22–25; and Timothy 6, 1–2.
>
> "I'm not coming to camp because I'm a Christian but because of my position in Christ of being a Christian," he said. "I'm not trying to follow God's word (in the Bible verses) by the law and be a servant to my master but through my love of Christ and wanting to serve God I've decided to report.
>
> "If I wasn't a Christian I wouldn't report because my own personal will is one of siding with the players on some of the issues."

The verses from Ephesians, Colossians, and Timothy all command slaves to be obedient to their masters. Five days earlier, while still on strike, Niland had told reporters that to the owners a player was just "a piece of meat."[95]

There were countless reasons to strike or not strike, but as the stand-off dragged on, at some point every player's narrow self-interest lay in his reporting to camp. Among many other lessons, the 1974 strike shone a harsh light on the well-worn platitudes about the importance of the team. Player after player, on abandoning the strike, told reporters something to the effect, "I had to make the decision that was right for me." Some players expressed defiance of their striking teammates.[96] Others agonized, often poignantly. Some were bitter at having been betrayed by those who quit before them.[97] Several explained that they had to protect either their job or their family's financial security.[98] And many waved the flag of personal freedom, or, as the Patriots' Hannah put it, "This is my own decision as an individual, and America is still a free country." In Dallas, as the Cowboys trickled into camp one by one, they seemed to be reading from the same script: "It's up to each individual to make up his own mind" (Harris); "This is an individual decision" (Staubach); "I looked at the situation from an individual standpoint" (Jordan); it is "just an individual decision" (Waters).[99]

One of the most arresting aspects of the 1974 strike and its coverage in the press was this repeated insistence on individual freedom to strike or not strike, as if the choices were equally honorable and had no effect on anyone else, and nothing were at stake beyond the individual's right to choose. According to Dick Connor of the *Denver Post*, it took equal "courage" either to strike or to report to camp. Bob St. John of the *Dallas Morning News* admired those on both sides for "standing up for what they believe."[100] Other writers charged the NFLPA with hypocrisy in demanding "freedom" from the owners while trying to keep individual players from exercising their own freedom of choice. Everyone should respect others' decisions and, presumably, shake hands afterwards.[101] Some players, while reporting to camp, actually insisted that they still supported the strike and their striking teammates (a pretense that earned the contempt even of Dick Young).[102]

Rugged individualism and the social compact have always co-existed uneasily as American ideals and in American life. The most powerful principle opposed to self-interest was simple loyalty to teammates or the union. The very notion of "team"—as in everyone contributes, from the greatest star to the lowliest scrub—was a sacred idea in football, as old as the game itself. Now, newspaper coverage made the expendability of "marginal" or "fringe" players a constant theme, along with the vulnerability of aging or injured players. Without intending to be debunkers, sportswriters were casting professional football teams as Darwinian jungles, rather than "families." Why so many veterans remained out of camp, despite the personal risk, seemed to mystify or irritate sportswriters who foresaw the union's defeat. The players were being misled by either a self-serving or a blindly militant Ed Garvey.

An NFL "team" was indeed a very unstable entity, governed by coaches' prerogatives, ruthless competition for limited jobs, and the whims of chance. Yet "team" and "teammate" had very real meaning for most football players of that era. Loyalty here was not an abstract principle but a visceral impulse. In one of the strike's great moments, All-Pro guard Larry Little, among the few Dolphins to hold out to the very end, told a *Miami Herald* reporter that he would have stayed out indefinitely, "even if it came down to just me and Doug Swift. I wasn't going to let Swift take it by himself." Linebacker Ron Pritchard said roughly the same thing about Pat Matson in Cincinnati: "I'm sticking with him," Pritchard told reporters just before the strike collapsed. "If I quit now for money, I couldn't hold my face up. I wouldn't be much of a person."[103]

As the strike dragged into August, it became harder to believe that the players still out of camp were merely greedy. The highly paid ones were losing a lot of money; the lower-paid ones were jeopardizing their careers. The strike, for the most post, was a confusing and frustrating affair, but every now and then a striking player distilled the entire ordeal into a simple statement like Little's and Pritchard's. Ray Chester put it this way: "There comes a time when you have to start thinking about the other guy and not always do what seems best for you." This was Pete Adams's explanation for striking: "It's just that I'm a member of the union." And Bo Rather's: "If I'm going to benefit I ought to play a part in the effort."[104]

The NFLPA's slogan in the summer of 1974 was "No Freedom, No Football." For me the words of these players—or of the Eagles' Bunting ("The reason I'm out here is that I'm in the union and we're on strike"), or of Bunting's teammate Tom Luken ("We agreed to stick together as a unit"), or of a third Eagle, Kevin Reilly ("The thing is, you can only play football so long. You have to be a man the rest of your life")—expressed the truer spirit of those who remained on strike.[105] Such loyalty was not "radical" but "traditional," though different from the NFL's traditional paternalism. The strikebreakers who insisted on their right to make a personal decision, or who more bluntly looked out for "Number 1"—the ones who put self above team or union— were actually the ones in the vanguard of a cultural revolution, as the 1960s gave way to the "Me Decade" of the 1970s.

"Cooling Off"

The beginning of the end of the strike came on August 3, when the Cowboys' Roger Staubach reported to camp. After Ed Garvey snapped to a reporter, "I'd hate to have been at Pearl Harbor with him," the fallout was immediate. Critics had singled out Garvey from the beginning, whether for his arrogance or his supposed radicalism. The jab at Staubach, the ex-Navy man and Vietnam veteran who was one of the most respected players in the NFL, alienated even some of Garvey's few admirers, including Edwin Pope and Rams' player rep Tom Mack.[106] On August 5, when three more starting quarterbacks, Bob Griese, John Hadl, and Terry Bradshaw, reported to camp on the same day, the slow trickle of defections now seemed one drop from a flood. The union made a last-ditch effort to persuade strikebreaking veterans to leave their training camps, but only the Cleveland Browns complied, as 13 of the 17 veterans in camp walked back out. (Chuck Heaton of the *Cleveland Plain Dealer* described the move as a slap at poor Art Modell, who "has learned the hard way that kindness, consideration and generosity to athletes doesn't [*sic*] pay off.")[107] This was much too little and too late. On Sunday, August 11, three days after Richard Nixon resigned from the presidency (replaced by a real football player, ex-Michigan center Gerald Ford, as sports sections everywhere reported), the NFLPA leadership announced that veterans would be sent back to camp for a two-week "cooling-off" period while negotiations continued.

No one felt very happy. Several coaches and owners balked at accepting the strikers, on the chance that they would walk out again in two weeks. Having filled their training camps with dozens of free agents for exhibition games, the clubs were now wary of depleting their ranks only to find themselves short-handed again. Sid Gillman flatly declared that he would not take the striking Oilers back on these terms, until a call from the Management Council to owner Bud Adams made it clear that this was not an option. Gillman relented but had his way when he cut seven veterans at the moment of their arrival. One of them, Paul Guidry, had driven 26 straight hours from his home in Buffalo. Gillman claimed that he had been unable to reach the players by telephone to prevent their wasting a trip, but as John Wilson, a writer actually on the owners' side, put it in the *Houston Chronicle*, "Gillman wasn't satisfied to win the strike. He wanted to apply the hobnail boot and crush the players."[108]

The situation in Houston became grotesquely fascinating, as the wire services again made it a national story. Once practices resumed, fights broke out between strikers and strikebreakers (as they did in the New York Giants' training camp).[109] Steve Kiner, the "Gillman loyalist" who had blasted his striking teammates as "crybabies" and "idiots" at the beginning of the strike, became a frequent target. Gillman infuriated his veterans when he put them through a murderous "cutting drill" in which six offensive linemen let seven defensive linemen get past them, then cut their legs (that is, blocked them from behind, at their knees). This tactic was widely recognized as the most brutal, and cowardly, thing one player could do to another, and it was later banned by the NFL because it caused so many career-ending knee injuries. Defensive end Elvin Bethea, a future Hall of Famer forced to risk his livelihood to satisfy Gillman's vindictiveness, was outraged. "There are people out there who hate Gillman's guts," Kiner told a reporter writing a syndicated story for *Newsday*.[110]

In Baltimore, general manager Joe Thomas was a more subtle tyrant. When it became clear that most of the Colts' strikers would wait until the last minute to report, Thomas announced that they would not be allowed in camp until Sunday, after the next exhibition game (and payday), because of logistical difficulties in administering physicals and assigning them to rooms in the dormitory. No one believed this, of course; Thomas was merely letting the hired hands know who was boss.[111] In Atlanta, Van Brocklin proved himself the most devious of all the hard-liners. He immediately announced that his 18 regulars who had remained on strike to the end would start on Saturday against the Cincinnati Bengals, after just three days of practice, "on national television." That last phrase clearly signaled Van Brocklin's intention, as a local reporter put it, "to teach his veterans a lesson or embarrass them before millions of viewers." (Though sputtering on offense, the Falcons played creditably in losing 13–7 in overtime, but Van Brocklin gave it a good try.)[112]

Immediately after the cooling-off period was announced, 12 members of the U.S. House of Representatives threatened "a thorough inspection of pro football's anti-trust status if a fair contract compromise with the players' association is not reached or if the union is injured as a result of the 44-day strike."[113] (Nothing came of the threat.) For the striking players, while most felt relief to have the ordeal over, many were angry or frustrated at having sacrificed so much for nothing. Veterans on each club held meetings and, in some cases, formal votes on what to do when the cooling-off period ended. Two-thirds of the Washington Redskins were prepared to walk out again, but they were the exception. In Minnesota, the unwillingness of his teammates to take the same stance provoked Alan Page to resign as player rep.[114] The union scaled down its demands but insisted on just a five-month contract, with negotiations on the key freedom issues to open again at the end of the season. The owners would not agree and offered their own new proposals that left the freedom issues untouched. On August 27, player reps rejected this offer by a 25–1 margin (only Buffalo voted for it), and the players now prepared for a season without a contract.[115]

Then the "housecleaning" began.[116] The Associated Press reported that 265 rookies had made their NFL clubs after the brief strike in 1970; 272 made it in 1974 (compared to 168 in 1973). The additional hundred rookies meant that a hundred more veterans were cut. Abandoning the strike did not guarantee the club's loyalty. Giants owner Wellington Mara claimed that of 200 veterans waived around the league, 109, or just over half, had crossed the picket lines before the end of the strike.[117] Many clubs unloaded everyone who had signed with the WFL. A few teams dumped players who had been too outspoken during the strike.

Union officials and player representatives were hit disproportionately hard. Eight player reps had been cut, waived, or traded within two years of the 1968 labor dispute, four more after the brief 1970 strike. Gwilym Brown of *Sports Illustrated* calculated in 1971 that "a player rep's chance of being traded, waived, or cut is about three times as high as that of a player who minds his own business."[118] Whatever the precise ratio, the pattern continued in 1974. All four union officers—President Bill Curry, Vice Presidents Kermit Alexander and Tom Keating, and Secretary-Treasurer John Wilbur—were cut or traded. Seven player reps—the Falcons' Ken Reaves, the Packers' Ken Bowman, the Colts' Rex Kern, the Browns' Frank Pitts, the Bears' Mac Percival, the Giants' Charlie Evans, and the Saints' Del Williams—were also sent packing, either cut, traded, or put on injured reserve against their will. Retaliation seemed obvious only with Curry, Reaves, Bowman, and Evans, but the possibility hovered over every case.[119]

Visits by "The Turk," the assistant coach assigned to inform players that they had been cut, were a painful part of every training camp. In 1974 those visits simply became more highly charged, and more noticed by the press. Most clubs made their cuts quietly and, when necessary, denied that they were in any way related to the strike. Not George Halas. After shipping out the team's player rep and its most vocal strikers, the Bears' owner exulted, "It's the greatest (bleeping) thing that's happened to the Bears in five years. We got rid of some of these malcontents. Great day."[120]

I was one of the marginal veterans visited by The Turk on the last day of cuts. After the Chiefs' striking veterans reported to camp, Hank Stram left us at home and took only his rookies and our five defectors to Los Angeles for an exhibition game. Watching the game with my teammates in a bar, I took a Doug Swiftian view of the proceedings: let the Rams beat Kansas City's rookies, who were after our jobs, like a gong. They did, 58–16. I then played in the final three exhibition games, after which every club had until September 10 to reduce its roster to 47 instead of the usual 40. On the 10th, I came to practice having read in the morning *Kansas City Times* that Mike McDaniel, the free-agent rookie center from Kansas State, had been waived. Now there were just two centers, Jack Rudnay and myself. But after I suited up for practice and reported for the offensive linemen's meeting, my line coach called me out of the room to tell me, "Hank wants to see you." That was The Turk's calling card.

So, yes, I was cut. And baffled by the fact that the Chiefs kept just one center, along with five offensive tackles and three guards (one of the tackles, Wayne Walton, would back up Rudnay). I was dropped along with four other veterans: Pete Beathard, Pat Holmes, Dave Smith, and Larry Marshall. (Left tackle Jim Tyrer, no marginal veteran like us five but a starter since 1961 and nine times an All-Pro, had already been traded to Washington and replaced by a rookie.) The afternoon *Kansas City Star* had a few words to say about each of us. It reported that I was "deeply hurt" by being waived, but that I would return to graduate school and had "no worry about [my] future."[121] Along with maybe another hundred marginal veterans, I ended up with neither freedom nor football, or rather with the freedom to do anything I wanted except play football in the NFL.

Though a casualty of the strike, I was no victim. For me, the strike had been an act of solidarity with my teammates and commitment to the union that represented me. I had not anticipated testing the free-agent market if only we could eliminate the Rozelle Rule. Until striking put my position at risk, I had felt secure in Kansas City but uncertain whether any coach around the league even knew that I existed. I also had my own master plan that did not include hanging on in the NFL as long as I could. After two more seasons, 1974 and 1975, I would qualify for my pension (my first year with the Chiefs did not count, since I spent all but one game on the taxi squad). I would also be ready to finish my Ph.D. at Stanford and begin looking for a teaching position. Given the tough academic job market, I had told myself that I could continue playing if I failed to find a teaching job, but if all went well, my NFL career would end in two years.

Being cut altered my timetable, but the stakes were lower for me than for many players. There were others like me. After the Colts waived him, Rex Kern told the *Baltimore Sun*, "I'll probably finish working toward my Ph.D. in administration at Ohio State." Chris Stecher, a second-year tackle from Claremont-Mudd and a former candidate for a Rhodes Scholarship, told reporters he would also likely return to graduate school.[122] These were signs of the time. Besides Tom Mack, the engineering executive with Bechtel, Ken Bowman was a practicing attorney; Kermit Alexander was working on a law degree; Bronco quarterback Charley Johnson had his doctorate in chemical engineering; Doug Swift and the Bengals' Tommy Casanova attended medical school; Casanova's teammate Ken Riley had a master's degree in school administration. (These are just the ones whose off-season pursuits were mentioned during the strike, and they did not include others, such as Alan Page who would begin law school the following year and finish in 1978, or the Cowboys' John Babinecz, another future doctor.) This was an era in which playing in the NFL while working toward a long-term professional career was a recognized option.

At the end of the 1974 season, Sid Gillman beat out Buffalo's Lou Saban by a wide margin to be named AFC Coach of the Year. The *New York Times* summed up the case for Gillman in this way: "Starting with a team that had won only two games in two years and cutting seven seasoned players for striking after they reported to camp, he led the Oilers to several upsets on the way to a 7–7 won-lost mark and second place in the Central Division."[123] (Losing seven "seasoned players," whom he released in a ruthless demonstration of power, was an obstacle that Gillman overcame!) Improving from awful to mediocre would not normally warrant Coach of the Year honors. It is hard not to read the vote of the nation's sportswriters as an endorsement of Gillman's hard-line stance during the strike. Yet 1974 was Gillman's last year as coach of the Oilers. Six other NFL coaches lost their jobs during or immediately after the strike season, including Stram, Van Brocklin, Nick Skorich in Cleveland, and Howard Schnellenberger in Baltimore (the Colts' volatile owner, Robert Irsay, not Joe Thomas, fired Schnellenberger after just three games). Five more coaches were gone after 1975, four more after 1976—a total of 16 out of 26 coaches losing their jobs within three years of the strike, in an era when such turnover was not yet routine. Coaches are fired for many reasons, but rifts opened during the strike undoubtedly took longer to heal on some clubs than on others. It seems likely that aging and marginal veterans were not the strike's only casualties.

NFL players lost in 1974 but started a process that would allow a later generation to win everything they fought for and more, including a guaranteed *average* salary greater than Joe Namath's (even in adjusted dollars). The most serious long-term casualty was the relationship between the players and the fans, as the 1974 strike opened wounds that would never completely heal. The love affair of fans with "their" football heroes had always been built on illusions, of course, on a willed innocence that would never again be quite as easy to maintain.

THE END
OF THE
ROZELLE
ERA

The failed strike in the summer of 1974 marked the begin-
ning of a period of conflict that would not be resolved for two decades (and
that has continued, though with owners now fighting each other instead of
their players). Peace between the NFL Players Association and management
arrived only after two more failed strikes and a series of NFLPA victories in
court, before a labor agreement was reached in 1993 that became one of the
cornerstones of the hugely prosperous new NFL. Al Davis initiated the owners' internal conflicts when he filed suit in 1980 for the right to move his
franchise from Oakland to Los Angeles, then won the initial jury decision in
May 1982. Following Davis's final victory in appeals court in 1984, Robert
Irsay moved the Colts from Baltimore to Indianapolis, and other owners
began contemplating their own future relocations. By 1986 journalist David
Harris could write a book about the rise *and decline* of the NFL. Pro football
was thriving on the field, with Bill Walsh's West Coast Offense creating a new
dynasty in San Francisco, Buddy Ryan and Lawrence Taylor revolutionizing
defensive play, and the Super Bowl acquiring its exalted place in American
life. But off the field the NFL seemed to be falling into chaos. The third major
strike, in 1987, became particularly damaging to the league's credibility,
when the owners disdained any concern for "the integrity of the game" by
opting to field scab teams (with what were euphemistically called "replacement players").

On top of this structural breakdown, arrests, indictments, and convictions
of NFL players for drug offenses—and suspensions by Pete Rozelle that followed—became a routine part of the sports news. Over the 1980s, football

fans were forced to adjust to some troubling new realities in the NFL. With players making hundreds of thousands of dollars yet still striking for free agency, while also periodically being arrested for buying, using, or selling cocaine, fans had to develop either indifference to nonfootball matters, a tolerance for ambiguity, or an ability to compartmentalize their feelings about NFL football.

The 1987 strike ended without a settlement and sent the Players Association back to court. Players' off-field behavior continued making regular headlines, and the new television contracts actually paid lower fees (in adjusted dollars) as ratings declined. When Rozelle resigned in 1989, two years before his contract would expire, the NFL seemed rudderless. Yet out of this chaos a new NFL would emerge in the 1990s, a financial colossus unimaginable just a few years earlier.

Reaching the Heights

The year 1981 marked a pinnacle for the National Football League. That season saw the highest overall television ratings in the league's history, culminating in the highest-rated Super Bowl ever. The NFL was delivering weekly each season the sport that Americans loved above all others. The Dallas Cowboys, with their glitzy uniforms and look-but-don't-touch cheerleaders, along with high-tech game plans and a God-fearing coach, had officially become "America's Team" in 1978, when someone at NFL Films came up with that title for the Cowboys' highlight film. The dominant team in the late 1970s was not Dallas, however, but the Pittsburgh Steelers, with four Super Bowl victories and a host of compelling personalities. Their Steel Curtain defense, led by a front four of L. C. Greenwood, Dwight White, Ernie Holmes, and preeminently "Mean Joe" Greene, radiated a terrifying glamour. (Greene played against type in one of the most famous commercials of all time, a Coca-Cola ad in 1979, in which the weary warrior, suddenly softened, tosses his game jersey to an awestruck kid who has given him his Coke.) The Steeler offense featured a pair of running backs, Italian–African American Franco Harris (he of the "Immaculate Reception" in the 1972 playoffs) and Vietnam veteran Rocky Bleier, whose personal stories were readymade for Hollywood screenwriters. Joining Harris and Bleier were a couple of astonishingly balletic wide receivers in Lynn Swann and John Stallworth, a throwback center in Mike Webster, a country boy quarterback with a rifle arm in Terry Bradshaw, and even a famously beloved owner in Art Rooney.

The Super Bowl became truly super over the late 1970s and early 1980s. TV audiences of 75–80 million leaped to 102 million for Dallas and Denver in

Super Bowl XII in 1978, then hit 110 million in 1982. More important than the size of the audience was the emerging status of the game as an unofficial civic holiday and festival of excess. *Time* and *Life* had both published pre–Super Bowl cover stories back in 1972, but of the routine kind for big sporting events. *Time*'s article featured the opposing quarterbacks; *Life*'s was just scouting reports on the two teams. Super Bowl X in 1976 marked a turning point, when timing and circumstances conspired to make it the kickoff for the year-long national Bicentennial celebration.[1]

Time followed with back-to-back cover stories in 1977 and 1978, then another in 1982 at the end of that magical 1981 season (*Newsweek* added its own in 1979 and 1982). The event was now much more than a championship football contest. *Time*'s 1977 cover proclaimed the Super Bowl to be "The Great American Spectacle," and the story likened it to Marshall McLuhan's global village, "the national town" where "all the inhabitants have gone to watch a game on the community screen." Now "the nation's single largest shared experience (except for electing a President or watching American astronauts walk on the moon)," the Super Bowl was altering the rhythms of American life. On Super Bowl Sunday, the magazine reported, Georgetown University Hospital installed TV sets in the labor room for expectant fathers. Supermarkets stocked up on potato chips. Calls to the police in Kansas City had dropped by 300 percent when the Chiefs faced the Vikings in 1970. On the eve of just the eleventh contest, *Time* wrote about *tradition* as the factor "that most nourishes Super Bowl madness."[2] The Super Bowl had become the quintessential American example of an invented tradition.

Such attempts by the media to express the magnitude of the Super Bowl have become utterly familiar, but this is the period when they began. For the 1977 game, the NFL also turned the halftime show over to the Walt Disney Company, a shift from marching bands to the lavishly choreographed productions that made the halftime entertainment a blockbuster event in itself.[3] By 1982 the spectacle was outstripping the game, and excess was becoming a major theme in the media coverage, including the excess in media coverage. Reporting from the scene of the 1982 game in Pontiac, Michigan, Ira Berkow of the *New York Times* described a scene that topped any of Gatsby's West Egg parties: 3,000 guests at the commissioner's $250,000 NFL Super Bowl party consuming 3,200 chicken breasts; with 2,000 reporters present to eat the NFL's chicken and drink its cocktails and find something to write about each day (including the presence of 2,000 reporters, three times the number for Super Bowl I). "The football game was no more the major attraction here than stale cigars are in the front of a bookie joint," Berkow wrote, sounding a theme that would be repeated before and after each subsequent Super Bowl. Writers like Berkow by this time regarded the orgy of consumption with considerable irony, but for the public relations–minded men who ran the NFL, excess had no downside. The Super Bowl had become not just an NFL championship game and an unofficial national holiday but also the NFL's own best advertisement for itself.[4]

Forebodings

The NFL's ride to the top had not been entirely smooth, of course. After steadily increasing since 1970, attendance dipped in 1974, the year of the players' strike, and did not fully recover until 1980. Labor relations with the Players Association remained strained, to say the least (more on that shortly). In January 1980, Al Davis announced that he was moving the Raiders from Oakland to Los Angeles, in defiance of NFL bylaws. Davis had been Rozelle's implacable enemy since the NFL-AFL merger in 1966, which left Rozelle solely in charge and Davis nursing a grudge. No longer a commissioner himself, Davis returned to Oakland for 10 percent ownership of the team (enough for a foothold from which he would drive out majority owner Wayne Valley by 1976). Davis and his Raiders now belonged to an NFL whose governing philosophy journalist David Harris has called "League Think." A supermajority requirement enforced the rules: 75 percent of the owners had to agree on major decisions. As Harris has documented in his history of the NFL in the 1970s and 1980s, agreement and compliance with the rules were never as uniform or harmonious as the public face of the NFL pretended, but a general principle of all-for-one-and-one-for-all survived repeated challenges through the 1970s.[5]

Then Davis announced that he was moving his Raiders to Los Angeles and the vacant L.A. Coliseum. Davis never had been a team player; his mantra, "Just win, baby," had always ruled off the field as well as on. Foreshadowing his later defiance of his NFL partners, in 1974, when NFL Properties generated little revenue and distributed all of it through NFL Charities for the public relations value, Davis withdrew from the arrangement and demanded the Raiders' one-twenty-sixth share.[6] He was thus not a "League Thinker" gone bad when he began private negotiations with the Los Angeles Memorial Coliseum Commission (LAMCC) in 1979. He was also not the first NFL owner to abandon a community. The Los Angeles market was open, after all, because Carroll Rosenbloom, frustrated by his lease on the L.A. Coliseum, arranged for the Rams to move to Anaheim for the 1980 season. In 1971, the

Cowboys had moved from Dallas to suburban Irving; the Patriots, from Boston to Foxboro; the Giants, from New York to the Meadowlands in New Jersey. And in 1975, the Lions left Detroit for Pontiac. Because the teams remained within their metropolitan areas, none of these actions required the other owners' consent. The Raiders' case was different. When Davis announced the Raiders' move to Los Angeles, without seeking league approval, he signaled a complete break from the NFL's fundamental principles. Neither owners nor players had a right to free agency until Davis simply claimed his.

Oakland's was a financially healthy franchise, with 50,000 season ticket holders and regular sellouts of the 54,615-seat Oakland Coliseum; but visions of luxury boxes, pay TV, and 20,000 more ticket-buying fans danced in Davis's head. The LAMCC had filed suit against the NFL in 1978, immediately after Rosenbloom announced his plan to move the Rams to Anaheim, and the league failed to produce a replacement. Davis joined that suit in 1979, even before the other owners voted 22–0 (with five abstentions) against his own prospective move to L.A. To defend themselves against Davis's lawsuit, representatives of the NFL argued that the owners were partners, not competitors, in a single entertainment enterprise. (To defend themselves against the Players Association, of course, the same representatives would argue that the owners were competitors, not partners who colluded in holding down salaries.) Rozelle had to feel himself the butt of one of fate's crueler jokes when Davis and the Raiders won the Super Bowl in 1981 as a wildcard team, and Rozelle had to present the trophy to an exultant Davis in the locker room afterward as millions watched on television.

The first round in the lawsuit ended in a mistrial in August 1981. Rozelle in early 1982 still had reason to hope that he could prevail in court or persuade Congress to define the NFL as a single entity with 28 partners, instead of 28 separate interests. (In 1976 Seattle and Tampa had joined the original 26 franchises from the NFL-AFL merger.) With such legislation the league would suddenly become immune to antitrust lawsuits, and Davis would be rendered powerless.[7]

Rozelle's other nemesis was Ed Garvey. Garvey received the brunt of the criticism before, during, and after the strike in 1974. His critics accused him of zealotry or excessive idealism at best, of serving his own political ambitions at the expense of the players at worst. Union officials and player reps publicly insisted that the players, not their executive director, determined the issues, but Garvey's vision (and ambitions) guided the union throughout his tenure, and certainly the union's aggressive stance toward the owners in 1974 came chiefly from him. Without Garvey, the players would likely have reached an agreement with the owners, though on the owners' terms as usual, with modestly improved economic benefits but the freedom issues untouched. The players could have followed what Edwin Pope called "the clubby, nicely-nicely route" as they had in the past, or they could demand their "freedom," but they could not do both.[8]

Garvey might have had romantic illusions about leading a united workers' front to victory, but I suspect that he actually knew in 1974 roughly what would follow: not that two more failed strikes and a tortuous path through numerous lawsuits and appeals would be required, but that the players' freedom would have to be won in court. By the time the strike collapsed, Garvey and the Players Association were already two years into the lawsuit in Minneapolis challenging the Rozelle Rule as a violation of antitrust laws. In addition, ex-Viking Joe Kapp's related suit in California would soon be decided, and a subcommittee of Congress's Joint Economic Committee was "considering a study of the sports business." Despite the obvious defeat in the strike, Garvey told one reporter that "we're sure as hell nowhere near losing," because "this was a strike for recognition," and the owners "would have to deal with the union from now on."[9]

Most observers at the time probably read Garvey's comment as one last bit of bravado. It became clear only in retrospect that Garvey entered the 1974 strike with a Plan A and a Plan B. In Plan A, a solid union would win the strike and force the owners to modify their restrictions on player movement. In Plan B, the strike would fail and the NFLPA would turn to the courts and Congress.[10] As a labor lawyer, Garvey knew that he could not afford to give away at the bargaining table what he could win in court. The NFLPA could not sue over the restrictions on free agency, as a violation of antitrust law, if it reached a compromise agreement on them in collective bargaining. At the same time, Garvey knew that the union would have to prove in court that it had bargained "in good faith" on these issues. Only when bargaining failed could the union resort to the judicial system. Plan B therefore required the failed strike. It required individual and present losses for the future strength of the union. Had Garvey known how much bitterness among players, toward players, and toward himself that the strikes would eventually produce, he might have had second thoughts about Plan B.

Garvey had eight years to get ready for the next strike. The 1974 season ended without a labor agreement, and as negotiations dragged on, 1975 nearly saw the second major work stoppage in two years, when the New England Patriots voted not to play their final exhibition game against the New

York Jets unless the owners came up with a reasonable contract offer.[a] The Patriots' "strike" received support only from the Giants, Jets (over Namath's opposition), Redskins, and Lions. With angry or disillusioned players abandoning the union, membership had dropped from around 1,300 to 950, leaving the NFLPA nearly bankrupt. (The Buffalo Bills had just 12 dues-paying members.) The Minnesota Vikings, without Alan Page as player rep now, had recently called for Garvey's resignation on a "near-unanimous vote." As the Patriot-inspired impromptu strike now played out more as farce than serious drama, Garvey admitted that the NFLPA was "losing control. Essentially we have 26 locals all taking action." After five days the Patriots and their few allies returned to practice, and the 1975 season ensued without a labor agreement, as did the 1976 season, though more quietly.[11]

Plan B was moving smoothly along other channels, however. In December 1974, as the regular season drew to a close, Federal District Judge William T. Sweigert ruled in the suit brought by former quarterback Kapp that the college draft and Rozelle Rule were "patently unreasonable and illegal." One year later, Judge Earl R. Larson ruled in the Mackey case that the Rozelle Rule violated antitrust law.[12] In July 1976, the NFLPA achieved its third major victory, when the National Labor Relations Board ruled that the NFL had engaged in unfair labor practices during the 1974 strike (including the use of "yellow-dog contracts" and the unilateral implementation of a new wage scale for preseason games, as noted in the previous chapter). In September, in yet a fourth separate case, this one filed in the name of Jim "Yazoo" Smith, Judge William B. Bryant declared the college draft illegal unless agreed to in collective bargaining. Finally, in October, the Eighth Circuit Court in St. Louis upheld Judge Larson's ruling in the Mackey case that the Rozelle Rule violated antitrust law.[13]

Strikes are wrenching events for the participants that play out as public spectacles. Judicial proceedings are tedious series of rulings and appeals with more profound consequences but no drama. Most football fans probably paid less attention to the rulings of Judges Sweigert, Bryant, and Larson than they had to the players picketing training camps in 1974, but the basic labor structure of the National Football League had now been ruled illegal. The union's victory was not quite complete, however. Like Bryant, the judges of

a. Earlier that summer, the commissioner exercised the Rozelle Rule in another high-profile case, in which the Rams initially were to give up their star running back, Cullen Bryant, for signing the Lions' wide receiver Ron Jessie; but after Bryant filed a lawsuit, Rozelle awarded first- and second-round draft choices to Detroit instead.

the Eighth Circuit "encourage[d] the parties to resolve this question through collective bargaining." Restraints on free agency were not in themselves illegal, the courts ruled; rules on free agency could be collectively bargained.

What followed was the major turning point in the history of NFL labor relations, a decision by Ed Garvey for which he would still be vilified in 1987, during the last of the major strikes and after he was long gone. The court rulings sent the owners back to the bargaining table, where Garvey in effect gave up the players' freedom (free agency and the abolition of the college draft) in return for a more powerful union.

The collective bargaining agreement reached in February 1977 increased the players' benefits, created an arbitration board for their grievances, and freed them from arbitrary hair and dress codes and the like. But on the key issues, where the players held the leverage they had won in court, it modified the college draft and replaced the Rozelle Rule but left their basic powers intact. The agreement reduced the number of rounds in the draft from 17 to 12 (leaving more rookies free to negotiate with the teams of their choice) and gave a player unhappy with the team that drafted him an opportunity after one season to play out his option (at a low salary). In place of the Rozelle Rule, it created a complicated "first refusal/compensation" system. After playing out his option, now at 110 rather than 90 percent of his old salary, a veteran player could negotiate with other teams, but his own club retained the right to match the outside offer. If his club declined, the player could leave, but his new team would have to pay compensation tied to a wage scale. A new salary under $50,000 required no compensation. For a player earning between $50,000 and $64,999, the club that signed him would have to surrender a third-round draft choice. Salaries between $65,000 and $74,999 warranted a second-round pick; between $75,000 and $124,999, a first; between $125,000 and $199,999, a first and a second; and over $200,000, two first-round choices. The average salary in 1977 was $55,300.[14]

The result was no player movement whatsoever, free agency in theory only. Over the five years covered by the agreement, rising television revenues drove up the average salary to $82,400. Any player in a position to play out his option likely had a salary that triggered compensation. Few clubs, assuming that they did not did not refuse to sign free agents on principle, would sacrifice a second- or third-round pick for a marginal player. A little higher up the scale, players at even the average salary cost their new teams a first- or second-round draft choice. At the top of the scale, Walter Payton, the league's best running back, received not one offer when he became a free agent in 1981. The owners insisted on their good faith, claiming that they had not anticipated in 1977 the growth in salaries that would make free agents too costly. Garvey argued that the owners with their full stadiums and shared TV revenues had no incentive to invest in top players. He also looked very much like a union leader outmaneuvered by management, despite the leverage he had won in court.[15]

The 1977 agreement also settled the Mackey lawsuit, as well as the companion class action suit filed in the name of Kermit Alexander on behalf of all players who had been affected by the Rozelle Rule since 1972. The 15 plaintiffs in the Mackey case shared $2.2 million, while roughly 2,000 players covered by the Alexander suit divvied up nearly $14 million, as determined by a point system. Each point was worth $2,330.[b] The 79 named plaintiffs received one point each. All players received a point for each season played from 1973 through 1976, and another for each of those seasons in which they played out their option.[16]

For many current players, particularly stars (and their agents), the 1977 labor agreement seemed close to a disaster, and it marked the beginning of the end of Garvey as executive director of the NFLPA. After the player reps unanimously approved the 1977 agreement, ballots were sent to the 863 dues-paying members of the union (out of about 1,400 total players). Just 593 voted, 91 percent in favor, which meant that 494 union members voted for the labor agreement that governed 1,400 players for the next five years. For those who did not vote, indifference seems inconceivable, sullen resignation more likely.[17]

For Garvey, the most important items in the agreement were the "agency shop" and "dues check-off." All NFL players now had to pay dues, which were automatically deducted from their paychecks. The union recovered its solvency, and for this Garvey was willing to sacrifice more radical freedom for the players. Throughout his tenure as executive director, Garvey pushed harder for across-the-board benefits and security for the rank-and-file than he did for the great wealth available only to stars through free agency. Most of all, Garvey wanted an organization powerful enough to run the NFL as an equal partner with the owners. Whether the players' collective welfare or his own power as the head of the union mattered more to him, only he and NFLPA insiders know, but in either case, the 1977 agreement rebuilt the union for future battles.

b. My share of the $14 million was $2,330, one point for playing in 1973. The first installment of what amounted to roughly 18 percent of my $13,000 salary as an English professor at Oregon State University arrived in my mailbox as a nice windfall. Many others likely found it poor compensation for what they had lost.

1982

In a long profile in *Sports Illustrated* in January 1980, Frank Deford hailed Pete Rozelle as "King" of his domain, "at the height of his powers." But Deford also portrayed Rozelle as essentially a man of the 1950s and early 1960s, perhaps not up to the league's new challenges—"brutality, safety, drugs, race, free agentry"—because he did not really understand them. In 1982 cracks in the foundation of the modern NFL suddenly widened into chasms all around the commissioner.[18]

George Orwell taught us to anticipate 1984 with grim foreboding, but 1982 turned out to be the NFL's nightmare year. It started well enough in January, with what remains the highest-rated Super Bowl ever, two weeks after "The Catch"—the pass from Joe Montana snagged by Dwight Clark at the back of the end zone to beat Dallas, 28–27, for the NFC championship—instantly entered football lore and endless TV replays. In the buildup to Super Bowl XVI, the press crowned 49er coach Bill Walsh, who developed Bengal quarterback Ken Anderson as well as Montana, as the NFL's latest sideline "genius." Whether Montana's cool or Walsh's inventiveness put San Francisco on top was the sort of controversy Rozelle could only love. The game itself turned on a play by reserve linebacker Dan Bunz, who stuffed a Cincinnati run at the half-yard line to assure the win and produce a Cinderella hero to share the glory with the cool quarterback and genius coach. What more could a football fan, or NFL commissioner, want? In March, Rozelle signed new five-year contracts with ABC, CBS, and NBC totaling $2 billion, an average of more than $14 million per team per year—more than double the fees under the expiring contracts. As Gerald Eskenazi pointed out in the *New York Times*, that $14 million represented two-thirds of the $20 million paid for the Denver Broncos franchise just two years earlier. Rozelle could look out on his creation and see that it was good.[19]

In early May, the *New York Times* assessed the state of the NFL and found a mix of good and bad, but a positive balance. Rozelle had been forced to withdraw the Senate bill intended to protect the league against antitrust claims. Davis's lawsuit would thus proceed to its conclusion in just a few days, while "worsening negotiations" with the Players Association raised the "specter" of another strike. On the positive side, though, league officials had persuaded Herschel Walker, the University of Georgia's sophomore running back, not to challenge the NFL's rule against drafting underclassmen. More important, the recent TV deals had infused much-needed millions into the weaker NFL franchises. (As in the 1974 bargaining sessions, owners would again claim meager or no profits, while the NFLPA would insist that every team made "substantial" money.) Rozelle still had his friends in Congress, in particular Senate Majority Leader Howard Baker of Tennessee. Remembering his deal with Senator Long and Representative Boggs in 1966, and knowing that the city of Memphis desired an NFL franchise, Rozelle had a reasonable hope of eventual success with his bill after some more legislative maneuvering. The *Times* also reported that, although Rozelle would not comment, he felt confident that the players would not back Garvey if he attempted to call for another strike. The state of the NFL? According to the *Times* headline, "It's Still Winning More Than It Loses."[20]

Then the sky fell in, not once but three times. On May 7, a jury in Los Angeles ruled in favor of Davis and the LAMCC. The NFL immediately appealed, of course, and Rozelle could still hope for congressional intervention, but the very real possibility that Davis would ultimately prevail now loomed over the league as it squared off against the Players Association.[21]

Following this blow, the announcement, on May 11, of yet another new rival league, the United States Football League, was a relatively minor aftershock in NFL offices. Even after the USFL signed a contract with ABC (for a modest $18 million over two years) and hired an experienced television man, Chet Simmons, as commissioner (bringing another $12 million from ESPN, the new cable company for which Simmons had served as president), the new league posed no direct competition for players and fans. By initially limiting player payrolls to $1.2 million—not enough for poaching on NFL rosters—and by playing in the spring, the USFL hoped to succeed alongside the NFL, not at its expense.[22]

The USFL would eventually consume considerable NFL energy and legal costs before disappearing, but it began in May 1982 as a minor irritant. The June 14 cover story in *Sports Illustrated*, on the other hand, was a blindside hit worthy of an Oakland Raider defensive back. On the magazine's first-ever nonpictorial cover (also reproduced in a full-page ad in the *New York Times* on June 10), the opening paragraph of a special report was typed out in the style of a police confession:

Cocaine arrived in my life with my first-round draft into the National Football League in 1974. It has dominated my life, one way or another, almost every minute since. Eventually, it took control and almost killed me. It may yet. Cocaine can be found in quantity throughout the NFL. It's pushed on players, often from the edge of the practice field. Sometimes it's pushed *by* players. Prominent players. Just as it controlled me, it now controls and corrupts the game, because so many players are on it. To ignore this fact is to be short-sighted and stupid. To turn away from it the way the NFL does—the way the NFL turned its back on me when I cried for help two years ago—is a crime.

The author (writing with the assistance of *Sports Illustrated*'s John Underwood) was Don Reese, a former defensive lineman for Miami, New Orleans, and San Diego. In the 1977 off-season, Reese and Dolphins teammate Randy Crowder had been arrested, then convicted, for selling a pound of cocaine to undercover cops. After missing the 1977 season, Reese signed with New Orleans, where he played for three years, before one final season in San Diego. At each stop, according to Reese's confession, cocaine use was rampant, and he named the players who partied with him. The article was a cry of self-loathing but also a finger pointed sharply at the NFL. "[D]rugs dominate the game," Reese charged, "and I got caught up in them." And he issued a warning: "The NFL is heading for catastrophe. Drugs are causing it."[23]

Drugs did not first enter the NFL in 1982, and drug use by NFL players is not a scandal. It becomes a scandal when the media report on it, and the major place for scandals to erupt in the 1970s and 1980s was on the cover of *Sports Illustrated*. Before cocaine, and soon steroids, there had been amphetamines, along with prescription painkillers and muscle relaxers, not to mention cortisone shots to speed up healing and Novocain and Xylocaine for numbing the pain long enough to play another game. Drugs fueled players and kept them on the field. "Pep pills" had been around for decades. Johnny Blood, the NFL's wild man of the 1930s, claimed to have been the first to use them, in 1935. But drugs in sport did not become a scandal until 1969, through a three-part investigative series by Bil Gilbert in *Sports Illustrated* describing a "startling" rise in drug use by athletes over the past ten years.[24] A rash of exposés by former NFL players published in 1970 and 1971—Dave Meggysey's *Out of Their League*, Bernie Parrish's *They Call It a Game*, Johnny Sample's *Confessions of a Dirty Ballplayer*, Chip Oliver's *High for the Game*— invariably included accounts of rampant use of "speed."[c]

The NFL finally banned amphetamines in 1973 and promptly faced its first drug crisis in early 1974, when Rozelle fined the San Diego Chargers and eight of their players for abusing them. Coaches and trainers distributed amphetamines (and steroids) to the players by the handfuls (there were bowls of steroids on the dining tables at training camp, next to the salt and pepper), and the Chargers were already facing a lawsuit by a former player, Houston

c. Though an insider at the time, I have only an outsider's knowledge of this issue. If popping uppers was common when I played, I never witnessed it.

Ridge, for juicing him up only to be crippled by injuries. The players felt more sinned against than sinning, but as with Karras and Hornung ten years earlier, Rozelle made them scapegoats for practices assumed to be common throughout the league. Ever the PR man attentive to the NFL's image, Rozelle also attempted to cast much of the blame on the psychologist hired by the club, Arnold Mandell, a respected department chair at the University of California, San Diego, School of Medicine, who admitted prescribing amphetamines, but only to protect the players from street drugs as he attempted to wean them from their addictions. (This was the case that an angry Mandell took to the public in an article in *Psychology Today* and a book, *The Nightmare Season*. The state of California subsequently found Mandell guilty of "overprescribing" drugs.)[25]

In contrast to amphetamines, cocaine was a "recreational drug" with no special connection to pro football or any other sport. Marijuana entered the NFL in the 1970s simply as part of the larger culture. Cocaine then became American society's yuppie drug of choice in the late 1970s and 1980s, and NFL players were among the young professionals who could afford it. What was becoming generically known as recreational "substance abuse" had a long tradition in pro football. Hard drinkers from Johnny Blood to Bobby Layne contributed to the mystique of larger-than-life men living large off the field as well as on. Whether in life or only in the popular imagination, bars were football players' natural habitat. But as the drug culture of the 1960s and 1970s turned the country once again, for the first time since Prohibition, into a nation of libertines and Puritans, football players who partied, now with weed or coke instead of beer and whiskey, were no longer doing the all-American thing.

Coaches and club officials did not really care what their players did off the field, so long as it did not affect their performance—until it made headlines or the cover of *Sports Illustrated* and became a "scandal," that is. Through the 1970s, the NFL dealt with drugs and alcohol as individuals' problems. Among the higher-profile cases, police busted Duane Thomas for possession of marijuana in 1972 and Lance Rentzel in 1973, and Joe Gilliam for heroin in 1976. In the third installment of *Sports Illustrated*'s three-part series on brutality in football in 1978, this one focusing on the role of amphetamines in fueling players' rage, Jack Danahy, the NFL's director of security, insisted to John Underwood that the league had no "drug crisis," just some individual users. In 1979 *Sports Illustrated* described the downward spiral of ex-Steeler quarterback Gilliam's life under drugs. In 1980 the league established a program to offer players rehabilitation, without penalty, and by the time of Don Reese's revelations, 17 players had enrolled, 7 in 1980 and 10 in 1981—including most notably Minnesota quarterback Tommy Kramer and Dallas linebacker Thomas "Hollywood" Henderson (the beginning of a long and well-publicized saga for Henderson). Like Gilliam's story, Henderson's public announcement of his cocaine addiction in February 1981, two years after he made All-Pro and played in the Super Bowl with the Dallas Cowboys, briefly rocked the NFL but appeared as an isolated case.[26]

Reese indicted the whole league, and his confession in *Sports Illustrated* had a remarkable impact. Over the rest of the summer of 1982, newspapers ran almost daily stories that seemed to confirm an entire NFL snorting lines before and after games. Local reporters investigated what could be discovered close to home, and the wire services sent the juicy bits to newspapers around the country. In just the first five days following Reese's revelations, the coach of the Denver Broncos admitted that his club had had to initiate drug-testing in training camp the previous summer; the *Orlando Sentinel* reported that 9 of the 150 collegians at the most recent scouting combine had tested positive for illegal drugs but had been drafted anyway; the coach and owner of the Cleveland Browns acknowledged that the team "had some problems with drug use over the years"; and the owner of the New Orleans Saints denied the extent of the problem claimed by Reese but estimated that "maybe 10 percent" of his players used cocaine while Reese was on the team. Over the next ten days, a grand jury in New Orleans began turning up the names of several Saints players involved in buying or using cocaine; investigative columnist Jack Anderson told a national audience on ABC's *Good Morning America* that "federal agents had secretly infiltrated a narcotics ring operating inside the N.F.L."; and Redskins running back Terry Metcalf, who had previously played in the Canadian Football League, told a reporter in Toronto that nearly half of the players on both sides of the border used marijuana, and almost as many used cocaine.[27]

Such flurries of bad news about the NFL have become routine; they began in the summer of 1982. Over that summer, several teams announced new drug-testing programs or their hiring of a "security director" with a declared role of counseling players but an implicit one of investigating their off-field behavior. In a front-page story in the *New York Times* on June 27, the NFL's assistant director of security and drug abuse declared that "only 17 players" had been identified as "chemically dependent," though probably another 40 or 50 were also addicted and hundreds "were using [cocaine], many of them regularly." As always, NFL representatives declared the "integrity of the game" their uppermost concern: in this case, the fear that an addicted player could be tempted to fix a game in order to pay for an expensive drug habit. League officials admitted they believed that five or six teams had serious problems, with a half-dozen or more "chemically dependent" players on each. The league hired Carl Eller, a member of Minnesota's Purple People Eater defense of the early 1970s and himself a recovering cocaine addict, to counsel current players. The new scourge, Eller explained, was freebasing, which made cocaine more potent and addictive. Freebasing gave players the same "incredible emotional high they can get on the field."[28]

Innocent players complained that they were now being stereotyped as drug addicts as well as dumb jocks, but as the summer played out, one incident after another seemed to confirm their new image:

- New Orleans's George Rogers (the NFL's leading rusher in 1981 after winning the Heisman Trophy at South Carolina) was named as a cocaine user.
- Ex-Saint Mike Strachan was identified as a supplier for his teammates.
- Cleveland running back Charles White (another former Heisman winner) was reported to be in rehab in Los Angeles.
- San Diego running back Chuck Muncie was banned from training camp until he completed treatment for his drug dependency.
- Atlanta tackle Warren Bryant was admitted to rehab (while three other Falcons confessed to experimenting with cocaine).
- Ex-Dolphin running back Mercury Morris was arrested for trafficking in cocaine, in order to treat the excruciating pain from a broken neck suffered during his playing days.
- St. Louis linebacker E. J. Junior was arrested for possession.[29]

Damage to the players' image, of course, damaged the league's as well, and these incriminating stories just kept coming and coming. For Pete Rozelle, the strike in September must have come as a relief.

Strike Two

Hardly. The pending players' strike was, in fact, Rozelle's chief worry over the summer of 1982.[30] It was also a worry wholly lacking in surprise. Rozelle had to see it coming virtually since the collapse of the last strike in 1974, yet no one could have seemed less prepared. At the center of the 1982 strike was Ed Garvey, not Rozelle, who became a mere bystander—a fact that did as much to undo his reputation as a strong commissioner as his suspension of

Hornung and Karras in 1963 had done to make it. In addition to culminating the NFL's nightmare year, the 1982 strike marked the beginning of the end of the Rozelle Era.

The 1982 strike was also the decisive event in the history of the NFL Players Association, marking the end of its Garvey era and the beginning of the long campaign for free agency. As I noted earlier, free agency under the conditions in the 1977 labor agreement proved illusory. When negotiations on the new contract opened in February 1982, the executive director of the Management Council acknowledged that of 555 players who had played out their options over the life of the 1977 agreement, 352 re-signed with their old clubs, 43 were traded or switched teams without compensation, 111 were not signed at all, and just one, Norm Thompson, moved to a new team with compensation involved. (He overlooked a second case, John Dutton's, and left 47 unaccounted for.)[31] Salaries climbed with the new TV deals, but no one was signing the multi-million-dollar contracts now routine in baseball, basketball, and hockey. Stars and their agents were furious with Garvey. In the spring of 1980, superagent Mike Trope had attempted to dump Garvey and organize a new union. In early 1981, a handful of player reps made another unsuccessful attempt. In December 1981, the union had to threaten Charger quarterback Dan Fouts and two Oakland Raiders, Ted Hendricks and Chris Bahr, with suspension for refusing to pay their dues. With dues now mandatory, the union was solvent but not at all unified.[32]

By 1982 Garvey had abandoned free agency, and he despised agents as a reactionary force serving individual clients at the expense of the union.[33] Instead, he demanded a percentage of gross revenues for the players, to be deposited in a central fund overseen by the Players Association and distributed according to a wage scale based largely on seniority. The average salary in 1982 was slightly more than $90,000, but the averages by position (as reported by the Management Council) ranged from $160,037 for quarterbacks to $79,581 for defensive backs and $65,779 for kickers. (Running backs averaged $94,948; defensive linemen, $92,996; wide receivers, $85,873; offensive linemen, $85,543; and linebackers, $85,205.)[34] The NFLPA proposal tied the wage scale to years of service, regardless of position or talent, then provided various adjustments for individual and team performance—bonuses for starting, for playing time, for playoff appearances, for All-Pro recognition, for selection by peers among the top 272 players in the league (roughly ten at each position). Seventy percent of the players' pool would go toward base salaries, 30 percent toward incentives.[35] In addition to placing the interests of the rank-and-file above those of the stars, such an arrangement would make agents superfluous.

Most important, the proposed model would make the NFLPA a full partner with management in running the National Football League. This was Garvey's ultimate vision and a proposition guaranteed to outrage the owners. Unlike in 1974, this time, because the league negotiated its new TV contract before the labor agreement, everyone had a clear idea of how much money was available, a whopping $2.1 billion over five years from television alone. The union calculated that players' salaries accounted for only 30 percent of the league gross, while the owners took home 36 percent in profits after paying out 34 percent in operating expenses. The players demanded 55 percent of the gross, the level supposedly reached during the NFL-AFL war of the 1960s. Garvey argued that the players were underpaid compared to other professional athletes, while the owners, by sharing 95 percent of revenues, had no incentive to pay players what they were worth. To Jack Donlan, the new executive director of the Management Council who came to the NFL from National Airlines with a reputation for union busting, the issue was simply control. The owners had it and were not about to give it up.[36]

The union this time targeted the regular season, when the owners' financial losses would be substantial. A poll conducted by the *New York Times* in April indicated that a majority of players would support a strike, but a much smaller one than Garvey and other union leaders claimed. In addition, several big-name players—Joe Montana, Terry Bradshaw, and Lynn Swann most notably—publicly opposed it. Eighty percent of the players polled also said that they had good relations with their owners, while just 53 percent approved of Garvey's handling of negotiations. (Seventeen percent disapproved of Garvey, and 30 percent didn't know or didn't answer.) As in 1974, the players were far less united than the owners.[37]

Players on opposing teams exchanged "solidarity handshakes" before preseason games, in defiance of the league rule against fraternization. (Also during the summer, one of the NFL's two newest teams, the Seattle Seahawks, proved that at least one NFL tradition remained strong: the club cut starting wide receiver Sam McCullum, who also happened to be the team's player rep.) When the Management Council finally responded to the union's demands with a serious counteroffer, it proposed a five-year, $1.6 billion deal, not guaranteed but projected in individually negotiated salary raises and including one-time bonuses of $10,000 per year of service since 1977 for each player. The union countered with a $1.6 billion package over four years rather than five (replacing the 55 percent of gross revenue with 50 percent of the TV contracts, plus some other monies). The differences were obviously negotiable, but the union's insistence on a fixed percentage to be managed by the union challenged the owners' power and control. As *Time* magazine put it, "Though both sides seem to be talking about the same amount of money . . . the philosophical difference on how that money should be allocated is a gulf without horizons."[38]

With the two sides again at an impasse, the players went on strike on September 20. The owners considered fielding teams with free agents and strikebreakers but decided on a lockout and canceled the games. A number of players denounced the strike and criticized the union, but unlike in 1974 they had nowhere to go.[39] The television networks filled their vacant time slots on Sundays with boxing, Canadian and small-college football, and a replay of the most recent Super Bowl, and on Monday nights with old movies and a "Superstars" competition. None of these earned ratings that approached an ordinary NFL game. The Players Association planned to offer "real" NFL football in a series of 19 All-Star games. Had these succeeded, a player-owned and -operated professional football league could have resulted: socialist pro football in the heart of capitalist America! The NFL sued, the NFLPA appealed, and while the appeal was being heard, two games drew all of 8,760 fans to RFK Stadium in Washington and 5,331 to the L.A. Coliseum. The judge upheld the NFL, putting an end to the series, "to the relief of all."[40]

After the predictable series of moves and countermoves, the union capitulated on November 16, after 57 days and 8 games (one of which would be made up by extending the season). The owners' final offer, announced at $1.37 billion, was, at most, marginally different from the one it put on the table in September. Instead of a wage scale, overseen by the union, the owners agreed to an "escalating minimum wage," ranging from $30,000 for rookies (increasing to $50,000 by 1985) up to $200,000 for 18-year veterans, without a fixed percentage of the gross and with substantial latitude for individual negotiations. In other words, control remained with the owners, and the NFLPA had never looked more ridiculous. The players gained almost nothing after sacrificing a half-season's salary (which basically accounts for the reduction from $1.6 billion to $1.37 billion). Only an immediate one-time bonus of $10,000 to $60,000 per player—which the owners had offered before the strike—made the final agreement at all palatable.[41]

Player reps in the past had always rallied around Garvey. This time, they initially voted to refer the owners' offer to their teammates without a recommendation. They eventually approved the final version by a 19–9 vote, and the players ratified it by a 3–1 margin, a significant level of disgust apparent in both tallies. The majorities undoubtedly voted to end the strike, not to celebrate the new contract. In approving the offer, the San Francisco 49ers also voted unanimously to ask for Garvey's resignation. Garvey's inner circle of union executives remained loyal, but he had less broad support than ever before.[42]

Absent from this account has been the name "Pete Rozelle." Whether or not Rozelle's role in settling the 1970 strike was exaggerated, his failure to intervene in 1974 or 1982 (then again in 1987) left him looking extraordinarily weak. Whether he opposed or supported the hard-liners on the Management Council, he had no role in negotiations, and the NFL was outgrowing its era when salesmanship and public relations were sufficient at the top. The owners "won" another strike but also failed once more to recognize how partnership with the players' union would strengthen, not weaken, their league.

The biggest loser in 1982 was Ed Garvey. After another unsuccessful attempt by a minority of player reps to dump him in February, Garvey resigned in June.[d][43] Whether or not his own power mattered more to him, with him went the possibility of the NFLPA as a workers' union, negotiating wages for all members, at the expense of stars. The strike's failure sent the union back to pursuing free agency in the next round of negotiations. Although another failed strike and nearly six years of litigation would ultimately be required, victory this time was assured, because the demand for free agency had antitrust law on its side.

The Dark Side

The NFL had been flying high when San Francisco nipped Cincinnati in the 1982 Super Bowl. A year later, in his annual press conference before the 1983 game, a noticeably somber Rozelle admitted that 1982 had been "a very distasteful year for the players, coaches, and owners of the National Football League."[44] On top of the strike, cocaine, and Al Davis's lawsuit, a PBS documentary just a week earlier had alleged that 12 NFL games had been fixed between 1968 and 1970, and that some current owners had a gambling connection to organized crime.[e] What more could possibly go wrong?

d. Garvey promptly entered politics as an assistant attorney general in Wisconsin, then was defeated for the U.S. Senate in 1986.

e. Out of this program on PBS's *Frontline*, "An Unauthorized History of the NFL," came the 1989 book *Interference: How Organized Crime Influences Professional Football*, written by Dan Moldea with the assistance of a producer of the *Frontline* program. *Interference* was largely ignored (by *Sports Illustrated* most notably), or criticized for "sloppy

As it turned out, a lot. Following the multiple muggings of 1982, the NFL became a wounded giant over the rest of the decade, with all the pygmies piling on. Whether a new generation of players was getting in more trouble, or a new generation of sportswriters would no longer let them get away with it, reports on failed drug tests and athletes' run-ins with the police became a routine part of sports reporting in the 1980s. Snippets from the wire services in the sports sections of most daily newspapers now included drug arrests along with injuries and trades. In part, pro football simply entered an era in which journalists took an adversarial stance toward powerful institutions of any kind, and sportswriters redefined themselves as serious journalists. In contrast to big-time college football schools, mostly located in small cities where the local sportswriters needed the team more than the team needed them, NFL clubs with the sole exception of Green Bay had to deal with a more aggressively adversarial metropolitan press.

The NFL also brought negative attention on itself, through its secrecy and arrogance. Rozelle and other NFL officials and owners had a long history of crying poor but refusing to open their books to the public, and of admitting to nothing that seemed in any way a flaw. Any reporter now who could dig out something juicy on the NFL was not about to keep it quiet. Even Rozelle's famous affability began to seem merely evasive, or dishonest, and sportswriters now seemed to enjoy his stumbles. How else can we understand the press's curious infatuation in the 1980s with Al Davis, who stole a football team from the city that most desperately needed it, but who also thumbed his nose at Rozelle and the rest of the NFL's old guard? Davis defied Rozelle and his fellow owners no matter what they decided, whether to give their proceeds from licensing to NFL Charities or to regulate the location of franchises. (Famous for reclaiming outcasts and for being a "players' owner," Davis also treated his players ruthlessly when they no longer pleased him.) Davis is surely one of the stranger folk heroes of the late twentieth century, but he served the needs of a press corps fed up with NFL smugness.

The Police Blotter

Paul Zimmerman's 1983 preseason report in *Sports Illustrated* was titled "An Overdose of Problems." According to Zimmerman, a year earlier the USFL

---

journalism" (*New York Times Book Review*, September 3) and for assembling "nasty allegations" without real evidence (*Washington Post Book World*, October 29). A brief review in the *Los Angeles Times Book World* (September 24) declared "the weight of evidence is overwhelming," but the book and its claims quickly receded into vague rumor.

had been Rozelle's Number 4 worry; drugs were Number 3, Al Davis's lawsuit Number 2, and the pending strike Number 1. Now drugs topped the list.[45]

Before Don Reese, drugs in the NFL were more rumored than documented. After Reese, regular reporting on drug arrests and convictions, punctuated by an occasional story about the cumulative problem or "crisis," created a popular perception of a drug epidemic in the NFL that no amount of public relations could alter. Reese's revelations also ended the no-fault era for the NFL's drug users. The labor agreement signed at the end of 1982 included the NFL's first leaguewide drug-testing program and a provision granting the commissioner the power of suspension.[46] For a league obsessed with its image, drug testing was a necessary curse. Not to test players for drugs would now seem horribly irresponsible. Unlike the old days, however, when no one was caught because no one tried catching, drug testing meant some failed tests. The NFL needed failed tests in order to prove its vigilance, but each one also became another black mark against the league's good name. The Players Association suffered with the public, too, whenever it resisted league efforts to root out the drug offenders. The issue for the NFLPA was power: it could not allow the NFL to do anything not agreed upon in collective bargaining. But the union must have often seemed to the football public simply indifferent to players' self-destructive and criminal behavior. The players' collective image suffered most, of course, as each arrest or suspension seemed to implicate all of them, not just the ones actually caught.

As the truncated nine-game 1982 season played out, following the disruption of the 57-day strike, in late October Don Reese was sent back to prison for violating his probation by continuing to use cocaine. Having decided "to do something right" in telling his story to *Sports Illustrated*, Reese was being punished for confessing that he had not yet whipped his habit and had thus violated the terms of his probation. A week later, Mercury Morris, the dazzling counterpoint to the efficiency and brutal pounding of Jim Kiick and Larry Csonka in the Miami Dolphins' Super Bowl backfields, was sentenced to a minimum of 15 years in prison for trafficking in cocaine. (In January, the judge set his term at 20 years; the conviction was overturned in 1986.)[47]

The new year continued the depressing litany of players and former players arrested for using, selling, or conspiring to sell cocaine. On July 25, Rozelle announced the first drug suspensions in league history: four games each for the Cardinals' E. J. Junior and the Oilers' Greg Stemrick, along with the Bengals' Pete Johnson and Ross Browner, both of whom had been convicted of nothing but had confessed to buying cocaine as witnesses during the trials of drug dealers. (Because they were in line with the collective bargaining agreement, the NFLPA and its new executive director, Gene Upshaw, supported the suspensions.) In early September, Rozelle suspended a fifth player, the Redskins' Tony Peters, after he pleaded guilty to conspiring to sell cocaine.[48]

In August a five-part series in the *New York Daily News* titled "The NFL and Drugs" claimed that, according to "well-placed sources within the NFL," 50 percent of the players in the league used cocaine recreationally and 20 percent, or 10 players per team, were "hard-core users." It also reported that as many as 50 players over the past year had gone through the NFL's drug-rehab program at the Hazeldon Foundation outside Minneapolis, the facility settled upon in the 1982 collective bargaining agreement. The extent of teams' problems supposedly ranged from two with none (New York's Giants and Jets) to the Dallas Cowboys with 34 known cases of drug use and "epidemic" use by the reigning Super Bowl champion 49ers, whose record had fallen to 3–6 in the strike-shortened 1982 season. Rozelle was launching a "three-pronged attack" on the league's problems: education, rehabilitation, and discipline. According to the *Daily News*, Rozelle and the "public-relations conscious NFL" were "highly concerned with its image."[49]

Along with the rest of the NFL, the Dallas Cowboys in 1983 entered their own new era. According to the series in the *Daily News*, the Cowboys had become "South America's Team," after published stories linked several players to a Brazilian drug ring. Neither the connection to the Brazilian ring nor another federal investigation eventuated in arrests, but the possible involvement of four or five Dallas players in this high-profile case kept returning to the news. A couple of weeks before the *Daily News* series, the *New York Times* reconstructed a history of the Cowboys' drug problems dating back to 1972. *Sports Illustrated* weighed in, too, with a story on the federal investigations and another on Harvey Martin, the current Dallas player whose life seemed in greatest danger of spinning out of control. The Cowboys' drug culture was real but also an especially attractive target for reporters put off by the club's long-standing arrogance. "Ever since Don Reese did that article on cocaine," Martin told *Sports Illustrated*'s Gary Smith, "it's like there's an all-out effort to catch us at something."[50]

In August *Sports Illustrated* added steroids to the list of the NFL's drug problems. Though primarily focusing on Olympic sports, *Sports Illustrated* suggested that "as many as 50% of the active NFL linemen and linebackers have used steroids." Steroids were not yet illegal or banned by the NFL, but they were becoming controversial elsewhere in the sporting world, and their spillover into the NFL did not help its already tainted image. An assessment of the state of the NFL in the *New York Times* at the end of the 1983 season wondered if the league had reached its peak in popularity. With the fallout from the 1982 strike and mediocrity on the field, as well as "continuing drug incidents involving players," there seemed a real possibility that the league's standing with the public would now steadily decline.[51]

After the blizzard of stories about drugs in 1982 and 1983, the pace slackened over the next two years, but the respite was brief. In May 1985 *Sports Illustrated* issued a special report, "Steroids: A Problem of Huge Dimensions." Only one NFL player, Tampa Bay and ex-Steeler lineman Steve Courson, would speak openly about using steroids, but he claimed that 75 percent of the NFL's linemen took them, and the magazine cited other estimates ranging from 40 to 90 percent of all players.[52] A few days before Super Bowl XX the following January, the Players Association announced the results of a survey of roughly three-fourths of its players, 29 percent of whom insisted that there was a drug problem in the NFL, while 32 percent claimed there was not (39 percent were not sure). The general public likely felt more certain about this issue when, the day after the game, the coach of the losing New England Patriots, Raymond Berry (an icon from the Unitas era in Baltimore), announced that at least five of his players had serious drug problems, and that he suspected five to seven more. Berry said that the team had voted to accept voluntary drug testing, a move that brought immediate objections from the Players Association as an action outside the collective bargaining agreement. Had Berry been the coach of one of the league's bottom feeders, his announcement would have been less shocking, but a Super Bowl contender with drug problems became a major story.[53]

Columnists again weighed in, and 1986 became a more image-bruising year than 1983, with seemingly one incident after another calling attention to the NFL's drug problems.[f] The worst incident was the death of Cleveland defensive back Don Rogers in June from an overdose taken at his bachelor party.[54] Reports of arrests and suspensions, and of players checking into rehab, continued into 1987, including big names such as the Redskins' Dexter Manley in March and the Rams' Charles White in August. Autobiogra-

f. In the midst of the ongoing reports on drug arrests, *Sports Illustrated* devoted most of its March 10, 1986, issue to a special report, "Gambling: America's National Pastime?," which again raised the specter of fixed NFL games and pointed to the hypocrisy of the antigambling stance taken by a league intimately tied to gambling and gamblers since its beginning.

phies by Lawrence Taylor and Thomas Henderson published that summer described in one case a club ignoring a star's problems with cocaine and alcohol, in the other a player snorting coke through an inhaler on the sidelines during the 1979 Super Bowl. On the steroids front, after the NFL finally banned them in 1987, the first round of testing that summer caught 97, or about 6 percent of the league's players. This was nowhere close to the estimates of 40, 50, even 75 percent, but with the tests announced well in advance, that anyone failed was the surprise.[55]

About 7 percent tested positive for steroids in 1988, the last year before players could be suspended for those drugs, as well as cocaine (in 1989, just 13 players would test positive). Media attention, including a five-part, front-page series in the *New York Times*, greatly exceeded the documented numbers, which no one believed anyway. How many NFL players actually used steroids, no one knew; somewhere between no one and everyone. But few football fans could have believed that the number was small, and insiders confirmed publicly that the NFL's drug-testing program was flawed, perhaps sometimes intentionally undermined by clubs that did not want their players stopped or caught.[56]

Cocaine remained the NFL's chief blight. By mid-September 1988, Rozelle had suspended 19 players for cocaine and other recreational drugs, including Manley and White, along with the Bears' Richard Dent and the Giants' Taylor (a front-page story in the *New York Times*). Manley and Dent were two of the NFC's top defensive linemen, Taylor the premier defensive player in the entire NFL, and White led the AFC in rushing in 1987. When *Sports Illustrated* included the story of White's addiction, "A Visit to Hell," in its NFL preview issue, drugs and their grim consequences became another routine topic for assessing the state of the game. In October, defensive back David Croudip of the Atlanta Falcons died from a cocaine overdose, the NFL's second such death in three years. (There would be another, David Waymer's, in 1993.)[57]

As the 1988 season played out, more suspensions followed. Five banned players, now reinstated, were to take the field for Super Bowl XXIII pitting San Francisco against Cincinnati, until the Bengals' Stanley Wilson missed a team meeting the day before the game and was found in his hotel bathroom, using cocaine. No suspension was ever more dramatic, and this one became permanent. (Manley and White would also eventually be among the NFL players banned for life.)[58] The aggregate number of suspensions never grew very large, and it was miniscule as a percentage of all players in the NFL. Athletes, league officials, and club executives argued that drug abuse in pro football was no more common than in society at large.[59] But the litany of names, appearing one or two or three at a time, week to week, month to month, some of them stars, created a sense of a continuous crisis. Stardom not only brought no immunity from illicit drugs or their legal consequences, it seemed to attract them. And each reported arrest, suspension, failed test, or fatal overdose was symbolic as well as actual, seeming to signify moral corruption at the heart of a sport once thought to build character.

Back in 1983, *New York Times* columnist Dave Anderson had worried about an opposite potential response: as drug arrests became so common, they would become no more troubling to fans than speeding tickets.[60] I suspect that football fans collectively in the 1980s were both appalled and indifferent. Football had always polarized the American public, breeding both passionate fans and equally passionate detractors. Drugs and criminality, on top of the labor wars, created new grounds for polarization in the 1980s, but they also created a dilemma for those who loved pro football. The NFL's continuing popularity suggests that most fans somehow adjusted, developing callousness to nonfootball matters or a capacity to compartmentalize the conflicting things they knew. NFL players could seem mercenary only when they were on strike, degenerate only when their names appeared in the stories about drug arrests. Once the games began, they could become "our guys" again. But the idea that football in itself builds character all but died in the 1980s.

Living (and Dying) with Pain

Among the reports of drug abuse in the 1980s, one atypical incident stands out. In 1984 former Denver Bronco running back Otis Armstrong was arrested and convicted (then put on probation) for fraudulently obtaining nearly 1,500 Percodan tablets from nine different doctors over a six-month period. Anderson was addicted to the painkiller after taking pills by the handfuls to relieve the agony from 17 upper-body fractures suffered during a seven-year career. As Michael Janofsky commented in the *New York Times*, "These difficulties reflect a dark side of professional football, a side barely known to anyone outside of those who play the game."[61] Anderson's addiction to Percodan (like Brett Favre's more-publicized addiction to the painkiller Vicodin in 1996) was less a vice than an occupational hazard.[g]

If we measure the dimensions of football's dark side by their degrees of separation from the game's own nature, cocaine is distantly related, abuse of

---

g. A survey of more than 1,400 former players by *Newsday* in 1997 reported that over half of them had been medicated to play with injuries, and roughly 10 percent suffered from drug-related complications after retiring.

performance drugs more closely connected, and serious injuries so intimately a part of the game as to be unavoidable. It is easy to condemn the use of steroids and amphetamines, yet they are likely less damaging to football players' bodies than the game itself, and on this issue our football culture is hopelessly schizophrenic. A sport that thrives on the "reckless abandon" of oversized and supercharged bodies cannot avoid high casualty counts. Performance-enhancing drugs contribute to injuries, while Novocain, Xylocaine, and other drugs put injured players back on the field too soon; but injuries are part of the game, with or without drugs. The hard fact that neither fans nor those who run the NFL can comfortably acknowledge is even harsher: injuries in football are *necessary*. Without them, the players' risk would not seem real, their heroism would be diminished.

Football fans watching *Monday Night Football* on November 18, 1985, were horrified to see Lawrence Taylor sack Joe Theismann and snap his leg, exposing his shattered tibia and fibula for endless TV replays . . . as they had been horrified in August 1978, when a blow from Jack Tatum left Daryl Stingley paralyzed . . . as they would be horrified in November 1991 and November 1992, when first Mike Utley and then Dennis Byrd lay paralyzed on the field at the end of a play. None of these incidents involved a personal foul.[h] In the late 1970s, the NFL banned Tatum's favorite "clotheslining" technique, as well as "spearing," or leading with the helmet in tackling, and enacted new rules to protect quarterbacks, but without making the game appreciably safer.[62] The injuries to Byrd and Utley verged on freakish. Byrd collided head-on with a teammate while rushing the quarterback. Utley simply lost his balance and fell forward, the front of his helmet striking the turf with all of his 315 pounds behind it. Fans would also be saddened in future years when star quarterbacks Steve Young and Troy Aikman would be forced to retire early, before one more concussion led to permanent brain damage. (Doctors in the 1990s would discover that what we had called "getting your bell rung" in my day— just shake it off—was potentially serious, even deadly.)

Serious injuries are so routine in football that fans likely become inured to the news of yet another one (except for those to their own favorite players), but occasional body counts in the media force the issue on the public's attention at least briefly. In 1986, in one of its periodic outcries against

h. While Tatum's blow was legal, he subsequently embraced his image as an "assassin" in not one but three autobiographies, where he described his contest with teammate George Atkinson in which they awarded each other two points for every "knock-out" and one point for a "limp-off."

violence in football, *Sports Illustrated* declared an "injury plague in the NFL," in which 183 starters had missed a total of 574 games over the first half of the season. In June 1988 the *Los Angeles Times* surveyed 440 retired players and found that 78 percent suffered from football disabilities. The previous March, the *Chicago Tribune* reported on two informal studies of NFL players' life expectancy. Len Teeuws, both an actuary and a former player from the 1950s, looked at data on 1,800 men who played at least five years between 1921 and 1959 and determined their average lifespan to be 61 years. Ex–San Diego Charger Ron Mix, now an attorney representing players in workmen's compensation claims, found an average life expectancy of 55 years in 800 cases. With their nonrandomized samples, none of these studies was statistically reliable, but the litany of familiar names of players who died in their 40s and 50s—headed by Bobby Layne and Norm Van Brocklin—had considerable shock value.[63]

On April 25, 1987, 30-year-old Larry Bethea, a former defensive tackle for the Dallas Cowboys, put a bullet in his head, four years after cocaine helped end a once-promising career. Bethea's was the first suicide in the NFL since September 15, 1980, when my own former teammate, Jim Tyrer, who left the Chiefs when I did but fell from a much loftier position, went to a Chiefs-Seahawks game in Arrowhead Stadium with his 11-year-old son. Afterward, Tyrer wandered the upper concourse of the empty stadium, then went home and, around 5:00 A.M. the next morning, shot his wife, then himself; while another son hid under his bed for more than an hour, thinking there were burglars in the house, before crawling out to find his parents' bodies. There are few more cavernous places than an empty football stadium. I am haunted by the image of big Jim, a man of tremendous dignity on and off the field during a long and distinguished career for which he was named to the All-AFL team, wandering around Arrowhead Stadium, looking down on an empty field where just a half-dozen years earlier he had played before cheering thousands. Suicides in the NFL are rare (though with at least eight more since Bethea's in 1987 not as rare as one might think) but long-term emotional as well as physical damage is well documented. Fifty-four percent of respondents to the *Los Angeles Times* survey in 1988 dealt with "emotional strain," ranging "from brief periods of despair and adjustment to serious thoughts of suicide."[64]

Studies in the 1990s and early 2000s would confirm these findings on the physical and emotional toll from pro football. In an effort to establish more reliable data on life expectancy, the Players Association commissioned the National Institute for Occupational Safety and Health (NIOSH) to examine the medical records of more than 7,000 NFL players from 1959 through 1988. Published in 1994, the NIOSH study would report a normal life expectancy but also find that football linemen were 52 percent more likely to die of heart disease than the general population (and three times more likely than players at other positions). The study would also confirm that the larger the player, the greater the risk, a fact also documented by the Living Heart Foundation and the Scripps Howard News Service in 2006. Scripps Howard tracked the deaths of 3,850 players born since 1905 and contacted medical examiners and coroners for the 130 born since 1955 who have died. Twenty-two percent of those 130 died of heart disease and 77 percent of them were medically obese. The Living Heart Foundation's two studies released in 2006, in collaboration with Mount Sinai Heart and the Pennsylvania State College of Medicine, confirmed that former linemen were 54 percent more likely than other players to have enlarged hearts, and also discovered that half of the linemen had "metabolic syndrome, a group of risk factors for cardiovascular disease that includes obesity, high blood pressure, low levels of protective cholesterol, and insulin resistance."[i] In contrast, just 20.3 percent of nonlinemen in the study had the syndrome, slightly below the national average of 21.8 percent.[65]

In 1985 William Perry, at 318 pounds, became a sideshow attraction as "The Refrigerator," an enormous lineman with the agility to play running back. In 1988 there were 17 300-pounders in the league; by 2002 there would be 331; in 2005, over 500. Why? The weight room? Steroids? "Natural" development? Whatever combination of factors have been at play, a little-noted rule change in 1978 was one of them. The bodies of football players have always been shaped in part by the rules of the game. Until the 1950s, top linemen (as determined by their selection to the NFL's All-Decade teams) played on both offense and defense, and they averaged less than 230 pounds. At 350 pounds, Les Bingaman from 1948 through 1954 had seemed a freak. (Bingaman "specializes in not moving," one sportswriter wryly observed in 1954. "He squats and waits.") When the NFL instituted two-platoon football in 1950, decreased demands on their endurance allowed the All-Decade linemen of the 1950s to balloon to 249 pounds, then add another nine pounds in the 1960s. At this point, linemen's average weight more or less stabilized, increasing just four pounds, to 262, in the 1970s.[66]

Then came radical rule changes on pass blocking in 1978. In my era,

i. The Living Heart Foundation was created in 2001 by Archie Roberts, a 1960s-era NFL player who went on to become a distinguished heart surgeon, expressly to address the medical problems of former pro football players.

offensive linemen could not open their hands or leave their arms extended. Pass blocking was a little like boxing: hit and recoil, move the feet, hit and recoil. In 1977 and 1978, responding to concerns that the game had become boring, the NFL passed rules allowing offensive linemen to extend their arms and open their hands in pass blocking, as well as new limitations on defensive backs' contact with wide receivers. These, along with other rules in 1979 and 1980 outlawing certain dangerous blows and protecting quarterbacks in particular, had two goals: to reduce injuries and open up the passing game. As scoring had fallen to a 36-year low,[67] pro football also again faced criticism for excessive violence. John Underwood reported in a three part series titled "Brutality: The Crisis in Football" in *Sports Illustrated* in August 1978 that 20 of the NFL's 28 starting quarterbacks suffered incapacitating injuries in 1977. Spearing, chop blocks (like Sid Gillman's "cutting drill" after the 1974 strike), and forearms to the head crippled dozens of players. Oakland defensive back George Atkinson's blow to Steeler receiver Lynn Swann's head on opening day in 1976 had provoked Pittsburgh coach Chuck Noll to accuse Atkinson of being part of a "criminal element" in the NFL, prompting Atkinson to sue Noll for libel.[68]

The goal of making football safer, though not so safe that it reduced fans' thrill in witnessing physical aggression and risk, remained elusive, but the moves to open up the passing game had immediate results. Scoring increased, and the restrictions on defensive backs made the crowd-pleasing West Coast Offense of the 1980s possible. But allowing offensive linemen to extend their arms and open their hands provides one of the great cases of the Law of Unintended Consequences. This new freedom made it easier to protect the quarterback. Fewer sacks meant more passes completed, but the rules on pass-blocking also literally changed the shape of NFL football, or rather of the men who played it.

Open fists and extended arms meant a radical transformation of linemen's job description. Now, instead of hit-and-recoil, they could hold their ground and ward off defenders with bulk and brute strength. Not immediately but over time, the advantage of sheer size became obvious. Offensive linemen's average weight rose to 270 pounds in the 1980s, then to 299 (for Pro Bowlers) by 1996.[69] By 1998, the mere 280- and 290-pound offensive linemen of the Super Bowl champion Denver Broncos were celebrated as undersized overachievers. Bigger offensive linemen could simply smother smaller defensive linemen, unless the defenders bulked up in tandem with the men who blocked them. Defensive linemen got bigger; offensive linemen got bigger yet. And as 300-pound defensive linemen and 330-pound offensive linemen became the norm, the long-term health risks associated with obesity could only increase. The bigger, faster, stronger players since the 1980s will become statistics in the studies of disability and life expectancy in 2015 and 2025.

Drugs did immeasurably more damage to the NFL's image in the 1980s, yet pain and injury and the sheer physical demands of playing the sport defined the NFL's true dark side. In 1988, *Jobs Rated Almanac* ranked 250 occupations according to such factors as working conditions, income, and security; professional football came in 247th. Thanks to free agency, escalating salaries would boost the sport to 220th by the third edition in 1995 and to 204th in the most recent edition, in 2002; but playing in the NFL would continue to rank among the worst occupations for working environment, security, and stress, and dead last, 250th out of 250, for physical demands. Over the six editions, actuaries ranked first, second, first, second, fourth, and second (ex-Bear Len Teeuws clearly made a sound career move). For a placid, comfortable life, one could become an actuary. Pro football offered a CEO's salary and incredible highs, but often at an equally high physical and emotional cost.[70]

The Games Go On

As pro football's dark side became an inescapable part of the NFL's image in the 1980s, the league did more than just survive. TV ratings peaked in 1981 but remained high throughout the decade. For fans, reminders of the physical and emotional toll on players more likely invested NFL football with tragic grandeur than discredited it. The more troubling litany of felonies and misdemeanors can seem overwhelming when separated out from the daily and weekly reporting on the regular season, playoffs, and Super Bowl each year, but they were just a small part of the NFL's story in the 1980s, and fans learned to live with them. In fact, the game on the field became the most exciting in years. After zone defenses in the 1970s had nearly eliminated long passes and even long runs from scrimmage, the rule changes of 1977 and 1978 freed receivers from suffocating defensive backs and gave quarterbacks more time in the pocket, as their linemen could now hold off pass rushers longer. The passing game, both short and long, opened up again, with quarterbacks like Dan Fouts and Joe Montana throwing to the likes of Kellen Winslow and Jerry Rice. The leaguewide pass-completion average of 54.1 percent in 1979 marked an all-time high, and it would never again drop lower. In 1980 pass plays outnumbered runs for the first time since 1969. The scoring average in 1983 was the highest since 1965.[71] Tight ends like

Winslow and Ozzie Newsome redefined their position and became stars in the passing game. As playing cornerback became more difficult, the best ones were drafted earlier and paid more than ever before.

The 1980s became perhaps the NFL's greatest decade for coaching innovations. The reigning offensive "genius" of the 1980s was Bill Walsh, whose West Coast Offense made San Francisco the team of the decade and was adopted or adapted throughout the NFL. Instead of hit-or-miss risk, the passing game became a ball-control offense that used multiple receivers to attack every part of the field, relying on short, safe passes punctuated by the occasional bomb. The West Coast Offense was more sophisticated and complex than any offensive scheme before it, and it made football more than ever a coaches' game of system and strategy. Quarterbacking, too, became more complicated than ever, but as an extension of the coach, who called all of the plays from the sidelines.

Despite the shift toward passing, the 1980s was also a great decade for running backs. Instead of a pair of backs sharing the ball—Paul Hornung and Jim Taylor, Larry Csonka and Jim Kiick, Franco Harris and Rocky Bleier—teams now tended to have a single featured back. Hugely talented stars such as Jim Brown, Gayle Sayers, and O. J. Simpson had always been "featured," but now the system itself made each team's primary ballcarrier a star. Walter Payton led the way, with Tony Dorsett, John Riggins, Eric Dickerson, Curtis Dickey, Marcus Allen, Curt Warner, and many others behind him. In 1984 Payton passed Brown's career rushing mark and Dickerson topped Simpson's single-season rushing record of 2,003 yards. (That same season, Dan Marino set new records for passing yards and touchdowns, and Art Monk for pass receptions.) For a brief moment, before an injury stopped him short of four complete seasons, Raiders' running back (and Kansas City Royals' outfielder) Bo Jackson seemed an athlete from another galaxy, toying with mere humans. In both subtle and not-so-subtle ways, NFL football on the field was shifting increasingly from a team orientation to a star system.[72]

Coaches had to develop defenses to stop the newly liberated offenses, whose coaches in turn had to develop new ways to exploit the redesigned defenses. Innovation begat innovation. Defensive strategists abandoned the simplicity of the 4–3 alignment for various versions of a 3–4, with designated pass rushers and extra defensive backs as dictated by down and distance (and by increasingly sophisticated computer analysis of the opponents' tendencies). The Chicago Bears' defensive coordinator, Buddy Ryan, became a celebrity as an assistant coach. Outside linebackers displaced middle linebackers as the key men on defense, led by the New York Giants' Lawrence Taylor, who redefined the position's possibilities and became an icon as "LT." At 6′3″ and 237 pounds, Taylor was big enough to stuff the run but also fast enough to cover receivers and, more important, to be a devastating pass rusher. Teams had to develop special game plans for neutralizing him. Like the offenses, defenses became less conservative. Instead of gearing up to stop big plays, with linemen holding their ground and backs dropping back into zones, defenses increasingly tried to create big plays of their own with more aggressiveness and more blitzing. (Blitzing linebackers and designated pass rushers also imperiled quarterbacks as never before, negating the intent of the rule changes meant to protect them.) Situational specialization—second and long, third and short, and so on—changed the roles of many players on both sides of the ball, and the enhanced overall complexity required more assistant coaches. The six or seven assistants of the 1970s began increasing to the 15 or 20 (or even more) that clubs have now.[73]

With more scoring and gambling on both sides of the line of scrimmage, NFL football became a more spectacular show for the fans. While the 49ers were the team of the 1980s, with Super Bowl victories in 1982, 1985, 1989, and 1990, the 1985 Chicago Bears most captured the public fancy, as a paradoxical collection of hip-hop throwbacks. Walter Payton ("Sweetness") had "the smile and voice of a choirboy" but also earned Jim Brown's praise as a "gladiator" when he broke Brown's career rushing record. (Brown did not pass out such accolades lightly.) Mike Singletary at middle linebacker was another pious assassin. Quarterback Jim McMahon, described by *Time* magazine in a pre–Super Bowl cover story as an "idiosyncratic punk rocker or just rocker or just punk," invented himself as a biker dude, wearing inscribed headbands on the field (in violation of NFL rules) and wraparound sunglasses off it. William "The Refrigerator" Perry, an unpolished rookie on the league's best defense, became a national phenomenon after his coach, Mike Ditka, began inserting him in the backfield for the goal-line offense. The Bears harked back to the rough-and-tumble teams of the Bronko Nagurski and Bulldog Turner eras. Ditka, himself famously combative as a 1960s-era player, then as a coach, labeled them "the Grabowskis." They also recorded a hip-hop track, "The Super Bowl Shuffle," that sold more than a half-million copies in Chicago by Christmas and became a signature statement in their pre–Super Bowl hype.[74]

The Super Bowl itself reigned in all of its overblown glory. In 1984 the country's premier sporting event and civic festival became the "Super Bowl of Advertising" as well, when Apple's single ad for its new Macintosh computer, an Orwellian "1984" directed by Ridley Scott that never even mentioned the product's name, caused a sensation as a media event, drew 200,000 consumers into dealers' stores the next day, and boosted sales 50 percent above Apple's goals over the next three months. The Super Bowl became the occasion for launching new product lines, introducing new marketing campaigns, winning unprecedented brand recognition for new or small companies (Monster.com, Master Lock, Mail Boxes, Etc., over the coming years). The year-to-year increasing cost of a 30-second spot became another measure of how high the NFL soared. The media began covering the ads in the same way as the games themselves, with pre-game anticipation and post-game reviews. Beginning in 1989, a *USA Today* Super Bowl Ad Meter registered viewers' preferences. Supposedly 1 in 10 TV watchers now tuned in for the ads.[75]

Polls in 1984, 1985, and 1989 confirmed that pro football was still Americans' favorite sport (by an increasing margin over the decade). Regular-season attendance remained strong. From 1982 through 1987, television ratings for the Super Bowl never dropped below 45.8, and a regular-season game between Chicago and Miami in 1985 set an all-time record for *Monday Night Football*. Yet at the same time, overall TV ratings declined from what turned out to be the all-time high of 1981, with *Monday Night Football* taking the hardest hit. Sportswriters speculated about the impact of the 1982 strike and drug arrests and of the new competition from cable, but they also complained about too many blowouts, too few games in doubt until the final gun. The NFL seemed thriving one moment, floundering the next.[76]

NFL football can seem a hopeless contradiction: alternately heroic and psychopathic, the worst of all occupations and the best of all experiences. Although the media celebrate NFL football one moment and excoriate it the next, the two sides are the dual faces of a single reality. And this duality became more sharply defined in the 1980s.

Strike Three: Scab Ball

As the five-year TV contracts signed in 1982 approached expiration, executives at the networks (which derived an astonishing one-eighth of their year's advertising revenue from the NFL) began talking about retrenchment. Observers estimated collective losses of roughly $150 million over the final two years of the contracts. Reversing a history of one huge increase after another, the NFL and the networks in January 1987 announced new three-year deals totaling $476 million per year, a slight drop from the $490 million that the league earned in 1986. Only reluctantly including the cable network ESPN allowed the NFL to fare as well as it did.[77]

The NFL's signing with ESPN would assure the long-term financial health of the league, as it also marked the coming-of-age of the all-sports cable network that would transform the entire sporting landscape in the 1990s. But none of that was apparent in 1987, when cable reached fewer than 50 percent of American households and was still generally known for picking up the scraps left by the broadcast networks. Accepting the cable network as a broadcast partner initially just allowed the NFL to keep revenues more or less flat as the league's fundamental structures were being assaulted elsewhere.

After Al Davis's victory in court in May 1982, he moved the Raiders to Los Angeles, where they would remain through 1994, though never on the terms that he envisioned. Promised improvements to the L.A. Coliseum never materialized; Los Angeles fans proved themselves much less passionate about the Raiders than Oakland's had been. Davis himself turned out to be a better "football man" than "finance man," more a renegade member of the old guard than one of the new breed of entrepreneurs he helped unleash on the NFL. By 1990 Davis was already announcing his intention to return to Oakland, where he was promised the luxury boxes, along with other incentives, that Los Angeles had never delivered. In what *New York Times* columnist Dave Anderson called "a rare triumph for civic sense over sports dollars," the Oakland City Council decided that the community needed better schools and housing, not to mention infrastructural rebuilding after the recent earthquake, more than a football team. After four more frustrating years in Los Angeles, and much talk of moving to various sites in southern California, Davis would take the Raiders back to Oakland in 1995 (and an expanded stadium, with luxury suites, in 1996).[78]

In the meantime, the league felt the first aftershock of Davis's successful lawsuit in March 1984, when Robert Irsay, the loose-cannon owner of the Colts, took his team to Indianapolis, literally stealing out of Baltimore in the dead of night.[79] Like Davis, Irsay had complained for years about his stadium, and he had repeatedly threatened to move his team to Phoenix, Memphis, Jacksonville, or Los Angeles, if not Indianapolis. Following Davis, Irsay knew that his fellow owners would not risk another lawsuit by vetoing his move. Next in line was Bill Bidwill, owner of the St. Louis Cardinals, who took his team to Phoenix in March 1988, this time with the formal approval of his fellow owners but only under the threat of another lawsuit. (Art Modell, Cleveland's future betrayer, spoke for those who felt extorted. "I would much prefer the Oakland Raiders instead of the Los Angeles Raiders and the Baltimore Colts instead of the Indianapolis Colts," Modell declared in defense of NFL tradition.) For preempting the league's potential "expansion opportunity" in Phoenix, Bidwell agreed to pay his fellow owners several million dollars. In return, he looked forward to 20,000 more seats and "about $2.5 million a year from luxury box seats." Relocation now offered a quick fix for the most ineptly run organizations, and the financial benefits of franchise free agency and new stadiums for all clubs were coming into focus.[80]

Three franchise shifts in six years hardly constituted a stampede, but the NFL was transforming itself in slow motion. Over the same period, Pete Rozelle and the NFL had to weather competition from the United States Football League that drove up salaries and culminated in another prolonged lawsuit, this one ending in another loss for the NFL but a damage award of just $1 for the USFL. Much more damaging to the NFL, both immediately and for the future, relations between the Players Association and a Management Council dominated by hard-liners remained as contentious and bitter as ever. Following Ed Garvey's resignation as executive director in June 1983, his replacement was NFLPA president Gene Upshaw, the All-Pro guard of the Oakland Raiders and protégé of Raider boss Davis. Whether or not Upshaw had absorbed Davis's contempt for Rozelle, the new five-year agreement signed in 1982 meant not peace but five years of waiting for another whack at the owners, and this time free agency would be prominently back on the table.

As long as the owners retained control, they were always willing to share some of their increasing revenues with their players. Player salaries soared between 1982 and 1987, not by the owners' choice but because of competition from the USFL. By signing more than 100 NFL players over its three-year life, the USFL forced NFL clubs to offer millions to their top draft choices and to current stars such as Lawrence Taylor and Joe Montana in order to keep them. Huge increases in the average salary for three years—38 percent, 23 percent, and 41 percent (according to the Players Association)—were skewed by these million-dollar contracts for a few. By the time negotiations began on the new agreement, NFL owners wanted to cut labor costs, while most players had received little of the new salary money. In August 1987, as strike talk intensified, rookie Brian Bosworth became the highest-paid defensive player in the NFL before he set foot on the field, when he signed a ten-year contract with the Seattle Seahawks for $11 million. Neither the owners nor the veteran players were happy.[81]

Whether Upshaw was deeply committed to free agency or, like Garvey, would have preferred some kind of wage scale, it was clear by 1987 that without competition from a rival league—the USFL was now defunct—only free agency could create a true market for football talent. And by this time there was a groundswell of player support. Despite modifications to the rules on compensation in the 1982 agreement, free agency was still an illusion.

Norm Thompson and John Dutton remained the only players in ten years to change teams with compensation (there would be a third and last, Wilbur Marshall, in 1988). The owners who, thanks to Davis, could now exploit their own free agency still adamantly opposed the players' having it. (Coaches, of course, also opposed free agency, because it would prevent them from developing the same personnel over several years.)[82]

With salaries inflated by the USFL and revenue from the new TV contracts flat, NFL owners did, in fact, have financial problems in 1987 that they had not faced in 1974 or 1982. In response to the players' demand for genuine free agency and the usual increases in benefits, the owners proposed modifications of the rules on free agency that would change nothing, offered not even slight increases in benefits, and insisted on rollbacks from the current level of compensation. They wanted to reduce payment for the option year and implement a wage scale for rookies (as well as extend the draft from 12 to 15 rounds, to tie up more first-year players). A wage scale! The owners now demanded something like what they had furiously opposed from Garvey in 1982. Of course, *they* would run it.[83]

The NFL's third and final strike began on September 21 and lasted just 24 days.[84] Upshaw and the union leadership called for a strike after the second game, apparently believing that owners would not receive their first TV payment until after the third. Instead, each club received its scheduled million-dollar payment from the networks on October 1, then sat back to outlast the striking players (for whom three games were required for the season to count toward their pensions). Unlike in 1982, the owners had decided to continue the season with strikebreakers and "replacement players." Unlike in 1974, the response in the press to the owners' willingness to field hastily assembled teams of "castoffs and retreads," as the Cleveland Plain Dealer termed them, was almost uniformly negative.[85] Even the paper once firmly in Modell's pocket now criticized the owners' position. As writer after writer pointed out, in trying to pass off scab ball as real NFL football the owners had permanently shattered any pretense that they were caretakers of "the integrity of the game." But when enough fans within the inevitably divided public proved willing to accept a mediocre substitute for real NFL football, yet another strike was doomed.

With missed games costing players an average of nearly $15,000 now, and the highest-paid players losing up to four times that amount, the fate of the 1987 strike, as a Washington Post headline put it, lay in "the alignment of the stars."[86] Among the players with the highest salaries, Boomer Esiason ($1.2 million), Jim Kelly and Warren Moon ($1.1 million), John Elway and Walter

Payton ($1 million), and Marcus Allen ($900,000) remained on strike to the end; but Joe Montana ($1 million) and Lawrence Taylor ($900,000) did not. Other big-name defectors included Randy White, Tony Dorsett (reluctantly), and Danny White of the Dallas Cowboys; Mark Gastineau, Joe Klecko, and Marty Lyons of the Jets; Gary Hogeboom of the Colts; Mike Webster of the Steelers; Howie Long of the Raiders; Steve Largent of the Seahawks; and Ozzie Newsome of the Browns. "Marginal" players were nearly invisible in the strike coverage this time, despite the fact that they again sacrificed the largest portion of their brief careers. Fewer players than in 1974, but still 261 out of nearly 1,600, broke from the strike over its three weeks, including 26 Raiders and 21 Cardinals, though not a single Redskin and just one Bear and one Chief. When Montana abandoned the strike on October 7, along with Dwight Clark, Roger Craig, and 9 more 49er teammates, the NFLPA was effectively beaten, although it held out for another week. On October 16, union leaders sent the players back to work without a contract.[87]

As in 1974, coverage of the strike exposed ambivalence about football players. Bill Brenner of the *Indianapolis Star* applauded quarterback Gary Hogeboom's "courage" in abandoning the strike, and David Casstevens of the *Dallas Morning News* adopted an ironic stance in "accusing" strikebreaker Randy White only of loving football, taking care of his family, honoring his contract, and looking out for himself.[88] But most writers now, even some who opposed the strike, were openly disdainful toward players who abandoned their teammates. George Vecsey of the *New York Times* declared that an "established player who walks through a picket line deserves the contempt of players and fans for the rest of his career."[89] The press particularly vilified "tiny" Doug Flutie, with cracks about "the five-foot-seven millionaire" and the "moral midget."[90]

Montana's defection was the most troubling. After the group of 49ers tried to quit striking earlier but were persuaded by Coach Bill Walsh to remain out with their teammates, *San Francisco Chronicle* columnist Glenn Dickey wrote an impassioned column about how strikes "bring out character." Dickey refrained from directly commenting when Montana finally did break ranks, but he reported that some of Montana's teammates were bitter, and he noted that "it won't ever be the same for Joe again." Columnists for the *San Francisco Examiner*, emphatically on the players' side this time (unlike in 1974), conspicuously said nothing about the defection of the 49ers' franchise player. Writers outside San Francisco treated Montana less gently. In Atlanta, the *Constitution*'s Dave Kindred, though contemptuous of the striking players, had even more scorn for their betrayers. As Kindred put it, "I don't like the strike. But I like the idea of hanging tough as a unit 1,500 strong. I like the dignity it takes to stay on the picket line even as you work within the union to make sense of the situation." The occasion was Montana's first game back, in Atlanta against the Falcons. When the "millionaire quarterback" refused to make himself available for an interview, Kindred had the last word: "Montana's a jerk in love with his checkbook. I'd rather dig ditches than look in the mirror and see Joe Montana." The 1987 strike tarnished several Hall of Fame careers.[91]

Kindred's opposition to the striking players put him in the minority among sports columnists in NFL cities. A new generation of sportswriters had arrived since 1974, more inclined to challenge the establishment than to support it. Such was the situation north of the 35th parallel, anyway; in southern cities like Atlanta, New Orleans, Dallas, and Houston, sports editors and columnists still tended to be antiunion.[j] It was hard to love an owner in 1987.[k] Carroll Rosenbloom had arranged to desert Los Angeles for Anaheim just before he died suddenly in 1979, leaving the club to his widow, Georgia, who proceeded to run it with all the football savvy of a former chorus girl. Davis, of course, had abandoned Oakland in 1982, after a protracted lawsuit. Two years later, after Irsay sneaked his Colts out of Baltimore, he announced to a welcoming party of 17,000 in Indianapolis, "It's not your team. . . . It's mine and my family's." Jets owner Leon Hess had already jilted New York for New Jersey (following the Giants), and as the strike played out, Bill Bidwell and Bud Adams, owners of the St. Louis Cardinals and Houston Oilers, respectively, were shopping their teams around. Joe Robbie had repeatedly undermined public efforts to refurbish Miami's Orange Bowl because he wanted a brand new, state-of-the-art stadium. Robbie succeeded, and opening day was October 11, 1987, the third Sunday of the strike. Although Art Modell would not abandon Cleveland for several more years, already he had squandered his good will in the city through his messy financial dealings. A sportswriter in Kansas City even took a potshot early in the strike at the famously bland (and rich) Lamar Hunt.[92]

The general attitude in 1987 seemed to be that the owners were doing what owners do: make lots of money, bust unions, and profess concern for "the integrity of the game" while dumping a fraudulent version of NFL football on a

---

j. The sports editor of the *New Orleans Times-Picayune*, Peter Finney, was an exception, although his paper offered plenty of contrary opinions.

k. The conspicuous exception in this case was the *Times-Picayune*'s Bob Roesler, a holdover from 1974 who was completely pro-owner.

gullible public. The 1987 strike was chiefly about the players: whether they were selfish, arrogant, foolish, and greedy; or very well paid, yes, but deserving of what they earned with their too-mortal bodies and of more if they could get it. In 1987 players faced stereotypes of their drug abuse as well as their greed. Antiplayer sentiments in southern newspapers (excluding the *Miami Herald*) were consistent with the region's conservative, antiunion traditions. Elsewhere, the press in NFL cities almost unanimously sided with the players.[1] Several sports columnists were more militant than the athletes. Instead of a Dick Young and Phil Pepe or a Dave Anderson and a Red Smith on opposing sides of the dispute, as in 1974, the *New York Daily News* and *New York Times* had Mike Lupica, Harvey Araton, Ira Berkow, George Vecsey, and others, all lining up with the players. Howard Cosell contributed scathing columns to the *Daily News* on strikebreakers, scabs, and scab ball. The *Cleveland Plain Dealer* was no longer Modell's house organ but the voice of a union town defending its own.[93]

While the striking players received most of the sympathy in the press, there was no lack of criticism for Gene Upshaw and the NFLPA. Even to many sportswriters on the players' side, the strike in 1987 seemed ill-conceived and unnecessary. While Upshaw and the union leadership repeatedly insisted that free agency was the key issue, management sources and some players insisted that such freedom, as opposed to pension and benefits, would only benefit a few. The fact that Upshaw was a former player, not a lawyer or career labor organizer, brought criticism. The fact that Upshaw was black, at least according to Upshaw and a few black players, raised the possibility that some of the criticism, and the resistance of the Management Council, was racially motivated. Whether Upshaw was serious or "playing the race card," he struck a nerve, provoking a flurry of anxious responses.[94]

The ace in the owners' deck, and the feature unique to the 1987 strike, was scab ball—or "sham ball," "fraud ball," "bogus ball," "sucker ball," or "bonzo football" ("You can drape chiffon on a chimpanzee and you still don't have a debutante"), as it was variously named.[95] Most sportswriters (outside the South again) loathed scab ball; some of them loathed the scabs. The rookies in camp in 1974 had had no reasonable option. They had to prove themselves good enough for the NFL before they could worry about how the NFL treated them. The players released during training camp in 1987, then called back to man the scab teams, had had their chance to prove their NFL quality and

1. Exceptions were Bill Brenner of the *Indianapolis Star* and Larry Felser of the *Buffalo News* (Felser was antistrike but not antiplayer).

failed. Now they were simply stealing someone else's income. In an "open letter to those who would cross the picket lines and play pro football," Cosell asked them if "there is a public price tag on your soul."[96] The strike's best wit also came from scab-ball trashing. Bernie Lincicome of the *Chicago Tribune* likened his relief on leaving a scab game early to "sneaking away from a dance recital in which none of the children are mine. If I have to watch someone dress up like a turnip and pick her nose, I want to be able to hug and scold her later."[97]

The opposing sentimental view of the "replacement players" was apparently crafted by Tex Schramm, general manager of the Dallas Cowboys and chief architect of management strategy during the strike.[98] According to the NFL's official line, the young men on the makeshift teams were "Walter Mittys," following their dreams.[m] The Associated Press, in a story likely carried in hundreds of newspapers, likened their experience to "attending a fantasy camp and getting paid for it before going back to their regular jobs as bartenders, stockbrokers, and high school coaches."[99] In one of the crueler ironies of the 1987 strike, striking players had to root for their own scabs— no hoping for the opposition to "beat them like a gong" when the results counted toward making or missing the playoffs. The defending Super Bowl champion New York Giants entered the strike 0–2 and came out 0–5, too far down to recover. Washington won all three of its scab games and went on to win the Super Bowl.

The owners and television networks jointly won the 1987 strike. Scab ball drew, on average, only 16,947 the first week, up to 25,627 the second, still less than half of normal attendance.[100] Yet fans polled in 1987 more decidedly took the side of the owners than in 1974 (no major poll had been conducted in 1982).[101] This preference says volumes about fans' ambivalence toward "mere" football stars. Television ratings also dropped for scab games, but not as sharply as the striking players hoped and expected.[102] Several advertisers (Miller Beer, Ford, General Motors, Chrysler, and Blue Cross/Blue Shield) pulled their ads, but the networks managed to fill their spots at discounted rates. The owners refunded a portion of their TV revenues to cover the networks' losses, while the networks did much more for the owners. Simply by carrying the scab games (no other programming could match their ratings), the networks guaranteed profits for the clubs. A handful of sportswriters did

m. The Walter Mitty version of scab ball would make a belated curtain call in the 2000 film *The Replacements*, a grotesque parody of the 1987 strike, astonishingly made by the most unionized industry in the country.

some investigative reporting completely missing in 1974, to show how paying minimum salaries to scabs offset lost gate receipts.[103] Lower profits were still profits. The only losers during the strike were the players.

The marriage of TV and the NFL left the union no real chance. (Mike Lupica of the *New York Daily News* viewed it more like a relationship of whores and pimps.)[104] The networks contributed over half of the NFL's annual revenue, in return for the most valuable programming to sell their advertisers. We sometimes demand of commercial television a "conscience" that it does not have, as if its role were public service or truth telling instead of selling its programs. Even specific instances of conscientious programming can be calculated acts to achieve bankable credibility. A mere football strike did not warrant such a calculated sacrifice. While individual sportscasters responded to this conflict of interest in varied ways, the mutual dependence of the networks and the NFL guaranteed that TV sportscasters in general would be kinder than print journalists to scab ball.[105] Moreover, television by 1987 spoke to and for its viewers in a way that the press no longer did. Many newspaper columnists in 1974 had presented themselves as advocates for powerless fans who would be forced to foot the bill for whatever the players won at the bargaining table. At least a few columnists in 1987 blamed the fans—attacked them, called them names—for letting the owners get away with the outrageous fraud of scab ball.[106] A more independent and critical sporting press meant a less powerful one. By 1987 more fans got their sports news from television than newspapers. The NFL now needed only television, as it had once needed the goodwill of the press. And with television on the owners' side, the players were utterly overmatched.

In hindsight the 1987 strike, like the one in 1974, appears unwinnable but necessary. The owners would never willingly let the players become free agents, but demanding free agency gave the union its only leverage. Owners' freezing or even reducing players' compensation would break no antitrust law. Denying them the right to choose their employers, on the other hand, would do so, as Judge Larson had ruled in 1976. As the union's critics in 1987 constantly reminded readers, however, Garvey and the NFLPA had willingly traded away free agency in 1977. The payoff had proven not worth it, and now they wanted it back. But contrary to the critics' assumption, the union could not simply go back to court and demand it. The absence of free agency resulted from collective bargaining, not the owners' monopolistic power. To get it back, the union had to bring it back to the bargaining table, fail to achieve it in good-faith negotiations, then turn to the courts for redress.

This is what Upshaw and the union did in 1987 and after. The day after the strike collapsed and the players returned to work once more without a contract, the union filed *Powell v. NFL* in the same federal court in Minneapolis in which it had won free agency in 1976. A complex lawsuit is not drafted overnight; clearly this one had been prepared in advance. Upshaw had a Plan A and a Plan B, as Garvey had in 1974. The owners would not yield at the bargaining table (Plan A), so the NFLPA went to court.

It took more than five years, and the NFLPA finally succeeded only by first seeming to surrender. In 1988 Judge David Doty ruled for the union in the *Powell* case. Confident that the league would prevail on appeal, the Management Council rejected Rozelle's attempt in early 1989 to broker a labor agreement, refusing to accept free agency even for players with seven years in the league. On November 1, 1989, the Eighth Circuit Court indeed overturned Doty's ruling on the grounds that players could not sue over issues collectively bargained in "good faith" and "at arm's length." The current restraints on player movement were still rooted in the 1977 agreement, which had been reaffirmed in 1982. The Management Council, however, had not anticipated the NFLPA's next move: in November 1989 it decertified itself as a collective bargaining unit. If the owners wanted to break the union in 1987, they were shortsighted. The owners needed a union, only a weak one. With no collective bargaining unit to represent them, the players became free to take the NFL to court, where they could not lose.[107]

Goodbye, Pete

In March 1989, at the annual league meeting, Pete Rozelle announced that he was resigning as commissioner, two years before his contract would expire. The lawsuits by Al Davis and the USFL (for whom Davis testified as a witness) and the inability to work out a collective bargaining agreement with the players had ground him down. Paul Zimmerman reported in *Sports Illustrated* that Rozelle had actually made his decision the previous October, when a new season meant not the usual joy of renewal but continuing problems: "the unresolved collective-bargaining agreement, the drug controversies, the growing specter of steroids and even a threat to his authority" from a bloc of owners. On March 22, after informing the owners in executive session, Rozelle left the meeting room tearful and broke down during the press conference that followed. Wellington Mara's voice also broke when he spoke with reporters afterward. The funereal event became surreal when Davis, as Zimmerman reported, "shook [Rozelle's] hand on the way out and then embraced him."[108]

Zimmerman summed up Rozelle's legacy: solvency, parity, public awareness, and his own decency. No one speaks ill of the deceased at a funeral.

Rozelle's considerable accomplishments were irrefutable, but a new NFL was emerging that required a different kind of leadership. In 1989 the league appeared beset with perhaps insurmountable problems and had appeared rudderless for some time before Rozelle resigned, yet within a year under new commissioner Paul Tagliabue the NFL would be moving confidently in a new direction. Two months before Rozelle announced his resignation, the *New York Times* reported several owners' fear "that his traditional strengths—friendly persuasion and public relations—may be antiquated in times that require greater legal and financial acumen." As the fabric of the modern NFL had been unraveling, Rozelle had not asserted his authority but "faded into the background behind lawyers and committees."[109]

The following October, the owners selected Tagliabue, the league's chief outside attorney since 1969, over Jim Finks, a longtime football man. The *New York Times* reported that this decision could mean "that the league may soon be managed more like a $1-billion-a-year entertainment business than a collection of money-losing tax shelters, as many outsiders have viewed it." A "new breed" of owners such as the Patriots' Victor Kiam and the Cowboys' Jerry Jones had come into the league, committed not to sharing and League Think but to "aggressive steps to raise revenues." Jones entered the NFL as Rozelle left it, and the extent to which the Cowboys' new owner would fundamentally alter the business of the National Football League would not be known for a few years, but his immediate firing of coach Tom Landry and general manager Tex Schramm, one of Rozelle's best friends and closest allies as well as the Cowboys' chief architect since the team's founding in 1960, shocked traditionalists. The old guard among the owners had always stressed holding player costs down; the new breed preferred to raise revenues. Half of the teams in the NFL supposedly lost money in 1989, when player salaries accounted for 50 percent of revenues. When free agency finally became a reality in 1993, the salary cap would be about 64 percent of revenues, and everyone would get rich.[110]

Everyone agrees that Rozelle's greatest contribution to the NFL was that first national television contract in 1962. Hindsight confirms that his greatest failure as commissioner came in labor relations, and Tagliabue's signature achievement would be labor peace, the task to which he immediately committed himself after his election. From the beginning, Tagliabue would deal with Upshaw and the Players Association as partners with the owners. Rozelle regarded the players as hired talent. Like a union-busting studio head of Hollywood's golden age, Rozelle valued them as the performers who drew the crowds, and he grasped the particular importance of marquee stars. But stars would come and go, because others always waited in the wings, and Rozelle could not accept the players as individuals with rights.

Rozelle's NFL remained the one he entered in the 1950s, run by a handful of strong-willed patriarchs who believed in their right to treat their players as either compliant or unruly children, depending on how they acted. Or worse: Tex Schramm, never an owner but as powerful as one, once told the players during negotiations, "You're the cattle, we're the ranchers."[111] Neither the owners nor Rozelle adjusted to the social changes of the late 1960s and 1970s. John Mackey, president of the Players Association in 1970 during the first brief work stoppage, later recalled his amazement at Rozelle's failure to grasp what had happened to the country. "We had Vietnam at the time," Mackey marveled, "turmoil everywhere, and a lot of things were changing. Any leader should have seen that the league was drafting players from those campuses, that pro football had to change, too, and be prepared for that. But Rozelle didn't. I never felt that he truly understood what was happening." Rozelle was "polite," "honest," and "sincere," but uncomprehending.[112]

In his formative dealings with players—with Paul Hornung and Alex Karras in 1963, with Joe Namath in 1969—Rozelle handled them like wayward children. When players later organized themselves and mounted strikes, Rozelle stayed in the background, either willing for the hardliners on the Management Council to have their way or powerless to stop them. Scab ball in 1987 exposed the philosophical bankruptcy of the NFL's old guard, who believed in "tradition," in the sanctity of "the game," and in the greater good of the whole, but who ultimately held their players, as well as the fans, in contempt. The new breed of owners who would be running the "new NFL" within a few years would ignore or take for granted the sanctity of "the game," but they would be extremely attentive to the fans—if only as their customers— and they would accept the players as partners in delivering their product.

The old guard's myopia is perhaps undeservedly obvious in hindsight. As player salaries soared in the 1990s, football fans would not seem unduly troubled, as they had been when already-well-paid players went on strike in 1974, 1982, and 1987. A poll conducted by the *New York Times* and CBS in December 1984 found fans generally satisfied with the game (except for the intrusion of too many commercials during telecasts), but nearly 50 percent felt that players were overpaid.[113] The Management Council had done its job too well. Convincing much of the public during the strikes of 1974 and 1982 that the players were greedy, while the poor owners struggled just to break even, hurt the league's image where it should have mattered most. Labor peace would be good for the image as well as the financial stability of the league.

The "modern NFL" initially thrived under a PR man; the "new NFL" required a lawyer with a marketing mentality. In a telling moment at the owners' annual meeting in March 1985, Rozelle had urged them, as the *New York Times* reported, to "generate a better public image in the aftermath of a strike, ownership changes, years of litigation, problems with Congress, players running afoul of the law, and competition with the United States Football League."[114] Unable to solve the NFL's problems, the PR commissioner focused on maintaining a positive public image that ignored them.

But the problems remained. In his first year as commissioner, Tagliabue established direct contact with Upshaw and began a sustained campaign to achieve a collective bargaining agreement. He also led the NFL in stretching the 16-game season over 17 weeks, adding two more wildcard teams for the playoffs, declaring college juniors eligible for the NFL draft to ward off a lawsuit, announcing future expansion and realignment, and negotiating new television contracts for nearly double the previous revenues. When he interviewed for the job, Tagliabue in a memo to the search committee had written, "Stadium economics are changing dramatically, and the entertainment marketplace is rapidly being restructured." Under Tagliabue, three-quarters of the NFL's teams would build new stadiums, renovate old ones, or contract for new ones. The new NFL was all about entertainment and revenue.[115]

The 1980s were "the league's most stressful decade."[116] Yet out of the seeming chaos emerged the colossus of the 1990s and the new millennium. Owners would thrive in the new NFL, with franchise values increasing more than six-fold (even in adjusted dollars) from 1989 to 2003. Collectively but unevenly, the players would thrive, too, though not quite to the same extent, as their average salary would nearly triple over that same period. Whether the fans and the sport itself have also benefited is a more challenging question.

THE
NEW
NFL

In 1989, when Paul Tagliabue replaced Pete Rozelle, the league took in $975 million in revenue and the average franchise was worth about $100 million. The most recent figures calculated by *Forbes* magazine in 2006 are $6.2 billion and $898 million (previous year's revenue, current worth).[a] For perspective, *Forbes* noted that the increase in franchise value since 1998 was 11 times the growth of the S&P 500 over that same period.[1] The "new NFL" that emerged in the 1990s had three cornerstones: labor peace, television contracts, and stadium revenue. (Leaguewide sponsorships and licensing added a smaller but still sizable pot of money, while favorable tax laws invisibly undergird the entire enterprise.) Labor peace arrived in 1993 after more than five years of litigation following the collapse of the 1987 strike. Ever-richer television contracts arrived with seeming inevitability, as the NFL always managed to have fewer TV packages than networks to bid for them. And the bounty to be extracted from stadium leases and local marketing was a gift to the NFL from its two "rogue" owners. Al Davis won for every owner the right to move his franchise for a better deal or extort generous stadium financing from the local community to keep him at home. Jerry Jones then showed everyone how to make a stadium pay.

Shrewdness, luck, and unintended consequences have all played a part in the new NFL's prosperity. Davis's fellow owners fought him in court until they lost completely, then they capitalized on the franchise free agency that he won for them all. Tagliabue understood the entertainment business and stadium

---

a. *Forbes* will have released a new set of estimates (in September 2007) at about the time this book appears.

economics far better than Rozelle, as well as the necessity of labor peace. Tagliabue also managed to hold together an increasingly contentious group of owners in an era when they thoroughly understood their legal rights at odds with collective policies. And television revenues soared, even as ratings slid, for reasons both within and beyond the NFL's control. The appearance first of cable and ESPN, then of the new Fox Network, guaranteed competitive bidding for NFL rights, but Tagliabue and the NFL helped themselves maintain their leverage by forming their own network as well.

Behind all of these developments lay the power of football itself and the passion of true fans, which could be manipulated and used for leverage but not simply created. In the new NFL, however, football became less completely a "sport" and more a "brand" and entertainment "product" to be moved by marketing men (and women, too), for whom NFL football was not fundamentally different from MTV videos or the latest blockbuster movie. How that marketing and branding of NFL football is related to the power of the game itself and the passion of the fans is the question for the following chapter. This chapter will consider the economic foundation of the new NFL.

Labor Peace at Last

In January 1989, as the NFLPA's suit worked its way through the judicial system, and realizing that free agency based on first refusal and compensation was not working, the owners unilaterally imposed so-called Plan B free agency. Each club could now "protect" (that is, restrict) 37 players each season, allowing the rest to become free agents (the 37 could still seek free agency under the old rules). Over the next four years, 718 players would change teams under this arrangement, for average salary increases of 70 percent or more; but Plan B did a lot less for stars than for journeymen.[2] Restricted players did see their salaries rise, as free agent signings altered the basic salary structure, but not nearly to the level that they could have negotiated if they were free. Under four years of Plan B, just three "protected" players received offers from other teams.[3] But Plan B backfired on the owners. It proved to the players that free agency could work for stars and journeymen alike, if only it were not restricted.

After winning the initial *Powell* decision, then losing the NFL's appeal in November 1989, the NFLPA by decertifying itself as a union gave up its right to sue the NFL on its own behalf, but it now could support individual players' antitrust suits. In April 1990, the NFLPA backed a new lawsuit in Judge David Doty's court in the name of New York Jets running back Freeman McNeil and seven others (all of whom had been "protected" players under Plan B).[4] This was the beginning of the end of NFL owners' absolute control over professional football.

Not without a fight. Behind the scenes, the league (through NFL Properties) went after the NFLPA's chief source for financing the lawsuits in the absence of union dues: its group-licensing agreement with the players. NFL Properties initially offered ten top quarterbacks (Jim Kelly, Warren Moon, Dan Marino, Phil Simms, John Elway, Bubby Brister, Boomer Esiason, Troy Aikman, Jim Everett, and Randall Cunningham) $500,000 each to turn their rights over to the NFL. It then went after other stars (Michael Irvin, Sean Jones, Steve Emtman, Ronnie Lott), eventually expanding the arrangement to include more than 700 players by 1992, for a minimum of $10,000 each.[5] Nonetheless, the NFLPA stayed afloat. The 50-day trial in the McNeil case that began in June 1992 ended with a jury deciding on September 10 that Plan B violated antitrust law. This was the decision that forced the restructuring of the NFL. The players' victory was not quite complete, however. The jury ruled Plan B too restrictive but did not rule out restrictions altogether, if collectively bargained. Doty told the two sides to agree on a system of free agency or he would impose one.

The NFL still had the option of appealing the McNeil decision. It would surely lose, but in the meantime the NFLPA's treasury would be drained as it kept paying legal costs. The NFL could also scrap Plan B, go to a less-restrictive Plan C, and start a new round of expensive legal proceedings. In other words, although the NFLPA now had the stronger hand, neither side held all of the cards. More so than Rozelle, Tagliabue believed in compromise, but it took Doty's rulings to convince the owners. (Tagliabue also created a more conciliatory Management Council by removing Jack Donlan as its head.) The two groups returned to the bargaining table in November 1992 and worked out a system of free agency by January, which Doty approved the following August. In the interim, the NFLPA became certified again as a collective bargaining unit and negotiated a labor agreement over the spring of 1993.[6] The National Basketball Association provided the model: free agency and a guaranteed percentage of gross revenue, but with the NFL's owner-friendly variations—a supposedly "hard" salary cap (that, in fact, proved to be semisoft though still harder than the NBA's) and nonguaranteed contracts. It had taken two full decades, but the players finally had both freedom and football.[b]

b. Under the terms of the agreement, all players became unrestricted free agents after five years. Restricted free agency was possible after three or four years, with the clubs holding the right of first refusal. Each club was allowed to designate one "fran-

Winners and Winners

On the day in 1993 that the NFLPA and the Management Council agreed on the free-agency plan, Gene Upshaw exulted, "For the first time, we're the partners of the owners." One interested observer, an attorney for the baseball players' union, said that free agency meant "citizenship." Upshaw's words recalled Ed Garvey's defiant (and erroneous) statement after the 1974 strike collapsed, that the players had not truly lost because "this was a strike for recognition," and the owners "would have to deal with the union from now on." Players struck in 1974 for "freedom and dignity." In 1987 the player rep for the Washington Redskins called the union's action a "dignity strike."[7] In one sense, the long campaign for players' freedom was a struggle for what Aretha Franklin (and Rodney Dangerfield) immortalized as R-E-S-P-E-C-T, and what countless athletes invoked whenever they felt that their opponents or the pollsters or the writers or the fans did not properly appreciate them (which was most of the time). With the 1993 agreement in place, Upshaw and the Players Association no longer had to snap at the table scraps but now sat at the table with the owners. Tagliabue began conferring regularly with Upshaw as a partner in all matters affecting the players.

Free agency also meant millions of dollars, to be sure, whether or not players changed teams or re-signed with their own. Players who had been collectively paid about 30 percent of league revenues in 1982 were now guaranteed twice as much of a much larger pot. In the first round of signings, the average salary of unrestricted free agents more than doubled, from $517,000 to $1.044 million. Restricted free agents did even better, seeing their average salary leap from $293,000 to $780,000. Not just marquee players but also backup quarterbacks, left tackles, and outside linebackers became millionaires. A defensive end, Reggie White, came out on top of the initial free-agent signing frenzy with a four-year, $17 million contract.[8] No longer was a rival league necessary. With a guaranteed percentage of most revenues, players' salaries were now driven by the size of the television con-

---

chise player," who was not fully free but was guaranteed a salary at least the average of the top five players at his position (and the team that signed him would have to give up two first-round draft choices). Alternatively, a club could designate a "transition" player restricted by slightly different rules. The terms of the salary cap required clubs to spend at least 58 percent of "designated gross revenues" on players (about 95 percent of gross revenues at the time) but not more than 64 percent (a limit that wealthy clubs quickly learned to circumvent). A defined pool for rookie salaries guaranteed a larger share for veterans; the college draft was left intact but reduced from 12 rounds to 7. And the league agreed to pay $195 million to settle all outstanding lawsuits.

tracts. After the initial jump in 1993 (and a slight dip in 1994), incremental average increases followed in 1995, 1996, and 1997, then a 35 percent leap in 1998 with the signing of new TV contracts, followed by more small advances until the next set of agreements would boost salaries again.

Despite the winner-take-all mentality on both sides of the prolonged labor wars, it was hard to find losers. The owners had been convinced in 1974 that freedom for the players would mean anarchy for the league, the undoing of 50 years of growth from a rinky-dink sideshow to the most popular spectator sport in the country. Instead, labor peace stabilized costs for player salaries and benefits, key elements in an economic structure in which the value of an NFL franchise could increase from $140 million in 1993 (for the expansion Carolina Panthers and Jacksonville Jaguars) to $530 million in 1998 (for the new Cleveland Browns) to $700 million in 1999 (for the Houston Texans). According to the Minnesota Vikings' owner, Red McCombs, the labor agreement meant as much as the television contract to the value of his franchise.[9]

The worth of the average NFL franchise, as calculated by *Financial World* and *Forbes*, rose from $125 million in 1993 to $898 million in 2006. Average revenue over the same period increased from $53.3 million per club to $192.5 million (in 2005). A fixed percentage of most of these revenues certainly made the players collectively richer, but in no way at the expense of the owners. Figures made public during one of Al Davis's many lawsuits against the NFL revealed that the clubs in 1999 averaged $11.6 million in profit. (That figure, of course, did not include the hidden tax benefits. An unrelated report claimed that Alfred Lerner wrote off half of the $530 million purchase price for the Browns on his personal income taxes.)[10]

The absence of the guaranteed contracts enjoyed by NBA and Major League Baseball players seems to make NFL players relatively less fortunate. According to the NFLPA, between 1995 and 2002, only about 40 players each season had some guaranteed base salary. In the overwhelming majority of cases, and even for most of the compensation negotiated by these 40, only signing bonuses were guaranteed.[11] Contrary to public perception, however, nothing in the NFL's collective bargaining agreement forbids guaranteed contracts, and nothing in Major League Baseball's or the NBA's requires them. Standard practices simply differ.[c] No NBA free agent would sign a contract that is not guaranteed, because he knows that some other club will offer one. Because football is less affected by individuals, few NFL players have the clout

c. David Meggysey, longtime western regional director of the NFLPA, corrected my own misconception on this point.

to command a guaranteed salary. Unlike in the NBA and Major League Baseball, where clubs must often continue paying on guaranteed contracts long after the player has stopped producing or even playing, "dead money" in the NFL is largely limited to signing bonuses.

There would seem to be an essential fairness in a system that rewards players only when they play, although such fairness seems ruthless in the case of career-ending injuries. The Standard Player Contract of my day is long gone, but players are still bound to their clubs for the duration of their contracts, while the clubs can release them at their discretion. (Beginning in their fourth year, veterans are guaranteed their salary for the current season once games begin.) Even here, the relationship has become less one-sided, as players can renegotiate their contracts at any time (the club must also be willing). The individual negotiating power that comes from free agency and the players' collective entitlement to a percentage of league revenues creates fairness in contracts today that was missing in 1974.

For both the NFL and the NFLPA as institutions, free agency plus salary cap has been an unalloyed blessing. The 1993 agreement—extended in June 1996, February 1998, December 2000, January 2002, and March 2006—has brought labor peace for 14 years and counting. Players and owners alike benefit from the public perception of harmonious relations between players and owners, instead of the unseemly spectacle of millionaires fighting billionaires for yet more money. For the NFLPA, the agreement has meant a full partnership in running the business of professional football. For the NFL, the new structure has created long-term stability as well as something close to true parity. With rosters changing each season through free-agent signings, no team (except for the New England Patriots in recent years) can remain dominant for long. Twenty different teams, nearly two-thirds of the NFL, played in the Super Bowl over the 14 seasons following the 1993 agreement. Fans of even the once lowliest franchises can renew their hope each season.[12]

For individual clubs, the new financial structure has been both a blessing and a curse. While shared revenues and the salary cap have guaranteed profits for any competently managed franchise, the cap and free agency have also made it extremely difficult to sustain excellence on the field. (Only the Patriots have so far solved the problem that has defeated everyone else.) The parity loved by the league has been hard on traditionally well-run clubs that can no longer develop their own players over many seasons. Once players achieve success, they are easily lost to free agency or become too costly to retain. Responsibility for the team's success has shifted significantly from the field to the front office, and within the front office from "football men" to "finance men," the "capologists" or "cap specialists" who now determine the strength of the roster from season to season. Coaching "geniuses" have become dependent on accountants. In the meantime, although "football men" may hate the cap, every owner has grown richer.[13]

For the players, now over 1,700 of them, compared to just 32 owners, the situation has been more complicated. A single collective bargaining agreement cannot serve the interests equally of all stars and journeymen, starters and reserves. The central fund demanded by Ed Garvey in 1982 favored the rank and file. In 1992, on the verge of the players' final victory in court, Garvey remained publicly critical of free agency as a benefit for stars (and their agents) at the expense of "career and decent wages for all players."[14] Under Gene Upshaw, whether by choice or necessity, the union opted for free agency with all its consequences. Every player now has a shot at free agency after four years, but half of the players in the NFL last fewer than three seasons.[15] In certain fundamental ways, both free agency and the resulting economic disparity among players have altered the meaning of "team." Clubs form and dissolve virtually from one year to the next. Individual performance always meant more than team success at contract-signing time, but the raised stakes have magnified that hard truth.

The collective benefits enjoyed by all players rose sharply with the 1993 agreement and its guaranteed percentage of revenues. At the same time, free agency separated football players into more distinct economic classes. Roughly 20 percent of the players' guaranteed revenue goes to shared benefits, the remaining 80 percent to individually negotiated contracts.[16] As a backup center in 1973, I made $27,000 while none of the Chiefs' starting linemen, even the All-Pros, made as much as $50,000. Today, a starting left guard making $300,000 can line up next to a left tackle who earns $6 million. In 2001, according to NFLPA data, there were 493 millionaires in the NFL (roughly 15 per team), earning an average of $2.86 million. With an average salary of $1,100,500 for all 1,729 players, a couple of simple calculations tell us that the remaining 1,236 players must have averaged a little over $400,000. In 2005, when the average salary was just under $1.4 million, the median salary was $569,000—a lot of money for everyone, but a whole lot more for some. As one NFL lineman has put it (with some exaggeration), "The problem is that there is no middle class in the NFL." An NFL "team" now more closely resembles a cast for a movie, with stars, supporting actors, bit players, and extras assigned their roles. For an ex-player from my generation, one of the strangest events in the new NFL is the off-season signing of backup quarterbacks. It may have been an obvious fiction in many cases, but in my day every position was supposedly up for grabs in training camp. Now the NFL has designated under-studies, paid accordingly.[17]

The 1993 agreement became a work in progress, with each extension attempting to address the flaws in the system. Under the 2002 extension, minimum salaries for veterans in 2004 started at $305,000 and increased between $75,000 and $125,000 for each season played. This meant that a solid sixth-year player, not a star, who would make $535,000 might well be dumped for a second-year player earning $305,000 in order to free up $230,000 under the salary cap. The five- or six- or seven-year career for merely solid players was in jeopardy. The 2002 extension addressed this issue by stipulating that veterans making the league minimum would not count more than $450,000 against the salary cap (thus affecting players in their fifth year and beyond). The new agreement also increased the fund for performance-based pay, bonuses for playing time that mostly benefited young veterans with low salaries who earned starting positions.[18]

Such details are nearly meaningless to outsiders but profoundly meaningful to the players affected. While free agency seems to mostly benefit stars, those designated "franchise" or "transition" players—not allowed to change teams, but compensated at the level of their highest-paid peers—can be particularly frustrated by their inability to capitalize on free-market bidding. The highest-salaried players sometimes become the most vulnerable to being released in order to create room under the salary cap for new free-agent signings. Upshaw has repeatedly had to argue that this is fair. No club is forced to release any highly paid player whom it wants to keep; players can renegotiate lower salaries; many of those released have gone on to sign with other teams for less money.[19] The hard, cold logic of the market rules. Running backs have become particularly vulnerable in the market-driven football world. A millionaire tackle who loses a step but can still protect his quarterback's blind side remains a valuable property. A running back who loses a step becomes instantly expendable. In 1982 only quarterbacks earned more than running backs. In 2000, among position players (that is, excluding kickers and punters), only tight ends earned less. In 2005 running backs had moved up but still earned less than offensive tackles, cornerbacks, and defensive ends as well as quarterbacks.[20] (Left tackles' becoming the highest paid players next to quarterbacks is its own story.[21])

Under the 1993 agreement, the Players Association became, in effect, an adversarial partner in running the NFL: collaborating when possible, pushing for players' rights and financial interests when necessary, though not to the detriment of the league's overall financial stability and not on behalf of the self-interest of every individual player. Some critics have charged that Upshaw has been "much closer to the NFL commissioner than a union boss ought to be."[22] Bryant Gumbel expressed this sentiment more bluntly on HBO's *Real Sports* in August 2006, when he advised incoming commissioner Roger Goodell to ask Tagliabue where he keeps his leash for Upshaw. The mild uproar that followed concerned whether NFL officials would try to censor Gumbel, their new play-by-play man on the NFL Network. In one of the most reasoned responses, Michael Wilbon of the *Washington Post* defended Upshaw instead. Wilbon pointed out that the overwhelming majority of football players are interchangeable parts of a highly successful league, not individual stars with marquee value. If the NFLPA tried to strike for guaranteed contracts, the owners would simply field replacement teams again.[23] The fact is, whether by necessity or conviction, Upshaw collaborated with Tagliabue in assuring a stable and prosperous NFL into the foreseeable future, to the benefit of future as well as current players, and of owners and fans, too.

To outsiders certainly, whatever financial inequities might affect some players seem insignificant in the context of their general prosperity. Careers remain short, but with a *minimum* salary increasing to over a quarter-million dollars, another strike became all but unthinkable, despite the posturing and delays preceding the most recent extension of the labor agreement. Yet even as the NFL, in the words of *Time* magazine in 2004, became the "American Money Machine," it continued to depend on a delicate balance. Relative parity has served the fans' rooting interests but at the cost of their long-term connection to favorite players, who come and go with each new round of free-agent signings. And the NFL so prospered that it reached a point at which its prosperity became a source of internal contention. As local revenues increased enormously but unevenly among clubs, less prosperous teams wanted more redistribution, while the Players Association wanted a share of those new revenues not included in the collective bargaining agreement.[24]

In 1970 just 4 percent of league revenue was not equally shared, and that figure changed little over the next two decades. In 2005 estimates of unshared revenues ranged from 10 to 20 percent, perhaps more than a billion dollars not shared among the owners or with the players. The 2002 collective bargaining agreement, set to expire after the 2007 season, had built-in incentives to settle: for the owners, the salary cap would disappear in the last year of the agreement; for the players, the years required for unrestricted free agency would be extended from four to six. But extending the collective bargaining agreement became entangled with a demand from the less-prosperous clubs for greater revenue sharing among the owners. As negotiations dragged on into 2006, approaching and then passing a March 1 deadline, Upshaw threatened to decertify the union again, making all players free agents and not likely willing to accept another salary cap. With too much at stake for both sides not to compromise, yet so much at stake that compromise would be expensive, the two sides seemed locked in what *SportsBusiness Journal* termed "a high-stakes game of chicken." Finally, on March 8, after repeated postponements of the deadline, by a 30–2 margin the owners agreed to shift about $150 million a year from the 15 wealthiest franchises to the less profitable ones and to share 59, 59.5, and then 60 percent of all revenues with the players over the six years of the agreement (the percentage rising every two years). Even Jerry Jones and Al Davis sounded like old guard League Thinkers in their comments to the press supporting the new arrangements. Upshaw and the NFLPA were the clear winners. Had the owners quit fighting each other and struck an agreement with the Players Association sooner, they would likely have given up less. Labor peace now extended through 2011, but only afterward did the outcome seem to have been inevitable.[25]

Stadium Games

The increasing disparity in club revenue and the shrinking of the players' share came from factors unforeseen in 1993. At that time, the NFL still derived most of its income from television and ticket sales, the revenues shared among owners and, as stipulated in the new labor agreement, with players. The tremendous growth after 1993 of unshared local revenues—from luxury boxes, club seats, seat licenses, naming rights, sponsorships, and local advertising—created a pool of funds outside the labor agreement. Much of it went into huge signing bonuses that circumvented the salary cap, creating an advantage for wealthier clubs and widening the gap between stars and ordinary players. It also threatened to undermine the "capitalistic socialism" on which the NFL had thrived since the first national television contract in 1962.

Television made every NFL owner rich in the 1990s beyond Pete Rozelle's wildest dreams. Davis and Jones made it possible for the shrewdest, luckiest, or most ruthless to become even richer. The free agency that Davis won for owners—the right to move their franchises and thus to extort sweetheart stadium deals from cities eager for "major league" status—had momentous financial consequences for the league unforeseen in 1982. Jones ("Davis Lite" to sports columnist Mike Lupica)[26] then showed his fellow owners the enormous profits to be made from their own stadiums. A stadium deal with an eager or desperate community, on top of the television contract, guaranteed riches for even "football impaired" owners.[27]

Cowboy Capitalism

When Jones acquired the Dallas Cowboys along with Texas Stadium in February 1989 for a reported $140 million, the Cowboys had just completed a season with the worst record in the NFL, and home attendance had been falling for five years. He had an immediate impact on the Cowboys: within a year, coach Tom Landry, general manager Tex Schramm, and player director Gil Brandt, the architects of "America's Team" since its inception in 1960, were all gone.[28] Jones had the Cowboys back in the Super Bowl by 1993, and twice more in 1994 and 1996, but his financial impact on the rest of the league had greater consequences. As a former oil wildcatter who leveraged his energy company to buy the Cowboys, Jones would not settle for just his share of the common revenue to honor a gentlemen's agreement.

The football-only (instead of multipurpose) stadiums built by the Cowboys and Kansas City Chiefs in the early 1970s had been the jewels of the league and, with their luxury suites, the envy of other owners.[d] The Houston Astrodome had introduced luxury boxes to the world of sport back in 1962, but few clubs had them for many years, and no one understood their financial potential until Jones showed the way. Jones promptly turned Texas Stadium into a playground for wealthy Texans, doubling the price of tickets, replacing 2,500 ordinary seats with 100 more luxury suites (on top of the present 289), and instituting seat licenses of up to $15,000, some of them for season tickets held by former Cowboy players and employees (profiteers cannot be sentimental). Jones's revenue from Texas Stadium went from $700,000 in 1992 to $30 million in 1993, when the Cowboys' gross revenue of $92.9 million exceeded the nearest NFL rival's by more than $18 million. Suddenly, every owner wanted a new stadium with all the trimmings.[29]

To enhance his revenue further, Jones went after NFL Properties. When NFLP was formed in 1963 (out of the original partnership with Roy Rogers Enterprises) to handle the licensing of team-logo merchandise, there was not much of a market. By 1970 the Dallas Cowboys were already on the way to becoming America's Team and accounted for nearly half of NFLP's revenue,

---

d. I recall running onto the field in Arrowhead Stadium for the opening game in 1972, feeling something like a gladiator's resentment as I looked up at the rich people watching us, I imagined, between sips of their daiquiris from behind the glass panels of their suites.

but the sums were too small for Schramm to mind sharing profits equally. (Schramm was a League Thinker all the way, in any case.) As noted in Chapter 3, an arrangement with NFL Charities in 1972 gave NFL Properties a public relations, not commercial, purpose. With the boom in sales of team-logo merchandise in the late 1980s, however, revenues could no longer be taken lightly. Teams' success naturally stimulated sales of their merchandise, as first the 49ers then the Bears ruled the 1980s, but an equal share in both good times and bad guaranteed a predictable return for all teams. With the Cowboys' return to glory in the 1990s, as Jones saw his team accounting for as much as a third of now very large sales, he was unwilling to settle for his 3 or 4 percent of $90 million in annual profit.[30]

Jones rocked the NFL boat for six years before unleashing his perfect storm. Only when he signed a ten-year, $25 million or $40 million agreement with Pepsi in 1995 (conflicting figures were reported), in defiance of the NFL's exclusive contract with Coca-Cola, did the financial structure on which the league had long thrived seem threatened. Miami as well as Oakland had opted out of the trust agreement with NFL Properties, and Jones was not the only owner to strike his own endorsement deals. (As *Sports Illustrated* reported, New England Patriot owner Robert Kraft signed a deal with Pepsi ten days after Jones did, "and no one seemed upset.") But Jones had shown contempt for Cowboy and NFL traditions from the day he bought the team. Now he was not just making his own marketing arrangements; with each one, he thumbed his nose at his fellow owners. After signing his next deal, with Nike, Jones punctuated the agreement by conspicuously walking the sidelines with Phil Knight during a *Monday Night Football* game; and the Cowboys' owner promised more deals to come. The NFL sued (for $300 million) to stop him; Jones countersued (for $750 million). A year later, the two sides dropped their suits, with Jones the clear winner.[31]

Technically, Jones's separate agreements with Pepsi, Nike, American Express, and other companies did not violate the arrangement with NFL Properties because they were with Texas Stadium, not the Dallas Cowboys. But Jones forced NFL Properties to change the way it did business. In negotiating new sponsorships in 1998, NFLP signed national agreements for less money than before, while reserving the right of individual clubs to negotiate their own as well. Coke, for example, remained the official soft drink of the NFL, but Pepsi (or Coke for that matter) could be the official soft drink of the Dallas Cowboys or the Tampa Bay Buccaneers or the New England Patriots. The league's new agreement with Coke reportedly dropped from $14 million a year to $4 million or so, but Jones told reporters that, with individual clubs negotiating their separate deals for $1.5 million or $2 million each, soft-drink sponsorships alone could bring between $60 and $70 million into the NFL. The best deals, of course, would go to those who aggressively pursued them. This compromise between club rights and leaguewide sponsorships was incorporated into the new "master agreement" when the 40-year-old NFL Trust expired in early 2004, but with Dallas, Miami, and Washington voting against the agreement, and Oakland, Philadelphia, and Tampa Bay abstaining, the fight over marketing and revenue sharing had clearly not ended.[32] (Jones also initially refused, in 2005, to abide by the league's ban on Regional Sports Networks, which would compete with its own NFL Network. After he relented, SportsBusiness Journal suggested that Jones might have grown "mellower" and become an NFL "insider."[33] Stay tuned.)

Let's Make a Deal

Though not quite as dramatic as 1982, 1993 was a pivotal year in the NFL's transformation in the 1990s. The collective bargaining agreement in the spring ended a quarter-century of labor strife and guaranteed several years of stable player costs. In the fall, the league announced expansion franchises for Charlotte and Jacksonville at a cost of $140 million each—up slightly from the $16 million paid by Seattle and Tampa in 1976. The inflated franchise price reflected the successively richer TV contracts, the latest of which, in 1990, bumped average annual revenues from $17 million to $32 million per club. It also reflected a new economic reality in the NFL, the enormous profits possible from new stadiums, now that owners had the leverage to exploit them. Existing franchises that sold for well under $100 million in the 1980s were now worth twice as much or more, attracting what Forbes magazine called the "new breed of debt-laden, swashbuckling owner" in the mold of Jerry Jones.[34] In 1994 the Patriots, Eagles, and Dolphins sold for prices ranging from $160 million to $173 million.[35] The NFL's most structurally tumultuous year followed in 1995. After the Tampa Bay franchise was sold in January, St. Louis lured the Los Angeles Rams with a package of stunning financial inducements, the Raiders returned to Oakland after 13 frustrating years in Los Angeles, Jones went to war with NFL Properties, Art Modell (a pillar of the NFL establishment) announced he was uprooting the Browns from Cleveland, and Bud Adams declared that the Houston Oilers would relocate to Nashville.[36] Modell just followed the trend, but his abandonment of Cleveland made him the most vilified sports owner since Walter O'Malley took the Dodgers from Brooklyn to Los Angeles in 1958.[37]

The professional sports league famous for its stability, and for its coopera-tive sportsmen-owners, was suddenly in chaos, and chaos had never been so profitable. Several of the league's worst-managed franchises instantly solved their financial problems by moving to new cities for better stadium deals. Los Angeles, the nation's number-two television market, went in one year from having two NFL teams to having none. With outrage in Cleveland so great, Tagliabue promptly promised the city an expansion franchise, which it awarded to Al Lerner in 1998 for $530 million. This created a 31-team league in need of a thirty-second team, with Los Angeles and Houston now lacking franchises. After trying long but unsuccessfully to find a suitable arrange-ment in Los Angeles, the NFL in 1999 awarded a franchise for the Houston Texans to Robert McNair for $700 million. The New England Patriots for several months in 1998–99 were destined for Hartford, Connecticut (the nation's twenty-seventh-largest TV market), before Massachusetts officials (with the intervention of Tagliabue) saved the team for greater Boston (the sixth-largest market). Owners in Cincinnati, Tampa Bay, Arizona, and Seattle all threatened to move but stayed put after extracting an agreement on a new stadium.[38]

Stadiums were the heart of the new NFL. Television remained the single most important source of revenue, but even as rights fees soared over the 1990s—from an average of $900 million per year from 1990 through 1993, to $1.1 billion from 1994 through 1997, to $2.2 billion from 1998 through 2005—nontelevision revenue increased even more. In 2003, when the televi-sion contracts provided $2.6 billion out of gross revenues of $5.3 billion, TV slipped under 50 percent for the first time since 1977. (The most recent television contracts, beginning in 2006, tipped the balance back to TV reve-nue.) Television continued to be the largest single pot of money, and it was guaranteed over the life of the contracts, but stadiums became the new eco-nomic engine driving the NFL into the financial stratosphere.[39]

Relocation enabled the worst-managed franchises (the Baltimore Colts, St. Louis Cardinals, and Los Angeles Rams) to become highly profitable. Threat of relocation, credible because the NFL was nearly powerless to prevent it, en-abled prosperous franchises to become tremendously more profitable. Be-tween 1992 and 2006, 18 teams moved into new stadiums (with three more, for the Indianapolis Colts, Dallas Cowboys, and New York's Jets and Giants in a joint venture, scheduled to open by 2010). Moving into a new stadium meant immediate increases in revenue ranging from 24 percent (for the Oakland Raiders) to 68 percent (for the Baltimore Ravens), with most clubs seeing gains between 30 and 40 percent (see Table 1, from which I derived my

Table 1. Franchise Values and Revenues, 1991–2006 (in Millions of Dollars)

Team/Owner and Date of Purchase	1991 Value	1991 Revenue	1992 Value	1992 Revenue	1993 Value	1993 Revenue	1994 Value	1994 Reven
Washington/Snyder '99	125	45.5	117	52.2	123	55.7	158	60.9
New England/Kraft '94	100	39.9	103	45.6	102	47.5	142	59.2
Dallas/Jones '89	180	52.5	146	55.8	165	55.1	190	92.9
Houston/McNair '99								
Philadelphia/Lurie '94	141	50.4	146	57.4	149	64.6	172	68.9
Denver/Bowlen '84	113	45.3	114	49.6	119	53.9	147	59.6
Cleveland/Lerner '98								
Tampa Bay/Glazer '95	114	43.9	113	46.7	118	51.2	142	60.1
Baltimore/Bisciotti '00	145	51.8	125	59.8	133	51.8	165	65.1
Chicago/McCaskey '20	126	50.4	139	56.6	136	55.8	160	65.4
Carolina/Richardson '93								
Miami/Huizenga '94	205	62.5	150	66	145	53	161	74.4
Green Bay/community	200	42.2	115	45.9	116	51.5	141	60.1
Kansas City/Hunt '60	122	43.7	123	50.6	130	54.9	153	64.8
NY Giants/Mara '25 Tisch '91	150	50.5	150	56.7	146	54.5	176	65.3
Seattle/Allen '97	130	46.4	130	52.6	137	52.9	148	58.9
Tennessee/Adams '59	119	45.9	128	56.8	132	55.4	157	62
Pittsburgh/Rooney '33	112	43.2	121	50.2	120	50.7	143	57.8
NY Jets/Johnson '00	125	44.3	117	49	119	50.1	142	59.2
St. Louis/Frontiere '72 Kroenke '95	135	49.4	126	51.6	128	53.1	148	59.4
Detroit/Ford '64	116	44.5	110	48.3	118	50.3	138	55.9
Indianapolis/Irsay '72	116	44.6	121	48.2	122	48.1	141	54.6
Cincinnati/Brown '66	125	44	115	53.9	128	49.4	142	54.4
Arizona/Bidwell '32	120	46.1	120	49.8	125	48.6	146	58
Buffalo/Wilson '59	126	48.3	125	61	138	56.4	164	64.9
Jacksonville/Weaver '93								
New Orleans/Benson '85	124	47.7	123	50.5	130	57.7	154	62.5
Oakland/Davis '66	135	46.2	128	51.9	124	51.3	146	58.8
San Francisco/DeBartolo '77	150	51.7	134	55.5	139	59.4	167	70.4
San Diego/Spanos '84	113	43.6	115	48.3	119	51.1	142	58.7
Atlanta/Blank '02	113	43.4	120	48.9	125	55.4[b]	148	59.8
Minnesota/McCombs '98 Wilf '05	119	45.8	120	60.5	123	51.8	147	60.9
TOTALS		1313.7		1479.9		1435.8		1752.9

Sources: *Financial World* from 1991 through 1997; *Forbes* from 1998.

Teams appear in the order of their 2006 franchise value. Franchises are listed by their current location: Baltimore (which was the Cleveland Browns through 1995), Tennessee (which was the Houston Oilers through 1996), St. Louis (which played in Los Angeles through 1994), and Oakland (which played in Los Angeles through 1994). Edward DeBartolo Jr. owned the 49ers from 1977 until 1998, when he was

1995 Value	1995 Revenue	1996 Value	1996 Revenue	1997 Value	1997 Revenue	1998 Value	1998 Revenue	1999 Value	1999 Revenue
151	58.1	184	64.7	200	70.7	403	115.1[b]	607	151.8
151	60.6	165	71.1	197	79.1	252	84	460	170.6
238	98.2	272	111.2	320	121.3	413	118	663	161.7
182	68.7	192	75.2	209	80.3	249	83	318	102.5
150	59.9	164	69.2	182	73.4	320	76.3	427	99.3
151	56.2	164	65.4	187	72.1	346	76.8	502	128.7[b]
163	64	201[a]	71.4	235	75.8	329	73.2	408	120[b]
161	65.1	184	73.5	204	79.5	237	79	313	100.8
		133	42.9	240	75.1[b]	365	83	488	128.5
186	72.3	214	82.2	242	95.4	340	103.1	466	127.5
154	59	166	65.8	186	74.9	244	78.8	320	103.2
172	64.4	188	72	204	82	257	85.6	353	110.4
168	66.5	183	71.5	211	80.6	288	82.3	376	107.5
152	56.9	154	62.4	171	71.2	324	77.1	399	99.9
158	58.1	159	63	193	65.7	322[a]	71.5	369	90
144	57.2	154	62.8	173	72.5	300	75.1	397	96.8
149	56.2	153	61.1	186	75.4	259	76.2	363	103.6
153[a]	57.4	193	76	243	85.8	322	91.9	390	111.3
141	56.1	150	61.3	181	69.4	312	74.2	293	97.6
134	52	145	60.3	170	69.7	227	70.9	305	98.3
137	54	171	62.1	188	72.1	311	69.2	394	91.7
155	59.7	166	66.9	184	71.1	231	76.9	301	100.4
172	63.3	188	73.1	200	77.7	252	78.7	326	101.9
		145	50	239	67.3	294	66.8	419	116.4
171	62.6	184	71.8	199	79	243	80.9	315	101.6
145[a]	57.3	162	70.8	210	79.3	235	78.3	299	100.4
186	69.6	196	77.7	218	85.9	254	84.7	371	109.3
153	60.3	169	68.3	191	75.6	248	82.5	323	104.2
156	57.6	167	68.2	191	79.2	233	77.6	306	98.7
154	58.3	167	66.7	186	74.2	233	77.7	309	99.7
	1729.6		2058.6		2256.2		2333.3		3085.6

pended for a year. After a legal battle, in 2000 he surrendered ownership to his sister, Denise Bartolo York, and her husband John York.

"Value" is estimated franchise value at the beginning of the season; "Revenue" is calculated from the vious season. "Growth" is franchise value in 2006 divided by franchise value in 1992 (some

Table 1. *(continued)*

Team/Owner and Date of Purchase	2000 Value	2000 Revenue	2001 Value	2001 Revenue	2002 Value	2002 Revenue	2003 Value	2003 Rever
Washington/Snyder '99	714	176.4	796	194	845	204	952	227
New England/Kraft '94	464	113.1	524	128	571	136	756	189[b]
Dallas/Jones '89	713	173.9	743	181	784	189	851	198
Houston/McNair '99							791	193
Philadelphia/Lurie '94	329	106.1	405	116	518	120	617	134
Denver/Bowlen '84	471	107.1	540	115	604	159[b]	683	171
Cleveland/Lerner '98	557	146.5	598	153	618	158	695	174
Tampa Bay/Glazer '95	532	132.9	582	146	606	151	671	168
Baltimore/Bisciotti '00	479	122.9	544	139	607	148	649	155
Chicago/McCaskey '20	319	102.8	362	113	540	124	621	132
Carolina/Richardson '93	513	128.1	574	144	609	152	642	161
Miami/Huizenga '94	472	131.2	508	141	553	145	638	159
Green Bay/community	337	108.7	392	119	474	132	609	152
Kansas City/Hunt '60	367	114.8	412	125	462	138	601	150
NY Giants/Mara '25 Tisch '91	387	110.6	419	120	514	134	573	143
Seattle/Allen '97	407	101.7	440	110	534	119	610	153[b]
Tennessee/Adams '59	506	126.4[b]	536	134	551	141	620	155
Pittsburgh/Rooney '33	414	96.4	468	109	555	142[b]	608	152
NY Jets/Johnson '00	384	109.8	423	121	512	131	567	142
St. Louis/Frontiere '72 Kroenke '95	418	116	448	124	544	136	602	150
Detroit/Ford '64	378	99.5	423	109	509	116	635	159[b]
Indianapolis/Irsay '72	332	107.3	367	118	419	127	547	137
Cincinnati/Brown '66	423	91.9	479	120[b]	507	130	562	141
Arizona/Bidwell '32	305	101.7	342	107	374	110	505	126
Buffalo/Wilson '59	365	114	393	123	458	131	564	141
Jacksonville/Weaver '93	460	121	500	132	522	137	569	142
New Orleans/Benson '85	324	104.6	371	116	481	139	585	146
Oakland/Davis '66	315	104.9	351	117	421	132	576	144
San Francisco/DeBartolo '77	379	111.6	419	120	463	129	568	142
San Diego/Spanos '84	393	109.2	416	119	447	131	561	140
Atlanta/Blank '02	321	107.2	338	113	407	120	534	133
Minnesota/McCombs '98 Wilf '05	322	103.9	346	112	437	123	542	135
		3475.8		3818		3983		4443

calculations for 1991 appear skewed—the high values for Dallas, Miami, and Green Bay, for example, that plummet the following year).

a. Year of a franchise relocation (the following year is the first with revenue from the new stadium).

b. First year of revenue from a new stadium (which opened the previous year) without relocation.

Table 1. *(continued)*

2004 Value	2004 Revenue	2005 Value	2005 Revenue	2006 Value	2006 Revenue	Growth
1,104	245	1,264	287	1,423	303	12.16
861	191	1,040	236	1,176	250	11.42
923	205	1,063	231	1,173	235	8.03
905	201	946	215	1,043	222	
833	198[b]	952	216	1,024	218	7.01
815	183	907	202	975	207	8.55
798	183	892	203	970	206	
779	175	877	195	955	203	8.45
776	172	864	192	946	201	7.57
785	175[b]	871	193	945	201	6.8
760	169	878	195	936	199	
765	170	856	190	912	194	6.08
756	168	849	189	911	194	7.92
709	159	762	181	894	186	7.27
692	154	806	175	890	182	5.93
712	158	823	183	888	189	6.83
736	164	839	196	886	189	6.92
717	159	820	182	880	187	7.27
685	152	739	172	867	179	7.49
708	157	757	176	841	179	7.67
747	168	780	186	839	178	7.63
609	145	715	166	837	167	6.92
675	150	716	171	825	175	1.17
552	131	673	153	789	158	6.57
637	152	708	173	756	176	6.09
688	153	691	169	744	173	
627	157	718	175	738	160	6
624	149	676	169	736	171	5.75
636	151	699	171	734	171	5.48
622	148	678	165	731	170	6.36
603	144	690	168	730	170	6.08
604	144	658	164	720	167	6
	4957		6039		6160	

To calculate the impact of a new stadium, take for example Washington's increase in revenue between 1997 (70.7 million) and 1998 (115.1 million) and divide the result (44.4 million) by the earlier figure (70.7 million). The increase is 63 percent.

calculations).[e] An additional eight stadiums underwent major renovations, some with comparable impact. (Green Bay's remodeled stadium meant a 36 percent increase in revenue within two years.) In 2006, when the Arizona Cardinals moved into their $455.7 million air-conditioned stadium ($310 million paid by the community and state)—with 88 suites going for $75,000 to $125,000 (over 90 percent sold), 7,501 club seats at $100–$325 each (100 percent sold), and naming rights purchased by an online university (!) for $154.5 million over 20 years[f]—they immediately began looking on paper like one of the NFL's well-run clubs. At this writing, four of the six franchises with the lowest values (and some of the oldest stadiums) are seeking to better their position. The Minnesota Vikings are working on legislative and voter approval for a new $675 million stadium, the 49ers are seeking approval for a controversial stadium/mall project, and the Chargers and Saints are exploring their possibilities.[40]

For what the financial press would term a "good deal," the club took the profits while the community paid the bills, as was the case for the Arizona Cardinals. Invesco Field cost Denver owner Pat Bowlen $100 million and taxpayers $301 million. The Cincinnati Bengals made out even better: the entire $452 million price tag for Paul Brown Stadium was paid for through an increased sales tax. A watchdog group called the League of Fans, founded by Ralph Nader, found that $4.6 billion of the $6.6 billion spent to build or renovate sports stadiums (not just for football) from 1990 to September 2003 came from public coffers. (The group's figure did not include the federal subsidies that came in three distinct forms: tax-free bonds for constructing them, tax breaks for financing them, and tax write-offs for renting their luxury suites.) *SportsBusiness Journal*, certainly no anticorporate publication, reported that for nine new NFL stadiums built between 2000 and 2006, the

e. The franchise values and revenues from *Financial World* and *Forbes* in the table tell some interesting stories in themselves: how Al Davis scarcely bettered himself by moving to Oakland, how well the Browns were doing in Cleveland (the ninth-most-valuable franchise in 1995, with the eleventh-highest revenue) before Art Modell uprooted them to Baltimore in 1996, how precipitously San Francisco declined from one of the NFL's most valuable franchises (ranked between second and seventh in value through 1997, under Eddie DeBartolo Jr.) to one of its least (plummeting to eighteenth in 1998, when Eddie was suspended by the league, then sliding downward to twenty-ninth by 2006, under Eddie's sister Denise and her husband John York). Not just stadium woes but also the change in ownership and accompanying deterioration on the field obviously contributed.

f. The purchase of naming rights for an NFL stadium by the for-profit University of Phoenix may be business as usual in the National Football League but is a stunning event in the history of American higher education.

public contributed $2.27 billion out of $4.24 billion (including at least two-thirds of the cost for six of the projects).[41]

Cities cut such deals with NFL owners despite evidence from economists, sometimes openly cited in the press, that sports stadiums were poor economic investments.[42] Communities courted or clung to NFL franchises through lavish public giveaways for the sake of "intangibles," the pride, recognition, and "big league feel" that come from having a team, or for what sociologists Kevin Delaney and Rick Eckstein have called "community self-esteem" and "community collective conscience" (shared values, beliefs, and experiences). Reporters and key figures involved in negotiations have sometimes spoken openly of these motives beyond, or despite, economic considerations. Voters in Tennessee approved a bond measure to lure the Houston Oilers as "a symbol of progress" for Nashville, despite projections of a "negligible direct impact on the city's economy" and concern about too-rapid growth. Hartford was prepared to build a $350 million stadium for the Patriots as a cornerstone for urban renewal but more importantly, as a state senator put it, to "turn around the image of Harford as a city in decline." A civic booster in St. Louis was blunter about the tradeoff: "Economically, you're better off with a bank or a factory. The impact of a team is minimal, but it buys a lot of emotional impact." In their study of stadium projects in nine cities, Delaney and Eckstein note a shift from economic arguments in the early 1990s to social-psychological arguments in the late 1990s and early 2000s.[43]

The most extravagant giveaways came not from the major metropolises but from cities such as Nashville and Hartford, second-class cities with first-class aspirations. By a strange calculus, American cities supposedly achieve status according to their number of big-league sports franchises. Portland, Oregon, with just one franchise (the NBA's Trailblazers) is somehow a lesser city than Indianapolis with two (the Colts and the NBA's Pacers). In Cincinnati, where the prostadium slogan in the campaign for public financing was "Keep Cincinnati a Major League City," the locals feared becoming another Louisville or Dayton. In Cleveland, the specter was Akron. The proposed sales tax in Cincinnati was headed toward defeat until opposition suddenly shrank when the Browns abandoned Cleveland and a similar fate for Cincinnati seemed possible. (Mike Brown—Paul's son, president of the Bengals, and a dug-in foe of Al Davis and Jerry Jones in NFL disputes in recent years— has Davis and Jones to thank for Hamilton County's reluctant generosity.)[44]

This calculus has not worked for the NFL in New York and Los Angeles, where civic pride does not depend on a football team, local politicians have more pressing priorities for public investment, and citizens have alternatives for spending their leisure time and money.[g] In 1999 the NFL would have much preferred Los Angeles to Houston, but Robert McNair's $700 million bid for a Houston franchise included $195 million in public money. Having to arrange his own financing for a franchise in Los Angeles, Hollywood superagent Michael Ovitz could come up with only $550 million. Los Angeles simply did not need the NFL as much as the NFL needed Los Angeles, the second-largest TV market.[45] On the other hand, the continuing absence of a franchise in Los Angeles has provided leverage for clubs in other cities—what *SportsBusiness Journal* calls "the Los Angeles card" that franchises in, say, Indianapolis or Phoenix can play to extort public financing "without needing to utter a threat."[46]

In 2005 New York State refused to put up $300 million for a nearly $2 billion stadium for the Jets (with New York City asked to kick in another $300 million). Potentially the most valuable franchise in all of sports but with a terrible stadium lease, the Jets had revenue of $172 million in 2004, $16 million below the league average and $115 million less than the Washington Redskins. A new stadium on the West Side would have made such a difference that the Jets were prepared to borrow more than $1 billion to build it. After the city rejected their bid, too, the Jets had to settle for sharing a new $900 million stadium (or $1 billion, or $1.2 billion, or $1.3 billion as estimates began climbing) in the Meadowlands with the Giants.[47]

The threat of losing big-city teams and their television markets (like Boston's) to the lure of stadium wealth in smaller markets (like Hartford) led to the NFL's G-3 program in 1999, under which clubs annually contributed $1 million each to a common fund for loans to build or renovate stadiums. Clubs that borrowed the money repaid it out of revenues they would normally have to contribute to the visitors' share of gate receipts, making the "loans," in effect, grants from the league. And the larger the market, the greater the possible loan. A $150 million subsidy through the G-3 program saved the Patriots for Boston, and Boston for the NFL. Small-market Green Bay qualified for only $13 million. Between 1999 and 2001, the league loaned $663 million for eight stadium projects, then put the program on hold until 2005, when it awarded another $76.5 million to Dallas and $34 million to Indianapolis. By this time, small-market teams complained that they were sub-

g. According to a survey published in *SportsBusiness Journal* in 2006, New York ranked last among NFL cities in "fan avidity level," with Los Angeles (as a prospective NFL city) ranked just above New York. In a separate poll, 37.31 percent of Angelenos supported using public dollars to renovate a stadium to secure an NFL franchise for Los Angeles, while 38.08 percent were opposed (and 24.62 percent were not sure).

sidizing the large-market franchises with vastly greater potential revenues that they would not have to share in return.[48]

The G-3 program notwithstanding, communities bore the greater financial burden, and as the state surpluses of the 1990s gave way to tight budgets and reduced spending on education, social services, and other public needs, battles over subsidies of sports franchises intensified. Even proposals to put the burden on visitors rather than residents, through new taxes on hotel rooms, rental cars, and restaurants, began receiving fierce opposition in many communities. Yet the residents of Arlington, Texas, after defeating referendums for public transit and an urban development project, voted in 2004 to pay half the cost of a new $650 million home for the Dallas Cowboys. After a $76.5 million "loan" through the G-3 program and a naming-rights agreement, the fans, not Jerry Jones, would pay the rest through a ticket surcharge and personal seat licenses assessed to season ticket holders. Jones could look forward to all of the future profits without paying any of the initial costs. By the time a final design was announced, the price tag for the 80,000-seat stadium was $1 billion and included 200 field-level and upper-level suites, each of them leasing for more than $350,000 annually—the most expensive in the NFL. That amounts to more than $70 million a year from suites alone.[49]

Games in publicly financed stadiums, of course, are unaffordable for much of the public. According to the annual "Fan Cost Index" calculated by *Team Marketing Report*, a family of four in 2005 had to spend from $229.49 (in Buffalo) to $477.47 (in Foxboro) to attend a game.[h] That's for general and club-level seats. Tickets alone for premium seats averaged $176.26 apiece and ran as high as $566.67 (again for the Patriots). The survey did not include luxury suites that cater to the business elites. In the words of a reporter for the *Washington Post* in 2006, "Today's NFL is built on corporate entertainment to the point that crowd size almost is secondary to suite sales and advertising signs."[50] The NFL still needs ordinary fans from all economic classes to maintain network TV ratings, subscribe to "Sunday Ticket" on DirecTV, and buy sponsors' NFL-themed merchandise, but new stadiums increasingly resemble all-inclusive resorts where the rich and well connected can party by themselves.

There is considerable irony in the fact that Davis, the man who made all of this possible, did not himself fully cash in on the opportunities he created for his fellow owners who fought him. Fundamentally old guard, Davis believed

h. The Fan Cost Index includes tickets, parking, drinks (two beers, four soft drinks), hot dogs, game programs (two), and two adult-size caps.

in the Raiders, not in the need for marketing them after he moved the club to Los Angeles, where they failed to arouse Oakland-like passions. After returning to Oakland, Davis either had alienated the community beyond repair, or he failed to rekindle those passions, or he priced the passionate ones out of the stadium, as 58 of 88 home games (through 2005) did not sell out. (From 2003 through 2005, just 68 of 756 NFL games were not sell-outs, and the Raiders and Arizona Cardinals accounted for 60 percent of them.)

A notoriously meddling owner, Davis also hurt his team on the field. As the Raiders settled into the NFL's bottom third in franchise values in the late 1990s, with "one of the worst stadium deals in the NFL,"[51] they also dropped from the top of their division. After winning three Super Bowls by 1984, the Raiders did not make another appearance until 2003 (losing to a Tampa Bay team coached by Jon Gruden, one of the many coaches Davis had driven away). Davis's intrusiveness in the football operation undermined his coaches. His litigiousness undoubtedly made current and prospective community partners wary. At NFL meetings, Davis usually abstained from voting, then sued the league for everything from "failing to promote the Raider brand" to allowing expansion teams to use the color black in their uniforms. He even filed a suit against the NFL to claim franchise rights in Los Angeles, several years after he abandoned the city. (At this writing, having lost the case and his appeal, Davis has taken it to the California Supreme Court.) The once feared Davis became a sad joke, his "maverick style and combative fearlessness" having "withered into a crotchety contrariness."[52] If the NFL has its own afterlife, Davis's nemesis Pete Rozelle is having the last laugh after all.

An NFL for Billionaires

In 2003 the Washington Redskins became the NFL's first billion-dollar franchise. The average franchise was worth $733 million, more than three-and-a-half times the $205 million average in 1996 and almost six times the $125 million average in 1991 (in constant dollars, three times and four times greater).[53] Television made every franchise hugely profitable. Even the Arizona Cardinals made a profit in 2003, despite averaging barely 36,000 fans at home (20,000 below the league average and 17,500 below the next-lowest team).[54] But local revenues created the widening disparity from top to bottom. Leaguewide stadium revenue increased from less than $50 million in 1986 to $576 million by 2002, but it was distributed very unevenly.[55] Through the mid-1990s all but a handful of teams made close to the league's average revenue. Beginning in 1998, ten teams or more made at least 10 percent more or 10 percent less than the average.[i] The number of luxury suites in NFL stadiums in 2003 averaged 143 but ranged from 68 (Arizona) to 381 (Dallas). The number of club seats averaged a little over 7,000 but ranged from 0 (Dallas, Minnesota, and San Francisco) to 15,584 (New Orleans), generating revenue of up to $33 million (Washington).[56] Seventeen teams received annual fees for stadium naming rights ranging from $620,000 (Jacksonville) to $10 million (Houston).[57] The lack of club seats did not prevent Dallas from holding its position as the NFL's second-richest franchise (slipping to third, behind New England, in 2006), but it undoubtedly contributed to Jerry Jones's belief that he needed a new stadium to keep up with the potentially richer Joneses.

The billion-dollar Redskins provided the model for making money in the new NFL. When Daniel Snyder purchased the team for $800 million in 1999, he also acquired a stadium (and its debt). The Redskins were already the NFL's second most valuable franchise (behind Dallas) when Snyder bought it, with revenue in 1998 of $141.1 million, $39 million of that derived from his stadium (compared to the $93.5 million from TV rights, NFL Properties, and the shared portion of gate receipts that every team received).[58] Snyder increased his revenue to $176 million in his first season by selling stadium naming rights to Federal Express for $207 million over 27 years; quintupling his marketing revenue through sponsorships with US Airways, Bell Atlantic, Amtrak, and Mobil; selling 3,000 additional club seats, leasing another dozen luxury suites, and adding 4,000 seats (including 1,000 front-row seats that brought in more than $3,000 each). By 2004 Snyder had raised his revenue to $287 million, $100 million or more above 19 teams. But can there ever be enough? In early 2005 the Redskins attempted to require fans to buy season tickets exclusively with the Redskins Extra Points MasterCard, with points redeemable for Redskins gear. It was a win-win proposition, with both wins going to the franchise. The policy lasted just one week, before officials at MasterCard objected, but in that week the new economic order in the NFL had been exposed with startling clarity. Shrewd business perhaps, as *Washington Post* columnist Tony Kornheiser noted, but "small and petty," too.[59]

Despite having to back down on its credit card plan, the Redskins managed to take in revenues of $303 million in 2005, at least $100 million above 25 teams. As the 2006 season opened, *Forbes* pegged the Redskins' value at

i. The 2005 season perhaps marked a reverse in this trend. If Washington with its $303 million is excluded, the remaining 31 clubs averaged $189 million in revenues; and with a range from $167 million to $250 million, four clubs bettered the average by more than 10 percent and just one club fell more than 10 percent below it.

more than $1.4 billion. *Forbes* attributed just 39 percent of that value to the revenues shared among all NFL clubs, with the Redskins' market, stadium, and brand management accounting for the other 61 percent. The average for the league was almost exactly the reverse: 60 percent from shared revenue and 40 percent from market and marketing. At the very bottom of the NFL, the Arizona Cardinals derived a full 80 percent of their franchise value from shared revenues. Yet a franchise that on performance deserved to be filing for bankruptcy was worth almost $800 million in the new NFL.[60]

To compete in the new NFL, a sweet stadium deal was essential for two reasons beyond simple profiteering: to pay down debt and to sign free agents. The 16 new owners who joined the NFL since 1993 borrowed varyingly large sums of money to purchase their franchises, some of them to build new stadiums as well. Snyder borrowed nearly $500 million to purchase the Redskins. As *Forbes* reported, Snyder's $49 million in operating income for 1999 would not even cover the $55 million in debt service.[61] In the 1970s and 1980s, league rules had placed strict limits on the amount of debt a team could carry (to prevent lending institutions from having power over decision making), but such limits would not work in the new NFL. The NFL's founding fathers had started franchises by scraping together a few thousand dollars and kept them solvent by pinching every penny. The new breed of owners entered the NFL already rich and ready to take on huge debts for the chance to become greatly richer. (According to *Forbes* in 2006, the NFL had 11 billionaire owners, ten of them with net worth between $1 billion and $2 billion, and Seattle's Paul Allen off in his own universe with his $22.5 billion.)[62]

The league raised the debt ceiling to $125 million but allowed owners to exceed that amount when assets other than the team, such as personal wealth or stadiums, secured it. Snyder, for example, in 2002 was allowed to consolidate all of his debt associated with the team, a whopping $700 million. *SportsBusiness Journal* reported on the same occasion that Robert Kraft owed $312 million on the Patriots' new stadium, and that Robert McNair owed somewhere between $300 million and $500 million on his purchase of the Houston Texans. When the New York Jets announced that they would borrow more than $1 billion to win the bidding on the site for a stadium on Manhattan's West Side, the idea that the NFL placed any ceiling at all on team's debt seemed ludicrous. Successive television contracts were chiefly responsible for the hugely appreciated values of NFL franchises, but finding additional sources of revenue from sponsorships, premium seating, stadium advertising, and naming rights had become not an option but a necessity. The money machine was also a monster with a voracious appetite.[63]

After debt service, what remained could be spent in the free-agent market. Because the rules of the salary cap allowed signing bonuses to be paid up front but amortized over the life of the contract for cap purposes, levels of cash flow created competitive advantages and disadvantages in the NFL for the first time. The Dallas Cowboys could give Deion Sanders a $13 million signing bonus in 1995, as part of a seven-year, $35 million contract, but count less than $2 million of it against the cap that season, on top of a base salary near the league minimum. Even after complaints from other clubs forced Jones to increase the amount of salary counting against the cap, the bulk of it was still deferred to the final years of the contract. Sportswriters and NFL rivals complained that Jones "bought the Super Bowl" that season by spending $61.9 million in salaries and bonuses when the salary cap was $37.1 million.[64]

Deferred salary eventually counted against the cap, however. A club might buy a Super Bowl but could not keep it year after year, because players like Sanders who received huge bonuses but mostly back-loaded salary had to be dumped before the full weight of their contracts came due. When the Cowboys released Sanders after the 1999 season for cap purposes, Snyder immediately signed him to a seven-year, $55 million contract with the Redskins, only to discover that large cash flows do not guarantee Super Bowls. With a salary cap of $62 million in 2000, Snyder spent $92.4 million in salary and bonuses, then watched as Washington finished third in its division. Snyder's fiasco proved the necessity of having the right coach and players, not just the most expensive ones, to buy a title. But the financial resources to back up shrewd free-agent shopping could provide an edge on the competition.[65]

With owners such as Jones and Snyder leading the way, the staid old NFL, run in the 1960s and 1970s by a paternalistic old guard, became part of the winner-take-all entrepreneurial economy of the 1990s. The leaders of the Players Association in 1974 had complained that the owners with all of their guaranteed television money and shared gate receipts had no incentive to go after the best players in order to win. Now, winning paid dividends in greater marketing potential. Yet, unlike in the larger economy, the winners in the NFL did not in fact take *all*. There was still that shared TV revenue, plus more new stadiums season after season. According to court documents, in 2002 the Cincinnati Bengals, with a 2–14 record but playing in a stadium financed entirely by taxpayers, earned enough profit to distribute $24 million in dividends to shareholders.[j] Red McCombs borrowed $100 million to purchase

j. Having paid for a new stadium to keep the crying-poor Bengals from leaving, Hamilton County commissioners filed an antitrust suit against the club after they

the Vikings for $246 million in 1998, failed to persuade Minnesota voters to build him a new stadium, settled in near the bottom of the league in franchise value because of that failure, then sold the team for $600 million in 2005, a pretty good return on a $146 million investment.[66]

At the close of fiscal year 2005 (covering the 2004 season, that is), the Green Bay Packers (because it is publicly owned, the only NFL club that discloses its financial records) reported TV revenues of $87 million, "other" shared revenue of $15 million, and local revenue of $89 million, resulting in a profit of $25 million. For the 2005 season, although profits dropped to $18 million due to "accounting changes and severance payments" to fired coaches, total revenues climbed from $200 million to $208 million, seventh best in the league according to the *Sports Business Journal*.[k] The profitability of the small-market Packers derived from having a facility funded almost fully by the public, with restaurants and shops that made Lambeau Field "a 365-day-a-year destination." With their twenty-first-century marketing of an old-school football image, the Packers epitomized the new NFL even more than the slicker Redskins and Cowboys did.[67]

The widening gap between high- and low-revenue teams, from roughly $150 million to $287 million in 2004, threatened to destabilize the league and became the key topic at owners' meetings over the winter of 2005–2006. By this time, according to *Sports Business Journal*, league revenues totaled close to $6 billion, 60 percent of which was equally shared national revenue, 20 percent came from gate receipts (34 percent of which was shared), and 20 percent derived from unshared local revenues. Even with rich clubs now collectively contributing $40 million to poor clubs, the poor complained that through the G-3 program they subsidized the wealthy and could not compete for free agents. The wealthy, in turn, complained that they needed high revenues to pay off debt and that more revenue sharing would benefit ineptly run franchises by penalizing those that marketed aggressively. Jones and the Bengals' Brown frequently represented the two sides in the reporting on the dispute, with Jones repeatedly pointing out that Brown had chosen to name his new stadium after his father instead of selling the rights. This seeming

---

learned about the hefty dividends. A judge threw out the suit in early 2006 on a technicality—it was not filed within the four-year statute of limitations—but the county has appealed.

k. *Forbes* estimated the Packers' revenues as $189 million in 2004 and $194 million in 2005 (thirteenth best in the league for both years), another reminder to take published figures as informed approximations.

conflict between greed and family values was complicated by the fact that Brown had essentially blackmailed the citizens of Cincinnati into building him a stadium at no cost to himself, then decided to memorialize his own father. The Bengals played in "Paul Brown Stadium," not "People's Park."[68]

Meanwhile, because local revenues varied so widely but all clubs owed the same minimum percentage to the players, the NFLPA's demand for a share of all revenues in an extension of the collective bargaining agreement threatened to create unequal burdens in player costs. The last-minute settlement in March 2006, under which the 15 wealthiest clubs agreed to shift about $150 million a year to the less profitable ones, temporarily salvaged functional harmony without resolving the tensions that put it in jeopardy. Whether it would last quickly became uncertain. Initially, the fact that the two nay votes came from small-market clubs (Buffalo and Cincinnati) seemed to suggest that the agreement still favored the rich franchises. Jacksonville's owner, with another small-market club, supported the agreement to preserve labor peace but worried that his franchise would not receive enough from other clubs to afford sharing a higher percentage of revenues with the players. *SportsBusiness Journal*, however, claimed that the high-revenue clubs made the largest concessions. It soon became public knowledge that Tagliabue had won the owners' support by inserting an "escape clause" in the agreement, which would allow them to reopen negotiations in three years if they "can't find new and better ways to make money, or if they decide they simply can't stomach paying so much to the players." According to the *Philadelphia Inquirer*, "several insiders expect that to happen." Keeping peace among the owners became one of the primary challenges facing the new commissioner, Roger Goodell.[69]

According to *Forbes*'s latest calculations, the widening revenue gap actually shrank in 2005, and this was before the infusion from the new television contracts to begin in 2006. Whether or not rough economic parity would prove less elusive than skeptics predicted, the bottom line had not changed: there were no economic losers in the new NFL, just degrees of winners.

TV and "Intangibles"

Richer or poorer, all NFL clubs made money because of television. The TV contracts that ran from 1998 through 2005 totaled nearly $18 billion, roughly half of the league's total revenue. The partner in the marriage, however, did not fare so well, as ABC, CBS, and Fox lost as much as $2 billion on NFL football over that period.[70] (Network losses, like NFL profits, were always estimates of closely held secrets.) The state of televised football at the turn of the twenty-first century was epitomized by the average of $550 million per year paid by ABC for *Monday Night Football*. In 1981, when the rights cost $46 million, *Monday Night Football* ranked twelfth among all shows in prime time, with an average rating of 21.8 (that is, 21.8 percent of the nation's TV households tuned in each week). That was its peak. Over the next 16 seasons, as rights fees climbed to $230 million, average ratings dropped to 15.0 (still roughly 21 million viewers), yet *Monday Night Football*'s prime-time rank climbed as high as number 4 among all network programs. Lower ratings meant reluctant advertisers and millions of dollars in losses for ABC. By then agreeing in 1998 to more than double its payments, in order to stave off NBC's attempt to grab the show for $500 million a year, ABC accepted likely greater losses in return for holding onto its prime-time position. Despite constant tinkering with the chemistry in the broadcasting booth, ratings steadily declined to 11.4 in 2001, where they held more or less steady for three years, then dropped to 10.9 in 2004 in the face of strong competition on Monday nights from CBS, then to 10.8 in 2005 for its final season. (The game that concluded 36 years as an American institution, the second-longest-running prime-time program in television history, earned a 9.2 rating.) *Monday Night Football* also slipped slightly from number 4 to number 6 in 2005 yet remained in the top 10 for the sixteenth consecutive year.[71]

That *Monday Night Football* could lose market share after 1981 but rank higher among prime-time programs told the story of network television in the age of satellites and cable. Broadcasting had become "narrow casting," as "mass markets" had become "niche markets" for advertisers. Ratings declined for NFL games on all of the networks. After peaking in 1981 at roughly 17 for the three networks combined (almost 22 for ABC, 17 for CBS, and 14 for NBC), ratings fell all the way to 11.5 by 1997, then continued slipping downward to 10.2 by 2005 (10.8 for ABC, 10.2 for Fox, 9.7 for CBS). Yet sports in general and NFL football in particular still offered the best opportunity for advertisers to reach a general audience (in 2005, all of the top ten network sportscasts were NFL games, and 22 of the top 25). Sunday afternoon NFL games outdrew the networks' prime-time shows, whose ratings fell even more precipitously over the 1990s.[1] Moreover, the NFL's fewer viewers in-

1. In 1993–94, ABC averaged 16.8 for *Monday Night Football* and 12.4 for the rest of its prime-time lineup; CBS averaged 12.9 for NFL games and 14.0 for its prime-time shows; NBC averaged 11.3 for football, 11.0 in prime time; and Fox averaged 7.2 in prime time but had no NFL. In 2005–6, *Monday Night Football* averaged 10.8, compared to 6.8 for ABC prime time overall; CBS averaged 9.7 for football, 8.1 in prime time; Fox averaged 10.2 for the NFL, 6.2 in prime time; and NBC averaged 6.3 in prime time and had no NFL football.

Table 2. Television Contracts, 1987–2006 (in Dollars)

Years	Average Annual Payment*	ABC	CBS	NBC	Fox	ESPN	TNT
1987–1989	468M (1.4B total)	147M	150M	120M	—	51M	—
1990–1993	900M (3.6B total)	237M	250M	188M	—	112M	112M
1994–1997	1.1B (4.4B total)	230M	—	217M	395M	131M	124M
1998–2005	2.2B (17.6B total)	550M	500M	—	550M	600M	—
2006–2011[a] (or 2013[b])	3.7B (20.4B total)	—	622.5M[a]	600M[a]	712.5M[a]	1.1B[b]	—

Sources: "N.F.L. Rights Fees through the Years," table accompanying Bill Carter, "N.F.L. Is Must-Have TV: NBC Is a Have-Not," *New York Times*, January 14, 1998; Barry Wilner, "NFL OKs 6-Year Extensions with Fox, CBS," *Washington Post*, November 9, 2004; Leonard Shapiro and Mark Maske, " 'Monday Night Football' Changes the Channel," *Washington Post*, April 19, 2005; Andy Bernstein, "NFL Restores NBC's Clout," *Street & Smith's SportsBusiness Journal*, April 25–May 1, 2005. For the year-to-year increases under the 1998–2005 contracts (from 1.75 billion to 2.8 billion), see *Street & Smith's SportsBusiness Journal*, April 15–21, 2002.

* Because annual payments escalate over the life of an agreement, the rise from the final year of one contract to the first year of the next is not as steep as the leaps in the averages, but the increases in the 1990, 1998, and 2006 contracts were nonetheless dramatic.

cluded the highest concentration of males, "the most precious commodity for advertisers." (Men were harder to reach because women watched more television.) Companies such as Anheuser-Busch, Ford, and Gillette needed a vehicle for pitching their products to young males. NBC, CBS, ABC, and Fox needed those male viewers of NFL games in order to entice them to watch their prime-time programs.[72]

In this new television climate, NFL football became a loss leader for the networks, so important in other ways that they sacrificed hundreds of millions of dollars rather than lose the rights. Because the numbers can quickly swim into a murky soup, another table might be useful. Table 2 shows the NFL's successive television contracts since 1987.

I would highlight Fox's average payment for 1994–97. ESPN and Rupert Murdoch's Fox Network, created in 1987, were chiefly responsible for the budget-busting rights fees that made every NFL franchise a gold mine by the end of the 1990s. Both increased the number of networks bidding. ESPN, despite its lower ratings on cable, could compete with the networks (and was uniquely profitable) because it could count on the subscriber fees it charged cable companies, on top of its advertising revenue. Fox bid unsuccessfully for *Monday Night Football* in 1987 and for the National Football Conference in 1990, then grabbed the NFC package from CBS in 1993 with what one analyst called a "drunken sailor bid" of $395 million per year, $100 million more than CBS bid after losing roughly $150 million over the previous four seasons on fees of $250 million per year.[73] With the ante now raised, CBS then became the wild card in the 1998 negotiations. Desperate to reclaim its place at the NFL table (despite declining football ratings on the other networks), CBS wrested the American Football Conference from NBC with a bid of $500 million per season, or double what it had paid for the NFC in the early 1990s when it lost millions. At the same time, Fox raised its bid for the NFC to $550 million, while ABC held off NBC's last-ditch grab for *Monday Night Football* by putting up another $550 million. With ESPN keeping its profitable Sunday night package for another $600 million, the NFL reaped $17.6 billion in TV revenues over the next eight seasons, while NBC rather than CBS sat out.[74]

The NFL's negotiating leverage came from five networks competing for four TV packages. (The cable network TNT shared the Sunday night package with ESPN from 1990 through 1997.) The networks' willingness—their desperation—to keep the NFL at any price owed something to "intangibles" of the sort that led communities to pour tax dollars into luxurious stadiums despite meager economic gain for themselves. The story of the new NFL that emerged in the 1990s was a dizzying progression of promotions and sponsorships and naming rights and lawsuits and TV ratings and TV revenues and negotiations with local governments and dozens of other deals conducted on several fronts simultaneously, whose outcome was an entertainment enterprise with gross revenues approaching $6 billion, shared unequally but generously among 32 very rich franchises. The underlying story was the power of "intangibles" beyond the control of marketing and negotiating that helped make this financial abundance possible.

One year into the 1998 contracts that left NBC out, the *New York Times* reported that male viewership for the entire prime-time lineup at ABC, CBS, and Fox had risen 2–3 percent, while NBC's dropped a whopping 26 percent (after losing *Seinfeld* as well as the NFL). The ratings for *Monday Night Football* had fallen about 5 percent from the previous year, yet it was the highest-rated prime-time program among male viewers, age 18 to 49. By the "new math of TV sports," the networks collectively were projected to lose $100 million a year on the football contracts, yet this was possibly the best of investments.[75]

In some ways the "new math" derived from cold calculations—the NFL's measurable impact on prime-time viewing generally—but it also incorporated intangible elements. There was a clear understanding within the television industry and among its observers that Fox had gained legitimacy and stability by acquiring NFL rights in 1993. "The network of Bart Simpson," with most of its channels on the weaker UHF range of the dial (above channel 13), instantly became the network of the National Football Conference, the more prestigious, larger-market half of the NFL, with a strong lead-in for its Sunday night programming and promotion for its entire prime-time schedule. (Fox's prime-time viewership immediately increased 7 percent after adding the NFL to its lineup.) In 1999 Fox's chairman acknowledged that "football helped build this network. The Fox sports brand, which is centered in the N.F.L., has been essential in building all of Fox." *Legitimacy*—that's an intangible. CBS, on the other hand, not only lost eight affiliate stations in 1993 (defecting to Fox to hold onto their football programming), millions of prime-time viewers (a 31 percent decline in two years), and a powerful lead-in to *60 Minutes* and the rest of its Sunday prime-time schedule (*60 Minutes* fell from the top ten), but the network also suffered a tremendous blow to *morale*—another intangible.[76]

In 1998 a reporter on the media for the *New York Times* proposed three possible explanations for the networks' willingness to take huge financial losses rather than lose the NFL. The first was sport's thorough penetration of American business culture as its primary metaphor ("game plans," "team-building," "big score," and all the rest), in the books by coaches read by business managers as how-to manuals, and through the hiring of athletes as consultants "to inspire the troops at conferences." The second was the "reflected glow that many executives feel from being around sports figures." And the third was the "deeply embedded masculine culture in the networks," which among other things made hanging out at the Super Bowl each year a highlight experience for executives. These seemed like three ways of describing the same thing—that male executives wanted to be associated with NFL football—without really explaining how it could drive supposedly rational business decisions. The chairman of a sports-marketing company pointed out that "television is a business of prestige and one-upmanship," a competitive sport in itself. Network executives declared that "sports coverage is good for corporate morale, and it keeps competitive juices flowing among rival employees." Why? The power of NFL football was obvious in its effects but essentially intangible, beyond explanation, in its causes.[77]

The relative importance of intangibles was itself intangible. As ratings continued to decline and losses mounted under the 1998–2005 contracts, NBC president Dick Ebersol defended his network's decision to dump its $150 million a year in losses on the previous football contract, while Leslie Moonves, the president of CBS, credited the NFL for pushing CBS past NBC to become the top-rated network. CBS received help from its affiliates in paying for NFL rights, and ESPN continued to enjoy the advantage of subscriber fees (the highest in all of cable television) on top of advertising revenue. ABC was not doing so well with *Monday Night Football*, however, and after writing off a $350 million loss in 1995 on its previous NFL contract, Fox had to write down another $387 million in 2002 (part of $909 million total losses for its sports programming) from the new one. For the first time, Peter Chernin, the president of Fox's parent company, News Corp, admitted that paying huge rights fees might no longer be in the network's interest. Having won legitimacy and higher prime-time ratings through association with the NFL, Fox might now have to pay more attention to its bottom line.[78]

As the 2005 expiration date approached, Paul Tagliabue and the NFL strengthened their bargaining position by expanding their ties to the satellite provider DirecTV. The NFL first made games available through DirecTV in 1994 to reach fans in rural areas. By 2001, between 1.2 and 1.3 million of DirecTV's 10 million subscribers paid $179 for the Sunday Ticket package, and a new contract was worth $150–200 million in annual profits to the NFL. In November 2003 the league introduced its own NFL Network on DirecTV, with 24-hour "news, analysis, and programming from NFL Films" and Steve Bronstein, former head of ESPN, as its president. Industry observers easily put the pieces together. The NFL's current five-year, $2 billion contract with Di-recTV ran to 2007, but the NFL retained the right to opt out two years earlier, when the contracts with CBS, ABC, Fox, and ESPN expired. Should those four balk at raising the current fees, the NFL would be in a position to sell its Sunday Ticket and NFL Network in the huge cable TV market. Despite the large losses at Fox and ABC (and with insiders doubting CBS's claims to be making money), the *Wall Street Journal* reported in September 2004 that the networks anticipated an increase of 3 to 7 percent in the new TV contracts, while the NFL saw 7 percent as the minimum. As a former sports executive at ABC described the NFL's ventures into its own programming, "This is about promoting the NFL, sure, but it's also about leverage."[79]

Leverage worked to a degree that stunned even insiders. In November 2004, CBS and Fox agreed to nearly 25 and 30 percent fee increases to extend their agreements through 2011, and DirecTV paid $3.5 billion for a five-year extension, through 2010. Although the copresident of CBS claimed that his network "made money on the last deal and will make even more on this deal," those who read the financial press knew the issue was more complicated. The chairman of Fox Sports now made no comment about profits and losses. *SportsBusiness Journal* expressed "shock" and "awe" at the new agreements, yet in what I assume was typical newspaper coverage around the country, a truncated wire-service story appeared in the *Portland Oregonian* alongside the week's injury reports in the sport section's "NFL Notebook." The NFL had just been launched into yet another unprecedented economic dimension, yet as so often happened, the most vital financial news appeared in nooks and crannies of the sports pages, public but barely visible.[80]

Five months later came the truly stunning announcement that, after 36 years, ABC would give up *Monday Night Football* to its cable partner ESPN for $8.8 billion over eight years. ESPN's $1.1 billion per year doubled what ABC had been paying while losing $150 million a year, and it nearly doubled ESPN's own current $600 million for Sunday nights. Having dropped from first to third in overall TV ratings, and to fourth (even behind Fox) among 18–49 year olds, NBC was returning to the NFL to pick up the Sunday night game from ESPN, for the same $600 million (for six years) but without the cable subscription fees that had assured ESPN's profits. Industry insiders questioned the wisdom of the networks but certainly not the good fortune of the NFL. At this point, the NFL looked forward to more than $3.7 billion per year, $117 million per club, up from $2.8 billion in the last year of the expiring agreements and nearly 70 percent higher than the $2.2 billion average over the life of the old contracts. With ratings slumping! *SportsBusiness Journal* reported that the new TV deals instantly increased the value of NFL franchises by $150 million, likely putting a quarter of the league's teams over $1 billion.[m] And the bidding remained open on a Thursday/Saturday package.[81]

Speculation about the Thursday/Saturday package dragged into January 2006 when, after considering bids from as many as nine media companies for sums reported to be as high as $440 million, the league announced that it would keep the package for its own NFL Network, part of a strategy to make the network more attractive to cable companies. (The NFL Network was currently available in just 35 million out of the 90 million households with cable.) With more than enough revenue from the other agreements, the NFL could afford to forgo short-term profits for building the long-term strength of its own network. (The decision also immediately created another contentious

m. According to *Forbes*'s calculations the following September, the average franchise value increased $79 million (10 percent), with five teams now topping $1 billion. Because *Forbes* uses revenue figures from the previous season, however, it is not clear whether the new television contracts are registered in the 2006 valuations. *Forbes*'s September 2007 numbers could be more revealing.

issue to be negotiated with the NFLPA, whose leaders contended that the package was worth $300 million, which should be added to the revenues shared with players.)[82]

As the 2006 season approached, speculation focused on how ABC would fare without the NFL and whether NBC would recover from its ratings freefall now that it was back in the game.[83] But additional uncertainties loomed for the future. It was hard to imagine NBC making a profit on Sunday nights. Despite its unique advantages, ESPN's "economics [would] be challenged" by paying nearly twice as much for Mondays as it had been paying for Sundays.[84] Whether Fox and CBS could hold their own while paying higher fees was uncertain, to say the least. All of the networks would attempt to extract more from their advertisers, of course (and early sales were strong),[85] but how long advertisers would find it in their interest to pay more in order to reach a declining share of the audience remained to be seen.

Yet . . . afternoon NFL games in 2005 clobbered the prime-time average ratings at all of the networks (by 20 percent for CBS and 65 percent for Fox), while Sunday and Monday night football remained the most potent vehicles for pitching prime-time programs to young male viewers. Even Fox's post-game show on Sundays outdrew its prime-time average, 7.2 to 6.1. The rights to NFL games might be too costly, but the cost of not having the NFL might be unbearable. The only certainty is that *very* profitable NFL franchises became even more profitable. And the double bonanza of the extension on the collective bargaining agreement and the new TV deals meant a 20 percent bump in the players' average salary, to $1.7 million.[86]

The "power" of NFL football is hard to pin down. The various psychological, sociological, anthropological, and cultural theories that can be employed in this effort are necessarily speculative and abstract. The $3.7 billion dollars put up by the TV networks, like the billions of dollars in public subsidies for stadiums, are decidedly concrete measures that do not explain themselves but confirm that the game's power, whatever its source, is real.

FOOTBALL
AS
PRODUCT

To a short list of milestones marking the creation of the new NFL—May 7, 1982, when Al Davis won the right to move his franchise; February 25, 1989, when Jerry Jones bought the Dallas Cowboys; May 6, 1993, when the owners and players finally signed a labor agreement—should be added July 12, 1994. On that day, the NFL announced that Sara Levinson, former copresident of MTV, had been hired as the new president of NFL Properties. This seemed like news of the you've-got-to-kidding sort. The president of a cable network feeding highly sexualized music videos to teenagers, and a woman as well, would head the NFL division that markets to fans of huge guys who grunt and sweat a lot. The significance of Levinson's hiring was perhaps mostly symbolic. MTV represented the cultural forces against which the NFL had held up a bulwark since the 1960s. The NFL was also, at all levels, overwhelmingly a men's club. Hiring Levinson to market professional football represented a decision at the highest levels that NFL football was no longer your father's Sunday pastime.

Explanations followed. MTV and Levinson represented two potential audiences that the NFL coveted, young people and women. Her hiring, however, confirmed something more fundamental: that the NFL now openly regarded itself as a "brand" and pro football as a "product" to be marketed.

Before Levinson: Public Relations and
the Iron John Super Bowl

Levinson's marketing and branding of NFL football built on the structures Pete Rozelle put in place in the 1960s. Having inherited the arrangement Bert Bell made with Roy Rogers Enterprises, Rozelle created the league's own in-house NFL Properties in 1963. The operation generated so little profit—gross revenues were just $1.5 million in 1969—that the owners agreed to Rozelle's suggestion in 1972 that all proceeds be turned over to a new entity, NFL Charities, for their public relations value. (In 1974 Al Davis withdrew his share from this arrangement.) In 1964 Rozelle also brought NFL Films in-house, to become "perhaps the most effective propaganda organ in the history of corporate America." More generally, over his tenure as commissioner Rozelle was preoccupied with protecting the game's image, whether it meant suspending Paul Hornung and Alex Karras for gambling, forcing Joe Namath to unload Bachelors III, and fining eight San Diego Chargers for using amphetamines, or enforcing uniform dress codes and rules against "excessive celebrations" on the field.[1]

Paul Tagliabue was no less attentive than Rozelle to the NFL's image. The ultimate example of league officials consciously crafting a certain image for their public has to be the 1992 Super Bowl between Washington and Buffalo, the one that should forever be known as the Iron John Super Bowl. Hypermasculinity had been an essential element in football's image virtually from the game's beginnings in the late nineteenth century, and with the rise of the women's movement in the 1960s and 1970s football was increasingly singled out by both critics and defenders of "traditional masculinity." In this climate, the NFL never looked more Neanderthal to its detractors than on September 17, 1990, when several New England Patriot players tauntingly exposed themselves to *Boston Herald* reporter Lisa Olson, who had the audacity to invade the male sanctuary of their locker room (a mere 12 years after a federal court had confirmed female reporters' right to do so). Patriots' owner Victor Kiam proved that the NFL's idiots were not only in the locker room when he defended his players by reportedly calling Olson a "classic bitch." (Kiam, the president of Remington Products, denied the charge in full-page ads in Boston and New York newspapers after the National Organization for Women threatened to boycott his company's razors and other items.)[2]

With roughly 500 working female sports journalists by this time, NFL officials had thought the issue long dead. Two weeks later, however, Cincinnati coach Sam Wyche barred another female reporter from his team's locker room, pushing the NFL deeper into damage control as football again sparked heated debate about women's rights and men's behavior. As routinely happens in the media coverage of Big Sport, these isolated incidents became a full-blown morality play, purporting to reveal broad truths about football, football players, and the general swinishness of men. Commissioner Tagliabue appointed a Harvard law professor to investigate the Patriots incident, fined Wyche $30,000, and reaffirmed the league's policy on access for all reporters. (Olson, it turned out, had the law on her side but not broad public sentiment. A poll conducted by CBS and the *New York Times* found both male and female respondents sensitive to women's occupational rights but more concerned about the players' personal privacy.) After the special counsel issued his findings in late November, Tagliabue fined Zeke Mowatt as the principle instigator, along with two teammates and the Patriots organization. Humiliated and distraught despite her vindication, Olson simply wanted to put the episode behind her; but after Kiam crudely joked about her at an all-men's dinner in February, she sued.[a] She also moved to Sydney, Australia, to take another job. From there, she agreed to an out-of-court settlement a year later.[3]

Such events do not take place in social and cultural vacuums. The harassment of Lisa Olson occurred as magazines like *Time* and *Esquire* reported on a growing sense of masculine crisis in the country. In *Time*'s fall 1990 special issue on women, an essay titled "What Do Men Really Want?" claimed that men were fed up with the feminist ideal of the "sensitive man" yet uncertain about what sort of men they were supposed to be. *Esquire*'s special issue, "The State of Masculinity," in October 1991 included a mocking account of the "weekend warriors" who gathered in forests to beat on drums and their sunken chests, chanting mythic incantations as they tried "to reclaim an inner, primal, ruddy Natural Man, the Wildman—the New Warrior's hairy mentor—who lumbers through Robert Bly's best-selling book *Iron John* . . . like an absentminded bigfoot with a degree in social work."[4]

A surprise best seller in 1990 and 1991, Bly's book, *Iron John: A Book About Men*, offered a "mythopoetic" exploration of men's ancient needs, and the failure of modern fathers to teach their sons how to meet them, that obviously resonated with thousands of the males described by *Time* magazine. For front-page news, 1991 more or less began with the Clarence Thomas–Anita Hill hearings and ended with the rape trial of the Kennedy cousin, Willie Smith. With the behavior of men and the relations between the sexes the top domestic news stories of the year, and with men supposedly agonizing over what it meant to be a man in a feminist or postfeminist world, NFL executives still smarting from the Lisa Olson incident must have held some fascinating

a. The owner who denied ever calling Olson a bitch and apologized profusely for her discomfort later joked with his fellow male diners: "What do the Iraqis have in common with Lisa Olson? They've both seen Patriot missiles up close."

meetings over the fall of 1991 to discuss what the cultural uproar over masculinity might mean for the league's image.

The result was what I am calling the Iron John Super Bowl on January 26, 1992. The game itself between the Washington Redskins and Buffalo Bills was one of the many forgettable Super Bowls, as the Redskins led 37–10 before the Bills scored twice in the last six minutes to make the final margin a little less embarrassing. But the packaging of the game was deeply revealing, and the concluding moments were simply astounding. The pregame show on CBS offered the usual mix of interviews, expert commentary, and highlights from NFL Films, but also a series of segments titled "Football the First Time," in which a Bill or Redskin player recounted his earliest memories of football, echoed by a mother or father or older brother. This reminder that violent NFL players were once little boys, in families like the viewers' own, set the stage for an introduction produced in NFL Films' high style. With music like the soundtrack from a fairy tale in the background, CBS's Pat Summerall introduced Super Bowl XXVI in the portentous manner of John Facenda as "football's ultimate field of dreams," where "grown men become little boys again, living out their fantasy in front of the entire world."

For the next three-and-a-half hours, only the Redskins lived out a fantasy; then came the closing minutes. With the outcome settled but the game still having to be played out, the TV cameras began panning the sidelines, as if for the usual shots of joyful winners and dejected losers. Instead, several players' children suddenly appeared. The cameras now lingered on enormous men, padded and sweaty, cradling toddlers in beefy arms or high-fiving with seven-year-olds who barely reached their waists. Winners and losers alike became fathers again, once the game ended. The scene was mind-boggling in itself and because it was so obviously orchestrated. Need it be pointed out that children are usually not allowed to wander onto the stadium floor during a Super Bowl? Even John Madden's lack of surprise had to have been planned in advance, his innocuous comments about kids and daddies, as if everyone were watching something altogether normal, the typical final minutes of a Super Bowl whose outcome was no longer in doubt. That final image of brawny yet sensitive and nurturing fathers was the NFL's perfect answer to the events of 1991, and a powerful fantasy for the millions watching the game and feeling a crisis in the state of American masculinity.

From PR to Brand Management

The Iron John Super Bowl was unprecedented and never duplicated—no more kids on the sidelines in the final moments—but it also strikingly illustrated NFL officials' conscious attention to the league's and players' image. With the hiring of Sara Levinson, a reorganized NFL Properties accelerated the shift from protecting the image into research-driven marketing and branding.

As noted above, NFLP's gross revenues in 1969 were $1.5 million. By 1979, they had increased to $100 million; by 1986, to $500 million. Profits could no longer be casually donated to charity for public relations. In the late 1980s, a "holy trinity" of the NBA, Nike, and Michael Jordan created the model for a sport that transcended sport to become a cultural and economic phenomenon. With team apparel becoming a national craze, Pete Rozelle directed NFL Properties to operate more as a business, and its growth continued under Paul Tagliabue.[5]

By 1993, the year before Levinson arrived, NFLP's gross revenues reached $2.5 billion, a five-fold increase since 1986. A marketing and promotions division sold corporate sponsorships, and a publishing division still produced the game programs sold in stadiums; but retail licensing, to some 350 manufacturers of 2,500 different items by 1991, generated the overwhelming bulk of revenues. Pro football's own appeal was still the given: the games and teams advertised NFL products, not the other way around. *Sports Illustrated* reported in 1992 that after Jets coach Joe Walton wore a certain NFLP-licensed sweater during a Monday night game, NFLP staff received more than 5,000 calls about it over the next few days. Likewise, the promotions division did not focus on selling NFL football but on helping major sponsors such as Coke, Hershey's, and Gatorade sell their own products through their ties to the NFL.[6]

NFL Properties was thus thriving before Levinson arrived. Profits to be shared among the clubs in 1993 exceeded $200 million, just 20 percent of the revenue from TV but still a considerable sum.[7] Under six years of Levinson's leadership, NFLP's revenues increased another 40 percent, not bad growth but nothing like the increases before she arrived (or the 21 percent she achieved in her own first year).[8] But Levinson's impact cannot be measured by the bottom line. In the commercialization of NFL football since the 1960s, Levinson's arrival contributed importantly to a "tipping point" for the league, the moment when incremental changes reached a magnitude that triggered a new way of thinking.[9]

The NFL's operating assumption, that football sold itself and could be used to sell other products, seemed to change when Levinson came in to promote NFL football itself more aggressively. Whether the hiring of Levinson, within months of a new labor agreement, new television contracts, and league expansion, was itself the tipping point or just the symbol of it, league officials in general and those at NFLP in particular began to talk more openly about NFL football as a "brand" in "the competitive business of sports and entertainment." The NFL now competed, one spokesman in 1995 explained, not just with the NBA, the National Hockey League, and Major League Baseball, but also with "Batman movies, 'Aladdin' and 'Pocahontas,'" the entire world of popular entertainment and leisure options. Owners and players took the same side here. As Gene Upshaw put it, NFL owners no longer competed for revenues against the NFLPA, but hand-in-hand with the NFLPA against "all the other entertainment choices out there: the movies, music, theater."[10]

As Jerry Jones pushed his fellow owners in the same directions, at NFL Properties the league's reorientation played out along two main lines. First, NFL football became less narrowly the game itself and more explicitly a "brand" to generate revenue from sponsorship partners. Second and more significantly, the games themselves became a "product" in a new way: not what the league *produced* (to satisfy the desires of serious fans) but what it *marketed* (to casual fans). That shift in the connotations of "product" contains a small revolution in presupposing that the games might not be sufficiently attractive in themselves. If that premise was and is correct, for all of the astonishing revenue it has generated as an entertainment product since the 1990s, NFL football has been losing power as a sport that historically resonated with the public much more deeply than mere entertainment. Or perhaps a profit-oriented NFL's sense of its product is simply wrong-headed.

What the hiring of Levinson meant to the National Football League was the subject of a shrewd essay in the *New Yorker* by John Seabrook in 1997. As Tagliabue explained to Seabrook, ESPN and Fox had introduced a new "attitude" in sport broadcasting, one "more youthful" and "iconoclastic." In addition, polls showed that kids had become more interested in basketball and soccer than in football, and more and more mothers did not want their sons risking injuries in contact sports. The bottom line was that those running the NFL could no longer take football's powerful appeal for granted, and they feared losing an entire generation of lifetime football fans (and that generation once lost might spawn another, then another). Millions still lived and died with their favorite teams each Sunday, but those passionate fans were aging, and there were other millions coming up behind them to be wooed. As Seabrook put it, Tagliabue "needed someone who could make football attractive to a new generation without disgusting the middle-aged bratwurst-and-beer types who enjoy going to games with their faces painted in the colors of their teams." Reporters for *Business Week* used similar language when they saluted the hiring of Levinson as "just what the NFL, that 75-year-old temple of testosterone, needs as it tries to score with a generation of channel surfers while holding on to its core Joe Sixpack crowd."[11]

During the years when NFL clubs, with little effort, had been selling out their stadiums and negotiating ever bigger television contracts, marketing had become an increasingly precise science elsewhere. Some observers therefore wondered how Levinson, coming from MTV, would adjust to the move from a "niche market" to a "mass market." With dozens of cable channels competing against the established networks, with more people watching TV but a smaller percentage watching any particular program, sports were often described as the sole remnant of a "mass" American culture.

With her former MTV colleague Howard Handler as her vice president of marketing, Levinson established an in-house consumer research unit whose initial "brand audit" ("the most comprehensive survey ever of sports fans") identified three distinct groups for the NFL to target: hard-core fans, women and children, and casual fans. As Seabrook explained, the NFL could take the first group for granted but must not alienate it. Levinson initiated or expanded programs to cultivate the other two. "Play Football" targeted kids, ages 6 to 15, with consumer products on the one hand and instructional clinics and flag-football programs in more than 20 NFL cities on the other. The purpose of this "experiential branding"—amazing term!—was "to turn kids into NFL consumers." Participation in the flag-football programs grew from 350,000 in 1994 to more than 5 million by 1999. A million of those were girls, some of whom also participated in new all-girl divisions of the long-running Punt, Pass & Kick program, with 175,000 competing the first year and more than 300,000 by 1999. Football 101 seminars and an "NFL For Her" product line targeted women, who made up 40 percent of the NFL's audience according to NFLP research.[12]

Levinson and her group also took on the challenge of marketing NFL football itself. To appeal to serious and casual fans differently, they developed a series of campaigns based on research-tested themes. "Pledge Allegiance" (to your favorite team) targeted the 40 million diehards; "Feel the Power" was for the 80 or 90 million casual fans, including women and teenagers. "Feel the Power" ran for four years. In 1996 the campaign's announced goal was to "use humor and hyperbole to humanize the league's incredible hulks." In 1997 the new campaign featured what Handler called "everyday people"—a tour guide at Lambeau Field, a secretary for the Tampa Bay Buccaneers—"who are like you and me but have meaningful roles with putting on the game." The 1998 campaign was aimed at the youth market, fans aged 18 to 34, emphasizing the "adrenaline-charged roller coaster ride" provided by the

NFL and exploiting the "argot and attitude" of black culture. In 1999, TV spots featured current stars alongside NFL legends to evoke the "timeless passion that brings people together" through football. In each campaign, the idea was to make casual fans with no deep commitment to football feel a human connection to the NFL.[13]

Behind these campaigns lay "Game Plan 1997," Levinson and Handler's master guide to all of their football marketing. Seabrook described it as their attempt "to put into marketing lingo the wordless passion of the gridiron." Marketing strategies would be based on NFL football's six "Core Equities," each of which could be evoked by a handful of "Key Symbols":

> Action/Power: hitting, elusive running, circus catches, the NFL Shield.
> History/Tradition: leaves, NFL legends, fathers and sons, tailgating.
> Thrill/Release: fans laughing, screaming, frustrated, exultant; players acting the same way.
> Teamwork/Competition: Green Bay Packers in the 1960s, 1969 Jets, the Steel Curtain.
> Authenticity: the ball (pigskin), the field, grass, mud, sweat, blood.
> Unifying Force: the team, friends, families, communities, tailgating.[14]

In other words, ads that used a particular symbol (hitting, elusive running) would evoke the corresponding "equity" (action/power) and sell the game.

The trade journal *Advertising Age* in March 1996 acknowledged Levinson's immediate impact by naming NFL Properties and its new president "Promotional Marketer of the Year."[15] But by March 2000, when Levinson announced her resignation, there were hints of conflict. As always, the NFL would not speak openly about its internal problems, but *SportsBusiness Journal* reported that Levinson's "leadership grip seemed to be slipping," after one of the league's apparel licensees appealed directly to several owners when Levinson declined to renegotiate the current agreement. (It is hard not to wonder if dealing with a woman spoiled for male clients some of the "intangible" charge of doing business with the NFL.) Levinson's departure prompted a reorganization in which the NFL consolidated its various business operations into a single entity, overseen by Roger Goodell, one of the league's vice presidents and Paul Tagliabue's likely successor.[16]

From the outside, the impact of the reorganization was invisible. Goodell dropped "Feel the Power" for a more generic "NFL 2000," a strategy, as the trade journal *Brandweek* described it, "with less emphasis on a brand message and more on specific marketing objectives: building the TV audience, boosting visits to NFL.com, pushing sales of licensed product, boosting attendance, stimulating youth interest and expanding participation in football, and enhancing players' image."[17] Some owners worried that Goodell "was too much in the thrall of revenue building" (one of them hated his use of "terms like 'monetize' and 'commoditize' "), but this had become the common language of the new NFL. In 2001 the league hired an outside ad agency for the first time, to develop a "quieter, lower-key campaign," with a theme ("This is what it's all about") redirected away from hard-core to casual fans. A spokesman for the ad agency explained the purpose as an attempt to call attention to football's "social currency," to the ways NFL football brings ordinary people together for a backyard barbecue or draws a farm kid to watch a game with his grandmother. What was different from Levinson's campaign themes is not apparent.[18]

The post-Levinson NFL moved away from having hundreds of licensees to having fewer, often exclusive, agreements in order to better manage the NFL brand. It also directed more resources into developing partnerships with fewer major sponsors—21 of them in 2003, each with its own product category.[19] The league certainly did not reduce its marketing efforts. Its most prominent new venture was "Kickoff Live," a Thursday-night live concert following "the world's biggest tailgate party," inaugurated in 2002 to launch the new football season. The first site was Times Square, with Bon Jovi as the headliner. In 2003 it moved to the National Mall in Washington, D.C., with Britney Spears. The league hoped to make "Kickoff Live" akin to a preseason Super Bowl, for which host cities would bid from season to season, but thus far it has had to settle for a more modest impact. According to the president of one marketing firm, the 2003 event was "broadly panned as an over-commercialized, undignified failure for the NFL" (unlike Super Bowl week?). After the uproar over Janet Jackson's "wardrobe malfunction" at the 2004 Super Bowl, the league toned down the third "Kickoff," then cranked up the volume again in 2005, with concerts in Los Angeles, Foxboro (home of the reigning champions), and Detroit (site of the next Super Bowl). The event outside the Los Angeles Coliseum, part of the league's courtship of the city for a new NFL franchise, featured NFL Hall of Famers, including local hero Marcus Allen, in addition to the musical performers and the USC marching band. ABC broadcast portions of the concerts on an "NFL Opening Kickoff" prime-time special, along with footage from the Rolling Stones' tour that served as an advertisement for the Stones' halftime performance at the Super Bowl five months later. (With the Stones at the Super Bowl, the NFL would be "mix[ing] monster brands.")[20] Oh, and a football game followed.

To track the NFL's ongoing and new marketing initiatives is a dizzying experience. The league has continued to work with sponsors on "big events" and season-long promotions, to enhance the interactive features on its website (launched in 1995, the same year as NFL Sunday Ticket on DirecTV), to sponsor youth football and fantasy football—much of this effort less for the revenue than for "fan development." The NFL formed a partnership with Nickelodeon, the kids' cable network, to showcase the Punt, Pass & Kick finals and contemplated producing "an NFL-themed animated series." Through NFL Europe the league attempted, not very successfully thus far, to create a desire for the product in untapped overseas markets. The rest of the world strangely persists in preferring its "football" to ours (while the 2006 Super Bowl drew a total television audience of 151 million, the World Cup Final that summer was watched by 603 million). A regular-season game in Mexico City between Arizona and San Francisco in 2005, however, drew 103,000 fans and led to showing Monday night games in Mexican theaters in 2006 and organizing youth flag-football tournaments there to develop young fans. It also suggested greater promise for one-time international events, beginning in 2007 with a regular-season game in London and an exhibition game in Beijing. (The NFL joined every other American corporation in lusting after the enormous Chinese market.) By 2002 the NFL was targeting the growing Latino population with special initiatives. In 2004 the league entered an NFL float ("Football as Americana") in the Macy's Thanksgiving Day Parade. As sports media in the early twenty-first century became a "three-screen world" of TV, computer, and hand-held wireless device (cell phone, PDA), competition for that "third screen" created a major new arena for future marketing. For its initial foray, the NFL in 2005 signed a five-year agreement with Sprint worth up to $600 million to deliver video highlights of NFL games to cell phones.[21]

With "NFL Kickoff" established as the season's opposite bookend to the Super Bowl, the league in early 2006 turned its attention to the college draft (already, according to the *Washington Post*'s Michael Wilbon, "the most overrated, overhyped, obsessively overcovered non-event in sports"). NFL marketers now envisioned the college draft, "NFL Kickoff," and the Super Bowl as the three key events in a "seasonlong brand campaign" in conjunction with corporate sponsors. Beginning in 2005, they also began branding individual seasons to reap the benefits from "expandable media and sponsorship platforms." After success with "XL" (for Super Bowl XL but also "Extra Large," as in larger-than-life), the "I" in Super Bowl XLI became a tagline for the 2006 season, beginning with the draft ("Dreams Start Here"), progressing to training camp ("One Game, Get Ready"), then to the Kickoff ("One Game, One

Dream"), then to Thanksgiving ("One Tradition"), and finally to the playoffs and Super Bowl ("One Game, One Dream, One Champion"). With sponsorship revenue having increased 70 percent over the past three years, the league in 2006 also embarked on a new initiative to sell "enhancements" for the first time since 1997: sponsorship of instant replay or the first-and-ten line or the red zone ("This instant replay is brought to you by Viagra"?).[22]

In all of this activity, the specific strategies and themes seem less significant than the strategizing and thematizing themselves. The danger of oversaturation is obvious: when there are too many "specials," nothing seems special anymore. The greater danger lies in devaluing the actual football games if they become simply part of a larger spectacle or a multipronged marketing campaign. While much of the NFL's activity is geared toward generating additional revenue through ties with sponsors and the staging of ancillary events, the efforts at "fan development" are the most revealing. Behind them lies an assumption that not just the spin-off events but also NFL football itself requires packaging and marketing to attract and hold uncommitted fans. One only has to listen to the NFL's marketers to hear the combination of doubt and faith in the sport's own hold on the American public. In 2003, as the league coordinated the "entertainment package" on the electronic scoreboards for the clubs, its director of entertainment programming explained, "Our game speaks for itself . . . but we want the whole presentation to be more of a spectacle."[23]

Whether the NFL's marketing efforts are effective will remain a mystery, because what would have happened without them can never be known. As the New York Times pointed out, given the sold-out games and soaring revenues at the stadium, NFL Properties in the late 1990s seemed to be promoting pro football to already true believers.[24] But NFL executives had to worry that yesterday's loyal fans were aging, while tomorrow's could not be taken for granted. The fact that John Madden NFL Football from EA Sports was the most popular sports video game in the country did not guarantee that its young addicts would become fans of the real thing.

Pro football first passed Major League Baseball as Americans' favorite spectator sport, by a narrow margin, back in 1965. In 2005 the margin was more than two to one over baseball in a Harris poll (33 percent to 14 percent). In a poll in 2003, 59 percent of American adults "followed" professional football. In both of these recent polls, every demographic group preferred pro football to every other sport—but younger fans to lesser degrees. In the 2005 poll, for example, 39 percent of those between ages 28 and 39 named pro football their favorite sport (down from 42 percent in a 2004 poll), but only 27 percent of those between 18 and 27 did so. Industry research typically found that just 31 or 32 percent of NFL fans belonged to the coveted 18–34 age group. Moreover, the overall 59 percent in 2003 was down from 66 percent in 1998. Yet the 33 percent who preferred pro football to all other sports in 2005 was up from 26 percent in 1998.[25]

Should those figures reassure or alarm those who run the NFL? Reading poll data for guidance has to feel like following the continuous loop of a Möbius strip, hoping for a conclusion that can never arrive. As the sporting public became more fragmented, football held its number-one position with a shrinking portion of an expanding audience, and the young in particular were more susceptible to novel entertainments. The most brilliant marketing campaign might have no effect on the NFL's future, or the league might thrive with no marketing at all. But it could not afford to gamble. With Jerry Jones leading the demand for more entrepreneurial marketing, and with Daniel Snyder and several other new owners needing to pay off enormous debts on their investments, and with competition for Americans' leisure time and dollars increasing every year, the NFL could no longer assume that owners only had to open their stadium gates and watch the fans pour in, then be pleasantly surprised every four or six or eight years with richer TV contracts. Arthur Blank, owner of the Atlanta Falcons, spoke for the entire new NFL when he told a reporter, "You must go out and find customers. You must provide good entertainment value irrespective of the product on the field."[26] *Irrespective of the product on the field.* Before *Monday Night Football* in 1970, no such "irrespective" was conceivable. Now, it informed the fundamental thinking of NFL owners and league executives.

Managing the Brand

For better and for worse, the NFL cannot completely control its brand, despite obsessive efforts to do so. When the league's own efforts backfire, the public often reacts with bemusement at the giant's chagrin. When the players on their own fail to present a sterling image as role models, the public response tends more to sadness or disgust, if not cynicism. Because NFL football is experienced overwhelmingly more often through the media rather than in person, the media have always wielded power beyond the NFL's control. "The media" since the 1960s, of course, means predominantly television, and the sports media in recent years have most conspicuously included ESPN. Whether the NFL or ESPN has had more influence on how the American public has viewed pro football since the early 1990s is a tough question to answer.

ESPN, Celebrity, and Irony

In 1979, before ESPN was launched, three TV networks broadcast an average of 18 hours of sports each week. After ESPN debuted on September 7, 1979 (in a mere 2 million households), and expanded to 24-hour broadcasting a year later, weekly sports programming increased by 168 hours. Initially the "sports" shown on ESPN were a slap-dash stew of no interest to the established networks: slow-pitch softball, high school lacrosse, tractor pulls, Australian rules football. The all-sports cable network started as a national joke, but as cable expanded, ESPN's reach expanded with it, to 10 million households by May 1981 and to 25 million by September 1983, the year it became the first cable channel popular enough to charge a subscription fee. Programming improved, too (including *The NFL Game of the Week* from NFL Films, hosted by Steve Sabol), as did its financial value. The initial investor, Getty Oil Company, lost $67 million before selling the network to Capital Cities/ABC in 1984 for $237 million. ESPN first made an operating profit, $1 million, in 1985. The following year, it earned $40 million.[27]

Conventional wisdom has it that ESPN fully arrived in 1987, when it acquired rights to NFL football games and the legitimacy that came with them. Despite Pete Rozelle's fear of tarnishing the NFL's image by association with cable, as I noted in the previous chapter the decision was a crucial step for the NFL in providing leverage to wrangle higher fees from the broadcast networks while opening up the new lucrative cable market. Once on ESPN, the NFL thrived more than ever, and ESPN thrived on the partnership, as *Sunday Night Football* immediately became the highest-rated show on cable and stayed there continuously through 2005, its final season. By the end of 1992, ESPN reached 61.4 million households, on the way to 90 million. When the Walt Disney Company purchased Capital Cities/ABC in 1995 for more than $19 billion, ESPN was no throw-in but the jewel. With several successful ancillary ventures—ESPN Radio (1992), ESPN 2 (1993), the ESPY Awards (1993), and *ESPN The Magazine* (1998)—among its more than 40 branded businesses, the former national joke was worth $20 billion by 2001, generating $2 billion of revenue as "the cash cow that drives Disney."[28]

ESPN's impact on the NFL and other sports has been enormous in both obvious and subtle ways. Beyond the economics, its highlights on *SportsCenter* have replaced the daily newspaper as fans' first source for scores and game reports. (The Internet now likely has that role.) Its more in-depth reporting has encroached on *Sports Illustrated*'s near monopoly on extended analysis. The network has often been criticized for offering only "sports lite," but it has not altogether shied away from investigative journalism and serious interview programs such as *Outside the Lines*. And it has simply offered more games of all kinds than any other network.

More profoundly, ESPN has altered the way we think about sports and athletes. ESPN has arguably become the major force in creating our broader celebrity sports culture, transforming athletes from mostly local heroes into national celebrities. With its vastly greater national audience, television as a medium creates celebrities in ways that newspapers and even magazines never could. With its 24 hours of daily sport, ESPN makes most starting players in the NFL at least minor celebrities. And at the top of the pyramid of celebrity making, *SportsCenter* produces the sound and sight bites that separate the major from the minor celebrities. The epitome of sports fame used to be a photo on the cover of *Sports Illustrated*; sometime in the 1990s it shifted to making the highlights on *SportsCenter*.[29]

ESPN turned the NFL draft into a media event, a debutante ball for quarterbacks and linebackers.[30] It made the personalities of many pro athletes better known than their performances. And competition from ESPN forced cable rivals and the traditional networks, joined now by Fox, to ratchet up their own coverage of pro athletes. It spurred HBO to turn training camp into reality TV. More generally, every game today has its on-the-field post-game interviews. Every player's appearance on TV is an opportunity for self-marketing, for performing live a certain personality and image before a national sports-obsessed audience. Every appearance on *SportsCenter* is an opportunity to see oneself as a star. I have often wondered if kids now dream at night not of scoring the winning touchdown in a big game but of watching themselves doing it on *SportsCenter*.

Extending Roone Arledge's vision, *SportsCenter*'s producers perfected the art of storytelling for short attention spans. The network's highlight coordinator once compiled a list of 17 different basic highlights, each telling a different story, from "Who Won?" and "Hail, Conquering Hero" to "Turning Point" and "Blue Collar." But at the same time that ESPN has glorified pro football players and other athletes as never before, it also deflates them with the hip irony that characterizes our so-called postmodern culture, particularly the youth-oriented part of it. An element of irony has always been present in the media's response to football—in the cartoons and jokes about dumb jocks, for example—but *SportsCenter* brought irony closer to the center. Keith Olbermann once joked to a reporter that he and Chris Berman, who attended prep school together, took "the same class in Wise Ass Sportscasting." Following Olbermann and Dan Patrick, it seemed that every *SportsCenter* anchor had signed up for the class through correspondence school.[31]

Berman became ESPN's first star, best known for the silly nicknames he assigned to athletes. Patrick and Olbermann transformed *SportsCenter* from an addiction for sports junkies to a cultural phenomenon, becoming known for irony-dripping catchphrases: "real men don't strut . . . and a mighty roar went up from the crowd . . . the use of unnecessary violence has been approved." Olbermann borrowed that last line from the John Belushi film *The Blues Brothers* to describe quarterback sacks and, as he put it, "other moments of mayhem." The violent play was invariably one of those ferocious hits that NFL Films would heighten and stylize by showing it either in super slow motion or in a gasp-inducing montage. The same blow shown on *SportsCenter* might likewise strike the viewer with awe, but Olbermann's deadpan irony would at the same time deflate it. The awestruck fan sees the athlete as larger than life; the hip-ironic fan sees him merely life-size, or smaller. And *SportsCenter*'s hip-ironic anchors became celebrities themselves, no mere reporters on games and athletes but the sporting world's Ed Sullivans or Bob Hopes, masters of ceremony more famous than most of the stars they introduced.[32]

The most powerful shapers of pro football's image today are NFL Films and ESPN, and the National Football League controls only the former. Footage from NFL Films appears everywhere, ESPN included, but ESPN broadcasts 24 hours a day. If NFL Films is football's epic poet, ESPN is half bard, half jester. NFL Films regards pro football with awe; ESPN laces awe with irony. The network's phenomenal popularity has been mostly good for the NFL, of course, and the NFL has been a key factor in ESPN's success. But ESPN also directs its irreverence at the NFL and, at times, indirectly upstages NFL games, when players such as Terrell Owens and Chad Johnson consciously perform for the highlights on *SportsCenter*. Without ESPN, the NFL's appeal to twenty-something males would undoubtedly be weakened, but irony deflates football's power. And *SportsCenter*'s mix of sport and entertainment, with "a little attitude and a little humor," created the model copied throughout the sports media as the NFL moved into the new century.[33]

Malfunctions

ESPN is just one of many forces beyond the NFL's control, despite the league's considerable effort in asserting it. In recent years, all NFL employees have attended "a three-hour brand-awareness seminar that stresses the league's values: tradition, teamwork, community, and integrity," to keep everyone "on message," as the political consultants would say. But NFL football also exists in the wider world, and protecting the brand has become a constant challenge, while a gleeful press reports all of the failures. The NFL looked merely ridiculous when fans in early 2005 could not buy a jersey with the name of New England's Randall Gay on the back, because "Gay" turned out to be one of the "naughty words" not allowed on team merchandise.[34]

The NFL has cooperated in the production of Hollywood films such as *Little Giants, Jerry McGuire,* and *Invincible,* allowing use of its trademark, helping to cast league personnel in supporting roles, and arranging product placement of NFL sponsors' merchandise.[35] But the league could do nothing to stop films such as Oliver Stone's *Any Given Sunday* from portraying a darker side of professional football. Apart from the game telecasts, much of what happens on television is also beyond the NFL's control. The new breed of yuck-it-up, testosterone-charged studio shows pioneered by the Fox Network in the 1990s, some of them with a hot "sports babe" to banter with the guys, drew young male viewers into the orbit of the NFL. These programs also erased whatever boundary once stood between sport and entertainment when their producers hired comedians like Jimmy Kimmel and Tom Arnold (followed by Dennis Miller on *Monday Night Football* and controversial talk-radio host Rush Limbaugh on ESPN) as studio commentators or analysts. However offensive to some personal tastes in league offices, all of this benefited the NFL if it drew attention to the games and developed the fan base. But then during the 2003 season Limbaugh charged that the media overrated Philadelphia quarterback Donovan McNabb because he was black. The problem was Limbaugh's and ESPN's, but it was also the brand-conscious NFL's, and everyone had to fall back again into damage control.

Courting the MTV generation has repeatedly proved risky. Like parents shocked when they finally listen to the lyrics of their kids' music, NFL Properties recruited the rapper Eminem for one of its ad campaigns only to discover belatedly that his song included references to drugs, rape, and assault.[36] Capitalizing on the craze for team merchandise in the early 1990s hit a snag when the marketers learned that "some of the company's best customers are inner-city gang members." (The league quickly countered with a program in which socially conscious rapper KRS-1 spread the word, as NFLP's director of communications put it, "that NFL merchandise is meant to be a message of goodwill and not a uniform of war and gangs.")[37]

The "Nipplegate" incident at the 2004 Super Bowl was the NFL's ultimate PR disaster. League officials in 1993 had adopted a new strategy for halftime shows to attract a younger audience, staging Michael Jackson in rock-concert format instead of the usual kitschy pageantry. In 2001 the NFL turned over production of the halftime show to MTV (featuring Aerosmith and 'N Sync)[38] and was pleased enough with the results to go with MTV again in 2004. This time, when Janet Jackson's star-tipped breast inconveniently "fell" out of her black leather bustier at the conclusion of her performance, NFL executives faced outrage from the public, the media, and even the FCC and Congress. Amidst the furious denials of ill intent by everyone remotely involved, the joke was clearly on the NFL. The league that wanted to seem a bit more hip than in the old days of "Up With People" and Carol Channing got a considerably larger dose of Gen-X or Gen-Y attitude than it bargained for.

Some critics judged the NFL merely hypocritical for expressing shock at Ms. Jackson's performance while using scantily clad cheerleaders and other sexual teases to attract those coveted 18- to 34-year-old males. (Cheerleaders' tops, of course, are so constructed that nothing would fall out in an 8.0 earthquake.) Within the NFL, at least one club executive questioned the wisdom of catering to the tastes of "the people who *least care* about the game," only to see the results "blow up in our face."[39] In November 2004, with Janet Jackson still a recent memory, *Monday Night Football* ran a pregame promo for its new hit series *Desperate Housewives* with one of its stars, naked, seducing Eagles wide receiver Terrell Owens in the locker room. More outrage, more embarrassment, more apologies.[40]

After Jackson's "wardrobe malfunction," the league reasserted control over Super Bowl halftime, opting for retro-hip entertainment with Paul McCartney in 2005 and the Rolling Stones in 2006. (Having the Stones in 1968, or in 1970 instead of Carol Channing, would have been a bit edgier.) Just to be safe, the NFL also now demanded a five-second broadcast delay, to give the networks an opportunity to edit if necessary. (ABC censored two naughty words from Mick Jagger's performance.) The NFL had to back down from its decision to limit fans on the field for the Stones' performance to those under 45, to minimize the likelihood of injuries and lawsuits. Baby boomers protested and won.[41] When planning for spontaneous excitement is turned over to corporate lawyers, the results sometimes play out like a skit on *Saturday Night Live*. And in their efforts to prove that NFL football is no longer just your father's Sunday pastime, league officials sometimes look like your 60-year-old father in low-riding baggy cargo pants and black wing tips.

Whether or not the air of artificiality and contrivance around the Super Bowl is eroding its power, for now it remains the NFL's most successful act of branding each year, its premier advertisement not just for its style of football but for its place in American life. The Super Bowl is both a brilliant invention and a happy accident. To some degree, the NFL simply capitalized on having the country's most popular sport and a single championship contest instead of a seven-game series, as in professional basketball and baseball. But the kind of event that the Super Bowl became was neither inevitable nor accidental. Its ties to patriotism, piety, and pop music came from conscious decisions made in league offices, as did the extravagant party hosted by the commissioner each year to cultivate relations with reporters, media executives, and corporate CEOs and eventually the two full weeks for pregame hype. But alongside this careful nurturing, an entire folklore also grew up around the game beyond the NFL's control:[b] a belief that cities' water systems are at risk when all of the country's toilets flush simultaneously at halftime, that two-thirds of all avocados are consumed each year in Super Bowl guacamole, that the most popular rides at Disneyland have no lines on Super Sunday.[42]

None of this was true, but all of it enhanced the league's own efforts to stage an event with mythic dimensions. Equally untrue but not so beneficial was a claim that emerged in the buildup to the 1993 Super Bowl: for women, Super Sunday was a "day of dread" when domestic violence soared. That assertion was later discredited, but not before it, also, had entered Super Bowl folklore.[43]

The Dark Side Once More

This claim in 1993 seemed plausible because of recent and ongoing events in the news, including the harassment of Lisa Olson and the periodic arrests of players for mistreating wives and girlfriends. Sexual violence defined the NFL's dark side for the public in the 1990s as cocaine had in the 1980s, particularly in the aftermath of O. J. Simpson's arrest and trial, which did for domestic violence what Don Reese's confessions had done for drug abuse in 1982.[44] News from the dark side over the 1990s and into the new century posed a constant challenge to the brand-conscious NFL. League officials in 2004 could pressure ESPN to cancel *Playmakers* after one season, despite the show's popular and critical success, but they could have little effect on the news of actual NFL players doing in life what the actors in *Playmakers* did on film.[45]

Race and celebrity, rather than O. J. Simpson's previous NFL career, dominated the media's initial coverage of his arrest in the summer of 1994 for the murders of his former wife and her companion, but over the following months investigative reporters explored a possible connection between football and sexual violence. The *Washington Post* searched newspapers in more

---

b. The *New York Times'* Leonard Koppitt also discovered that the stock market for several years tended to rise after former AFL teams won the Super Bowl and to fall after victories by original NFL teams, though anyone who trusted this as an investment strategy should not have been allowed to have children.

than 40 cities, along with police and court documents, for a front-page story in November 1994 reporting that 56 current or former NFL players (along with 85 collegians) had been reported to the police for violence toward women since the beginning of 1989. The following July, a *Sports Illustrated* cover story titled "Sports' Dirty Secret" cited media coverage that "suggests that a majority of the nation's domestic abusers play college or professional sports." In December 1995 the *Los Angeles Times* ran a front-page story (which spilled over into a full ten pages in the sports section) reporting on 252 criminal incidents involving 345 athletes or team employees—all found in court documents and newspaper or wire-service reports in 1995 alone.[46]

Experts cited in these stories proposed various reasons for sexual violence by athletes, including alcohol abuse, childhood poverty, the culture of entitlement and male exclusiveness in sports like football, and the abuse of mood-altering drugs. I suspect that a significant portion of the public in the 1990s came to accept the idea that football and sexual violence were intimately related. Yet the data, for all the front-page and cover-story notoriety, did not support that conclusion. The 56 NFL players identified in the *Washington Post* over a nearly six-year period translated to roughly ten per year out of 1,600 players in the league. For context, William Nack and Lester Munson in *Sports Illustrated* reported estimates that between 8 and 12 million American women were assaulted by their partners each year. The surveys by the *Post* and the *Los Angeles Times* included acquittals and unresolved cases along with convictions. Various authorities pointed out that the figures cited in these reports might over- or underrepresent the actual problem, since high-profile athletes were both more easily targeted and more readily exonerated than other groups, but clearly the numbers alone were not as damning as they seemed.[47]

The *Washington Post*'s Bill Brubaker acknowledged that experts "agree there is no statistically reliable way to determine on a national basis whether football players are committing more violent crimes than other men." Mary-ann Hudson in the *Los Angeles Times* made the same acknowledgment about athletes in general. Yet in both cases, the disturbing details in the stories overwhelmed the cautionary note.[48] The one scholarly study cited in these reports was a survey of sexual assaults on ten university campuses in the early 1990s, whose data the principal author later admitted were inconclusive. This admission appeared in 1999, several years after the initial reporting and not in the *Washington Post* or *Los Angeles Times* but in the academic journal *Quest*.[49]

One of the coauthors of the original study also collaborated with a sportswriter from *Sports Illustrated* on a book in 1998 titled *Pros and Cons: The Criminals Who Play in the NFL*, the ultimate indictment of NFL players as sexual predators and thugs. Jeff Benedict and Don Yaeger contended that a full 21 percent of the players on NFL rosters in 1996–97 had been charged with a serious crime, basing their conclusion on the available criminal records of 509 NFL players (out of roughly 1,700), 109 of whom had accumulated a total of 264 arrests.[50]

The "crimes" ranged from disorderly conduct, drunk driving, and boating while intoxicated to rape and murder. The truly violent ones included 2 homicides, 7 rapes, 4 kidnappings, 45 cases of domestic violence, and 42 aggravated assaults. Again, these numbers did not differentiate among convictions, acquittals, and dropped or pending cases. After a trained statistician subsequently worked with Benedict to reexamine the data, they reported that NFL players were arrested half as often as the general population (20-year-old males were the control group), and that this was true for both black and white players.[51] (With blacks constituting a two-thirds majority of the league's players, the majority of those arrested were also black, undoubtedly feeding stereotypical ideas about black male criminality.)[c] As happened with the earlier study of sexual assaults on college campuses, *Pros and Cons* was widely reviewed in the popular press and cited in newspaper reports on athletes' sexual violence. The correction appeared a year later, but in the academic journal published by the American Statistical Association. Does anyone wonder which had the wider impact?

Faulty or misleading statistics do not make football irrelevant to the sordid events described in *Pros and Cons*, but how the sport is related to such crimes is simply not obvious. The seamy details of the sexual violence recounted at length in the book, while distasteful to read, in some cases usefully exposed the ambiguity of acts that the daily press tended to report simply as brutal assaults. Celebrity status, which can begin in college (or before college) and continue into the NFL, certainly instills in some players a warped sense of entitlement, including entitlement to women. But celebrities, whether athletes or rock stars, also attract "groupies," and whether the player is predator or prey in those encounters is not always clear. The most disturbing stories in

---

c. The authors of *Pros and Cons* openly disavowed the significance of race, calling attention instead to the violent, dysfunctional backgrounds of the criminal players. The arrest of a high-profile white player such as Green Bay's Mark Chmura (indicted in 2000 for raping his family's babysitter, then acquitted under circumstances that left unanswered questions) could complicate lazy racial judgments, but likely without dispelling them.

Pros and Cons involved women apparently seduced by their own fantasies into entanglements with NFL players, only to find themselves helpless to stop the men from going too far. The violent nature of football was not the problem here, but a celebrity culture that distorted personal and sexual relations on both sides.

Not just football but sport in general has become, in the words of a reporter for *Sports Illustrated*, "the stage where all the great moral issues have to be played out."[52] The media use events such as Don Reese's confessions, the Lisa Olson incident, and the O. J. Simpson case to construct morality plays on issues of concern well beyond the world of sport. (Another rash of incidents over a seven-month period in 1999–2000, with Rae Carruthers and Ray Lewis indicted for murder and Mark Chmura for sexually assaulting his 17-year-old babysitter at a prom party, repeated the process.) *Sports Illustrated*'s own cover stories "Sport's Dirty Secret" and "Paternity Ward" (May 1998, on deadbeat fathers) conspicuously served this purpose (as did the more recent national reporting of the Duke lacrosse rape case in 2006).[53] While these media-made morality plays usefully draw the public's attention to serious social and economic issues, at the same time they easily distort the truth about the athletes and sport that provide the story. NFL officials can offer countless denials and objections, but these morality plays take on a life of their own.

The NFL, in fact, responded more forcefully than other professional sports organizations to domestic and sexual violence. In the summer of 1994 (the "summer of O. J."), the NFL began sending counselors to training camps to talk about domestic violence. (Topics for its seminars to prepare rookies for life in the NFL included date rape and the dangers of unprotected sex, but also warnings about women with schemes for getting impregnated so that they can sue for child support.)[54] In 1997, the NFL instituted a policy on violent crime that gave Commissioner Tagliabue absolute power to administer punishment, from fines to suspensions, for any conviction, no-contest plea, or other legal finding of guilt. The league reported that the number of players arrested for violent crimes declined from 38 in 1997 to 26 in 1999. In 2000 it broadened the policy to include nonviolent crimes as well. For an NFL concerned about its image, the numbers of arrests were both small and too large, since each one was highly publicized, at least locally. To his credit, Tagliabue declared criminal acts by NFL players to be a "substantial" issue "of player conduct," not an "image" problem. But they also mattered to the NFL for what they did to its image, its brand.[55]

Reporting on domestic violence included athletes in many sports, but football players, trained to be violent, seemed particularly dangerous to women. Yet in its 1995 survey, the *Los Angeles Times* found the NFL no more implicated in violent crimes than Major League Baseball, and less so than the National Basketball Association.[56] All of the major professional sports foster competition and aggressiveness—but so do business, law, and politics. Pro athletes also exist in the same culture of wealth and celebrity with movie and TV stars, pop musicians, and even some sports broadcasters. Nonetheless, the NFL could do nothing to prevent the emergence in the 1990s of something close to a consensus, at least in the therapeutic community and among sport sociologists who write about gender issues, that football in its very nature was antifemale, an idea captured by the title of Mariah Burton Nelson's much-cited 1994 book, *The Stronger Women Get, the More Men Love Football.*[57]

I had the strange experience of seeing my own encounters with football violence cited in a 1997 book on male depression as a case study of the psychological crippling of young football players. In a football memoir I had written in 1982, I described playing as a walk-on on the scout team at Notre Dame, desperate to prove myself by making my varsity teammates ache at night from the pounding I gave them in practice. I described how I could not truly *know* my teammates while taking out my frustration on them. Once they became real people to me, I could no longer regard them simply as objects for my self-assertion. At that point, football became more psychologically complicated for me.

I thought I had described the internal dynamics of the football experience, how one typical player discovered the uses and limits of aggression within the boundary of the rules and the practice field. Instead, the author who quoted me saw a young athlete who learned "to love publicly dominating others" at the expense of "rich, nourishing forms of interpersonal intimacy." I was likely "a confused, lonely boy who felt at his best in those rare moments of approved violence played out before an adoring crowd." And a few pages later: "It is a short step from Michael Oriard's thirst for public domination as a 'salve' for his adolescent wounds to the dynamics of battering or other forms of dominance."[58]

Whoa! To see my own experience transformed into a cautionary tale about dysfunctional males, and myself cast as a football-damaged soul likely to become a batterer and tyrant, would have been infuriating had it not been ludicrous. It also brought home to me how easily football can be pathologized on the basis of large assumptions and little understanding. Football is violent, and some violent males do gravitate to football. Other males are not prone to violence but act violently on the football field, as required, perhaps with satisfaction or even pleasure, then return to their normal lives after the game.

Acknowledging that pleasure without pathologizing it can be a challenge. It does not "make sense." Nor does it conform to prevailing views of what humans *ought* to enjoy. Americans who do not like baseball tend to find it boring. Americans who do not like football tend to find it personally and socially destructive.

NFL football has been transformed since my playing days by a broader celebrity culture. Sudden wealth and celebrity can indeed be a toxic mix, yet most players manage to maintain their immune systems. As one who has shared the general dismay at the reports of athletes' misbehavior over the years, I have always found myself parting from the critics who blamed football itself. Football is sometimes brutal but not inherently brutalizing; it (mostly) excludes females but is not inherently antifemale; it hurts people but does not make them hurt others off the field. NFL football is believed to be inimical to marriage, yet a survey of 1,425 retired players conducted by researchers at Ball State University and published in *Newsday* in 1997 found that 14 percent of them divorced during their careers or in the first year afterward, compared to 13.5 percent for all males aged 24–29 in the 1990 census.[59] After surveying or interviewing 75 other NFL wives, one coach's spouse concluded that there is no typical pro football experience among women and families, and that she finally did not know whether players and coaches are more or less faithful and violent than other males.[60]

The occasional story in the press about an NFL player who misses a game to be with his wife in childbirth, or the one about kamikaze linebacker Chris Spielman's retiring altogether to nurse his wife through cancer, reminds the public that football players can be ordinary husbands and fathers, too.[61] Much more often, however, the media-made morality play has no such uplifting message. And as the NFL's criminality index rises and falls with events in the news, NFL officials can do little more than watch the story run its course.

But What's the Product?

Noting the limits on the NFL's control of its brand only begs the more intriguing question, the one that gets to the heart of NFL football's place in American life in the past, present, and foreseeable future. Midway through his 1997 account of Sara Levinson and NFL Properties, John Seabrook suddenly asks: "What, exactly, is Levinson selling, in selling football?" Weighing the various marketing strategies he sees Levinson implementing, Seabrook decides that "the game I knew and loved was not exactly the game she was planning to sell." He senses that gender is a key factor. Someone at NFL Properties discovered, well before Levinson arrived, that women made up about 40 percent of the NFL's fan base. Given the great to-do since the 1970s about "*Monday Night Football* widows," there must have been a real "Eureka!" moment for the researcher who first came up with that number. It has been repeatedly confirmed, but how to explain it has proven trickier. One of Levinson's colleagues at NFL Properties, a man working on its Women's Initiative, told Seabrook (sheepishly, it would seem), "Our research indicates that women like the tight pants on the players. They like, um, their butts." I suspect that there's a bit more to it.

Seabrook distinguished his wife's pleasure in "the ballet part of it: the perfect passes, the circus catches, the great breakaway runs," from his own experience playing football, that "the essence of the game is hitting, not ballet." His wife "thinks that tackling should be banned from the sport." He believes that "football is about hard work, pain, and losing," and that this "most immutable aspect of football" is the hardest to sell. "Football," Seabrook asserts, "is the only common language we have in which to talk about the pitiless, hit-or-be-hit side of America."[62]

Seabrook's wife may be no more representative of female fans generally than the ones who supposedly tune in for the cute butts in tight pants.[d] *Washington Post* columnist Sally Jenkins observed before the 2005 Super Bowl that, for some women, watching football might be a subversive act, while for others it might simply be "a gratifying experience," perhaps on the same terms as for men. Arguably the NFL's number-one female fan in 2007 is Condoleezza Rice, U.S. secretary of state under President George W. Bush. Rice grew up black and female in segregated Alabama in a family of well-educated high achievers. She learned to do many things, besides love football, to break down barriers. There is nothing typical about Condoleeza Rice, but there is also no reason to assume that her passion for and knowledge of the game are unique, a renunciation of her sex.[63] The quiet reemergence of women's professional football in recent years is worth noting here,[e] as well as

---

d. In a segment of the Super Bowl pregame show in 2000, the women from the morning talk show hosted by Barbara Walters, *The View*, offered their opinions on that 40 percent of the Super Bowl's viewers who are female. "It's all about the butts," Meredith Viera insisted, as if to validate what the NFLP spokesman told John Seabrook. Two of her cohosts, however, were more serious fans (while Walters declared herself simply baffled by football's appeal). The segment ended with the announcement that viewers could log onto ABC.com and answer the question, "Would women watch the Super Bowl if the players' pants were looser?," with the results to be reported during the next morning's program. I'm afraid I missed it.

e. In 2006 three professional women's leagues sponsored a total of 80 teams, but a the large number of girls who play on high school teams (nearly 1,300 in 2005).[64]

Right or wrong about women, Seabrook had it half right about football's fundamental nature. I would counter that the *tension* between the hit-or-be-hit side and the ballet side defines the essence of football: not the perfect pass or circus catch alone, nor just the obliterating tackle, but the catch made despite the tackle; or the disappearance of a 5' 11" running back into a mass of 300-pounders, then his burst out the other side into the open field and freedom. For many fans, no doubt, there is no greater charge than the head-on collision or the blindside massacre, but for most, I suspect, the eluding of annihilation is more satisfying. (It also matters a great deal whose team is doing the eluding and the annihilating.) Whether this is a guy thing, or whether women respond to the same tension for either the same or different reasons, no reliable survey or "brand audit" that I know of has determined.

Seabrook's larger point was that NFL football exists apart from its packaging. Those who respond to its fundamental nature will remain fans no matter what the packaging, while those who respond to the packaging may be briefly attracted but will not become real fans.

Football's power from its beginnings derived from the players appearing larger than life and meeting physical demands that seemed heroic in contrast to ordinary human experiences. It would be hard to overstate the strangeness of football's sudden emergence as a spectator sport in the late nineteenth century.[65] Not organized until the 1870s, and played initially only by students at elite northeastern universities at a time when just 1 or 2 percent of Americans even went to college, football by the 1890s drew crowds of 40,000 in New York and became a local sensation everywhere in the country. This was the era of "yellow journalism," and the popular press described football and football players in extravagant, overwrought metaphors and analogies (the sort of sportswriting that would lead to Grantland Rice's famous christening of the Notre Dame backfield in 1924 as the Four Horsemen of the Apocalypse). Football players in the 1890s were cast as gladiators performing in the Circus Maximus of Manhattan Field or the old Polo Grounds in New York, to thrill the "vestals and senators, patricians and plebs" in the stands (all of this from the front page of William Randolph Hearst's *New York Journal* in 1896).[66] The simplest explanation for the appeal of such bombast is that by restoring epic combat to an overcivilized age, football addressed a general

---

huge crowd was around 4,000, and unsuccessful efforts to find a national sponsor or a TV contract left the leagues' future uncertain.

"crisis of modernity" and accompanying "crisis in masculinity," as factories, corporations, and bureaucracies diminished individual human beings and eroded males' traditional sense of independence and meaningful labor. The now-familiar epigram would not appear for many decades, but its meaning was already true: modern sport was life with the volume turned up. And this was particularly true for football.[67]

Since those beginnings, changing conditions in the United States have always affected football's social and cultural role. Football resonated during the Depression in different ways than it had in the Roaring Twenties, or than it would during the Second World War, the postwar boom, or the turbulent 1960s.[68] In the 1950s, as pro football emerged as the king of American sports, its shrewdest observers saw it as an antidote to the "rat race" for success and the banality of everyday life, a tonic of excess, of physical and emotional self-expression, for people trapped in little boxes. By the 1990s and early 2000s, football seemed part of an entire culture of excess, evident also in popular music, blockbuster films, reality TV, even the verbal sparring of the political "chattering classes" during presidential elections and national crises —all of it seemingly premised on a belief that, with the volume of everyday life already so loud, it was necessary to raise the decibel level several notches just to be heard. Here's the point: while the NFL developed strategies for competing in an amped-up and crowded entertainment marketplace, football's enduring power derived from its authenticity. Games were unscripted. Both the physical wonders and the brutal injuries were real, not acted, without the benefit of focus groups, market testing, or computer-generated imagery. Football players really were as big, fast, strong, and talented—and in constant physical danger—as they seemed.

If sport is life with the volume turned up, football in the 1990s became sport with 500 watts per channel and a massive subwoofer. Remember the XFL, the Extreme Football League that existed briefly in 2001? As the brainchild of Vince McMahan, CEO of the World Wrestling Federation (before it became World Wrestling Entertainment), the XFL must have looked good on paper: give football the WWF treatment—more violence, more trash-talking, more sexual titillation on the sidelines—to attract the WWF's millions of rabid 18- to 25-year-old male fans. A predictable disaster followed. The WWF itself parodied a sport whose authentic form had no following beyond the parents and friends of high school and college wrestlers. The XFL offered parody, too, but of the most popular sport in the United States, which already pushed against the boundaries of the permissible and the possible in terms of the body's physical limits, of acceptable violence, of spectacular display, of media saturation, even of sexual titillation. Like the folks at NFL Properties, Mc-Mahan viewed football as a product. Unlike the NFL, all he had for sale was tastelessly gaudy packaging.[f]

The XFL failed because the NFL delivers the same charge more powerfully, at a time when a lot of people seem to want or need it. Like John Seabrook, I believe that gender is a key factor here. The Iron John Super Bowl of 1992 came at the end of a year of crisis but also near the beginning of a period in which a desire for larger-than-life football heroes has seemingly again become acute. *Esquire* magazine in May 1994 announced the arrival of the "post-sensitive man" and, in October 1996, "the second coming of the alpha male." Announcements in popular magazines of shifts in the zeitgeist are always suspect, but the 1990s indeed saw a multipronged reassessment of men's roles and identities. "Angry white males" became a political force in the 1994 congressional elections and made talk radio (including sports talk radio) a phenomenon. Gatherings of Promise Keepers filled football stadiums in the mid-1990s, and Louis Farrakhan's Million Man March drew hundreds of thousands of African American men to the National Mall in Washington, D.C., in October 1995. On an entirely different front, in September 1996 *Newsweek* ran a cover story on synthetic testosterone as the new antiaging, performance-enhancing wonder drug for midlife males. Viagra, the ultimate male performance drug, hit the market in 1998 to redefine the normal aging process as dysfunction.[g] (Levitra and Cialis followed Viagra, all

f. I managed to miss the XFL's entire inaugural/final season, but I did tape the opening game and finally got around to watching it for writing this chapter. The production was even sillier than I expected. It would have been enjoyable as a *Saturday Night Live* spoof, were it not so amateurish. It looked like a couple of B-squads, televised by NBC interns and cheered on by apprentice showgirls, all of them struggling to remember their lines and cues. With everyone in the stadium miked up, and Jesse Ventura bellowing in the broadcast booth, it succeeded only in being louder than an NFL game.

g. Recognizing Viagra and its clones as performance drugs also casts athletes' use of anabolic steroids in a clearer light. During the furor over steroids in baseball over the winter of 2004–2005, some commentators pointed out that steroids in sports were not unlike the Ritalin taken by high school seniors to score higher on their SATs, or the beta blockers taken by classical musicians to banish stage fright—fuel for a "performance culture" that extended well beyond the world of sport. As the title of a book by John Hoberman put it, we now live in a world of "testosterone dreams," in which aging is a disease and doping oneself to improve professional productivity, sexual performance, and general sense of well-being is the sensible person's choice. As in so many other matters, sport simply casts a bright light on the more general condition. And today's athletes using steroids are already contemplating tomorrow's genetic engineering. Hoberman foresees a crisis in our near future over what it means to be "normal" and human.

three of them marketed through ties to NFL football.) The title of another cover story on testosterone in *Time* in April 2000 asked, "Are You Man Enough?" What it meant to be a man, and how to be one, was becoming a national preoccupation, fueled by anxiety, not certainty.[69]

Livin' Large

This is the context for considering a remarkable series of profiles in *Esquire*, *Sports Illustrated*, and other magazines in the late 1990s and early 2000s that celebrated NFL players such as Brett Favre, Bill Romanowski, Warren Sapp, Tony Siragusa, and Jeremy Shockey for "livin' large."[70] From Pudge Heffelfinger in the 1890s to Bingo Bingaman, William "The Refrigerator" Perry, and the herds of 300-pounders in recent years, there have always been literal football giants who embodied the fantasy of livin' large. Entire lines—Buffalo's "Electric Company" (for "plugging in" The Juice, O. J. Simpson) and Washington's "Hogs" on offense, and the Los Angeles Rams' "Fearsome Foursome," Minnesota's "Purple People Eaters," and Pittsburgh's "Steel Curtain" on defense—have collectively done the same. But these magazine profiles pushed that image to new extremes. All of their authors employed an overstuffed Tom-Wolfe-on-steroids prose style to match their subjects, as if they attended the same workshop on How to Write About Larger-than-Life Football Players. Lesson one: use compound adjectives. Tony "The Goose" Siragusa, the Baltimore Ravens' 340-pound "mammoth run-stuffing, face-stuffing defensive tackle," as Michael Silver described him in *Sports Illustrated*, became the poster boy for livin' large in 2001 after Baltimore won the Super Bowl. Silver also called Siragusa "the Ravens' massive, gap-plugging, run-stopping, life-loving defensive tackle," as well as "wide-bodied, wisecracking, potbellied, potty-mouthed, bighearted, large-living" for good measure. Siragusa anecdotes sounded like tales of Paul Bunyan or John L. Sullivan. He drank up his $1,000 signing bonus at Ross Brothers' Tavern on the day he received it. He refused to learn his college fight song because, as he yelled at his coach, "If I wanted to learn a school song, I would've gone to Notre Dame or Penn State. I want to kill people on the football field. That's why I came to Pitt."[71] If American males felt constricted by new social norms, football players like Siragusa showed what was possible with an oversized body and an attitude to match.

The Goose and his kind "lived large" both on and off the field. The writers celebrated their enormous appetites for beer, food, jokes, and horseplay (sometimes for women, but this was a more complicated matter), as well as the joyful violence with which they played football. They always *played* football, and life, too. As Siragusa's 5'1", 105-pound wife Kathy told Silver, "His objective in life is to enjoy every moment without regrets." The formula for these magazine profiles also required hardships overcome (Siragusa blew out two knees, saw his father die from a heart attack at 48, and had to win respect in the NFL as a slow-footed run-stuffer instead of a lightning-quick pass-rusher). And there had to be a glimpse of a tender side (in Siragusa's case, a brief moment relaxing with Kathy and their two daughters). But Siragusa was a role model only for a life of carefree, gargantuan excess. The Siragusas and Warren Sapps and Jeremy Shockeys ("a nightclubbing, skirt-chasing, politically incorrect Okie")[72] embodied a longing to feel unfettered physically, emotionally, and psychologically—a loud complaint against society's demand to be nice and do good.

The All-Madden Teams selected in the 1990s by the popular sportscaster to honor the NFL's toughest players, the ones most willing to wallow in blood, sweat, and dirt, evoked this same spirit. Icons of livin' large also appeared in Super Bowl pregame shows, not surprisingly led by Fox, the network known for excess. Fox's presentation of an All-Time All-Madden Super Bowl Team before the 1997 contest wallowed in rugged-guy stuff and was accompanied by a segment in which a half-dozen former Oakland Raiders sat around a poker table, smoking cigars and telling wild tales of the Silver and Black. Over the next several years, NBC and CBS copied Fox, and Fox repeated itself, with features on Vince Lombardi's Packers, the 1985 Chicago Bears, and more All-Madden Teams. The Raiders, Bears, and old-time Packers represented something very different from, say, the glamour of the San Diego Chargers or San Francisco 49ers.

Livin' large sometimes meant out of control or against the law, crippled by injuries or pumped up on steroids. Although the media keep the two sides of pro football entirely separate, the NFL's dark side is an inverted mirror of its larger-than-life grandeur. A polarized public responds to one side or the other, and fans continue to compartmentalize their feelings, but the two sides are inextricably linked. Korey Stringer, the gentle giant of one *Esquire* profile, turned out to be literally too large for life when he died from heatstroke during training camp in 2001. (Massive body weight also contributed to the sudden death of 49ers offensive lineman Thomas Herrion in 2005). Steroids produced mammoth bodies but also "'roid rage" (and Lyle Alzado blamed them for his brain cancer, a dubious assertion that gained wide currency while he was dying). The titles alone of Lawrence Taylor's two autobiographies, *LT: Living on the Edge* (1987) and *LT: Over the Edge* (2003), described a too-familiar NFL morality play. Pro football resides at the limits of the desired and permissible, and the fact that some individuals topple over to the far side should surprise no one. Football players who act out their fellow citizens' collective fantasies are themselves only human, which is to say, sometimes overwhelmed by their roles. That so many keep their bearings should be the surprise.[73]

Guy Culture

The magazine and TV profiles of players livin' large belonged to what some commentators at the beginning of the twenty-first century were calling a new "Guy Culture." The political columnist David Brooks in early 2003 wondered what to make of "the return of the pig" in the retrosexism of the so-called lad magazines *FHM* and *Maxim*, cable programming such as Comedy Central's *The Man Show* (with its "Household Hints of Adult Film Stars" and bikini-clad women bouncing on a trampoline), and Hooters as just another restaurant chain. He might also have mentioned hit movies such as *American Pie* and *There's Something about Mary*, and any number of programs on Fox Network stations (including the testosterone-drenched *Best Damned Sports Show, Period*). Blatant sexism and vulgarity seemed running amok, yet tongue-in-cheek playfulness and wink-wink self-awareness signaled irony or parody, a chance to be a pig and mock piggishness at the same time. Brooks wondered if, instead of marking the end of civilization as we know it, this Guy Culture simply marked a stage in men's accommodation to a new gender order. Another writer called Guy Culture "an understandable reaction to a vast industry of Oprah-fied women's media, based (as guys perceive it) on gross sentimentalism, political correctness, and the dearth of a sense of humor." Perhaps it revealed a new generation of nonsexist males who had been thoroughly Oprah-fied but were declaring their "independence on certain patches of social territory."[74]

Like football. The occasion for the latter ruminations was the debut of the Extreme Football League in 2001 with its intention "to shrug off the 'proper' constraints of the NFL and encourage its audience to embrace the violence and sex that football engenders." The XFL, of course, proved to be unnecessary as well as uninspired, but it pointed to a role that the NFL already played. Mariah Burton Nelson's title, *The Stronger Women Get, the More Men Love Football*, might be apt in a way not intended: suggesting not that loving football is pathological but that it might help men compensate for a loss of male prerogative and power in social realms where there is more at stake. (If so, Nelson ought to love football, too.)

NFL football met Guy Culture head on in the lad magazines, those imports from England adapted to the American scene, with a focus on sports, alcohol, gadgets, and babes in lingerie. *Maxim* was launched in the United States in April 1997 and offered a fairly ordinary NFL preview that September. After a similar but briefer one ("for short attention spans") in September 1998, the September 1999 issue departed from the formula with an "NFL hit man's" confession, "I get paid to break legs." *FHM* (For Him Magazine) then obliterated the genre in September 2001 with its "Big Football Blowout! 20 Pages Dedicated to the Only Sport Worth Watching." Instead of routine predictions for the upcoming season, the "Blowout" began with a Q&A session with the ubiquitous Tony Siragusa, revealing the inside dope on such matters as the time he nearly crapped his pants during a game. A pictorial and interview with Rebecca Grant, the hot babe from Fox Sports' *NFL Under the Helmet*, revealed which NFL players hit on her when she interviewed them. *FHM* did not rank NFL teams but their fans: for Dedication, Intimidation, and Rowdiness. A survey of women's responses to football-related questions revealed that 33 percent claimed to have performed oral sex on a guy while watching a game. "A fan's guide to who's hurt and who's a puss" separated players who vomited on the field under stress or were sidelined by turf toe from those who played despite a lacerated kidney, mangled fingers, or a severed biceps.[75] *FHM* offered a similar concoction each subsequent September, and *Maxim* adopted the new style with its 2002 preview.

NFL officials must not know whether to cheer or cry. NFL football, *FHM* and *Maxim* seem to say, is an essential part of a young man's life. But football itself seems considerably less important than the gargantuan excess that it generates, and than the football babes on the sidelines and in TV studios (Rebecca Grant, Lisa Dergan, Lisa Guerrero, Leeann Tweeden, Jillian Barberie, and Jill Arrington have all appeared, mostly undressed, in these magazines, and NFL cheerleaders regularly, too). *FHM* and *Maxim* must pose a fascinating conundrum for the folks at the NFL, as they see their brand embraced by the most desirable demographic in the media universe but on terms that must produce more than a little uneasiness. We have arrived again, by a different route, at the hip irony so central to our current popular culture. Not just *FHM* and *Maxim*, along with *SportsCenter* and Fox Sports, but also *ESPN The Magazine* and even *Sports Illustrated* have seemingly embraced the credo, "Be hip or die." In response to ESPN's bid to grab the younger part of their readership with a bit of lad-magazine hip style, the editors at once-venerable *Sports Illustrated* had to adopt the new ironic mode, too, stuffing the beginning of the magazine with short takes on players' tattoos, pregame rituals, most embarrassing moments, and the like.

Hip irony even invaded the most sacred of all NFL football events, the Super Bowl, or at least the Super Bowl pregame show. Along with the usual mix of analysis and features, ABC's program in 2003 included comedian Jimmy Kimmel's interview with Raider linebacker Bill Romanowski, who had left Denver for Oakland as a free agent that season. In perfect deadpan, Romanowski earnestly explained that he did it for the money, and he described the anguish of looking for a mansion to buy in a new city after being uprooted. Most painful of all was finding his goldfish Splashy dead in its bowl one day, apparently from homesickness. Would winning the Super Bowl ease his pain, Kimmel asked, equally deadpan. Romanowski responded with quiet stoicism: "In the back of my mind, I know that bowl will never be full." The piece mocked the human-interest features included in every Super Bowl pregame show, including ABC's own (when the studio hosts returned to the air, they did not seem amused). If young fans now wanted hip irony, the media would deliver it, and the NFL would reap at least short-term benefits. But Paul Tagliabue, Roger Goodell, and their colleagues at NFL headquarters must have had some misgivings, knowing that long-term football passions are not usually built on irony.

The Power and the Glory and the Pain

The question "What's the product?" can have no simple answer, but whatever football *is*, what it means to those who care most passionately about it—and those meanings change with the times—cannot be artificially created. John Seabrook made this point by telling a story. After describing Sara Levinson's revolution at NFL Properties, Seabrook concluded with an account of attending the 1997 Hall of Fame induction ceremony in Canton, Ohio, where the "visceral side of the game—the old, premarketing world of football—is on display each year." Seabrook arrived in Canton as "a New York smart-aleck in Kitschville," only to lose his "force fields of irony" as soon as he found himself in the presence of his boyhood heroes, the Hall of Famers who returned each year to welcome the new class. One of the 1997 inductees, Mike Webster, was a throwback to that earlier era. Webster played center for the Pittsburgh Steelers from 1974 through 1990, in short sleeves even in freezing weather, in pain and despite injuries (and while others remained on strike in 1987, Seabrook could have added). Webster's post-football life had then become the grimmest of cautionary tales: he lost his money, his house, his wife; he lived for days at a time in his car; he suffered from convulsions and spasms, and from a varicose vein condition in his legs that caused even tiny cuts to "squirt blood everywhere." While still married, Webster and his wife "would sometimes cover his veins with Super Glue, to prevent them from popping in the living room."

To present him at the induction ceremony, Webster chose his old teammate, Terry Bradshaw, the Hall of Fame quarterback who had become, in Seabrook's words, "the football buffoon on Fox's N.F.L. broadcasts." Bradshaw told the Canton crowd raucous tales of Webster "ripping eye-watering farts as Bradshaw squatted over him," then concluded by hollering to his old center, "Jes' one mo' time!" Webster came to center stage, removed his jacket, and squatted over the ball in his old stance, as Bradshaw took his position behind him.

Following this moment of Fox-studio high jinks, the battered old Steeler himself took the podium and offered his own "simple, sincere" remarks to the crowd. As Webster talked, friends and admirers erupted repeatedly into cries of "Miiike!," sounding like the painted warriors saluting their leader in the recent film *Braveheart*. Horribly damaged, as everyone knew, but uncomplaining and quietly dignified, Webster spoke almost mystically of "finishing the game," while "fans up on the hill bellowed savagely 'We love you, Mike! We're with you, Mike!'" Seabrook confessed: "I found myself joining in the din: 'Miiike!'"

The point of the story was unspoken but clear: anyone not horrified yet awed by the stoicism of the used-up warrior felt no deep connection to football. Webster's was not a pretty story, and his kind of suicidal valor has little practical value in our new-millennial world. But Mike Webster embodied in exaggerated form something central to football, a link to some biological imperative or to some imagined larger-than-life barbarian past. That link is the ultimate "intangible," and it is mostly a fiction, but it is the fiction on which football first seized the American imagination in the 1890s and then became the number-one spectator sport in the United States by the 1960s.

Both in the damage to his body and in the stoicism with which he endured it, Webster was exceptional yet also typical. A 1990 study conducted for the NFLPA by researchers at Ball State University and another at Harvard University in 1997, as well as a survey of 1,425 former players by *Newsday* in 1997 and investigative reports by the *Los Angeles Times* in 2000 and the *Arizona Republic* in 2003, confirmed and amplified the findings from the 1980s cited in Chapter 3. Sixty-five percent of the players in the Ball State study had suffered a "major injury" during their careers. Sixty-three percent of respondents to the *Newsday* survey reported permanent injuries. As players have grown bigger, stronger, and faster, their collisions (Force = Mass $\times$ Velocity) have become increasingly violent. The current generation of oversized players is the next generation of more extreme cripples.[76]

Putting flesh on the statistics, a *Sports Illustrated* cover story in 2001, "The Wrecking Yard," examined the medical condition of seven retired players, including everyone's favorite icon of the old NFL, Johnny Unitas, along with Hall of Fame running back Earl Campbell, Joe Jacoby (one of the original "Hogs"), and Curt Marsh, a former offensive lineman for the Los Angeles Raiders. The greatest passer of his era now had no control over his right hand. (To play golf, he wrapped it around the club with his good hand and secured it with Velcro.) Campbell could barely walk; Jacoby could not bend over. Back surgeries and hip replacements were the norm. The most shocking photograph showed Curt Marsh's stump, where his right foot had been amputated as the result of misdiagnosis and improper treatment while playing for the Raiders. Campbell was 46 years old when the article appeared (another of the seven, Chris Washington, was just 39). All seven players faced "a lifetime of disability and pain."[77]

Football fans are not sadists, but a sport in which players did not risk such consequences would not have football's primal appeal. Nor are players masochists, yet football and pain have an intimate relationship that every player comes to know too well. On the one hand, football's culture of toughness is indeed dangerous, as it drives players to risk crippling injuries to earn the respect of coaches, teammates, and themselves. In addition, pain is intimately related to drugs, the fistfuls of Vicodins and other potentially addictive pain relievers that players pop as casually as vitamins just to get through the season.[78] But the experience of pain is also deeply personal, a private testing of the will and probing of the body's limits. It might not "make sense," but it is also not simply pathological.

In the face of what sometimes seems an American culture of victimhood, the NFL's damaged former players share a remarkable unwillingness to blame others for what happened to them. The one great exception arises when they feel betrayed by their clubs. Many are bitter about the official neglect of their medical needs in retirement. (At his induction into the Hall of Fame in 2006, among fellow inductees who now limped through life on artificial knees and hips, ex-Giants linebacker Harry Carson implored the NFL and NFLPA "to look after the product you have up on this stage.")[79] But the NFL's cripples also tend to refuse regret. Among the seven in *Sports Illustrated*'s "wrecking yard," only Campbell admitted that he might not have played in the NFL had he known how much he would hurt afterward. Fully 90 percent in the 1997 *Newsday* survey said that, if given the opportunity, they would play football again. One player described the "goose bumps and the rush of adrenaline when those fans are roaring." Another described a football game as "three hours of complete euphoria." The most addictive drug in the NFL is NFL football itself.[80]

Football makes little sense according to the rules we learn to live by in our modern world. That is why it appeals so powerfully, not just to working stiffs wearing dog masks and barking in the end zone seats in Cleveland, but also to TV executives and CEOs in luxury suites. (The Dallas Cowboys' new stadium will have an interesting feature: two sideline clubs available only to premium-seating customers, through which the opposing players will walk between their locker rooms and the field. For a very large sum of money, wealthy Cowboy fans can buy an exclusive up-close experience of NFL players in all of their uniformed and sweaty glory.[81]) Football ultimately is what it is and what its fans make of it, no matter what efforts go into the packaging. It is deeply ironic that the NFL has become a financial colossus but can no longer afford to trust football's own power. The league needs those 80 or 90 million casual fans, on top of its passionate 40 million, to feed the money machine it has created. Yet without that inherent power all the marketing in the world would be pointless.

To actually play football in the NFL demystifies it, but players are not immune to its larger-than-life mystique. That mystique is probably what drew them to the game in the first place and, apart from huge salaries, what sustains them through the miseries of long seasons. But some pay an exorbitantly high price. Five years after Canton, Mike Webster was dead, at age 50.

FOOTBALL
IN BLACK
AND WHITE

Whatever the product the NFL was selling in the 1990s and early 2000s, it came predominately in shades of black. The commercialization and racialization of NFL football have proceeded hand in hand since the 1960s, as pro football's thrills have been disproportionately provided by African American players. The number of black players in the NFL increased from 12 percent in 1959 to 28 percent in 1968, 42 percent in 1975, and 49 percent in 1982, the last season that African Americans constituted a minority in the NFL. The black majority grew to 54 percent in 1985, 61 percent in 1990, and 68 percent in 1992, where it has more or less stabilized (fluctuating between 65 and 69 percent).[1]

The Miami Dolphins' Larry Csonka and Jim Kiick in the early 1970s made up the NFL's last white glamour backfield, known for power and grit, not grace and speed (Mercury Morris provided the speed and received less credit). Since then, the runners providing most of the highlights on *SportsCenter* have been Walter Payton, Tony Dorsett, Earl Campbell, Eric Dickerson, Marcus Allen, Barry Sanders, Emmitt Smith, Edgerrin James, LaDainian Tomlinson . . . the list could go on. White quarterbacks have continued to throw most of the long, arcing touchdown passes loved by NFL Films and fans alike, but the players on the receiving end have also been mostly black. For every Steve Largent, the ultimate white "possession receiver," there have been several Harold Carmichaels, Art Monks, Jerry Rices, Michael Irvins, and Terrell Owenses. Players such as Bruce Smith, Lawrence Taylor, and Ronnie Lott even redefined the positions for the guys who make the crushing hits.

From such evidence it would seem obvious that the National Football League, along with the National Basketball Association, represents the absolute triumph of merit over racial prejudice. The reality, of course, is more complicated, not just because the men with the headsets on the sidelines remain disproportionately white and those in the owners' suites exclusively so, but also because race itself is so burdened with loaded significance in the United States. NFL football since the 1960s has provided a stage on which a sort of racial theater has been performed. As the nation disavowed the racism in its past and officially embraced color-blind equality, racism has persisted without official sanction, and in our professed color blindness we continue to see color but are reluctant to talk about it publicly. In NFL football, as in American society at large, race still matters, but exactly how is less clear than in the days of segregated public facilities and Jim Crow laws.

Barriers

Pro football was marginally integrated from the NFL's beginning until 1933—with no more than five black players in any one season—when an unofficial "gentleman's agreement," apparently demanded by George Preston Marshall, owner of the Boston (soon Washington) Redskins, kept the league lily-white through 1945. In 1946 Paul Brown signed Bill Willis and Marion Motley for his Cleveland Browns in the new All-America Football Conference, while pressure from black groups and others in Los Angeles forced the Rams to sign Kenny Washington and Woody Strode. These four were the collective Jackie Robinson of professional football, still a minor sport whose integration received little public attention while Robinson was turning the "American Pastime" upside down.[2]

Over the late 1940s and 1950s, integration in pro football proceeded slowly and fitfully, with Marshall's Redskins holding out against increasing pressure (even from the Kennedy White House) until 1962. Black players in the 1950s and 1960s were disproportionately stars, since it was much easier to justify making room for a great running back than for a mediocre tackle. The increasing number of African Americans over the 1960s was to some extent led by the rival AFL,[a] and it now conspicuously included players from the all-black schools in the still-segregated South. In 1949 Tank Younger became the first athlete from a black college to play in the NFL. In 1970 NFL clubs drafted 135 players from black schools.[3] Grambling, the small agricul-

a. Besides making Grambling's Buck Buchanan the league's first draft pick in 1963, AFL clubs had pro football's first black starting middle linebacker (another Kansas City Chief, Willie Lanier, in 1968) and first two black starting quarterbacks (Denver's Marlin Briscoe in 1968 and Buffalo's James Harris in 1969).

tural college in Louisiana whose football team was coached by Eddie Robinson, became a phenomenon in the 1960s for sending more players into professional football than any school except Notre Dame.

Black players well into the 1960s faced the blatant racism that still scarred our national life—cheap shots and racial slurs on the field, taunts from the stands, quotas on their own teams, and discrimination at hotels and restaurants on the road and in housing at home. Until Jack Olsen's landmark five-part series in *Sports Illustrated* in 1968, "The Black Athlete—A Shameful Story," there was almost no reporting on these incidents. Olsen focused more on college sports, but in the final installment he offered a detailed portrait of the NFL's St. Louis Cardinals, torn apart by an aggressive "white supremacist cell" within the team that openly harassed black teammates. The Cardinals appeared to be the worst of the NFL's teams but at the same time representative of more general problems throughout the league.[4]

Black college athletes in significant numbers began speaking and even acting out around 1967, but pro athletes with salaries and careers at risk mostly kept quiet. Along with Bill Russell and Muhammad Ali in other sports, Jim Brown was an early exception, and his outspokenness was not welcome. Brown's comments on racism in his 1964 autobiography, *Off My Chest*, and his defense of the separatist, antiwhite Black Muslims, led *Time* magazine in 1965 to call him a candidate for "Most Controversial Athlete of the Year." Despite the fact that Brown was also, as *Time* put it, "without argument the greatest runner in professional football," this cover story was a rarity. The media of the day reported on Brown's football prowess without probing very deeply into his social and political views. Brown appeared regularly on the cover of magazines such as *Pro Football Illustrated* and *Pro Football Almanac*—with stories about the athlete, not the man—but the best football player of his generation appeared only once on the cover of *Sports Illustrated*, early in his career, to introduce a brief primer on the tricks of his fullback trade. (Now-forgotten white wide receiver Tommy McDonald appeared three times over the years when Brown played.) Sportswriters "never felt completely at ease" with Brown, as one of them admitted.[5]

The most significant act of racial protest in pro football in the 1960s took place in the upstart AFL, not in the established NFL where it would have had a greater national impact. As black players began arriving in New Orleans for the AFL's season-ending All-Star game in January 1965, they found that taxis would not pick them up and nightclubs on Bourbon Street would not admit them, in what seemed an orchestrated campaign. Whether they felt less constrained than peers in the NFL, or they simply seized an occasion when it arose, 21 black players voted to boycott the game, despite pleading from New Orleans officials anxious about the city's image as it sought its own NFL team. (Pete Rozelle's deal to win congressional approval of the NFL-AFL merger would give New Orleans a franchise in 1967 anyway.) Facing his own public relations dilemma, AFL commissioner Joe Foss moved the game to Houston, where it was played without incident.[6] Although the episode received little attention in the national press, it sent a clear signal to civic leaders. Through the combination of its economic clout and the collective influence of its black players, professional football became a force for antidiscrimination. (The NFL would not have to invoke this power again until 1991, when Phoenix lost a chance to host the Super Bowl after Arizona voters rejected the state holiday honoring Martin Luther King Jr.)

The boycott in New Orleans by AFL All-Stars marked the end of pro football's official accommodation with segregation, when black players were often housed separately from their white teammates on the road. More subtle and less public forms of discrimination did not disappear so easily. Black players with white wives or girlfriends received frosty stares on the streets. Stardom on the field did not translate into endorsements or post-football employment opportunities for black players as it did for whites. Most directly insulting were the apartments and houses suddenly not available when the owner actually met the dark-skinned potential renter with whom he had been speaking on the phone. At the same time, NFL salaries were increasing, with black running backs making more money than everyone except for white quarterbacks, creating a generation of first-class black football players who remained second-class American citizens.

That contradiction lessened over the following decades without altogether disappearing, as has been true more generally for successful African American professionals—business executives, doctors, lawyers, and university professors—whose anger and resentment has perplexed many whites in recent years. To reach the top of one's profession yet still be subject to casual racist slights—suspicious scrutiny in stores, stops by the police for "driving while black"—may be less "serious" but more personally insulting than the gross inequality that remains at the lower ends of the economic ladder. When recognized, NFL players are treated as celebrities; when not, they live in that same soul-bruising world. (Deion Sanders has described such incidents during his own career.) And for all their millions, black stars see in their mostly white head coaches and club executives reminders of the limits beyond which they cannot easily pass.[7]

Discrimination on the field and in the locker room also persisted less overtly beyond the end of segregation. In his series "The Black Athlete," Jack Olsen quoted a white player who described "the strange and subtle forms" that racial prejudice could take in the NFL:

> I can say in complete honesty that I can never remember a coach mentioning a guy's race or color. I can't cite a single case of a player who was cut because he was black. I can't remember a single Negro-white fistfight, except one or two that had nothing to do with race. But the prejudice is there. The league reeks of it. The way the teams are composed. The way the locker rooms are laid out. The way Negroes are criticized more than whites. The way they're not supposed to know how to play certain positions. The way the white players are allowed to boss them around and criticize them. . . . If I were a Negro I'd go nuts trying to fight it, because you can't fight it. Where do you start? It's like attacking a wall of mushroom soup.[8]

To fight it meant having a "bad attitude," a sure exit from the NFL (except for players as talented as Jim Brown).

Olsen also described the "rigid patternization of black athletes" in the NFL: no black centers, 3 of 32 starting guards, 3 of 45 starting linebackers, but three-fourths of the starting cornerbacks. Olsen explained this evidence of "quotas" in terms of the typical general manager's dilemma: to balance the need for star performers against the need for white star performers with whom white fans would identify. Sport sociologists in the 1970s would call this racial distribution "stacking," the most visible sign of apparent discrimination, because anyone could count the players and draw conclusions. As in baseball, where the athletes in the "central" positions of catcher, pitcher, shortstop, and second baseman remained overwhelmingly white, the absence of black quarterbacks, centers, and middle linebackers in the NFL led to a conclusion that coaches excluded blacks from football's "central" positions as well. These were the "thinking" and "leadership" positions, the ones requiring athletes to call the plays and the blocking schemes, responsibilities not to be trusted to "athletic" but less intelligent black players.[9]

I have always been skeptical about one part of this argument. To someone who played the position, center never seemed to me as "central" as quarterback or middle linebacker. When I joined the Chiefs in 1970, the center on their previous season's Super Bowl team had been E. J. Holub, a 225-pound linebacker shifted to center after too many knee surgeries had destroyed his mobility. Hank Stram kept E. J. on the field because of his great football heart, despite his failing body. At center, his liabilities would be minimized. There were no black centers in my era, but I always believed that it was because top athletes were not drawn to the least glamorous of all positions, while coaches did not want to waste a talented black player at a position where he was not needed.

Even after Miami's Dwight Stephenson emerged in the 1980s as the best center in the NFL, African Americans continued to be underrepresented at that position (and to a lesser degree at the other offensive line positions). In 1993, when 92 percent of running backs and 90 percent of wide receivers were black, 47 percent of offensive tackles, 32 percent of guards, and just 18 percent of centers were also black, and those figures have changed little since then.[10] Yes, centers must recognize the defenses and call the blocking schemes, but this is not quite the same as doing differential equations in your head. However it happened that most centers and a majority of offensive linemen have remained white, whether through self-selection, coaches wanting their best athletes elsewhere, or whatever, I am not convinced that racial prejudice, either conscious or unconscious, has been a key factor.

The exclusion of blacks from middle linebacker was real for a time, however, and it made more (racist) sense. The middle linebacker was the captain and signal caller of the defense, and the 4–3 alignment devised by Tom Landry as a New York Giants assistant coach in the 1950s and adopted throughout the NFL in the 1960s made him the star. (The defensive tackles tied up the guards and center, keeping the middle linebacker free to track down the ballcarrier.) My teammate Willie Lanier was the NFL's first black middle linebacker (and one of its best ever), and he was followed in the early 1980s by the Chicago Bears' Mike Singletary, at a time when the position made glamorous (and "central") by Sam Huff, Joe Schmidt, Ray Nitschke, and Dick Butkus was essentially disappearing. In the 1980s, Lawrence Taylor reinvented the position of outside linebacker as the primary destructive force in the new 3–4 defenses. Linebacker, whether inside or outside, became just another position increasingly filled by African Americans. Not quite half of all linebackers in 1983 were black; by 1993, nearly three-quarters were black.[11] What was once at stake with middle linebackers was no longer an issue.

Quarterback was and remains the one unambiguously central position, and it inevitably has had the most highly charged racial history. The first black quarterback in the NFL, Willie Thrower, played briefly for Chicago in 1953. The second black quarterback, Marlin Briscoe, did not take the field until 1968, only to be shifted soon to wide receiver, the fate of many black quarterbacks entering the NFL well into the 1980s. Some of these were the great wishbone quarterbacks from schools like Oklahoma and Nebraska who were fundamentally runners, not passers. Others, like Eldridge Dickey from Tennessee State, never had a chance.[b] And others, like James Harris and Joe Gilliam, were given an opportunity to play quarterback but no real opportunity to develop. Black quarterbacks into the 1980s received no apprenticeship; they either succeeded immediately or returned to the bench. (In an interview during the Super Bowl pregame show in 1996, Gilliam insisted that he lost his briefly held starting job in Pittsburgh in 1974 because of his race; and Terry Bradshaw admitted that, at the time, he believed Gilliam to be the better quarterback.)[12]

Some coaches in the 1960s and 1970s undoubtedly shared the racist assumption that blacks were not intelligent enough to play quarterback in the NFL. Potential black quarterbacks were also held back by resistance to their leadership by white teammates, not all of them from the South, and by fans who would not tolerate their inevitable bad games. The arrival in the NFL of Doug Williams in 1978, then Warren Moon in 1984 and Randall Cunningham in 1985, began the gradual emergence of the black quarterback into nearly normative status. Williams made history in the 1988 Super Bowl when he was named MVP after leading the Redskins to a lopsided victory. (A back injury that required surgery cut short Williams's career little more than a year later.) Still, never more than 9 percent of NFL quarterbacks were black until 1999, when three were drafted in the first round and the overall number jumped to 21 percent.[13]

Well before this time, because the white public wanted to believe that racism was a problem of the past, charges of racism in the NFL always came as a surprise. Jerry Rice's complaint to a San Francisco television reporter after his record-setting performance in the 1989 Super Bowl—that he received less media coverage than Joe Montana or Bill Walsh—struck a nerve in Bay Area newspapers. The *San Francisco Examiner* ran the story on the front page on consecutive days (the *Chronicle* covered it in the sports section), including defensive remarks not only from the sports editor but from the executive editor, as well. Montana, not the Super Bowl MVP Rice, had also been selected for the $50,000 Disneyland ad filmed immediately after the game. Rice only implied that race was a factor, but Harry Edwards, the Berkeley sociologist and sports activist who served as a consultant with the 49ers, bluntly charged racism.[14] As the national press picked up the story, Rice denied that he had intended to make race an issue. Ron Fimrite in *Sports Illustrated* dismissed

b. Dickey was briefly my teammate in Kansas City, after failing in Oakland, and I saw with my own eyes that he had what sportswriters like to call a "cannon" for an arm.

race as a factor and read Rice's complaint instead as another sign that the modern athlete no longer played for the love of the game but for the commercial endorsements—"the hero as huckster."[15]

Unfortunately, there was a general truth in Rice's charges, whether it applied to his own case or not. The very fact that advertisers have given us the term "crossover star" to describe a small handful of African American celebrity athletes (most notably pre-1994 O. J. Simpson in football, along with Magic Johnson, Michael Jordan, and Tiger Woods) acknowledges that for most black athletes there is a boundary they cannot cross. It is highly unlikely that decisions made at the highest levels of commerce and advertising in this country are affected by what most people would call "racism," but one would have to be astonishingly naïve to think that they are not affected by race. If nothing else, Rice's outburst hinted at how African American players might see their place in the football cosmos very differently from what the white public assumes.

In 1991, when *Sports Illustrated* attempted to reassess the condition of the black athlete 23 years after its groundbreaking 1968 series, the magazine received just 301 responses to questionnaires sent to the 2,290 players in the NFL, NBA, and Major League Baseball. That's 13 percent, and in no way a statistically reliable random sample. The reassessment, consequently, had little of the power of the original. In the second paragraph of his first article, Olsen had quoted the athletic director at the University of Texas at El Paso, who offered the stunning observation that "the nigger athlete is a little hungrier" than the white athlete.[c] Olsen's interviewees made his case for him; what athletic administrator would have said such a thing in 1991? Several black players for the St. Louis Cardinals in 1968 had also spoken openly about their treatment by racist white teammates (who also spoke openly, but anonymously). In 1991 the only black voices in the *Sports Illustrated* survey were of retired athletes. The likely explanation should be obvious. In 1968 the average salary in the NFL was around $20,000; in 1991 it topped $450,000— and not guaranteed—with the stakes comparably higher for off-the-field opportunities as well. The risk of appearing to have a "bad attitude" had become very costly.

The lead writer on the 1991 story, William Oscar Johnson, acknowledged that the low response rate produced statistically meaningless results, but then

---

c. UTEP was Texas Western in 1966 when its all-black basketball team beat all-white Kentucky for the NCAA championship. The 2006 feel-good film about the episode, *Glory Road*, ignored the on-campus racism reported by Olsen.

proceeded to present the findings as if they were meaningful. And certainly they seemed so. Large percentages of the black players reported still being treated worse than their white teammates, while whites overwhelmingly claimed that all were treated the same.[16] Was one side right, the other wrong? One hypersensitive or the other oblivious? The players most likely to respond to the survey, of course, had strong feelings—blacks resentful, whites defensive—and the views of the 87 percent who did not participate could not be known. Racial incidents that made the news were rare in the 1990s, though they were sometimes chilling. Miami linebacker Bryan Cox was racially taunted by Buffalo fans at a game in 1993, then fined by the NFL after he flipped them off. The following summer, Cox filed a civil rights lawsuit against the NFL for failing "to maintain a working environment free from racial harassment, intimidation or insult." Just days before the Super Bowl in 1996, someone firebombed the church in Knoxville, Tennessee, in which Packer defensive end Reggie White preached.[d] However infrequent these incidents, they pointed to a world in which black players lived that felt very different from the one inhabited by their white teammates.[17]

On one issue nearly half (43 percent) of the white respondents to the *Sports Illustrated* survey agreed with their black teammates: that African Americans had worse chances of moving into management positions than did whites. That situation is changing with glacial speed. By 2004, the final racial barrier on the field was thoroughly breached, as Donovan McNabb, Michael Vick, Daunte Culpepper, Steve McNair, Byron Leftwich, and Aaron Brooks were all starting NFL quarterbacks and six other African Americans were backups. (In some ways these six were the most significant: black quarterbacks at last enjoying the right to be just competent, or to be long-term projects who might develop into starters.) The proliferation of black quarterbacks since 1999, in turn, generated dozens of articles celebrating the end of stereotypes in the now "color-blind" NFL.[18] But in one area the barriers are only beginning to crack. Art Shell became the NFL's first black head coach in 1989, when 60 percent of NFL players were African American. There were two by 1991, three by 1995, but no more until 2004, when there were five. A sixth in 2005 and a seventh in 2006 meant 22 percent in a league with two-thirds of the players African American. The number of black assistant coaches increased from 50

d. Another incident that received national attention (in 1997) involved white Carolina quarterback Kerry Collins, who assumed the same freedom to use a racial epithet with a black teammate that he enjoyed with a number of African Americans on the team, only to find himself nearly in a fight and having to apologize.

to 154 (32 percent) over that period, 14 in 2004 holding the position of offensive or defensive coordinator. Progress has been real, but slow.[19]

The wall is tremendously higher between the field and the front office. While the commissioner's office increased its minority support staff from 16 percent to 49 percent between 1995 and 2002 (the last year reported), top executive and administrative positions for both the league and the clubs remained overwhelmingly white. Likely due not to overt racism but to an "ol' boy networking cycle," NFL management, in the pithy phrase of African American legal scholar Kenneth Shropshire, remains a "black-bottomed pyramid." Although black players with their high salaries but no guaranteed contracts rarely spoke out, William Rhoden reported in the *New York Times* in 1999 their "growing resentment" over the "granite ceiling" that kept them from moving into management. Rhoden himself has been outspoken. In *Forty Million Dollar Slaves: The Rise, Fall, and Redemption of the Black Athlete* (2006), he granted that integration has made certain individual black athletes rich but also argued that it has left them powerless, replicating something akin to an Old South plantation. Rhoden judges integration overall as a disaster for the black institutions that might not have thrived but at least survived during the era of separate-but-(un)equal segregation. Rhoden argues that integration has had the consequence, intended or not, of "practically eliminating every black person involved in sports—coaches, owners, trainers, accountants, lawyers, secretaries, and so on—except the precious on-the-field talent." Among the subtler ways that racism can work, Shropshire has pointed out that even sports agents are predominantly white, because black players believe that "they need the Man to talk to the Man in order to get a fair deal." The only part of the pro football establishment that resembles the racial makeup of the athletes has been the NFL Players Association, where in 2003 African Americans made up 64 percent of the Executive Committee, 80 percent of the vice presidents, 41 percent of the department heads, and 54 percent of the support staff.[20]

For critics outside the league, the paucity of black head coaches has been the primary target. Not only public figures like Jesse Jackson and black sports columnists for the major dailies but also voices, both black and white, throughout the media released a steady stream of criticism over the 1990s and early years of the new century, culminating in a report commissioned in 2002 by two black lawyers, one of them the celebrity attorney Johnny Cochrane, backed by the implied threat of a lawsuit. The criticism (and threat?) bore fruit in the so-called Rooney Rule, named for Pittsburgh Steelers president Dan Rooney, who chaired the NFL's committee on diversity. The Rooney

Rule requires NFL clubs to interview at least one minority candidate for every head-coaching vacancy. At the very least it gives black offensive and defensive coordinators an opportunity to impress those with the power to hire. The Rooney Rule likely contributed to the adding of a handful of black head coaches since 2004, but no NFL bylaw governs front-office hiring.[21]

Black Is Best

NFL officials in the early twenty-first century like to describe their league as color-blind, and at least the evidence on the field seems indisputable. As black players became a majority in the NFL, then a supermajority, it would be nice to think that old prejudices also gradually disappeared, that the presence of black players in great numbers and at all positions by the 1990s impressed upon the entire white football public the reality that blacks were as varied as whites in their abilities and character traits. We like to believe that sport, with its "level playing fields," is an agent of racial progress; that it not only provides opportunities based on merit alone, but also promotes racial understanding and tolerance in the larger society.

It is difficult to know how far we have progressed in this area. With the country officially committed to racial equality since the 1960s, contrary views have necessarily remained unspoken (except among frank bigots and white supremacists). These contrary views remain unspoken, however, not un-thought, except on those rare occasions when someone blurts out an impolitic viewpoint and provokes an uproar. Despite having championed Cassius Clay/Muhammad Ali while much of the mainstream press still refused even to call him by his Muslim name, Howard Cosell was publicly lambasted after a *Monday Night Football* game in 1983 for carelessly referring to the Redskins' Alvin Garrett (with admiration) as "that little monkey." Cosell survived his blunder, but CBS commentator Jimmy "the Greek" Snyder did not, after offering his views in January 1988 on how slavery bred blacks for athletic success. Snyder and Al Campanis, the baseball executive who suggested in a 1987 interview that blacks might not have the "necessities" for management positions, became the poster boys for an American racism in sport that would not go away. In his 1988 remarks, Snyder did not say anything that others had not said before him, including some prominent black athletes, but by this time for someone in the sports media to say such things openly was guaranteed to provoke a furor. Silence might not be golden, but on matters of race in sport it became much safer.

But race still matters. In addition to the gradual emergence of black quarterbacks since the 1960s, football's racial theater has followed two other main plots: the sometimes blunt but often subtle questioning of whether black athletic achievements are due to "natural" ability or social and cultural factors, and controversy over on-field behavior that seems related to a distinctive "black style." The stakes in both cases extend well beyond football, to competing ideas about African American humanity held by blacks and whites alike.

Following Jack Olsen's explosive series on the black athlete in 1968, documenting open racism in sometimes shocking detail, Martin Kane's "An Assessment of 'Black Is Best' " in 1971 became a different kind of landmark for *Sports Illustrated*, gaining instant notoriety for reinforcing stereotypes of blacks' "natural" athletic ability, implicitly (however unintentionally) opposed to whites' intelligence and effort. Most sports fans today would be shocked to learn that before the 1930s, African Americans were stereotyped as physically *inferior* to whites. That changed in the 1930s, not gradually but suddenly, out of a need to account for Jesse Owens and his fellow African American sprinters. Since the beginning of the century, exceptional black athletes such as the cyclist Marshall "Major" Taylor and the boxer Jack Johnson had occasionally prompted tests and speculation on their anatomy to account for their achievements. But in the 1930s, the phenomenon of black sprinters, along with black boxers led by Joe Louis and Henry Armstrong, a handful of black college football stars at northern schools, and even the black baseball and basketball players restricted to their own leagues and barnstorming teams, for the first time suggested that athleticism might be a mark of the entire race.[22]

Now, in 1971, summarizing arguments that had been offered since the 1930s (when they were also first refuted, chiefly by Dr. Montague Cobb at Howard University),[23] Kane cited the "anthropometric" research about body proportions (blacks' shorter trunk and longer limbs "on average"), bone density (greater for blacks), distribution of muscle and fat (more of the former for blacks, less of the latter), lung capacity (greater for whites, to aid distance runners), and "hyperextensibility" or double-jointedness (to account for blacks' jumping ability). Then came the explanations: American blacks' origin in West Africa (not East Africa, home to the world's best distance runners) and their ancestors' breeding under slavery. Kane alluded to alternative sociological and psychological arguments, and noted the importance of motivation (the attraction of sport or show business as "a way out of the despair of the slums"), but the article's attention to physical traits overwhelmed these complicating factors. Kane presented himself as a racial progressive who looked optimistically to the future for black Americans. Besides their marked success in sports already, he predicted that "other doors will surely open." But intentionally or not, Kane's essay declared loudly that black athletic success was more a gift than an achievement.[24]

Kane's analysis provoked both endorsement and outrage among *Sports Illustrated*'s readers[25] and a stinging reply from Harry Edwards in the journal *Black Scholar*. Edwards, the sociologist at Berkeley who led the black movement to boycott the 1968 Olympics in Mexico City, systematically refuted each of the supposed innate physical and psychological differences cited by Kane. Even "survival of the fittest" under slavery, a seemingly plausible idea, became more complicated when Edwards pointed out the obvious fact that many slaves survived "due to their shrewdness and thinking abilities," not their strength or stamina. More fundamentally, Edwards cited the scientific research since the 1930s that challenged the very concept of "race," in light of the greater differences among individuals within so-called races than between races. For African Americans in particular, after the interbreeding under slavery, the notion of a "pure" race was nonsensical. Edwards characterized the popular view of "the black male's racially determined, inherent physical and athletic superiority" as a "myth" deeply imbedded in "the Negrolore and folk-beliefs of American society." The true explanation of black athletic achievement, he insisted, lay in "a complex of societal conditions" that "channel a proportionately greater number of talented black people than whites into sports participation."[26]

With Kane's article and Edwards's response, lines were drawn and positions staked out that would change little over the next 30 years.[27] The stakes were high. Belief in natural black athleticism denied black athletes credit for the hard work and "character" traditionally linked to athletic success. More pernicious, as Edwards pointed out, whites could easily acknowledge black athletic superiority because they could then believe in a corollary claim of black intellectual inferiority. While a few scientists at this time were measuring muscle mass and the length of tendons, another handful was comparing black and white IQs and test scores. Scientists in the two groups acted independently and published in different journals, but the discussions of black athleticism were always haunted by the claims of Alfred Jensen, William Shockley, and others that test scores proved that blacks were naturally less intelligent than whites. The debate over the causes behind black athletic success was not about fast-twitch muscles or elongated heels but about black humanity.

IQ and 4.3 Speed

The issue of black athleticism was thus explosive, but it would not go away. In 1977 *Time* magazine addressed "the black dominance" represented by O. J. Simpson, Julius Erving, Joe Morgan, and the entire 65 percent of NBA players and 42 percent in the NFL who were African American. *Time*'s anonymous writer (articles in the magazine were still unsigned at this time) noted that just asking for an explanation "makes some people uncomfortable," because "racist arguments" about intelligence "can distort any discussion of racial differences." (Why journalists and publications felt the need to raise the question under these circumstances is the puzzle.) While reputable scientists had become reluctant "to study the physical differences between whites and blacks," a number of prominent black athletes did not share their unease. In Kane's assessment for *Sports Illustrated*, Dallas Cowboy running back Calvin Hill had proposed the argument about "survival of the fittest" under slavery that would get Jimmy the Greek fired 17 years later. Now in *Time*, O. J. observed that blacks "are built a little differently, built for speed—skinny calves, long legs, high asses." While such expressions of black pride ignored the darker implications of racial difference, other athletes quoted by *Time* seemed fully aware of them. Baltimore tight end John Mackey attributed black speed to childhood "opportunities and exposures." Cleveland wide receiver Paul Warfield pointed to the absence of alternatives for black kids in their neighborhoods.[28]

Time's piece was the last in the mainstream media for several years. Stephen Jay Gould's award-winning *The Mismeasure of Man* in 1981 temporarily routed the scientists working to prove the relationship between race and intelligence, neither of which was the measurable reality that they claimed, and cast the entire effort to identify racial differences in an unsavory light. The remarks of Howard Cosell, Al Campanis, and Jimmy the Greek in the 1980s, when the stakes in the discussion of black athleticism had become clear, might not have been denounced so swiftly and thoroughly had they occurred a decade earlier. "Folk belief" in the innate physical superiority of African Americans undoubtedly persisted, however, but by this time it was being expressed only indirectly. Broadcasters in the 1980s still sometimes slipped into describing black football players as "athletic" or "naturally" talented. Before the 1989 Super Bowl, for example, *Boston Globe* columnist Derrick Jackson invited readers to listen carefully to the TV announcers. Jackson had documented the commentary of Terry Bradshaw for a game three weeks earlier between Philadelphia and Chicago. Bradshaw had gushed over the Eagles' Randall Cunningham: "This guy is an athlete! He's not a quarterback,

he's an athlete! A guy who has the ability to run and to break tackles."
Bradshaw described the Bears' Mike Tomczak, on the other hand, as a "smart"
quarterback with "his head in the game." (The "athletic" Cunningham passed
for 407 yards in beating the Bears.) Bradshaw presumably intended nothing
racial in his comments and meant to praise both Cunningham and Tomczak.
Jackson's point was that the terms of praise that readily came to mind had
insidious implications with a long history. In all, Jackson analyzed seven NFL
games and found that 77 percent of the adjectives describing white players
related to mental abilities, while 65 percent of those describing blacks referred
to physical skills.[29]

With the stakes increasingly clear, the decision by news anchor Tom Brokaw to take on the issue for an NBC special in April 1989 is fairly astonishing.
The program, "Black Athletes—Fact and Fiction," whose script could have
been written by Martin Kane 18 years earlier, was named Best International
Sports Film at the International Sports Film Festival; it also caused a new
eruption of the old controversy. Again, the scientists with their data seemed to
validate what sports fans saw with their own eyes, while the social scientists'
arguments about cultural and social factors lacked measurable evidence. Brokaw's producer for the special was Jon Entine, who for some reason over the
next decade came to believe that the country desperately needed to embrace
the scientific explanations for black athleticism. The result would be *Taboo:
Why Black Athletes Dominate Sports and Why We're Afraid to Talk about It*,
published in 2000, the fullest elaboration of the arguments made by Martin
Kane and Harry Edwards in 1971, *Time* magazine in 1977, and Brokaw's NBC
special in 1989.[30]

By the time *Taboo* appeared, the biological argument had largely lost public
sanction. Following the uproar over Brokaw's program, in 1991 *USA Today*
ran a four-part series titled "Race and Sports: Myth and Reality," which
looked at the issue from a wide range of perspectives in dozens of short
articles. On the question of black athleticism, it noted the various explanations for black success in sports but clearly emphasized the social and cultural explanations. In 1997, in a reassessment of Martin Kane's original
exploration of the topic, the title of a *Sports Illustrated* article asked, "Is It
in the Genes?," this time essentially answering, "No." (Also in 1997, John
Hoberman's scholarly account of racist science in *Darwin's Athletes: How
Sport Has Damaged Black America and Preserved the Myth of Race* was less
widely read but received considerable attention in the popular press.) By now,
black dominance was so overwhelming in some sports—basketball, sprint-

ing, and certain positions in football—that a new concern had emerged. In challenging Kane, Harry Edwards had noted in passing that belief in black athletic superiority would ironically handicap white athletes who might give up trying to compete against black "supermen." That point lay dormant in the ensuing debates until *USA Today* included the "white flight" from speed sports (or "white fright" of black dominance) in its survey of racial attitudes about sports. The centerpiece of *Sports Illustrated*'s 1997 reassessment was not a new look at black athleticism but an inquiry titled "What Ever Happened to the White Athlete?"[31]

Sports journalists and broadcasters by this time had become noticeably cautious in dealing with racial issues, validating what Jon Entine would call a "taboo" against talk of African Americans' "natural" abilities.[32] But even as the biological argument retreated from public discussions of sport, a dramatic "return of biology" seemed to be playing out everywhere else in the 1990s, in the writings of the zoologist Richard Dawkins, the philosopher Daniel Dennett, and dozens of others.[33] In the ongoing debate over nature and nurture, nature had always had its advocates, from the social Darwinians of the late nineteenth century to Edward O. Wilson and his fellow sociobiologists of the 1970s. In the 1990s, evolutionary psychologists provided the new voice, and what was remarkable this time was the flood of popular books that brought their ideas to the general public. Having been mostly out of fashion since the 1930s, the "Party of Nature" returned in force.

In *How the Mind Works*, one of the leaders in the field, Steven Pinker, argued that not just reasoning, emotion, and social relations, but even "biologically functionless activities" such as art, music, literature, religion, and philosophy are products or byproducts of evolution. *Mean Genes: From Sex to Money to Food, Taming Our Primal Instincts* (2000), written by a biologist and an economist, described the instinctual basis for greed and infidelity; for going into debt, getting fat, abusing drugs, and taking risks; for our most deeply personal responses to beauty and our relations with family, friends, and enemies. In *The Truth about Cinderella: A Darwinian View of Parental Love*, the first volume in the series Darwinism Today published by Yale University Press for general readers, two psychologists explained how parents' abuse of stepchildren is rooted in our evolutionary past. Books about love and sexual relations in particular poured out of the major publishing houses. Biologists and anthropologists had been writing about the evolutionary basis for male aggression and violence for decades. Now, in books with titles or subtitles such as *The Myth of Monogamy*, *The Evolution of Human Mating*, and *The Science of*

Romance, we were informed that fidelity and monogamy are unnatural and that love as well as lust, romance as well as rape, are rooted in our genes.[34]

The most notorious contribution to this "return of biology" was Richard Herrnstein and Charles Murray's *The Bell Curve: Intelligence and Class Structure in American Life* (1994), an 800-page argument for the intellectual inferiority of African Americans.[35] *The Bell Curve* was a very different kind of book from these others, in perspective and intention as well as subject matter. The authors of *Mean Genes* offered their work as a self-help book for readers who needed to know what they were up against in trying to stay slim, balance their checkbooks, or keep their marriages intact. On the first page of *The Myth of Monogamy: Fidelity and Infidelity in Animals and People* (2001), the authors announced that "aspiring monogamists are going against some of the deepest-seated evolutionary inclinations with which biology has endowed most creatures, *Homo sapiens* included." Whether it felt discouraging, reassuring, or unconvincing to be told that our self-indulgences and bad habits are not entirely our fault, these books purported to explain a common humanity. Even Daniel Dennett's controversial assaults on religion and everything spiritual or metaphysical addressed a general human condition. *The Bell Curve*, on the other hand, was written by and for members of one group about another group, and its kind of thinking had less personal, and more political, implications for a society splintering into permanently separated economic classes. It would be comforting for an overclass to believe that genes largely determine success or failure, and that a genetically inferior underclass cannot be rescued by expensive social and educational programs.

Stephen Jay Gould responded to *The Bell Curve* with an updated edition of *The Mismeasure of Man*, and this time he made explicit the connection between the stereotypes of intelligence and athleticism. Pointing out that the best available evidence shows that Africans are the oldest humans on the planet and consequently the most genetically variable, Gould drew this conclusion: "I suggest that we finally abandon such senseless statements as 'African blacks have more rhythm, less intelligence, greater athleticism.' Such claims, apart from their social perniciousness, have no meaning if Africans cannot be construed as a coherent group because they represent more diversity than all of the rest of the world put together."[36] Gould clearly signaled that sport was an arena in which the "pernicious" fallacies of race science played out.

Not just the explorations by Tom Brokaw, *USA Today*, and *Sports Illustrated*, but also *The Bell Curve*, the revised edition of *The Mismeasure of Man*, and the entire "return of biology" provide the context for Jon Entine's resuscitation of the genetic argument for black athleticism. *Taboo* is a puzzling book. Entine seems to have been caught between the new romance with biology and his own uneasiness over the older racist science. His subtitle, *Why Black Athletes Dominate Sports and Why We're Afraid to Talk about It*, suggests a crusading purpose, to break down public reluctance to discuss something indisputably true. Yet his book also offers a full account of the appalling race science that flourished from the middle of the eighteenth century to the middle of the twentieth, culminating in the Holocaust and legitimating American slavery along the way. In the book, Entine disavows the continuing attempts by scientists such as William Shockley and Arthur Jensen in the late 1960s and early 1970s, and Herrnstein and Murray in *The Bell Curve* more recently, to "prove" the intellectual inferiority of the black race. Entine casts himself as a racial progressive who believes that the time has come when we can look at the differences between races without prejudice, for our collective good.

Exactly why it is important to address the issue of black athletic superiority, and what we would gain as a nation by doing so, *Taboo* never makes clear. Entine claims that acknowledging the differences between black and white is "the first and most important step in bridging them," as if Americans ever had a hard time believing in racial differences.[37] What *is* clear is that the explanations for supposed racial differences remain as vexed as ever: not just the competing claims of "hard" science and "soft" social science, but also competing claims within the biological sciences, including the long-standing dismissal of the very category of "race."[38]

Entine acknowledges that race is a "fuzzy concept" that historically has been "almost always reflective of a social agenda." Yet he endorses current race science as the disinterested pursuit of truth while accusing the Gouldians of sacrificing their scientific understanding to their social and political values. He insists at the beginning of the book that "the importance of the individual remains paramount," only to spend the rest of it generalizing about "populations" and "races." He acknowledges that "the relationship of nature to nurture remains beyond us for now," then proceeds to argue for the primacy of nature. He admits that the evidence is inconclusive, yet insists on drawing conclusions. Having traced the sorry history of belief in black athletic superiority as a corollary to the belief in black intellectual and moral inferiority, he proceeds to make the case anew for black athleticism. And at the end of the book, he disavows again "the familiar if erroneous calculus" by which "IQ and athleticism are inversely proportional," asserting that the time has come "to decouple intelligence and physicality." If only it were so easy.[39]

I am no expert; nor is Jon Entine, Tom Brokaw, or Martin Kane. Both the real and the supposed scientific experts disagree among themselves. This is not an issue like evolution or global warming on which the scientific evidence is overwhelming and disagreement is merely ideological. The expertise of the "experts" on black athleticism is invariably narrow, based on some intriguing data or an understanding of certain biological mechanisms from which broad conclusions are extrapolated. In the absence of actual proof of a gene or genes for athleticism, as also of the measurable impact of social and cultural factors, those on both sides of the debate *choose* what to believe for whatever reasons matter to them. For the general public, "folk belief" undoubtedly remains more powerful than science. Here, the basis for belief is the seemingly self-evident facts from the world of sport. In the case of football, all positions in the NFL, except for quarterback (for its own complex reasons), are disproportionately black, most of them overwhelmingly so, particularly if they require speed. It appears simply obvious that African Americans are "naturally" superior athletes.

I can add nothing to the scientific debate, but perhaps I can throw a few drops of "common sense" against the tide of folk belief. The overwhelming dominance of African American athletes in the 1990s, compared to the late 1960s and early 1970s when *Sports Illustrated* first addressed their striking successes, ironically challenges the conclusion it seemingly demands. When blacks were restricted to certain positions in football, it might have seemed plausible to identify a hereditary physiological trait to account for their superiority within their supposedly limited scope. Now consider today's NFL. Consider the different shapes and sizes of black bodies in the NFL. Consider the different requirements for each position. Consider what is needed for just one position, say wide receiver: "soft hands," quick judgment, fearlessness, concentration, intelligence (to read defenses), discipline (in running routes) —oh, and 4.3 speed. This should be the "common sense" of the football world. But which of these abilities constitute "athleticism"? Which of these are inborn? Which are developed through repetition and hard work? Which are more characteristic of African Americans generally?

Speed seems the one irrefutable indicator of natural black athleticism. One of Entine's more dazzling factoids is that blacks of West African ancestry hold the 200 fastest times in the hundred-meter dash.[40] But even here the case is not simple, and not just because black sprinters do not all have the same physique or share a common ancestry. The extreme genetic variability ("polymorphism") among Africans that Stephen Jay Gould emphasized in *The Mismeasure of Man* means that a racial "average" is virtually meaningless.

Echoing Gould in a 1997 essay in the *New Yorker*, "The Sports Taboo," Malcolm Gladwell cited research on Pygmies from Zaire and the Central African Republic, whose DNA reveals "more genetic variation than in all of the world put together." (Raised in Canada by his English father and Jamaican mother, Gladwell himself embodies a challenge to racial categories.) Gladwell reasoned that the genetic variability of those of African descent means greater numbers at the extremes, including the extreme of athleticism. Here "common sense" can contribute again. *All* elite athletes are genetically advantaged to varying degrees. Success in athletics, as in virtually any difficult endeavor, depends on varying combinations of "talent," "effort," and "luck," with "talent" standing for whatever the individual was born with, "effort" for everything within the individual's control, and "luck" for, well, luck. Talent is doled out unequally, of course. Likewise, some individuals work harder than others, though no one makes it to the highest levels and sustains a career without working hard. And some need more luck than others, although everyone needs at least a little, if only to remain free of serious injuries. To think that something as complicated as athletic success might be reduced to a gene or some unvarying combination of genes, which are common to a "race," defies common sense. And as yet, science has not trumped common sense on this matter.

Gladwell's alternative terms for "effort" in his essay are "desire" and "caring," the motives behind the effort. "Athletic success," he wrote, "depends on having the right genes and on a self-reinforcing belief in one's own ability. But it also depends on a rare form of tunnel vision. To be a great athlete, you have to *care*." Gladwell held Canadian age-group records in the 1,500 meters in his teens, and he concluded his essay with a story from his own sixteenth year, when he trained in St. Johns, Newfoundland, with two white distance runners. At the end of a long workout his two friends proposed running up a hill, "as steep as anything in San Francisco," backward. This turned out to be a turning point in the young athlete's (and future writer's) life. "They ran up the hill backward. I ran home."[41]

Gladwell quit running competitively at 16. A quarter-century later, he is a distinguished journalist and the author of two acclaimed best sellers, *The Tipping Point: How Little Things Can Make a Big Difference* (2000) and *Blink: The Power of Thinking Without Thinking* (2005). Whether or not he foresaw the University of Toronto, the *Washington Post*, the *New Yorker*, and these books in his future, at 16 Gladwell clearly saw options. In its 1991 series on race and sports, *USA Today* reported on a survey of 159 blacks and 395 whites conducted by a professional pollster, which found that both groups rated black athletes higher than whites for speed, strength, and excellence in "instinct" sports, and gave whites their highest scores for "leadership" and excellence in "thinking" sports.[e] For its 1997 report on the disappearance of the white athlete, *Sports Illustrated* commissioned a survey of 1,835 middle school and high school students, among whom 34 percent of the black males agreed with the statement, "Whites are not as good athletes as African Americans." Forty-nine percent of the black kids playing football believed they were good enough to play in the NFL (compared to 27 percent of whites, with a wider gap for basketball). These surveys document the American folk belief, unaffected by what the "experts" say. And such ideas have consequences. If a black kid grows up believing that he has a genetic advantage in sports, simply due to his race, why should he not try to exploit that advantage rather than face the riskier challenges of school and the professions to which only education can lead?[42]

As Harry Edwards and others have been repeatedly warning, black athletic myths have their most pernicious effects in black communities. Some white kids may be giving up prematurely on football and basketball; too many black kids may be giving up on everything else.

Black Style, or Thirteen Ways of Looking at an End Zone Dance

Into the 1970s, black players were still proving that they could compete in the NFL. Since the 1980s, black players have been reinventing the game as their own. Black receivers and black cornerbacks have transformed the passing game on both offense and defense. Huge but mobile black linemen and linebackers have changed play along the line of scrimmage. With African Americans comprising roughly two-thirds of NFL players since the early 1990s, has the game become culturally as well as physically blacker? Or more simply: just how "black" has NFL football itself become?

What I have in mind here is the popular sense of "black" and "white" styles in playing football, which I assume are widely shared by football fans. For me, they have long raised questions without simple answers. How real are they? Do they have any consequences for the meaning of NFL football, or for racial relations in the country more broadly? Compared to black athlet-

---

e. Whites ranked themselves considerably higher than blacks both for "leadership" and for excellence in "thinking" sports. Blacks ranked whites higher than themselves for "leadership" but put themselves marginally above whites for "thinking" sports (7.3 to 7.2 on a scale of 10).

icism, the stakes are not nearly as high in "black style," nor as obvious, which makes it unusually interesting as racial theater.

The possibility of a distinctive "black style" in football dates from the 1920s and 1930s, when commentators first criticized or celebrated players at all-black colleges for a "tendency to be theatrical or play to the grandstand," or for being "natural showmen."[43] Following Jesse Owens and his fellow black sprinters, who suddenly made speed seem to be a black trait, Joe Lillard and Oze Simmons in the 1930s, Jackie Robinson and Buddy Young in the 1940s, J. C. Caroline and Ollie Matson in the 1950s, among many lesser stars, reinforced an emerging idea that black running backs were somehow unique. A stereotype of black ballcarriers was well in place by the late 1950s, when I began playing football: they had speed, grace, and agility, along with a tendency to fumble and a willingness to risk a loss for the sake of a long gain. They would run sideline to sideline, often in defiance of their coaches' bedrock belief in straight-ahead football. They would swing the ball away from their bodies (for balance as they made their cuts), while their coaches screamed at them to "tuck it in" and grumbled about "showboating." Fumbles happen in football, but fumbling by black running backs became viewed as a racial trait and character flaw.

"Black style" in sports became explicit in 1967, when black at last was beautiful. In an essay in *Esquire*, George Frazier wrote about "the lazy amble with which Jimmy Brown used to return to the huddle; the delight the late 'Big Daddy' Lipscomb took in making sideline tackles in full view of the crowd and his way, after crushing a ball carrier to the ground, of chivalrously assisting him to his feet." Frazier pointed out that this athletic style expressed a more general Negro style, known to anyone "who was ever in a Harlem dance hall like the Savoy of the stomping years," or who listened to Miles Davis or read Ralph Ellison. Frazier also quoted the African American writer and critic Albert Murray, who declared that "nowhere in United States life has there ever been a richer mixture of vitality and elegance than in the Negro idiom, whether in sports, speech, dance, or everyday style and manner." In an essay in 1974 in *Ms.* magazine (of all places), Clayton Riley contrasted a white obsession with winning with a black emphasis on style. "White boys only want to know what the final score was," one of Riley's black friends told him. "They're only interested in the results. Brothers want to know what happened in the game, like 'Did O. J. dance?' "[44]

No "white style" existed in football until a "black style" defined it by contrast. "White" could have no particular style when it included WASPs and Irish,

Germans and Poles, Italians and an occasional Greek or Hungarian, the so-called melting pot of Anglo-Saxons and old and new immigrants who dominated college and professional football from the 1920s into the 1960s. Football in the 1920s and 1930s was understood to be a force for the "Americanization," not the whitening, of the new immigrant stock. Modesty and sportsmanship were middle-class, not white, values (despite their origins in the British aristocracy). An American obsession with winning derived from a winner-take-all political and economic system, not from whiteness. But the black minority eventually made the rest of the multiethnic country "white," and a black athletic style had the same effect. Through football, many working-class sons of millworkers and coal miners, with names like Nagurski, Savoldi, and Wojciechowicz, learned the manners of the college-educated middle class in the 1920s and 1930s. In the 1960s, Joe Namath conspicuously broke from this pattern, when he carried the swagger and "cool" learned on the streets and in the pool halls of his multiracial Pennsylvania mill town into the American Football League.[45] "Black style" did the same, reversing football's traditional process of socialization. Instead of embracing the dominant sports culture, black style reinvented it in the outsiders' own image.

Over the 1970s and 1980s, while the National Basketball Association became the primary arena for black style in sports, what most conspicuously constituted one in football were end zone celebrations and the various antics following quarterback sacks and big hits by the defense. My teammate on the Kansas City Chiefs, Elmo Wright, as a rookie wide receiver in 1971 performed the NFL's first end zone dance, a simple high-kneed chopping of his feet, followed by spiking the ball, a routine that he brought with him from the University of Houston. Oakland's defensive backs were so charmed by Elmo's little dance that they tried to take his head off when he caught a pass. With the arrival of the Houston Oilers' wide receiver Billy "White Shoes" Johnson in 1974, Elmo's simple end zone two-step morphed into a choreographed routine; and Johnson's "Funky Chicken" spawned the "California Quake" and "Colorado Moonwalk" (Butch Johnson), the "Ickey Shuffle" (Elbert "Ickey" Woods), the "Electric Slide" (Ernest Givens), the "Highlight Zone" (Andre Rison), and on an on, down to Chad Johnson's latest creation.[46]

Thomas "Hollywood" Henderson in the late 1970s introduced comparable antics to defensive football, and a decade after Namath assaulted the Frank Merriwell code of modesty and sportsmanship before Super Bowl III, Henderson shattered it completely by taunting the Pittsburgh Steelers and their quarterback Terry Bradshaw before the 1979 Super Bowl. (Henderson declared Bradshaw so stupid that he couldn't spell "cat" if you spotted him the

"c" and the "a.") In 1980 New York Jets defensive end Mark Gastineau introduced his "Sack Dance," immediately infuriating opponents and embarrassing teammates. The anger became physical in a Jets-Rams game in 1983,
when L.A.'s offensive tackle Jackie Slater shoved Gastineau in mid-prance to
trigger a brawl that led to fines for 37 players. One aspect of the mêlée was
nonpartisan: *Sports Illustrated* reported that some Jets rushed the field "hoping to see Slater clean Gastineau's clock." The 1983 season also saw two more
near brawls: the first, when two Dallas Cowboy defensive backs took exception to an end zone celebration by the Washington Redskins' "Fun Bunch";
the second, when some New York Jets objected to Miami Dolphin defensive
end Mike Charles's mock levitation of the Jets' quarterback he had just
sacked. That offseason, the NFL revised its Code of Conduct to ban "overly
demonstrative acts by players."[47]

Given the brawl and two near brawls, the overt issue was not racial identity
but sportsmanship and potential violence. The Oakland defensive backs who
took retaliatory cheap shots at Elmo Wright were as African American as
Elmo. The Cowboys' defensive backs and Redskins' Fun Bunch likewise were
equally black. Gastineau, who danced, was white; Slater, who objected, was
black. As another (white) offensive lineman put the Gastineau case, "Gastineau was a jerk. He tried to embarrass people."[48] But race was usually the
subtext. Gastineau was an anomaly, as both sack dances and end zone celebrations became predominantly black things. Because they dominated the
positions of running back, wide receiver, defensive end, and outside linebacker by this time, African American players scored most of the touchdowns
and made most of the sacks. But somehow black players also seemed more
"natural" in showcasing their moves. Try to imagine Steve Largent shaking
any part of his anatomy in the end zone. The king of the sack dancers was not
Gastineau but Bruce Smith, whose repertoire of the "Pee-wee Herman,"
"Fred Sanford Sack Attack" "Hammer," and "Pose" made Gastineau look like
an amateur with no sense of rhythm. It came to seem that white men not only
could not jump but also did not dance.

The NFL faced a dilemma in the 1980s. League officials wanted their game
to be entertaining, but they needed to please both fans who loved and fans
who hated "excessive celebrations." In 1988, after Cincinnati's rookie running back Elbert "Ickey" Woods broke into his "Ickey Shuffle," the NFL immediately banned it from the end zone, so Woods took his act to the sidelines.
The following August, the NFL decided to ban it there as well, only to relent
after discovering that fans loved Ickey and loved the shuffle, which seemed
not a taunt but a spontaneous eruption of pleasure. In 1991 the league in-

creased the penalty for a second excessive-celebration offense to 15 yards, prompting *Sports Illustrated* to ridicule the NFL as the "No Fun League" run by narrow-minded fool's logic.[49]

By the new rulings, "spontaneous expressions of exuberance" were permissible, but not the "prolonged, excessive, or premeditated" kind. *Sports Illustrated* interpreted the initial rule in 1984 as an attack on "nonconformists" and "individualism," and the 1991 revision as the sign of a generation gap, the action of "Geritol-guzzling, fuddy-duddy relics, rooted in the late 1950s and '60s, when the NFL exploded upon the American consciousness featuring that legendary party animal, Vince Lombardi."[50] The image of NFL football was still at stake, but by now whether the issue was sportsmanship (celebration as taunting) or race (celebration as black self-expression) was uncertain. While league officials always cited sportsmanship, some outspoken black critics declared the ban an attempt to keep a white NFL from becoming too conspicuously a "Negro Football League." One writer in a black weekly newspaper complained about calling the initial legislation the "Gastineau Rule," as if Gastineau, not Elmo Wright, were the creative genius; and he pointed out that "the Jets' defensive end is basically the only white practitioner of this rapidly-fading art form."[51] Such critics viewed "black style" in basketball and football in the context of African American cultural traditions, as George Frazier and Albert Murray first proposed in the 1960s. The Funky Chicken derived from the same black expressive culture that produced the blues, Toni Morrison's novels, and hip-hop. As one African American sociologist bluntly put it (in a conference paper cited by *Harper's* magazine), "NFL rules against end zone celebrations were initiated to curb black athletes' expressiveness."[52]

A Brief History of Taunting and Boasting

As a former offensive lineman from an earlier generation, I have always instinctively belonged to the Party of Disapproval on this issue. Celebrations draw all of the attention to *me*, not to the team. Too many players preen in the end zone after sailing in untouched after a perfect pass, or beat their chests after routine tackles. But I also know enough history to understand that such "poor sportsmanship" and "disregard for tradition" is more complicated than that. Athletic style, loosely defined, has a long pedigree, dating at least from the Renaissance, when the nobility consciously adopted a proper manner of disporting to distinguish themselves from the lower classes. In the role of Miss Manners for knights and noblemen, treatises such as Castiglione's *Book of the Courtier* (1528) prescribed how and with whom gentlemen should compete in athletic contests. In the nineteenth century, the British elite effectively appropriated this courtly tradition in formulating our modern notions of "amateurism" and "sportsmanship," and did it with the same motive: to maintain the boundaries between the classes.[53] Literally, "amateurs" competed for the love of sport rather than any material reward, but the codified definition of "amateur" in nineteenth-century England explicitly excluded manual laborers (supposedly because their physical occupations would give them an unfair advantage). Sportsmanship complemented amateurism as the code of gentlemen for whom winning was less important than how one comported oneself. Sportsmanship thus created a "style" informed by a particular ethic but also a class bias. British gentlemen, of course, were winners at life from birth. They could afford to be good sportsmen because winning athletic contests truly did not matter.

Despite much lip service, Americans never bought into the unimportance of winning. In the late nineteenth century, when football and other sports were first organized in this country, the spoils of the larger society most certainly went to the victors, not to those who competed fairly. In sports, Americans unapologetically acknowledged that they followed the letter of the rules, not their spirit. This American "gamesmanship" could seem amoral or unethical, but it was also democratic in ways that British "sportsmanship" was not. At the same time, advocates for youth and school sports professed the importance of sportsmanship, proclaiming that the values learned on the playing field would make the athlete a better person and lead to success off the field. (The fictional character Frank Merriwell epitomized both these values and their rewards.) Former athletes did, in fact, walk into well-paying jobs on employers' assumptions about their character as well as their athletic fame. (It goes without saying that black athletes rarely received the same payoff as whites on that unwritten contract.)

Sportsmanship, in short, historically served the interests of insiders, not outsiders. And this history of sportsmanship as a "style" signifying class distinction reflects with obvious irony on a black athletic style rooted in the self-assertions of an underclass ignoring or even defying white standards of decorum. For black Americans, first under slavery, then during the long century of legal discrimination, expressions of style in dress, manner, speech, movement, and attitude were certainly not symbols of power or social superiority. Rather, they asserted collective identity and personal worth in the face of political and economic powerlessness. George Frazier, Albert Murray, and

Clayton Riley understood the stylishness of black athletes on precisely those terms in the late 1960s and early 1970s.[f] More recently, William Rhoden has described the "graceful ease and 'cool' " of black athletes as both a transformation of athletic performance into art and a signal of detachment from a white racist power structure.[54]

Football has always been more resistant than basketball to black style. In basketball, it is organic to the game, not tacked on after the action stops. Behind-the-back passes, crossover dribbles, and swooping dunks might be excessive but they also put points on the scoreboard. (The fact that Bob Cousy and Pete Maravich were early innovators cautions us against judging a certain basketball style to be exclusively black.) Sack dances and end zone celebrations merely added exclamation points. That was the rub for NFL officials: the exclamation came at the expense of players on the other team.

Taunting and trash talking have an even longer pedigree, going back to the boasts of epic heroes as they departed for battle or confronted their enemies. Greek, Roman, and Anglo-Saxon epic heroes were not team players, but the hero's paramount ambition for personal glory committed him to acts of bravery that rallied his followers and benefited them, too. The ritual boast expressed that commitment; actions then had to follow the words.[55] And the boast was related to flyting, the epic form of trash talking: the trading of insults between rivals, with the inventiveness of the insults valued in itself.[56] Scholars have traced the importance of flyting and epic boasting from Homer's *Iliad* and *Odyssey* and Virgil's *Aeneid*, to the Anglo-Saxon *Beowulf*, certain medieval literary genres, and comic tales of the ring-tailed roarers of the American West—the half-horse, half-alligator, I-can-whip-my-weight-in-wildcats titans of frontier legend. (My generation grew up with a sanitized version of this figure in Big Mike Fink, the keelboat captain and Davy Crockett's rival in the Disney series.) With no past buried in antiquity and myth, we Americans invented our Heroic Age out of our frontier experience. In valorizing physical prowess and honor, gargantuan appetites and violent playfulness, this mythic frontier defined the heroic world of men living large that pro football still evokes at its deepest levels.

In the sporting world, John L. Sullivan and his fellow bare-knuckle brawlers of the nineteenth-century prize ring came from this heroic frontier

f. The question becomes yet more complicated by the long tradition of privileged rebels affecting outsiders' styles. Today's suburban white kids with their hip-hop music and clothing styles, acting "black" on the court or playing field, follow generations of wannabe bohemians safely rebelling against their proper upbringing.

mold.[57] But over the twentieth century, this sort of thing disappeared from mainstream sports, as even the professional versions gained middle-class respectability, while taunting and boasting became the antithesis of sportsmanship. Viewed in this heroic-age context, the taunting and boasting in the NFL since the 1970s make football more archaic and elemental, more like epic combat than sanitized entertainment. Against coaches' warnings to say nothing that the other team can post in its locker room for motivation, players such as "Hollywood" Henderson and Chad Johnson (like Joe Namath before them) have played the role of Achilles and Hector before the walls of Troy, or Beowulf in Hrothgar's meadhall boasting about what he will do once he gets his hands on the monster Grendel.

This harking back to ancient warfare, the hero taking upon himself the burden of victory or defeat, touches on one of the underlying sources of football's appeal. We no longer live in a Heroic Age, our values have changed, yet football itself is an expression of a longing to recover the heroic. The fact that today's trash-talking football "heroes" are self-selecting, rather than ordained by their exploits, can trivialize this connection, however. Also, football is sport, not war or a brawl, precisely because it is governed by rules and a spirit of play. Yet most end zone celebrations are decidedly playful, some of them genuinely creative. There always seems to be another possible twist in the competing arguments. Ultimately, whether such actions belong in football or violate its true spirit is not self-evident.[g]

Like style, taunting has a distinct history in black experience. The rich African American oral traditions of "signifying," "loudtalking," and "playing the dozens" created within black communities an art of verbal contest that was playful as well as serious, sportive rather than sportsmanlike.[58] Taunting was always riskier in dealing with the outside white world. Jack Johnson, the first African American heavyweight boxing champion, infuriated the white public mostly by his actions (particularly with white women) but also with his words, taunting his opponents and the white bigots at ringside. When Joe Louis in the 1930s regained the heavyweight championship for black America, after a generation of black fighters had been denied a shot at the title, he consciously presented himself as a soft-spoken "good Negro" and "a credit to his race." When Cassius Clay / Muhammad Ali then proclaimed himself "The Greatest" and trashed his opponents, he violated not only the Frank Mer-

g. Some players have simply gone too far for anyone's taste. No one was more creative, or more offensive, than Seattle's John Randle, who raised his leg like a peeing dog over a fallen Brett Favre after sacking him in one game.

riwell code of modesty and sportsmanship but also the unwritten pact to which black athletes since the 1930s had agreed for a chance in integrated sport. Ali's boasting and taunting in the 1960s were as radical as Jack Johnson's, in part because they defied the demand to be a "credit to his race," in part because they were coupled to Ali's political defiance.[59]

Sack dances and end zone celebrations by African American players belong to the same cultural traditions. Or do they? In the highly commercialized modern NFL, and even more so in the "new NFL" of billion-dollar franchises and millionaire celebrity players, the issue cannot be so simple.

From Broadway Joe to Neon Deion

It is easy to see self-styled white rebels like Mark Gastineau, Jim McMahon, Brian Bosworth, and Jeremy Shockey as descendants of Joe Namath. But in certain key ways, Terrell Owens and Chad Johnson—and before them, Michael Irvin, Deion Sanders, Bruce Smith, Ickey Woods, and generations of black players going back to "Hollywood" Henderson, "White Shoes" Johnson, and Elmo Wright—are also more the heirs of Namath than of Ali. Ali defied white expectations of black athletes at a time when "uppity Negroes" could still be lynched. He also defied the U.S. government. Namath introduced the superficial elements of style, such as long hair and white shoes, and he asserted individual personality against the anonymity and egalitarianism of the team. It is difficult to find Ali's radical significance in end zone celebrations and sack dances. Instead, although Namath may not have directly inspired Wright, Woods, and Sanders, he freed them, as the 1960s mantra put it, to do their own thing.

Their "thing" may have expressed a black cultural heritage and, as Gerald Early has argued, a more pragmatic need "to distinguish themselves from whites" and "a reaction to racism," but for many black players the more open motive has been self-promotion and marketing.[60] Hidden under helmets and padded uniforms, and removed from the crowd, football players are the most anonymous of professional athletes. Those who have embraced their role as entertainers rather than warriors and pursued the potential payoffs in the new celebrity culture have understood the value of defining their personalities in ways that the public can instantly recognize. As William Rhoden put it in *Forty Million Dollar Slaves*, "having an 'attitude' was the kiss of death for African American athletes" in the 1950s and 1960s. Today, attitude is "hip and bold," a marketable commodity.[61]

Self-promotion for commercial purposes was part of Ali's act, too, learned from the wildly theatrical professional wrestler Gorgeous George (the spiritual godfather of today's World Wrestling Entertainment). Though already known as the "Louisville Lip" when he met George at age 19, the young Clay, in the words of one of his biographers, "elevated bragging as an art form to a new level" after the encounter.[62] Ali's act was no less political for being profitable, but no less commercial for being political.

For white players in the 1980s, acting out was all about commerce and celebrity. Gastineau told *Sports Illustrated* after the NFL first tried to clamp down on him that "the dance has paid off for me" in a huge contract and endorsements. Chicago Bears quarterback Jim McMahon resented authority —whether it came from his parents, the Mormons at Brigham Young University, or Pete Rozelle—but he also sought celebrity by inventing himself as a biker dude with shades and a headband. Brian Bosworth parlayed a self-invented image as a spike-haired, loogy-spitting punk rocker into the NFL's richest rookie contract in 1987, and into a movie and broadcasting career after he proved a bust on the field.[63]

Black players have likewise grasped the economics of self-promotion. As early as the 1970s, before he became "White Shoes," Billy Johnson gave himself a more revealing nickname, "Box Office Billy."[64] "Hollywood" Henderson received his name from sarcastic Dallas Cowboy teammates, when he began showing up for practice in a limousine and generally acting like a movie star. But Henderson had arrived in Dallas with Elvis Presley, Muhammad Ali, and Joe Namath as his heroes; and he embraced the new name and played it up, devising what he called his "antics on the field" to promote himself when he felt the Cowboys' PR man was ignoring him.[h] By Henderson's own account, his taunting of Terry Bradshaw and the Steelers before the 1979 Super Bowl had the same purpose, to "put on a show" for sportswriters. The act worked. Henderson no doubt exaggerated when he claimed that 442 of 500 sportswriters in the interview room "crowded around my table," but he was the face of the Dallas Cowboys in the pregame media coverage (he shared the cover of *Newsweek* with Bradshaw). To an agent he met at a pre–Super Bowl party, Henderson announced, "They think I'm a football player but I'm still an actor."[65]

There are many similar stories. Butch Johnson sought the help of a professional choreographer in developing his "California Quake."[66] Whatever Ickey

h. Henderson also became another poster boy for the NFL's dark side when he was caught smoking crack cocaine with two teenaged girls in 1983 and went to prison for 27 months. Rehabilitated, he launched a career preaching against drugs, then burst into public consciousness again in 2000 when he won $28 million in the Texas state lottery. Henderson's has been among the more eventful NFL and post-NFL careers.

Woods's private motives, the "Ickey Shuffle" literally became a commercial success, when a shuffling Ickey and his mother filmed a television ad after his rookie season. Whether or not this was Ickey's goal all along, players around the league would have had no trouble recognizing the potential payoff from what NFL rules called "planned demonstrations."

And then there was Deion Sanders. Sanders hated the nickname "Neon Deion," conferred on him by sportswriters, but "Prime Time" was his own creation: an image employing gaudy gold jewelry, outrageous talk, and an arrogant strut into the end zone, all of it fashioned at Florida State University before Sanders arrived in the NFL as a black Brian Bosworth. (Unlike Bosworth, who preceded him by two years, Sanders backed up his self-hype by becoming the dominant cornerback in the league.) In his autobiography, Sanders describes sitting in his dorm room on the day when he first realized how little cornerbacks earned in the NFL and created "Prime Time" on the spot as a way to become rich. Having already acquired the nickname in high school, Sanders now "decided I was going to do something with [it]. This character, this persona, was going to be much more than an athlete. He was going to be a total entertainer." "Prime Time," in Sanders's words, meant both an "on-the-field routine" and "being very outspoken and flashy and flamboyant" in his public life (in stark contrast to his real temperament). "I'm a businessman now," he told *Sports Illustrated* during his rookie year, "and the product is me, Prime Time."[67]

"Prime Time" made Sanders arguably the most successful athlete of his era, Michael Jordan included, in exploiting the commercial possibilities of his persona. Jordan earned much more from endorsements than Sanders did, but Sanders's $25 million in total income in 1995 put him second behind Jordan among athletes, without dominating his entire sport as Jordan did his. At least one unimpressed writer felt that Sanders "has been rewarded more for his image than for what he has accomplished . . . the echo rings louder than the sound that produced it." After the video game manufacturer Sega signed Sanders to a $2 million deal in 1995, the company's vice president for licensing and character development acknowledged that Sega was paying "not for the football talent but for the Prime Time persona." "It's hip, it's edgy, it's close to being over the top," she told a reporter. "We're always trying to push the envelope, and to see him out there trying to do new things, to do 10 things at once, that's perfect for us."[68]

Sanders was extraordinarily successful but also broadly representative in viewing himself as a one-man act in a show-business world. Listen to the players themselves. Clarence Verdin, a wide receiver for the Indianapolis

Colts with an end zone routine modeled after Michael Jackson's moonwalk, complained about the NFL's new restrictions in 1991: "I mean, we're supposedly in the entertainment business, and all I'm trying to do is entertain." Albert Lewis, a cornerback for the Kansas City Chiefs, told *Sports Illustrated* in 1993, "The days of scoring a touchdown and throwing the ball to the official are over. When a guy scores now, he is promoting something for TV, a new dance. It's for marketing." Sack-dancing Warren Sapp told *Esquire* that football games were his "showtime." Chad Johnson in 2005 promised a new skit after every touchdown and invited fans to offer suggestions. "I no longer play football," Johnson told reporters. "I'm an entertainer." Johnson's quarterback teammate, Carson Palmer, admitted that he could not do such things himself, but he always looked forward to watching Johnson's performances on *Sports-Center*.[69]

SportsCenter was Carnegie Hall for the new generation of football performance artists. As the show's popularity soared, players began choreographing routines specifically for the evening highlight shows. (Note the name of Andre Rison's signature end zone strut, the "Highlight Zone.") ESPN in general and *SportsCenter* in particular became center stage for a vastly expanded celebrity sports culture in the 1990s, with millions to be made by players with marketable personalities. One small corner of this media culture particularly intrigues me. NFL players now appear not just on trading cards but also in video games, whose strangeness dawned on me when I read in my local newspaper about a high school senior signing a letter of intent to play at a Division I-A university. As he contemplated college, the young man realized that instead of "being" Matt Leinart or Jason White while playing NCAA *Football*, "I can finally be myself."[70]

NFL players can "be themselves," too, on EA Sports' Madden NFL Football, the most popular of all sports video games. It must be an uncanny experience for athletes to watch their digitized selves on computer monitors, TV screens, or electronic game devices, as characters in a vast fantasy world also inhabited by monsters, wizards, and comic-book action heroes. Fans, of course, often confuse TV stars with the roles that they play, but NFL players truly straddle the worlds of fantasy and reality, because what they do on the field is real. I used to wonder what it felt like to be William Perry while constantly meeting people who saw him as "The Refrigerator." Today, more NFL stars than ever must have to deal with a divided self-consciousness, a sense of "being" both the persons they are and the roles they perform, with the distinction sometimes blurring. Deion Sanders, for one, acknowledged that "Prime Time" became a "monster" that nearly destroyed him.[71]

But self-promotion pays. The fact that salaries for wide receivers and corner-backs rose sharply in the 1980s and 1990s mostly reflected their heightened importance in the new pass-oriented game.[i] But notoriety as performance artists may have contributed, and it paid in endorsements and post-football opportunities in at least a few conspicuous cases. Sanders and Irvin, two of their era's most flamboyant stars, both ended up with jobs in television, alongside the white quarterbacks and coaches who did not need to act out in order to become celebrities. Immediately after the Philadelphia Eagles in 2005 suspended Terrell Owens for behavior damaging to the team, a spokesman for Fox announced, "Any time he wants to come in, we'd love to have him. If he wanted to do the weather, we'd let him help out." After the season, a television producer tried to interest the networks in a T.O. talk show. Chad Johnson in 2006 was profiled in a Halloween cover story in *Sports Illustrated* (also in *Maxim*'s NFL "preview with balls"), as well as featured in a series of commercials for *SportsCenter*.[72]

Owens took end zone performances into uncharted territory in 2002, when he pulled a Sharpie pen from his pocket to autograph the ball after scoring a touchdown. Many have followed him there. In 2003 Joe Horn placed a call on his cell phone, and Chad Johnson pulled out a sign that read, "Dear NFL: Please don't fine me again." By 2005 Johnson was creating a new act each Sunday, set up with teases for the media during the week. He performed CPR on the football, putted with an end zone pylon à la Tiger Woods (worth a $5,000 fine from the league), staged his version of Michael Flatley's *Riverdance*, and proposed to a cheerleader. In other venues, Steve Smith impersonated a sword-fighting pirate and Shaun Alexander cradled the football like a baby and burped it.[73]

After the 2005 season, the NFL yet again revised its rules, this time banning the use of props and requiring the player to remain on his feet. Dancing was in, snow angels and proposals on bended knee were out. The competition committee was becoming a parody of medieval theologians, parsing the fine distinctions between mortal and venial sins. Associated Press reporter Jim Litke recommended hiring "a panel of celebrity judges for every game to review the celebrations and score them, à la 'American Idol,'" with "markdowns for lack of originality, rhythm, taste, etc." Chad Johnson responded

i. In 1982 wide receivers earned lower salaries than quarterbacks, running backs, and defensive ends. In 1999, starting receivers were topped only by quarterbacks. Cornerbacks' stock rose even higher. In 1982 they earned less than everyone except for kickers; in 1999 only quarterbacks and receivers earned more. (In 2005, however, cornerbacks trailed offensive tackles as well as quarterbacks and were followed by defensive ends, running backs, and then receivers.)

with a public message to the committee, that "you can't cover 85, and there's no way you can stop [me] from entertaining." Tony Dungy admitted that he "look[ed] forward to seeing what Chad Johnson comes up with." Not Marvin Lewis. The Bengals' African American coach imposed a gag order and no-dance rule on Johnson in 2006 (ironically as ESPN ran a series of commercials in which *SportsCenter* anchors offered him new ideas for routines). Johnson compensated by sporting a blonde Mohawk, a rubber replica of which (a "Chad Mohawk Head") fans could buy for $30 in the team gift shop.[74]

The blonde Mohawk was pure marketing, but were Johnson's and Owens's end zone performances "black self-expression"? One African American sportswriter in 2001 had expressed disgust with NFL players' "absurd 'look at me' showboating" and "phony theatrics" after "ordinary plays," much of it "aimed at getting exposure on TV news highlights and on ESPN's popular *SportsCenter*." A colleague writing in the same black weekly newspaper defended Terrell Owens in 2004 for understanding "that being a showman on the field is part of the African-American experience." A third black sports columnist, Michael Wilbon of the *Washington Post*, expressed his admiration for the Indianapolis Colts in 2005 for, among other things, their lack of "egomaniacal, end zone strutting prima donnas." In his 2006 book, William Rhoden of the *New York Times* celebrated the long history of black athletic showmanship, only regretting that it did not translate into real power. No consensus, even among African American sportswriters who might have a personal stake.[75]

Nor is there a consensus among black coaches and team executives. Back in 1985, Pete Rozelle had fined Bears quarterback Jim McMahon for wearing adidas headbands in defiance of the league's contract with Nike. (McMahon retaliated by wearing a headband with "Rozelle" embroidered on it in the Super Bowl.) In 2001, when the competition committee moved to ban stocking caps and bandannas, it openly targeted African American players. As the *New York Times* reported, "Bandannas and stocking caps are linked to the hip-hop rap culture and also to gangs. They are, too, simply a fashion statement for some." Vikings coach Dennis Green, Ravens general manager Ozzie Newsome, Jets coach Herman Edwards, and Buccaneers coach Tony Dungy—all African Americans—supported the ban. Bob Wallace, a black vice president for the Rams, opposed it. (White coaches Marty Schottenheimer, Mike Holmgren, Brian Billick, and ex-coach Bill Walsh pushed for a compromise to allow skull caps.) Tony Dungy and Marvin Lewis in 2006 viewed Chad Johnson's antics differently. Disagreement among the most prominent black leaders in the NFL challenges the idea of a uniform black voice or single black culture. Away from football, many African American intellectuals have celebrated hip-hop culture for its rebelliousness, while others have condemned it for embodying a code and swaggering style that might be helpful for surviving on the streets but not—except in the case of pro athletes and the hip-hop artists themselves—for escaping them.[76]

Even to an outsider, no single "black style" seems capable of expressing what is most authentically "black" in African American culture. A sociologist who interviewed black college football players who either were or were not particularly expressive on the field found that the difference usually derived from the players' family backgrounds and early role models.[77] From Walter Payton to Barry Sanders to LaDainian Tomlinson, there have always been premier black running backs who simply flip the ball to the referee after scoring a touchdown and trot to the sidelines. They "act like they've been there before." Setting up a dichotomy between "black" and "white" codes of behavior insults African American players raised to value restraint. The consequences are worse if white fans who hate showboating read racial character into actions that are merely playful or self-promoting.

Black and white observers alike bring their own values to the NFL's racial theater, which has no simple plot or single theme.

The Racial State of the Game

The past three seasons have offered numerous signs of how far we have come in matters of race, but also how far we have to go. In 2004 there were six black starting quarterbacks and five black head coaches. The NFL's top five quarterbacks that season were Peyton Manning, Tom Brady, Donovan McNabb, Daunte Culpepper, and Michael Vick, two whites and three blacks. A sixth black coach arrived in 2005, when arguably the three best in the league were Tony Dungy, Marvin Lewis, and Lovie Smith. Art Shell, who became the NFL's first black coach in 1989 and the first to be fired in 1995, made it seven in 2006, when Al Davis rehired him.

Shell's second tour with the Raiders lasted just one season, and when Arizona also dismissed Dennis Green, only five black coaches were left standing for 2007, but two of them, Dungy and Smith, made history when they faced off in the Super Bowl. After Pittsburgh hired Mike Tomlin, to bring the total back to six (Steelers' owner Dan Rooney making good on the Rooney Rule), the total remained low, but at least the hiring, firing, and rehiring of black coaches was beginning to resemble the treatment of white ones. The NFL *almost* acquired its first black majority owner in 2005, until Reggie Fowler failed to qualify financially and had to settle for a minority partnership in the Minnesota Vikings. The league could not yet escape its perverse resemblance to an Old South plantation with millionaire field hands.

Other developments have been less easily measurable. The new critical mass of black quarterbacks in 2004 and what transpired at that season's Super Bowl illustrated how thoroughly racialized NFL football remained, even as race seemed to matter less. In what had become the Year of the Black Quarterback, the *Washington Post*'s Michael Wilbon was particularly sensitive to fans' temptation to see quarterbacks in black and white. Wilbon knew well that there were many ways to be a "white" quarterback: gritty, like Brett Favre; overachieving, like Jake Delhomme; commanding, like Peyton Manning; efficient like Tom Brady. He also knew too well that there had long been only one way to be a "black" quarterback: athletic. In a column during the playoffs, Wilbon asked readers to consider the widely varying styles and abilities of the league's six African American starters. Daunte Culpepper, he wrote, "has a pulling guard's body, John Riggins's speed, and Terry Bradshaw's arm," while Byron Leftwich "is a lead-foot pocket passer, the antithesis of what bigots suggested for decades a black quarterback had to be." Only the lightning-quick and athletic Michael Vick fit the stereotype at all, while Donovan McNabb had consciously made himself less a runner, more a drop-back passer, to resist the traditional linking of black quarterbacks to "athleticism." (McNabb was not the only member of the new breed of black quarterbacks to complain about the curse of "athleticism" and of being typecast as "running quarterbacks" in a league that most celebrated its great passers.)[78] Within the crowded field of black quarterbacks, McNabb seemed to be Wilbon's particular black hope in 2004. The previous season, Rush Limbaugh had made McNabb the lightning rod for all black quarterbacks when he accused politically correct sports broadcasters of overrating him *because* he was black. Now Wilbon sympathized with McNabb's decision to stay in the pocket, while also noting that an African American colleague at the *Philadelphia Inquirer* thought it a mistake to restrict his running abilities in this way. As McNabb and Vick prepared to square off in the playoffs, Wilbon found it "refreshing that these two black starting quarterbacks in Sunday's NFC championship game are free to play the position in such radically different ways."[79]

Once Philadelphia defeated Vick and Atlanta, McNabb's opponent in the Super Bowl became Tom Brady and the New England Patriots. Here I cannot document my claims, because no one would have been foolish enough to write such things, but I am certain that in 2004 Brady (and Peyton Manning) appeared whiter to football fans than any white quarterbacks before them, because of the many black quarterbacks jockeying with them for NFL supremacy. I am also sure that the Patriots were coded white, the Eagles black, in the racial theater of the 2005 Super Bowl, and not just because of Brady. As the media constantly reminded us over the course of the season and through the playoffs, under Bill Belichick the Patriot players did not celebrate, they put the team ahead of themselves, and several of them signed for less money to remain with the club. Their most notable off-season acquisition, running back Corey Dillon, had arrived with the reputation of a selfish troublemaker only to be reborn as another Patriot team player. Dillon was black, as were key Patriots such as Willie McGinest, Richard Seymour, Rodney Harrison, and Deion Branch. The Patriots were black and white, like every other team in the NFL. But they seemed the whitest team in professional football because what they stood for had been coded "white" in a racial mythology that began in white bigotry, persisted less openly with the end of segregation, and had been fed in recent years by black showmanship.[80]

The Patriots won with Deion Branch, not Tom Brady, as the MVP, while McNabb passed for 357 yards, as Philadelphia kept the score closer than expected. But McNabb also had three interceptions after throwing just eight all season, and in the closing minutes, with the Eagles needing to score twice, he seemed remarkably casual about letting time run off the clock. The Fox broadcasters expressed amazement as time ticked away, not singling out McNabb but wondering why no one on the sidelines did anything to hurry up the offense. (A columnist for the *New York Amsterdam News* judged that the Fox announcers' comments "did not contain racial overtones" but "merely reflected [McNabb's] sub-par play.")[81] The newspaper accounts the next day made much of McNabb's impressive yardage and three touchdown passes, and they downplayed the interceptions and wasting of precious seconds between plays. But I happened to hear an hour of sports talk radio, the voice of white guys in a medium that at least one scholar claims is "always implicitly about race in America."[82] The host and three out of every four callers berated McNabb for poor decision making (the interceptions) and lousy clock management. Not one of them mentioned McNabb's race, but those phrases were haunted by decades of racial history.

The 2005 season on the field was not as racially charged as 2004. Injuries to McNabb and Daunte Culpepper, and the dominance of Peyton Manning and the Indianapolis Colts for most of the season, limited the possibilities of symbolic racial drama; and Seattle-Pittsburgh in the Super Bowl bore none of the racial baggage of the previous matchup. The season's ugliest controversy pitted a black receiver (Terrell Owens) against his black quarterback (McNabb) and team. When Owens in an interview on ESPN said that Philadelphia would be better off with Brett Favre as quarterback, McNabb initially held his tongue, but after the season he called Owens's comment "black-on-black crime."[83] No black quarterback today can be unconscious of the racial role he plays, but McNabb must feel particularly burdened by it. In a companion story that played loudly only in Philadelphia in 2005, J. Whyatt Mondesire, the outspoken head of the local NAACP and publisher of the black weekly *Philadelphia Sun*, ripped into McNabb, calling him a "mediocre quarterback" and bizarrely accusing him of "playing the race card" in refusing to scramble to avoid being stereotyped as a black running quarterback.[84] To run or not to run, that was the question. To run meant embracing one's African American uniqueness; to drop back and throw strangely meant "playing white." Fran Tarkenton and Steve Young never had to make such a choice.

Playing the position most weighted with racial history, black quarterbacks will remain lead actors in the NFL's racial theater for the foreseeable future. In July 2006, Warren Moon toppled one more symbolic barrier when he became the first African American quarterback elected to the Pro Football Hall of Fame. Then, with Daunte Culpepper newly installed in Miami and Steve McNair in Baltimore, Donovan McNabb still in Philadelphia but without Terrell Owens, Michael Vick still running wild but throwing erratically in Atlanta, and Vince Young drafted third overall out of Texas as an "athletic" but unpolished prize rookie, the 2006 season opened with many potential scripts.

The Terrell Owens Show in Dallas played out more as soap opera than serious drama (best episode: the publication in November of Owens's children's book *Little T Learns to Share*, the first in a series projected to include *Little T Learns What Not to Say* and *Little T Learns to Say I'm Sorry*). The season's most intriguing early story, instead, came out of Jacksonville, where "lead-footed" (and black) Byron Leftwich was paired with athletic (and white) Matt Jones, a 6'6", 238-pound running quarterback from Arkansas, converted to wide receiver to take advantage of his 4.3 speed and 40-inch vertical leap. Michael Wilbon could not have conceived a more promising premise: "a stereotype-defying, in-the-pocket quarterback with zero speed but a cannon of an arm" throwing to "a stereotype-defying, field-stretching wideout." And there was more. Leftwich's two backups were also black, so that three black quarterbacks played "in a small Southern town in the sport traditionally most resistant to cultural change." And even more: the vice president in charge of player personnel who drafted Jones as a converted receiver was James Harris, a former black quarterback who had been a victim of the NFL's more rigid stereotyping in the 1970s. As Harris told Wilbon with wry understatement, "Looks like we have a little bit of role reversal going on down here."[85]

The Leftwich-Jones story could not take hold, as Jacksonville settled into the middle of the pack and Leftwich's season ended early with an injury (as did Culpepper's). Instead, Donovan McNabb initially took center stage once more, playing like the NFL's best quarterback over the first six games. More tellingly, after rushing for just 55 yards over the entire 2005 season, in the fourth game of 2006 McNabb scrambled for 47 yards and two touchdowns. "I decided to go back to my style of play," McNabb told reporters, "and if the opportunity is there, take full advantage."[86] McNabb did not say that he would no longer try to prove himself not a "black" quarterback, but his actions spoke for him. After his magnificent start, however, in the seventh game McNabb threw three interceptions, two for touchdowns, and threw up in the huddle. *Philadelphia Inquirer* columnist Rich Hofman groaned, "Every bad image of this quarterback and his inability to catch his breath in the huddle near the end of the Super Bowl—and all of the attendant implications about leadership and such—will now be re-examined."[87] On that same Sunday, Joey Harrington also threw three interceptions; Jake Plummer, Jon Kitna, and Matt Leinart, two each; but history dictated that only McNabb's performance had any racial implication.

McNabb's season ended with a torn-up knee in the Eagles' tenth game, and as his backup Jeff Garcia played well over the rest of the season, William Rhoden wondered in the *New York Times* "whether Eagles fans will remember McNabb."[88] Michael Wilbon likewise speculated about the memory of white fans in Atlanta, where "the Michael Vick Dilemma" played out with Vick brilliant one week and dreadful the next. After Vick flipped off the booing hometown fans at the end of one awful game in late November, Wilbon wondered "how all of this will play out on different emotional levels in and around Atlanta, relations and history being what they've been over the decades."[89] Elsewhere, Tennessee's Vince Young was brilliant often enough to be named Rookie of the Year but finished the season still a star for the future. Leftwich's replacement in Jacksonville, David Garrard, played well at times, as did Jason Campbell for Washington after Mark Brunell was benched, adding two more names to what was becoming a long list of black starting quarterbacks in the NFL. The most consistent of them all in 2006 turned out to be Baltimore's Steve McNair, but in a role overshadowed by his team's dominating defense, and in a season that ended prematurely in the playoffs.

In the absence of a starting black quarterback, the key African American figures at Super Bowl XLI were Tony Dungy and Lovie Smith, the first two black head coaches to make it to the NFL's ultimate game. A racial narrative can emerge almost spontaneously from the contrasting styles of white and black rivals, but Dungy and Smith were as alike as two coaches could be, and both black. The issue would consequently have to be more subtle, as when Selena Roberts framed it for readers of the *New York Times* on the eve of the conference championships pitting Dungy and Smith against Bill Belichick and Sean Payton. "Somewhere today," Roberts wrote, "a voice from a TV booth will celebrate Smith and Dungy for their motivational skills but not their mental acuity, leaving the thinking-man's adjectives for Belichick or the Saints' Sean Payton. It's not purposeful, or meant to be disrespectful, but think of it as black quarterback stereotyping when applied to coaching."[90]

The contrast worked better for Belichick than for Payton, whose close relations with his players resembled Dungy's and Smith's with theirs. And in fact, Dungy had been celebrated for his brilliant defensive schemes in his first head-coaching job in Tampa Bay. What distinguished Dungy and Smith from coaches like Belichick and the Cowboys' Bill Parcells was their emphasis on *teaching*—on not screaming or cursing or belittling but helping their players succeed. Iron-fisted and benevolent coaches—"Biff" and "Pop" in dozens of magazine stories and movies[91]—had defined contrasting styles since the 1920s. In 2006 two coaches with a management style marked by calm dignity triumphed over the NFL's my-way-or-the-highway autocrats and dour technicians. (Might they also have demonstrated that coaches, including reputed geniuses, succeed through their players, not their game plans?) The fact that it was two African American coaches who had these values was a consequence of their own character and experiences (including their personal friendship), not racial destiny. But at this moment in the NFL's history, whatever black coaches or black quarterbacks did was inevitably read as a revelation about race.

When asked about the significance of two black coaches reaching the highest level, Smith spoke of a future when such achievements would go unnoticed.[92] Earlier in the season James Harris spoke about an extreme "role reversal" in Jacksonville that circumstances prevented from playing out. Rather than a Black Hope—a single stereotype-busting African American quarterback or coach—the cumulative impact of thousands of black players and dozens of coaches seems more likely to convince the general football public that athleticism, intelligence, and character are attributes of individuals, not races. But how often roles must be reversed in the NFL before no one notices remains to be seen.

CONCLUSION

Paul Tagliabue's announcement on March 20, 2006, that he was stepping down as commissioner presented an obvious occasion for assessing the state of the National Football League after nearly 17 years of his guidance. Tagliabue broke the news just 12 days after the owners resolved their dispute over revenue sharing, in principle anyway, in order to extend their collective bargaining agreement with the Players Association through 2011. This was the commissioner's last piece of unfinished business, and it was most fitting that this was so, because Tagliabue's principle legacy to the NFL, and the achievement he claims most to prize, is labor peace. Tagliabue strengthened all three pillars of the new NFL. In a considerably more complex media environment than Pete Rozelle ever faced, Tagliabue positioned the NFL for one astonishingly lucrative set of agreements with the television networks after another. Al Davis and Jerry Jones initially drove the pursuit of new and upgraded stadiums, but Tagliabue through the G-3 program and in other ways nurtured the stadium boom while applying at least a little friction to the franchise free agency that could have been much more disruptive than it was. As new technologies transformed the media landscape, Tagliabue repeatedly positioned the NFL to take advantage of the latest and most profitable. His one notable failure—to place a franchise in Los Angeles after 1995—seems driven by factors beyond his control.[1]

According to *Forbes* magazine, Tagliabue's greatest achievement was "the creation of a tremendous amount of wealth for his bosses."[2] But labor peace was Tagliabue's highest priority on becoming commission, and I am convinced that history will judge it to be his most important legacy. Labor peace created the stability that freed owners to pursue new revenue streams and spared fans yet another troubling spectacle of millionaires striking for more money. For Tagliabue, agreeing with Gene Upshaw and the Players Association on the extension in 2006 was easy. Persuading the feuding owners to accept more revenue sharing to make the extension possible marks his major triumph in keeping alive the league-first philosophy on which the NFL has uniquely prospered. (Although Tagliabue was subsequently criticized for conceding too much to the players, the fault belonged entirely to the owners, whose delaying past the deadline left them no real choice but to leap at Upshaw's final offer.)

In a slightly different assessment of Tagliabue's accomplishments as commissioner, *SportsBusiness Journal*'s Daniel Kaplan mentioned labor peace along with revenue growth and record TV contracts, as well as "a strict steroids policy," but he put above all of them Tagliabue's "transforming the very entity he leads from what was essentially a football league with some TV contracts into something approaching a full-scale media company."[3] It is telling that in the early weeks after Tagliabue's announcement, speculation on his successor included not just insiders Roger Goodell and Rich McKay but also possible candidates from outside the NFL, perhaps an executive from an entertainment, media, or technology company. Kaplan contended that "refereeing how media and digital rights are divided locally and nationally will be one of the key tasks of the new commissioner." He also noted, though, "While the league may look to someone with more media experience to drive the league, there will be a strong emotional pull to ensure that the person has a firm connection to football."[4]

This remains the tension at the heart of the NFL today. Has the NFL become primarily a media company, or is it still, above all, a national *football* league? It is both, of course, but the balance has been shifting, and how the new commissioner will manage that balance over the coming years will be the story of the post-new NFL, whatever it will be called. The eventual naming of Roger Goodell, an NFL insider with broad experience but particularly in marketing and media, was both predictable and fitting. The modern NFL thrived under a PR man. The new NFL required a corporate attorney. As the NFL now moved deeper into the new century, it operated more and more as a multimedia entertainment business, and in Goodell it chose the man who replaced Sara Levinson in overseeing what was then called NFL Properties. (The owners selected Goodell over Gregg Levy, the league's outside counsel, the position Tagliabue held before succeeding Rozelle.)[5]

Goodell took over the most successful organization in professional sports, soaring on an upward trajectory with the apogee not yet in sight. News from the latest polling had to be mostly encouraging, though not wholly free from reasons for worry. Slightly under 30 percent of the total American population were "avid sports fans," while slightly over two-thirds had "an interest" in NFL football. One million boys played high school football in 2004, up 14 percent since 1990. A third less played soccer, although that represented more than a 90 percent increase since 1990. Two-thirds of 12- to 17-year-old boys and roughly 45 percent of girls had an interest in the NFL, in both cases the highest for any professional sport.[6] The pipeline of future NFL fans seemed to be flowing more or less smoothly, while labor peace, another extraordinary set of TV contracts, and new or refurbished stadiums for nearly all NFL teams guaranteed extraordinary profits at least for the next several years.

Goodell brought his own style to the commissioner's job—more outgoing with the media than Tagliabue (though not quite the second coming of Pete Rozelle), less inclined to "backroom deals and power cliques" in working with owners.[7] But there were no signs of a new direction for the NFL in Goodell's initial season. The Arizona Cardinals' new stadium was the league's showcase in 2006, as stadium-building continued to offer both rewards and challenges. The proposed $1.2 billion stadium to be shared by New York's Jets and Giants created a dilemma for other owners, who approved a $300 million grant through the G-3 program only after Gene Upshaw agreed to reduce the salary cap by $1.6 million a year for 15 years. (With a $100 million increase in annual revenue projected for each tenant of the new stadium, every one of the 32 clubs would owe the players an additional $3.6 million. By reducing the cap for each club by $1.6 million, Upshaw assured a deal that would still benefit the players by $2 million per club. Once again, the owners and the union acted as partners in managing the complex economics of the new NFL.) At the same meeting, the league also allocated $42.5 million to the Kansas City Chiefs to renovate Arrowhead Stadium, but the San Francisco 49ers were not faring so well on their own. When the club broke off stalled negotiations over a new stadium/ mall project for Candlestick Park and began looking to the south for other options, a state assemblyman threatened to block any attempt to take the San Francisco name with them. Perhaps the NFL has the Silicon Valley 49ers (or Gigabytes) in its future. Or new ownership in San Francisco.[8]

The NFL's prospects for Los Angeles also remained uncertain, though Goodell insisted he was not giving up; and more ominously, the 2006 season ended without a formula for revenue sharing. The league even suffered unaccustomed defeats in dealing with media partners, first in trying to keep cable operators from placing the NFL Network on a special sports tier with poor market penetration, then in renewing the rights to NFL.com for something close to the $120 million over five years from the expiring agreement. Regarding the NFL Network, after rejecting cable companies' bids for its Thursday-Saturday package, the NFL expected those same companies to pay a premium price for its own telecasts of the games. Expressing confidence that they would win the "stare-down," league officials ran newspaper ads in NFL cities urging fans to complain to their local cable provider. But the initial Thanksgiving Day telecast—which earned a 6.8 rating for its coverage area but just a 2.3 national rating—provoked "no reports of major fan ground-swells demanding the channel," and none arose over the rest of the season.

As the titan of pro sports took on the giants of the cable industry, under the watchful eye of congressional subcommittees, the amount of concern expressed by both sides for the little guy—the ordinary NFL fan, the ordinary cable subscriber—was quite touching. (The NFL Network topped that opening 6.8 only once, ending the season with a 5.4 average rating.)[9]

When the bids for NFL.com proved unacceptable, the league brought its Internet production in-house, too. This new reluctance to give the NFL all it wanted was having the effect, as *SportsBusiness Journal* saw it, of pushing its "transformation from a sports property to a media company." A few weeks later, when the league banned local TV crews from the sidelines, at the same time that clubs were developing their own media operations, the NFL indeed seemed more like a rival to Disney and Time Warner than to the NBA and NASCAR, with a goal of controlling both the content and the delivery of its entertainment product. An ultimate fantasy for owners and league executives seemed to be coming into focus: a single portal for access to all things NFL, with themselves collecting tolls and policing traffic.[10]

For now and into the foreseeable future, however, the NFL still depends on its broadcast and cable partners, whose own fortunes improved slightly in 2006. In the first year under the new TV agreements, NBC's *Sunday Night Football* averaged an 11.0 rating, slightly higher than ABC's 10.8 for *Monday Night Football* in 2005, though below the mid-11 range that NBC promised advertisers before the season. The network's sports chairman Dick Ebersol declared *Sunday Night Football* the "cornerstone of the prime time turnaround at NBC," increasing male viewers, strengthening its Sunday night programs overall, and promoting the new hit series *Heroes* in particular. Whether this was $600 million worth of benefits had to be calculated with the "new math."[11]

Over at ESPN, average ratings in its first season of *Monday Night Football* dropped from ABC's 10.8 in 2005 to 9.9. (Moreover, an ESPN rating represents fewer viewers than the same number for ABC and the other broadcast networks because ESPN's ratings are calculated on a "coverage area" roughly 17 percent smaller than the national TV market.) Nonetheless, ESPN's 9.9 was nearly 40 percent higher than its 7.1 average for *Sunday Night Football* in 2005, and *MNF*'s 17 games in 2006 included several of the largest audiences for sports in the history of cable television. To recover its $1.1 billion investment, ESPN also used Monday night games for programming across its range of "platforms," from ESPN.com to *ESPN The Magazine*, and to studio shows such as *Pardon the Interruption*. Ultimately how profitable the venture was in its first year was the network's secret, but it certainly strengthened ESPN's dominant position among sports media. With CBS's football ratings up 1 percent and Fox's up 5 percent, all four networks posted gains, but with overall rights fees up about 24 percent, the new math was still clearly needed here, too.[12]

For fans, the stars and teams and games were likely all that mattered: LaDainian Tomlinson's record 31 touchdowns, Cinderella seasons for Philip Rivers and Tony Romo (with midnight chiming for both young quarterbacks in the playoffs), the rise of the New Orleans Saints from the devastation of Katrina (sentimentalized initially to the point of ignoring the devastation that remained), and the rest of a typical season's many familiar yet unanticipated stories.

The news from the dark side in 2006 was typical though unusually frequent—at least three dozen players arrested, including nine Cincinnati Bengals—but the various reports of disorderly conduct and drug offenses never reached crisis stage or generated the media's next morality play. As the regular season came to an end, a neuropathologist's report that multiple concussions contributed to the depression and suicide of 44-year-old Andre Waters was followed by a program on HBO's *Real Sports* and a flurry of articles, including a front-page story in the *New York Times* about former Patriot linebacker Ted Johnson, 34 years old and already suffering from Alzheimer's-like symptoms. (Johnson charged that his coach, Bill Belichick, forced him to participate in a hard-contact drill just four days after suffering a severe concussion, resulting in a second concussion before the first had healed.) The grim stories reminded the football public (as well as Roger Goodell and Gene Upshaw, more pointedly) of the physical and mental costs paid by millionaire players—without lessening interest in the playoffs and Super Bowl, of course.[13]

For its four-hour Super Bowl pregame show, CBS opted for inspiration (last year's MVP Hines Ward embracing his roots in Korea, Bears running back Thomas Jones honoring his coal-mining mother) over desperation (no mention of the damaged and angry former players who had been much in the news all week). The Super Bowl itself was unusually uplifting, marked by the dignity of Tony Dungy and Lovie Smith and by Peyton Manning's exorcising the one demon haunting his career: his supposed inability to win the big games. All in all, another unique yet typical season in the new NFL.

As 2006 receded into history, the NFL's most urgent immediate need was to resolve the standoff over revenue sharing. As has been the case since the 1974 strike, it was hard to believe the supposed "startling development" that some clubs in the $6 billion NFL were losing money, as their owners claimed.

Nonetheless, the dispute between obscenely rich and merely rich owners was becoming "increasingly personal and contentious" as the offseason commenced.[14] I must end my chronicle before the owners' meeting in March. Perhaps by the time this book appears the owners will have resolved their differences. Perhaps not, but as with the deadlock over the latest extension of the collective bargaining agreement, it is also hard to believe that, with so much at stake, the parties will not hammer out a compromise.

Beyond the challenge posed by revenue disparity, the NFL's colossal success as an entertainment business makes it seem strangely vulnerable in a more fundamental way: more than ever hostage to television, to the marketplace, and ultimately to the public that supports the entire enterprise. Like all sports, football has the advantage over other forms of entertainment of being unscripted. Games, seasons, and careers follow no predetermined plots. These appear only afterward, and only then seem inevitable. NFL football (along with other sports) is the true "reality TV" (with brutally tough and selective auditions). If it ever becomes merely entertainment, or "product" or media "content," its future is uncertain. Entertainment fads come and go. If football continues to appeal to something deeper in its fans, it will survive as long as their lives require it, with or without brilliant marketing by the NFL.

The National Football League has never existed in any meaningful way without the media. (Even in its earliest years, without local newspapers NFL games would have been the philosopher's tree falling in the forest that nobody hears, except for a few hundred "sports" with bets on the outcome.) Today, the routine televising of games expands the NFL's weekly audience from a million to tens of millions; ESPN makes pro football a year-round drama; and the packaging and production of game telecasts, along with the steady outpouring from NFL Films and the magazine and TV profiles of football heroes "livin' large," enhance the power inherent in football itself. Packaging alone has little power, however, and while media events such as Super Bowl halftime shows and NFL Kickoff Live concerts may attract their own audiences, they are not necessarily audiences for the sport. Several million young males buy each new edition of Madden NFL Football. Something like 11 million belong to fantasy football leagues. Uncounted millions bet on NFL contests each week.[a] But unless these varied passions ultimately lead to, or

a. Since its debut in 1989, 53 million copies of Madden NFL Football were purchased by December 2006, including 2 million copies over the first weekend of the latest release; and a record $94.5 million was wagered legally in Nevada on the Super Bowl in 2006, in addition to however many millions were bet illegally or privately. Claims about unregulated betting vary widely. One pair of writers estimated in the late 1990s that 30 derive from, a passion for actual NFL football, it is hard to imagine their lasting.[15]

Our contemporary culture is full of signs that a longing to live large still characterizes our times (for those with the luxury to obsess about their quality of life beyond bare survival). Not only NFL football but also NASCAR, World Wrestling Entertainment, and various extreme sports are marketed in that spirit. It provides the premise behind all of the *Survivor*-type reality TV shows. Whether as a sly joke or for wish fulfillment, the creators of the hugely popular Sims video games even brought out a *Livin' Large* version, which introduced fantasy elements into the original's simulation of ordinary life.

On a recent wait in my doctor's office I happened to pick up a copy of *Outside* magazine with a cover story titled "50 Ways to Live Large," ranging from the exotic (climbing Yosemite's El Capitan, walking the 211-mile John Muir Trail, shark diving in the Caribbean) to something for everyone (keeping fit, planting an organic garden, building a tree house).[16] The psychic charge from these activities would seem to be highly variable, but they suggest that to live large, on whatever terms are possible, is a widespread desire. Football's psychic charge is available to everyone, if only vicariously.

The NFL "brand" has never been stronger, the "product" never more profitable, than in the early years of the new century. Research conducted in 2003 on "brand resonance"[b] found the NFL's to be the strongest in sports.[17] But moving product in an expanding entertainment marketplace is a lot more challenging than just offering games on Sundays that several million fans would not miss for anything. Despite all of the variables of pro football economics, this simple matter of caring remains the key. On the day that the NFL owners selected Goodell to succeed Tagliabue, observers named the many challenges facing the new commissioner—marketing for new media, revenue sharing, sustaining labor peace, and the rest. Goodell himself declared that the principal lesson he learned from his two mentors, Pete Rozelle and Paul Tagliabue, was "the importance of the game." In blessing his successor, Tagliabue added, "As he said, you need to focus on the game and focus on the players. He'll do fine."[18]

---

million Americans bet on the Super Bowl each year, their total wagers over that decade amounting to $3 billion. Another writer claimed at least $25 billion annually on all NFL games.

b. Brand resonance "combin[es] several factors related to a brand's power, including the attachment a user feels to the brand and the extent to which users of that brand represent a community with shared interests and values."

The job is to market the game, without letting marketing get in the way of the game, which mostly sells itself anyway. For all of its marketing efforts, the NFL still depends on Peyton Manning hitting Marvin Harrison for 21 yards on third-and-19 with 43 seconds on the clock and the Colts down 20–14. And on Jason Taylor or Brian Urlacher stuffing the running back at the goal line as time runs out. For the National Football League to hold onto its enormous audience, NFL football—the game on the field and the men who play it—must continue to matter.

Corvallis, Oregon
February 2007

AFTERWORD

I concluded *Brand NFL* in February 2007 with an observation that the National Football League was thriving yet strangely vulnerable. Three years later the NFL still thrives, yet it is now more vulnerable than at any time since 1993, more profoundly vulnerable than it has been since its struggles to survive in its earliest years.

None of this has been apparent on the field. After rooting for or against New England's quest for perfection in 2007 (following the embarrassment of "Spygate"), fans the next year could follow an aging Kurt Warner's improbable return to the Super Bowl with Arizona. The victory of the New Orleans Saints in the 2010 Super Bowl then capped the NFL's ultimate feel-good season. After two off-seasons of waffling over retirement, alienating even some of his most loyal fans, forty-year-old Brett Favre produced the highest passing percentage and quarterback rating of his career in leading the Minnesota Vikings into the NFC championship game. Even Favre's badly thrown interception to end the Vikings' run tarnished only slightly a remarkable achievement on behalf of aging professionals everywhere. Nothing at all tarnished the Saints' victory over Indianapolis two weeks later, bringing joy to a city still recovering from Hurricane Katrina and validating, for a brief moment anyway, the most extravagant claims about the power of an NFL franchise to renew a community's spirit.

With the economy slumping badly, NFL attendance in 2009 dropped 2.6 percent from 2008 but was still 95.5 percent of capacity for the league overall (and just slightly under the 96 percent in 2006, before the recession hit).[1] Even better, after two seasons of roughly flat TV ratings, viewership for 2009 was the strongest in years. Fox, NBC, and ESPN reached their largest audiences ever (total viewers, not ratings); CBS, its largest since 1993. The audience for NBC's *Sunday Night Football* was up 17 percent over 2008; Fox and CBS were up 12 percent and 7 percent, respectively; and *Monday Night Football* on ESPN up 20 percent. The league's own NFL Network saw its highest ratings ever, after finally reaching an agreement with Comcast that provided millions more potential viewers.[2] Strong ratings did not translate directly into more revenue for the NFL, of course, but they boded well for the next round of negotiations with the networks. Total league revenues continued to rise each season, from $6.5 billion in 2006 to $7.1 billion in 2007, to $7.6 billion in 2008 (with 2009 yet to be reported). The value of NFL franchises (as estimated annually by *Forbes* magazine) likewise rose, from an average of $957 million in 2007 to $1.04 billion in 2008, then remained flat in 2009—an achievement in the midst of widespread economic decline. *Forbes* valued nineteen of thirty-two franchises in 2009 over $1 billion, compared to just one in 2004.[3] If the NFL was not quite recession-proof, it was weathering the recession considerably better than other sports organizations and the country overall.

Off the field, Roger Goodell strengthened his reputation as a tough-on-crime commissioner with his handling of the usual incidents from the NFL's dark side, along with the unusually ugly case of Michael Vick, imprisoned for running a brutal dogfighting operation. Giants receiver Plaxico Burress also landed in prison for accidentally discharging an illegal handgun in a nightclub, and Titans quarterback Steve McNair was murdered by his girlfriend under tawdry circumstances that shattered the public image of one of the NFL's exemplary citizens. But the media treated each of these as an isolated incident, not part of a pattern that indicted NFL players in general.

The NFL's vulnerability in 2010 comes from elsewhere, and the immediate crisis is self-inflicted. As the deadline for the last extension of the league's collective bargaining agreement with the Players Association approached in March 2006, it seemed unthinkable that the two sides would not preserve the labor peace on which everyone had grown rich since 1993. It turned out that, by posturing and delaying, the owners were rushed into an agreement that they did not want. By opting out of the agreement in May 2008, then letting the March 2010 deadline pass for negotiating a new one, they have indeed thought the unthinkable: a lockout of the players in 2011 (following a 2010 season without a salary cap).

Labor relations were further complicated when Gene Upshaw died suddenly from pancreatic cancer in August 2008, just three days after it was diagnosed, leaving the Players Association without a clear successor as executive director. Seven months of rumor and in-fighting ended in March 2009 when the players selected a Washington attorney, DeMaurice Smith, over former players Troy Vincent and Trace Armstrong, the presumed frontrunners. Smith immediately began working to unify the membership and reach out to angry retired players, who had viewed Gene Upshaw as their enemy. (Upshaw's blunt dismissal of retirees' complaints seemed driven by his knowing what the NFLPA had won for them since 1993 that they had failed to win for themselves through solidarity on the picket lines.) But Smith's immediate and most pressing challenge was to negotiate a new collective bargaining agreement while preparing for a possible lockout.

As I write, the owners are claiming losses of $200 million since 2006 and demanding that the players reduce their overall compensation by 18 percent (the size of the figure is disputed). As always, the owners are also refusing to open their books to prove their losses, and published figures do not back up their claims. In winning a share of local as well as national revenue in 2006, the players obviously should have upped their portion, while the owners' went down; the question is whether the decline still leaves a reasonable profit or creates real hardship. In the first year after the March 2006 extension, the players' total salaries (as reported by *USA Today*) unsurprisingly rose from $2.63 billion to $3.2 billion. Also unsurprisingly, the clubs' overall profits, or operating income (as reported by *Forbes*), declined from $984.5 million to $587.5 million. But over the next two years, as player salaries rose to $3.23 billion, then $3.62 billion, operating income also rose, to $789 million and then $1.03 billion. In other words, profits were rising, not falling, when the owners opted out of the collective bargaining agreement while claiming financial distress.[4]

Although a full accounting for the 2009 season is not yet available, nothing so far has justified the owners' demand to roll back player compensation as much as 18 percent, and whether *any* rollback is reasonable cannot be known without the clubs opening their books.[5] Tax law is too complicated for debt obligations to be simply understood as expenses. Clearly, local revenues vary widely across the thirty-two franchises, and the range has widened with the new suite-laden stadiums in Dallas and other cities. That player costs create crushing financial burdens on low-revenue clubs is not so clear. Despite the salary cap, player payrolls vary as much as revenues do. In 2008, for example, while total revenues ranged from $208 million to $345 million, total payroll ranged from $84 million to $152 million. In 2009, just one club exceeded the salary cap of $128 million, while nineteen failed to meet the guaranteed minimum of $111 million.[6]

At best, these published figures only approximate actual revenues and expenses, but in the absence of more definitive data—which the owners alone can provide—the most reasonable conclusion is that the owners' problem is with each other, not with the players.[7] Whatever the precise figures, the players' guaranteed share rises and falls with fluctuations in total revenue. It can only be the high-revenue owners' unwillingness to share with the low-revenue clubs that jeopardizes the economics of the league overall. Perhaps some low-revenue teams can indeed afford their salary obligations only with the help of their richer partners. These "partners," however, are unwilling to share their millions from seat licenses, luxury suites, naming rights, and local sponsorships. The owners' problem is with each other, but they want the players to pay for it.

The alternative to more sharing is to operate without a salary cap and guaranteed minimum for the players, as will happen in 2010. Should this arrangement continue, for the potential long-term consequences one need only look at Major League Baseball, where the richer clubs sign most of the best players and only a handful of teams each season genuinely compete for the playoffs and World Series. The situation would not be as severe in the NFL, where shared national TV revenue narrows the gap between richer and poorer, but the balance that has helped fuel fan passions since 1993 would tilt and stay tilted.

Owners such as Jerry Jones and Daniel Snyder might welcome that new imbalance, but it is hard to believe that the supermajority needed to make such decisions would actually want this. Perhaps the threat of a lockout in 2011 is a bluff; if so, it has been well orchestrated. The owners hired as their lead attorney the man who guided the National Hockey League in its successful lockout of players in 2004–5. Provisions in the league's TV contracts guarantee payments in 2011 even if no games are played, and in September 2009 *SportsBusiness Journal* reported that clubs were putting clauses in their employees' contracts regarding nonpayment in case of a work stoppage. Most tellingly, the NFL is once again seeking freedom from antitrust law, this time in a lawsuit before the Supreme Court brought by the apparel manufacturer American Needle over the league's exclusive merchandising agreement with Reebok. The NFL actually won the lower court ruling but supported American Needle's appeal on the chance of winning broader immunity from antitrust law. At the heart of the case is the NFL's claim that it should be legally recognized as a single entity rather than as thirty-two teams competing against one another. A favorable ruling, among other consequences, could undermine free agency and allow the league to adopt policies without bothering with collective bargaining. (The Court heard the case in January 2010 and will likely issue its ruling in late June.)[8]

Even this conservative-leaning Court seems unlikely to give the NFL such broad antitrust exemption. Perhaps NFL leaders realize this but are hoping to see telltale cracks in the players' resolve, as negotiations drag out, before getting serious about bargaining. If so, they may find themselves dealing with an unfamiliar NFLPA. The players' chief problem, like the owners', though on different terms, has always been with themselves: their unwillingness to stick together during the work stoppages of 1974, 1982, and 1987. But this time, and for the first time ever, it is the owners who are demanding a greater share of the profits, who are more likely to seem "greedy" to fans put off by the whining of the rich. The players are asking only to continue an arrangement that works well for everyone, in the face of claims about a financial problem that the owners will not (cannot?) prove is real. With both the public and the media behind them for a change, and stronger leadership within their ranks, the players are likely to stay more united than before.

Whether the NFL preserves labor peace and the general prosperity it underpins is completely within the owners' control. Not so the league's long-term crisis. The news from the dark side that now threatens the very foundation of the National Football League was just emerging as I finished *Brand NFL* in 2007—in the reports of former players suffering from brain damage. That summer, Roger Goodell convened a "concussion summit," out of which came new standards for assessing head injuries and the 88 Plan for assisting retired players, named for the jersey number worn by John Mackey, the Hall of Fame tight end now living in a perpetual fog. The urgency of the issue then abated until the beginning of the 2009 season, with the release of the findings from an NFL-funded survey conducted by researchers at the University of Michigan. Former players over fifty reported symptoms of dementia at six times the rate of their peer group, while those between the ages of thirty and forty-nine were nineteen times more susceptible. Reporting by Alan Schwarz in the *New York Times* over the following months, along with long essays by Jeanne Marie Laskas in *GQ* and Malcolm Gladwell in the *New Yorker*, segments on ESPN's *Outside the Lines*, and countless blog postings, introduced the public to "chronic traumatic encephalopathy," or CTE, first identified in the brown stain of tau proteins in the brain tissue of Mike Webster, the sign of the same the "punch drunk" syndrome that has long afflicted an estimated 20 percent of former prizefighters.[9]

The inexplicable suicides and violent deaths of former players in their forties and early fifties—Webster, Terry Long, Justin Strzelczyk, Andre Waters, and several others (perhaps including my old teammate Jim Tyrer?)—now had an explanation; and Webster's death at age fifty, sad enough on its own terms, now became a watershed moment in NFL history. Football had been Webster's life, and he gave his life for football—a Faustian bargain that would approach classical tragedy had he had any idea what his end of the bargain would be. Worse, the research suggested that not only was *every* NFL player at risk, so might be the thousands who play football each season in college, the 1.2 million who play in high school, and even the 3 million who play in youth leagues. An NFL problem had become a national health issue.

As was their customary practice in managing the brand, Roger Goodell and other NFL spokesmen denied the growing medical consensus until denial became more damaging than the indisputable evidence. After an embarrassing public hearing before the House Judiciary Committee on October 28, 2009, Goodell and the league finally changed course. Stricter standards for treating concussed players, revisions to the rules to reduce "big hits," technological improvements to helmets, more generous care for damaged players, replacement of the compromised chairmen of the NFL's concussion panel—Goodell vowed to do whatever might reduce the danger.[10]

But what if football itself is the problem?

Football's "necessary violence" has been celebrated since the 1880s and openly or tacitly acknowledged ever since. As pro football has ridden its own wave of popularity since the 1950s, the game's violence has validated the larger-than-life prowess of the players and offered fans an intense experience missing from their own lives. Among the former players testifying before Congress late in the 2009 season was Kyle Turley, one of the poster boys for "livin' large" in an *Esquire* profile in 2002, now a spokesman for brain-damaged former players and seemingly one of them himself, suffering from vertigo, vomiting, and brutal headaches less than two years after retiring.[11] Turley's vivid testimony confirmed that livin' large for a few years in the violent world of the National Football League could mean living horribly damaged afterward. As the NFL now confronts rule changes, technological improvements to helmets, and medical procedures committed to players' health rather than team success, it also confronts fundamental unknowns. How important are violent collisions to the wild enthusiasm of NFL fans? If the game can be made safer—and that it can is not obvious—how much safer can it be without losing its psychic charge? Imagine football as a game of skill, rather than skill-plus-violence: is it a kind of football that millions of Americans will love?

Moreover, if big hits can be minimized without damage to the game, what about all of the little hits? From the reporting in the fall of 2009 the public now knows about the research at the University of North Carolina that has measured the impact of head blows, the dozens of routine hits in practices and games, perhaps a thousand for a lineman over the course of a season. The "g force" of these blows ranges from the teens and twenties to over a hundred (the equivalent of a head hitting a windshield in a twenty-five-mile-per-hour collision), and neurologists are suggesting that this "repetitive sub-concussive trauma" may be as dangerous as full-blown concussions.[12] If further studies should prove them right, football would shrivel at its roots.

What if parents not letting their sons play youth football becomes as sensible as strapping them into car seats when they are toddlers? Even if the NFL itself can be made safer, how can it survive if the pipeline dries up?

I conclude this new afterword much as I concluded the original book, but with a more acute sense of the NFL's vulnerability, and more pointed uncertainty. In writing *Brand NFL* I attempted to make sense of that astonishing phenomenon, the National Football League. In writing about the current labor situation for this afterword I am stymied by the fact that the owners' actions simply do not yet make sense. Yes, the NHL survived a lockout in 2004–5, but with much less at stake. The NFL's last work stoppage, in 1987, was extraordinarily ugly. While the players have always been handicapped in labor disputes by their brief careers and lack of institutional memory, the latter may be a challenge for today's owners as well, just nine of whom were in the NFL in 1987. "League think" is a distant memory for even fewer.

In a few weeks a decision by the Supreme Court in *American Needle v. NFL* will clarify whether the league will be allowed to operate as a "single entity." The 2010 season will then play out without a salary cap. In the meantime, owners and union leaders will resume meeting, on the chance of reaching an agreement before a 2011 lockout becomes possible. Jeopardizing nearly two decades of labor peace remains unthinkable to me—surely rational self-interest will ultimately prevail. Or not. As the intentions of the owners and the resolve of the players emerge more clearly over the next several months, the immediate future of the NFL will come into focus.

That's the short term. For now, evidence of CTE can be detected only in autopsies. In the absence of new diagnostic technologies, a generation or two of statistically representative NFL players must die and have their brains autopsied before neurologists can make definitive judgments about the long-term risks. Findings from this research could be devastating to the NFL, yet the league must support it rather than appear indifferent to the well-being of its own players and the millions playing at lower levels who take their cues from the NFL. Can the NFL be safer yet remain thrillingly violent, retaining its essential tension between violence and artistry? If so, how safe can it be if not just concussions but also repeated head blows of even mild force may have long-term consequences? These questions will haunt the NFL until this most fundamental issue is resolved.

May 2010

NOTES

Abbreviations

AJ	Atlanta Journal
AP	Associated Press
BS	Baltimore Sun
CE	Cincinnati Enquirer
CT	Chicago Tribune
DMN	Dallas Morning News
DP	Denver Post
GBPG	Green Bay Press-Gazette
HC	Houston Chronicle
LAT	Los Angeles Times
MH	Miami Herald
NFLPA	National Football League Players Association
NYDN	New York Daily News
NYT	New York Times
PI	Philadelphia Inquirer
SBJ	Street & Smith's SportsBusiness Journal
SDU	San Diego Union
SFE	San Francisco Examiner
SI	Sports Illustrated
UPI	United Press International
WP	Washington Post

Introduction

1. Thomas B. Morgan, "The Wham in Pro Football," *Esquire*, November 1959. This essay was the first full-blown manifesto of pro football's new dispensation.

2. Ibid.; "A Man's Game," *Time*, November 30, 1959 (the issue featured Sam Huff on the cover); Bobby Layne as told to Murray Olderman, "This Is No Game for Kids," *Saturday Evening Post*, November 14, 1959; "The Violent Fact of Pro Football," *SI*, October 24, 1960. Cover stories in *Life* emphasizing heroic violence ran on December 5, 1960; November 17, 1961; October 14, 1966; December 13, 1971; and October 6, 1972. The November 1965 issue of *Esquire* included Thomas B. Morgan's "The American War Game" along with articles titled "The Fifteen Dirtiest Plays" and "The Toughest Customers" (the issue also featured a story revealing how the players' elaborate equipment fails to protect them). Similar stories in *Look* appeared around this same time, including "Operation Meat Grinder," October 19, 1965; "A Game for Madmen," September 5,

1967 (the first of a two-part article written by Vince Lombardi with journalist W. C. Heinz); "War on Sunday," November 26, 1968; "Mad Dogs and Football Men," October 7, 1969; and "Mayhem on the Line," December 29, 1970.

3. Neil Steinberg, Jack McCallum, and Richard O'Brien, "He Could Always Move Merchandise," *SI*, July 27, 1998; Michael MacCambridge, *America's Game: The Epic Story of How Pro Football Captured a Nation* (New York: Random House, 2004), 144–45, 183–84.

4. Art Donovan's *Fatso: Football When Men Were Really Men* (1987) was followed by Sam Huff's *Tough Stuff* (with Leonard Shapiro, 1988) and Stuart Leuthner's *Iron Men* (1988). Donovan became a favorite on late-night talk shows. *The Game of Their Lives: Pro Football's Wonder Years*, produced by NFL Films for HBO in 2001, and *Johnny U: The Life and Times of John Unitas*, Tom Callahan's 2006 biography, confirm that the mystique of the 1950s NFL remains alive.

5. Stephen Mahoney, "Pro Football's Profit Explosion," *Fortune*, November 1964.

6. Brett Pulley, "The $1 Billion Team," *Forbes*, September 20, 2004; Stefan Fatsis, "Can Socialism Survive?," *Wall Street Journal*, September 20, 2004; Ari Weinberg and David Dukcevich, "NFL's Highest-Paid Coaches," *Forbes*, January 24, 2003. Average ticket price is from the Fan Cost Index calculated by *Team Marketing Report* (online).

7. MacCambridge, *America's Game*, 212.

Chapter One

1. Michael MacCambridge, *America's Game: The Epic Story of How Pro Football Captured a Nation* (New York: Random House, 2004), 135–38, 157–58; Gerald Eskenazi, "The State of the N.F.L.: It's Still Winning More Than It Loses," *NYT*, May 2, 1982.

2. David Harris, *The League: The Rise and Decline of the NFL* (New York: Bantam, 1987); MacCambridge, *America's Game*, 171–73.

3. Tom Barnidge, "The NFL on TV," in *Total Football II: The Official Encyclopedia of the National Football League*, ed. Bob Carroll, Michael Gershman, David Neft, John Thorn, and the Elias Sports Bureau (New York: HarperCollins, 1999), 511–13.

4. Tex Maule, "Players Are Not Just People," *SI*, April 29, 1963; Kenneth Rudeen, "Sportsman of the Year," *SI*, January 6, 1964.

5. Leonard Shecter, *The Jocks* (Indianapolis: Bobbs-Merrill, 1969), 253–54; John Underwood et al., "The Biggest Game in Town," *SI*, March 10, 1986; Dan E. Moldea, *Interference: How Organized Crime Influences Professional Football* (New York: William Morrow, 1989), 27–38, 91, 199, 360.

6. MacCambridge, *America's Game*, 381.

7. Ibid., 287.

8. Tom C. Brody, "C. B. DeMille of the Pros," *SI*, November 20, 1967; William Taaffe, "Footage That Can Go to Your Head," *SI*, September 5, 1984; Ben Yagoda, "Not-So-Instant Replay," *New York Times Magazine*, December 14, 1986; Glen Macnow, "NFL Films Is Scoring High," *Nation's Business*, September 1988; Robert Strauss, "Catching Football on Film," *NYT*, October 29, 2000; David Lidsky, "Innovators: This Is NFL

Films," *Fortune Small Business*, August 22, 2002; Allen Barra, "On NFL Films' Home Turf," *Wall Street Journal*, October 18, 2006.

9. Brody, "C. B. DeMille of the Pros"; Robert Strauss, "An Empire Built on the Ballet of Football," *Electronic Media*, December 4, 2000; Tom C. Brody, "Fearless Tot from Possum Trot," *SI*, November 22, 1965; Jeff Bond, "Blood, Sweat, and Tunes," *Film Score Monthly*, January 1999.

10. Chris Pizzello, "On Touchdowns, There Are No Second Takes," *American Cinematographer*, October 1995; Strauss, "Catching Football on Film"; Strauss, "An Empire Built on the Ballet of Football"; Bond, "Blood, Sweat, and Tunes."

11. Bond, "Blood, Sweat, and Tunes."

12. Ibid.

13. Brody, "C. B. DeMille of the Pros." NFL Films has documented its own history in a series of videos featuring cinematographers and sound crew members, along with Steve Sabol, talking about their craft. See *The Stylists and the Storytellers* (1995), *Silent Soldiers: The Cinematographers* (1996), and volumes 1 and 2 of *Lost Treasures of NFL Films* (2000, shown initially on ESPN Classic Network). See also *The Idol Makers: Inside NFL Films*, a documentary film produced by National Geographic Television in 2000; and *Tight on the Spiral*, produced by Veras Communications for PBS in 2001.

14. Barra, "On NFL Films' Home Turf"; Jim Longo, "A Voice That Will Live on Forever," *Marion Star*, September 26, 2004; Bond, "Blood, Sweat, and Tunes." Yoshio Kishi receives credit in volume 2 of *Lost Treasures of NFL Films*, but his contribution is omitted from the various print tributes to the company. A compact disk recording, *The Power and the Glory*, has a rich sampling of Sam Spence's music.

15. Pizello, "On Touchdowns, There Are No Second Takes"; Bond, "Blood, Sweat, and Tunes"; Yagoda, "Not-So-Instant Replay"; Strauss, "An Empire Built on the Ballet of Football"; Strauss, "Catching Football on Film"; Lidsky, "Innovators: This Is NFL Films."

16. *The Idol Makers: Inside NFL Films.*

17. For a wry account of Lawrence Taylor "talking and bellowing and screaming" when he was miked for one game, see Tim Green, *The Dark Side of the Game: My Life in the NFL* (New York: Warner, 1996), 136–39.

18. Pizzello, "On Touchdowns, There Are No Second Takes."

19. Tom Hedden, quoted in Bond, "Blood, Sweat, and Tunes."

20. Ed Gruver, *The American Football League: A Year-by-Year History, 1960–1969* (Jefferson, N.C.: McFarland, 1997), 7–19.

21. Ibid., 20–37, 48–49, 54, 56; Roone Arledge, *Roone: A Memoir* (New York: Harper-Collins, 2003), 64.

22. Arledge, *Roone*, 66; Gruver, *The American Football League*, 125. For attendance figures, see Roger Treat, *The Encyclopedia of Football*, revised ed. (Garden City, N.Y.: Doubleday, 1977), 685.

23. Gruver, *The American Football League*, 156–62; MacCambridge, *America's Game*, 229–30.

24. Gruver, *The American Football League*, 35.

25. Super Bowl TV ratings are easily found on the Internet. See <http://www.philly burbs.com/pb-dyn/news/66-01252006-603201.html>.

26. Ira Berkow, "Once Again, It's the Star-Spangled Super Bowl," *NYT*, January 27, 1991.

27. "Scalpers Soaked as Rains Pass," *NYT*, January 12, 1970; Ira Berkow, "Much More Than a Football Game," *NYT*, January 19, 1985.

28. Berkow, "Once Again, It's the Star-Spangled Super Bowl."

29. Terry Lefton, "Big Game Will Keep with America's Mood," *SBJ*, January 28–February 3, 2002.

30. For a critical view of the show, see John Tierney, "Beer, Football, and a Glut of Patriotism," *NYT*, February 5, 2002.

31. William Nack, "A Name on the Wall," *SI*, July 23, 2001; MacCambridge, *America's Game*, 12.

32. Donald Jackson, "Bald Case in Point: Pro Football's Magical Immunity," *Life*, December 9, 1966. The "case in point" was part of a larger story titled "Ducking the Draft—Who and How."

33. On Pat Tillman, see Barry Wilner (AP), "NFL Pays Tribute to Tillman, 'Hero to All,'" *Portland Oregonian*, April 25, 2004; Josh White, "Tillman's Parents Are Critical of Army," *WP*, May 23, 2005; Josh White, "Tillman Killed by 'Friendly Fire,'" *WP*, May 30, 2005; Gary Smith, "Remember His Name," *SI*, September 11, 2006.

34. Marc Gunther and Bill Carter, *Monday Night Mayhem: The Inside Story of ABC's Monday Night Football* (New York: William Morrow, 1988), 28–30; Steve Rushin, "The Titan of Television," *SI*, August 16, 1994.

35. Arledge, *Roone*, 30–32.

36. Randy Roberts and James Olson, *Winning Is the Only Thing: Sports in America since 1945* (Baltimore: Johns Hopkins University Press, 1989), 114.

37. Gruver, *The American Football League*, 35; Arledge, *Roone*, 65.

38. Richard Sandomir, "One Night in 1970, the Revolution Was Televised," *NYT*, November 23, 2005.

39. Arledge, *Roone*, 31; Gunther and Carter, *Monday Night Mayhem*, 18, 54.

40. Roberts and Olson, *Winning Is the Only Thing*, 121.

41. Gunther and Carter, *Monday Night Mayhem*, 63.

42. Ibid., 67, 348; Erik Spanberg, "TV Nets Fine-Tune a Winning Playbook," *SBJ*, April 23–29, 2001.

43. Roger Kahn, "Emperors and Clowns," *Time*, January 10, 1977.

44. David Maraniss, "When Football Mattered," *Esquire*, September 1997.

45. Charles P. Pierce, "Does Football Matter?," *Esquire*, September 1997.

46. Thomas B. Morgan, "The American War Game," *Esquire*, October 1965. This essay essentially repeats the argument Morgan made in "The Wham in Pro Football," *Esquire*, November 1959.

47. For the fuller story, see David Maraniss, *When Pride Still Mattered: A Life of Vince Lombardi* (New York: Simon & Schuster, 1999).

48. See Tex Maule, "Vince Brings Green Days to Green Bay," *SI*, October 19, 1959; "The Drillmaster," *Time*, December 19, 1960; and Tim Cohane, "The Packers Pay the Price," *Look*, October 24, 1961. In *When Pride Still Mattered*, Maraniss calls Cohane Lombardi's "great mentioner" and the "historian of the Lombardi myth" (275, 295). Maraniss also sets the record straight on Lombardi's law school experience (68).

49. Bill Furlong, "New Day in Green Bay," *SI*, December 12, 1960.

50. Ibid.

51. The most complete telling of this story is in Herbert Warren Wind, "Packerland," *New Yorker*, December 8, 1962.

52. Maule, "Vince Brings Green Days to Green Bay"; Maule, "The Drillmaster"; Cohane, "The Packers Pay the Price"; Wind, "Packerland."

53. "Vinnie, Vidi, Vici," *Time*, December 21, 1962.

54. Many of these anecdotes were included in *Run to Daylight!* (Englewood Cliffs, N.J.: Prentice-Hall, 1963), written by Lombardi and journalist W. C. Heinz in the typical manner of "as told to" autobiographies. The book is full of stories and comments from previously published writings because Heinz had to cobble it together with little help from Lombardi, who had a poor memory for details. See Maraniss, *When Pride Still Mattered*, 318. Other sources of Lombardi lore are Vince Lombardi and W. C. Heinz, "A Game for Madmen," *Look*, September 5, 1967; and Vince Lombardi and W. C. Heinz, "Secrets of Winning Football," *Look*, September 19, 1967.

55. Quoted in Leonard Shecter, "The Toughest Man in Pro Football," *Esquire*, January 1968.

56. Jerry Kramer and Dick Schaap, "The $25,000 Block," *Look*, September 3, 1968.

57. Shecter, *The Jocks*, 107; Larry Merchant, *And Every Day You Take Another Bite* (Garden City, N.Y.: Doubleday & Company, 1971), 101, 103; Robert Lipsyte, *SportsWorld: An American Dreamland* (New York: Quadrangle/NYT, 1975), 54.

58. Jerry Kramer and Dick Schaap, "Green Bay Diary," *Look*, August 20, 1968; Richard Schickel, "On Pro Football," *Commentary*, January 1969; "Proud Fathers, Proud Sons," *Time*, September 14, 1970.

59. Merchant, *And Every Day You Take Another Bite*, 106; Lipsyte, *SportsWorld*, 57.

60. Maraniss, *When Pride Still Mattered*, 279.

61. Dick Schaap, "The Rough Road Ahead for Paul Hornung," *Sport*, November 1961; Maraniss, *When Pride Still Mattered*, 277–78.

62. This is essentially a summary of Maraniss's portrait in *When Pride Still Mattered*.

63. Davis's comment appeared in a segment of NBC's pregame show. See also Merchant, *And Every Day You Take Another Bite*, 105.

64. Maraniss, *When Pride Still Mattered*, 216.

65. Joe Namath with Dick Schaap, *I Can't Wait Until Tomorrow, 'Cause I Get Better-Looking Every Day* (New York: Random House, 1969), 51.

66. Lipsyte, *SportsWorld*, 52–53.

67. Merchant, *And Every Day You Take Another Bite*, 115; Lipsyte, *SportsWorld*, 52.

68. Robert H. Boyle, "Show-Biz Sonny and His Quest for Stars," *SI*, July 19, 1965.

Like Lombardi, Namath has been subjected to full biographical treatment. See Mark Kriegel, *Namath: A Biography* (New York: Viking, 2004).

69. John Lake, "Two for the Football Show: The Swinger and the Square," *New York Times Magazine*, November 5, 1967; Larry Merchant, "Mirror, Mirror, on the Wall, Who's the Fairest in the Fall," *Jock New York*, November 1969.

70. John Underwood, "Fabulous in Defeat," *SI*, January 11, 1965.

71. Kriegel, *Namath*, 130–39.

72. Boyle, "Show-Biz Sonny and His Quest for Stars."

73. Stuart Smith, "A Joint for Next Season," *SI*, February 8, 1965; "The $400,000 Knee," *Time*, February 5, 1965.

74. John R. McDermott, "The Famous Mustache That Was," *Life*, December 3, 1968.

75. Paul Hornung as told to William F. Reed, *Golden Boy: Girls, Games, and Gambling at Green Bay (and Notre Dame, Too)* (New York: Simon & Schuster, 2004), 234.

76. Leslie Fiedler, *No! in Thunder: Essays on Myth and Literature* (Boston: Beacon Press, 1960); Robert Daley, "Football's Marvelous Misfit," *SI*, December 5, 1964; Marshall Smith, "Bad Boy of the Pros," *Life*, October 22, 1965.

77. Boyle, "Show-Biz Sonny and His Quest for Stars."

78. Dan Jenkins, "The Sweet Life of Swinging Joe," *SI*, October 17, 1966.

79. Leigh Montville, "Off Broadway Joe," *SI*, July 14, 1997; Boyle, "Show-Biz Sonny and His Quest for Stars"; Jenkins, "The Sweet Life of Swinging Joe."

80. Jenkins, "The Sweet Life of Swinging Joe"; Arthur Daley, "Namath and the Draft," *NYT*, December 10, 1965; "A Uniform Draft Policy," *NYT*, December 18, 1965.

81. Jenkins, "The Sweet Life of Swinging Joe."

82. Ibid.

83. See Gerald Astor, "Namath the Game," *Look*, November 29, 1966; John Skow, " 'Joe, Joe, You're the Most Beautiful Thing in the World,' " *Saturday Evening Post*, December 3, 1966; Barbara Long, "Joe Namath," *Vogue*, February 1, 1967; Judy Klemesrud, "The Penthouse of Joe Namath: First There's the Llama Rug," *NYT*, December 12, 1967.

84. Smith, "A Joint for Next Season"; Jenkins, "The Sweet Life of Swinging Joe."

85. Skow, " 'Joe, Joe, You're the Most Beautiful Thing in the World' "; Lake, "Two for the Football Show"; Edwin Shrake, "The Plays Go for the New Joe," *SI*, October 16, 1967; Merchant, *And Every Day You Take Another Bite*, 116. Mark Kriegel has shown that the resentment of some teammates never ended; see Kriegel, *Namath*, 225.

86. "Battle of the QBs," *Time*, September 17, 1965; Charles Moore, "Mr. Big of the Bonus Baby War," *Life*, January 15, 1965; McDermott, "The Famous Mustache That Was."

87. Bill Mathis, "The Joe Namath I Know," *Esquire*, September 1968; and Al Hirshberg, "The Joe Namath I Know," *Esquire*, September 1968. Namath (as told to Larry King) responded to Hirshberg's charges in the December issue.

88. Tex Maule, "A Go Pattern vs. a Stop Team," *SI*, January 13, 1969.

89. Tex Maule, "Say It's So, Joe," *SI*, January 20, 1969.

90. Al Lightner, "Sportslightner," *Oregon Statesman* (Salem), January 14, 1969.

91. Sandy Smith, "Broadway Joe: Rebel with a Nightclub for a Cause," *Life*, June 20, 1969; "Bugging Joe Namath," *National Review*, July 1, 1969. See also "A Surfeit of Surveillance," *Christian Century*, July 9, 1969.

92. "Joe's Tearful Good-by," *Newsweek*, June 16, 1969; "Blues for Broadway Joe," *Newsweek*, June 23, 1969; "Broadway Joe's Return," *Newsweek*, July 28, 1969; William Johnson, "Mod Man Out," *SI*, June 16, 1969; Nicholas Pileggi, "The Game Was Up at Namath's," *SI*, June 23, 1969; Gary Ronberg, "To Be a Good Joe, It Takes a Hard Sell," *SI*, July 28, 1969; "Bachelors II," *Time*, July 25, 1969.

93. Kriegel, *Namath*, 299, 309.

94. "Namath of the Jets," *Newsweek*, September 15, 1969. The articles in *Newsweek*, like *Time*, were unsigned in this period, but the magazine's sports editor, Pete Axthelm, was identified on the contents page as the author.

95. Kriegel, *Namath*, 356, 361.

96. Rick Telander, *Joe Namath and the Other Guys* (New York: Holt, Rinehart and Winston, 1976), 49. Telander's chronicle of the 1975 season is particularly informative regarding Namath's relationships with teammates (mostly good) and sportswriters (mostly bad) and the special status he continued to have among both teammates and opponents, even toward the end of his career.

97. Long, "Joe Namath."

98. Murray Kempton, "Sports," *Esquire*, October 1972.

99. "Pain Pays the Bills for Joe's Good Life," *Life*, November 3, 1972; Dick Schaap, "I Still Do What I Want to Do—Only I Don't Want to Do as Much," *Life*, November 3, 1972.

100. James Reston, "Joe Namath, the New Anti-Hero," *NYT*, August 21, 1970; Jack Richardson, "Joe Namath and the Problem of Heroic Virtue," *Esquire*, October 1969.

101. Quoted in Merchant, *And Every Day You Take Another Bite*, 117.

102. Kriegel, *Namath*, 285.

103. Dave Anderson, "Vietnam Victims Gain Namath's Salute," *NYT*, February 16, 1969; Dave Anderson, "Political Football," *NYT*, July 1, 1973.

104. Art Spander, "Joe Namath, the Man and the Myth," *Sporting News*, September 21, 1974.

105. Herman L. Masin, "Jet Age Hero," *Senior Scholastic*, November 17 and November 24, 1969; Rose Namath Szolnoki with Bill Kushner, *Namath: My Son Joe* (Birmingham, Ala.: Oxmoor House, 1975).

106. John Pekkanen, "The New Cincinnati Kid," *Life*, October 10, 1969; Gerald Astor, "Charger Goes Groovy," *Look*, December 2, 1969; Marty Domres and Robert Smith, *Bump and Run: The Days and Nights of a Rookie Quarterback* (New York: Bantam, 1971); Kay Gilman, "Sports Stars: The New Sex Symbols," *MH*, August 11, 1974. On his effect on women, see Kriegel, *Namath*, passim.

107. Kriegel, *Namath*, 338, 358. Kriegel's biography fully documents the marketing of Joe Namath throughout and after his football career.

108. William F. Buckley Jr., "Toward an Imperfect Understanding of the Namath Affair," *Esquire*, October 1969; Richardson, "Joe Namath," *Esquire*, October 1969.

109. Bernie Parrish, *They Call It a Game* (New York: Dial Press, 1971), 289–90.

110. Prescott Sullivan, "It's an Expensive Truce Time for 49ers and for Youth Fund," *SFE*, August 18, 1974; Ron Hudspeth, "A New Look," *AJ*, July 22, 1974; Cameron C. Snyder, "Young, Eager, Insecure Colts to Face Steelers," *BS*, September 14, 1974.

Chapter Two

1. Edwin Pope, "Strike May Become Dolphin Triumph," *MH*, August 8, 1974. On Robbie's tightfistedness, see David Harris, *The League: The Rise and Decline of the NFL* (New York: Bantam, 1986), 199.

2. Joe Williams, "Players Threaten Pro Grid Bosses," *New York World-Telegram*, February 7, 1957; Lester Rodney, "On the Scoreboard," *Daily Worker*, December 4, 1957.

3. Michael E. Lomax, "Conflict and Compromise: The Evolution of American Professional Football's Labour Relations, 1957–1966," *Football Studies* 4 (October 2001): 5–39; Bernie Parrish, *They Call It a Game* (New York: Dial Press, 1971), 245–68.

4. Lomax, "Conflict and Compromise," 29–31.

5. NFLPA, "About Us," <http://www.nflpa.org>; William N. Wallace, "Football Talks Resume Today," *NYT*, June 28, 1968; Sam Goldpaper, "N.F.L. Club Owners and Player Group Reach Agreement," *NYT*, July 15, 1968; Lomax, "Conflict and Compromise"; Parrish, *They Call It a Game*, 271–85.

6. William N. Wallace, "Rozelle Moves to Avert Strike," *NYT*, July 8, 1970; "N.F.L. Players Told: Skip Camp Awhile," *NYT*, July 10, 1970; "Pro Football Camps Open for Rookies Only Today as Controversy Continues," *NYT*, July 14, 1970; William N. Wallace, "Football Tie-Up Enters 4th Day; College All-Stars Resume Drills," *NYT*, July 17, 1970; William N. Wallace, "It's Fourth Down and 100 Yards to Go as Pro Football Pension Dispute Hardens," *NYT*, July 19, 1970; William N. Wallace, "N.F.L. Club Owners Agree to Join Mediation in Their Dispute with Players," *NYT*, July 23, 1970.

7. Dave Anderson, "N.F.L. Owners Open Camps Tonight to Seasoned Players," *NYT*, July 30, 1970; Joseph Durso, "Most Regulars Shun Football Camps and Vote to Strike against Owners," *NYT*, July 31, 1970.

8. Dave Anderson, "Pro Football Club Owners and Players Agree to 4-Year Pact, Ending Strike," *NYT*, August 4, 1970. On Rozelle's minimal role in the strike, see Harris, *The League*, 194.

9. Leonard Koppett, "Sports of the Times," *NYT*, August 4, 1970.

10. See, for example, Joe McGuff, "Sporting Comment," *Kansas City Star*, July 5, 1974.

11. Position papers from the opposing sides are Theodore W. Kheel, "Owners: A Grave Threat to Structure of the Game," *NYT*, May 26, 1974; and John Mackey, "Athletes: Freedom Placed above Economic Desires," *NYT*, May 26, 1974. See also William N. Wallace, "N.F.L. Clubs Dispel 'Myths' of Big Profits," *NYT*, June 7, 1974; Tom Seppy (AP), "NFL Players, Owners Break off Bargaining," *WP*, June 27, 1974; UPI, "Firm Line Is Drawn on 'Freedom Issues,' " *WP*, June 30, 1974; "The Issues," *WP*, July 2, 1974.

12. Gwilym S. Brown, "Because of a Clause, a Cause," *SI*, May 1, 1972.

13. Jeff Meyers, "Rozelle Neutral on Grievances," *St. Louis Post-Dispatch*, July 21, 1974.

14. William N. Wallace, "Rozelle Rule Found in Antitrust Violation," *NYT*, December 31, 1975.

15. Meyers, "Rozelle Neutral on Grievances"; Jeff Meyers, "Players Say Rozelle Gave Them Crumbs," *St. Louis Post-Dispatch*, July 23, 1974.

16. AP, " 'Freedom' Is Key in Players' Strike," *Cleveland Plain Dealer*, June 28, 1974.

17. Furman Bisher, "Fan Union, Local No. 1.5," *AJ*, July 5, 1974; Jack Murphy, "Little Public Support for Striking Athletes," *SDU*, July 17, 1974; Len Wagner, "Out of Bounds?," *GBPG*, July 18, 1974; Neil Amdur, "Merits of Cooling-Off Period Debated," *NYT*, August 12, 1974.

18. For example, see Phil Pepe, "Players, Pepe in Minority," *NYDN*, July 21, 1974; "NFL Strike: Fans Will Pay" (editorial), *Boston Evening Globe*, August 6, 1974.

19. Skip Myslenski, "With 90 Issues Unresolved, NFL Strike Is Imminent," *PI*, June 23, 1974.

20. Myslenski, "With 90 Issues Unresolved."

21. Harris, *The League*, 95.

22. Red Smith, "You Can't Pay Me Enough," *NYT*, May 29, 1974.

23. George Solomon, "Curry: NFL 'Restrains Rights'; Curtis: 'I'm Spoiled,' " *WP*, June 28, 1974; "Curtis to Defy Pickets," *HC*, June 27, 1974.

24. "NFL Picket Crossing Due to Begin Today," *WP*, July 3, 1974.

25. Dave Brady, "Players' Symbol Clinches Opposition," *WP*, June 30, 1974; Bisher, "Fan Union, Local No. 1.5"; "Klein Denounces Garvey's Tactics," *SDU*, August 1, 1974; Dick Young, "What's Going on Here?," *NYDN*, August 7, 1974; Ron Hudspeth, "The Picket Line," *AJ*, August 5, 1974. On Van Brocklin, see Lewis Grizzard, "Norm Van Brocklin: The Dutchman Right or Wrong, but Always the Dutchman," *AJ*, July 16, 1974. See also Douglas Hartmann, *Race, Culture, and the Revolt of the Black Athlete: The 1968 Olympic Protests and Their Aftermath* (Chicago: University of Chicago Press, 2003), 188–89.

26. Tom Callahan, "All Seems Serene," *CE*, August 15, 1974.

27. Jerry Magee, "Charger Rookies Defy Player Strike, Report," *SDU*, July 4, 1974; Jack Murphy, "Carnival Atmosphere as Picketing Begins," *SDU*, July 4, 1974; Jerry Magee, "Klein Charges Strikers with Violence Threats," *SDU*, July 5 1974; Jack Murphy, "Folks Not So Cordial on Strike's Second Day," *SDU*, July 5, 1974; Jerry Magee, "No. 1 Draft Pick Goode Joins Charger Pickets," *SDU*, July 6, 1974; Jerry Magee, "Goode Ends Strike Role, Rejoins Camp," *SDU*, July 7, 1974.

28. Red Smith, "With Certain Inalienable Rights," *NYT*, July 8, 1974.

29. "N.F.L. Held in Labor Code Violation," *NYT*, July 1, 1976.

30. "NFL Strike Brings All-Star Game Cancellation," *WP*, July 11, 1974; Edwin Pope, "Love Letters," *MH*, July 16, 1974.

31. Bill Van Smith and Terry Galvin, "Dolphins to Meet on All-Star Fate," *MH*, July 3, 1974; Bill Braucher, "Morris' Talks Snag on Injury," *MH*, July 13, 1974; Edwin Pope, "Monday Looms Key Date for Breaking Strike," *MH*, July 25, 1974; Bill Braucher, "No Additional Vets Report; Dolphins Warned on Bonuses," *MH*, July 30, 1974.

32. See Dick Forbes, "Strike Won't Delay Bengals' Camp," *CE*, June 28, 1974; and Tom LaMarre, "Otto to Cross Picket Line?," *Oakland Tribune*, July 16, 1974.

33. See Dick Forbes, "Bengal Veterans Speak," *CE*, July 14, 1974, and other *Cincinnati Enquirer* reports over the succeeding days.

34. Jack Murray, "Bengal Split Piles Pressure on Pat Matson," *CE*, July 14, 1974; Dick Forbes, "Matson Most Hurt by Bengals' Division," *CE*, July 20, 1974; Jack Murray, "The 'Brotherhood' Aligns with NFL Strikers," *CE*, July 25, 1974. For others receiving hate mail, see AP, "Bowman Seeks No Sympathy," *GBPG*, July 16, 1974; and John Hall, "Who's Boo Hoo?," *LAT*, August 23, 1974.

35. Bill Braucher, "Dolphins' Vets Will Meet Friday," *MH*, July 4, 1974; Bill Braucher, "Swift Needs All the Wit He Can Find These Days," *MH*, August 7, 1974; Edwin Pope, "Another Side of Don-and-Doug Show," *MH*, August 1, 1974.

36. Richard Goldstein, "Wellington Mara, the Patriarch of the N.F.L., Dies at 89," *NYT*, October 26, 2005; Daniel Kaplan, "Pro Football Loses a Giant Leader," *SBJ*, October 31–November 6, 2005.

37. Jerry Magee, "Charger Vets Seek Trades," *SDU*, July 11, 1974; John Hall, "The War Games," *LAT*, June 25, 1974; "Judgment for Sweeney," *NYT*, January 23, 1997.

38. Robert Markus, "Presidential Pardon for Abe Gibron?," *CT*, September 12, 1974. See also Don Pierson, "Hard to Find a Happy Bear in Camp," *CT*, August 22, 1974.

39. Jeff Meyers, "Mulligan in a Stew about Being Sent to Bears," *St. Louis Post-Dispatch*, August 25, 1974.

40. For a portrait of Irsay during his Baltimore years, see Harris, *The League*, 105–7, 224–25, 565–69, 713–19.

41. Alan Goldstein, "Ted Hendricks Signs with Sharks of WFL," *BS*, August 9, 1974; "Colts Deal Drougas to Saints," *BS*, August 18, 1974.

42. Hal Lundgren, "Gillman Sold on Inexperienced Ellenbogen," *HC*, July 12, 1974; Hal Lundgren, "The Gillman Approach: Total Control, Authority," *HC*, July 14, 1974; Jerry Wizig, "Gillman Foresees No Problems with Vets," *HC*, July 16, 1974; Dick Peebles, "Quick to Forget," *HC*, July 17, 1974.

43. Bob Whitley, "Walden Crosses Picket Line, Mum on Why," *Pittsburgh Post-Gazette*, July 17, 1974.

44. Jeff Meyers, "Striking Unity Among Big Red," *St. Louis Post-Dispatch*, August 1, 1974.

45. Jim Klobuchar, "Page Accuses NFL Owners of 'Reprisals,'" *Minneapolis Star*, August 31, 1974.

46. Dick O'Connor, "Turner, Ralston Keep the Peace," *DP*, July 14, 1974; Dick O'Connor, "Bronco Vets 'Too Organized,'" *DP*, July 24, 1974; Dick O'Connor, "Pressure off as Bronco Veterans Don't Ask Boycott," *DP*, July 31, 1974; Dick O'Connor, "Summer Unity Might 'Make' '74 Broncos," *DP*, September 4, 1974.

47. Len Wagner, "Freedom Has New Meaning for Vets," *GBPG*, July 26, 1974; Don Pierson, "Green Bay Police Arrest 19 Pickets," *CT*, July 26, 1974.

48. Jesse Outlar, "This and That," *Atlanta Journal and Atlanta Constitution*, July 21, 1974. This combined Sunday edition of the two Atlanta papers also had five other stories about the trade.

49. Gordon Forbes, "Eagle Vets Prepare to Greet Rookies with Pickets," *PI*, July 9, 1974; Gordon Forbes, "Players Misguided, Eagles Owner Says," *PI*, July 13, 1974; Gordon Forbes, "Picketing 'No Fun' for Veteran Eagles," *PI*, July 14, 1974; Gordon Forbes, "Next Step in NFL Strike Seems to Be Up to Owners," *PI*, July 17, 1974.

50. Gordon Forbes, "Coach, Eagle Vets Hold Team-Unity Meeting," *PI*, July 22, 1974; Gordon Forbes, "Some Eagles Feel Gabriel Let Them Down," *PI*, August 11, 1974.

51. Gordon Forbes, "Eagles Drill—Minus Gabe," *PI*, July 23, 1974; Gordon Forbes, "Freedom Issues Soured Gabriel on NFL Strikers," *PI*, July 27, 1974; Gordon Forbes, "Eagles Vote to Stay Out, but Kramer, Germany Go In," *PI*, July 27, 1974; Gordon Forbes, "Blame Any Eagles' Split on Tose, Says Dempsey," *PI*, August 4, 1974; Forbes, "Some Eagles Feel Gabriel Let Them Down"; Gordon Forbes, "Tose Set to Cool Off but Dempsey Isn't," *PI*, August 12, 1974.

52. Cliff Christl, "Nystrom Finds 'Scab' Label Hard to Bear," *GBPG*, July 13, 1974; Tom LaMarre, "Three Raider Vets Report; Blanda Next?," *Oakland Tribune*, July 25, 1974; Walt Daley, "Raider 'Outs' vs. 'Ins': Wide Rift," *SFE*, July 27, 1974; Norm Miller, "Three Giants Defect; Mates Vow Strike Support," *NYDN*, August 7, 1974.

53. Jack Saylor, "Lions Coach McCafferty Dies," *Detroit Free Press*, July 29, 1974 (see also the four other strike-related articles or commentaries in that day's sports section).

54. Larry Felser, "Labor-Scented Air Fuels Football Fire," *Buffalo Evening News*, July 26, 1974; Jeff Meyers, "What's Dawning in Canton—Labor Test or Fete?," *St. Louis Post-Dispatch*, July 26, 1974.

55. Don Pierson, "Pickets Picket Pickets, but Fame Game Goes On," *CT*, July 28, 1974; Dick Young, "Of Soft Heads and Hard Hearts," *NYDN*, August 1, 1974; Dave Anderson, "Nostalgia Enters the N.F.L. Strike," *NYT*, August 1, 1974.

56. Jim Graham, "Players' Union Creates Bad Image," *DP*, July 7, 1974.

57. George Solomon, "Baugh Slings Some Arrows at the NFL Players Association," *WP*, July 25, 1974; AP, "Ex-NFL Greats Criticize Players Strike Demands," *HC*, August 3, 1974; "Lane Raps Establishment," *PI*, July 28, 1974.

58. "N.F.L.'s Preseason Crowds Are off by 256,748; Gate down $1.8 Million," *NYT*, August 5, 1974.

59. George Minot Jr., "NFL Parley: No Progress," *WP*, July 21, 1974; "Players' Barrier Beginning to Display Ragged Edges," *WP*, July 28, 1974; Nancy Scannell, "End of NFL Strike Seen 'Soon,'" *WP*, July 30, 1974; Nancy Scannell, "NFL Factions Try Again," *WP*, July 31, 1974; Nancy Scannell, "NFL Talks Are Intensified," *WP*, August 1, 1974; Nancy Scannell, "NFL Talks Recess until Tuesday," *WP*, August 2, 1974; Leonard Shapiro, "Redskins Hold Line in NFL Player Strike," *WP*, August 4, 1974.

60. Jim Caffrey, "10 Colt Veterans Cross Picket Line at McDonogh Camp," *BS*, July 26, 1974.

61. Wallace, "N.F.L. Clubs Dispel 'Myths' of Big Profits"; "N.F.L. Data on Profits Disputed," *NYT*, June 8, 1974; Edwin Pope, "Time for Both Sides to Get Sensible," *MH*, July 30, 1974; Red Smith, "Figures Don't Lie, Very Often," *NYT*, June 21, 1974.

62. "Sports Salaries and Benefits," *NYDN*, June 30, 1974.

63. Roger G. Noll, ed., *Government and the Sports Business: Papers Prepared for a Conference of Experts* (Washington, D.C.: Brookings Institution, 1974); UPI, "How Team Owners Rip Off the Paying Public," *SFE*, July 21, 1974.

64. Edwin Pope, "Monday Looms Key Date for Breaking Strike," *MH*, July 25, 1974.

65. "N.F.L. Held in Labor Code Violation," *NYT*, July 2, 1976. This was the ruling that also restored the signing bonuses of striking players.

66. Pope, "Time for Both Sides to Get Sensible."

67. Tom Callahan, "The View from Wilmington: What's to Strike About?," *CE*, August 2, 1974. See also Jack Murphy, "Strike May Cost Vets Season's Pay—Klein," *SDU*, July 2, 1974; Pepe, "Players, Pepe in Minority."

68. Bisher, "Fan Union, Local No. 1.5."

69. The ten newspapers wholly critical of the strike were the *Atlanta Journal, Chicago Tribune, Cleveland Plain Dealer, Dallas Morning News, Houston Chronicle, Los Angeles Times, Minneapolis Star, New Orleans Times-Picayune, Pittsburgh Post-Gazette,* and *San Francisco Examiner.*

70. Others with opposing views at the same newspaper (with the prostrike columnist named first) were Richard Basoco and Bob Maisel of the *Baltimore Sun,* George Puscas and Joe Falls of the *Detroit Free Press,* Jeff Meyers and Bob Broeg of the *St. Louis Post-Dispatch,* Cliff Christl (with some ambivalence) and Len Wagner of the *Green Bay Press-Gazette,* Dick Connor and Jim Graham of the *Denver Post,* and Jack Murphy (only at first) and Jerry Magee of the *San Diego Union.*

71. These included the *Boston Globe, Buffalo Evening News,* and *Cincinnati Enquirer.*

72. Hal Lebovitz, "Rookies Will Report, We Will Play," *Cleveland Plain Dealer,* July 14, 1974.

73. Wells Twombly, "The Most Absurd Dispute in Recent Memory," *SFE*, July 15, 1974; Wells Twombly, "Football Freaks Need Their Own Bill of Rights," *SFE*, July 29, 1974; Wells Twombly, "NFL Strike Becoming a Loser's Delight," *SFE*, August 23, 1974. See also Dick Young, "Independence Day and Players Rights," *NYDN*, July 4, 1974; Young, "Of Soft Heads and Hard Hearts"; Young, "What's Going on Here?"; and Dick Peebles, "Strike Three," *HC*, July 3, 1974.

74. Tom Callahan, "PR Is for Owners," *CE*, August 6, 1974.

75. Smith, "You Can't Pay Me Enough"; Smith, "Figures Don't Lie, Very Often"; Smith, "With Certain Inalienable Rights"; Red Smith, "In Pro Football's Cradle—Pickets," *NYT*, July 29, 1974; Red Smith, "And in Some Cases Erroneous," *NYT*, August 7, 1974.

76. Edwin Pope, "Don't Pin Whole Rap on Players' Union," *MH*, July 12, 1974; Pope, "Love Letters"; Edwin Pope, "Time for Both Sides to Get Sensible," *MH*, July 30, 1974; Edwin Pope, "A Slight Omission of the Central Fact," *MH*, August 7, 1974.

77. "Poll Shows Fans on Players' Side," *NYT*, August 24, 1974.

78. "Poll Favors Owners over Players," *NYT*, July 16, 1974.

79. Chuck Heaton, "NFL Owners Won't Call Off Season," *Cleveland Plain Dealer*, June 28, 1974; Chuck Heaton, "NFL Strike Has Coaches on Spot," *Cleveland Plain Dealer*, July 7, 1974; Don Langenkamp, "Fans Anti-Player in Barber Poll," *GBPG*, June 29, 1974; Len Wagner, "Fan Apathy Roots Deeper Than Strike," *GBPG*, July 25, 1974; Clint Roswell, "Fans in Street Brush Off the NFL Strike," *NYDN*, July 12, 1974; Jack Murphy, "Little Public Support for Striking Athletes," *SDU*, July 17, 1974; Dick Forbes, "Some Lady Fans Falling Out of Love with Football," *CE*, July 20, 1974; Dick Forbes, "Striking Bengals Get No Sympathy at Riverfront," *CE*, August 4, 1974; Glenn Schwarz, "Bay Area View: Players Asking for Too Much," *SFE*, July 21, 1974; Ed Levitt, "A Voice for Fan Freedom," *Oakland Tribune*, July 24, 1974; Pope, "Time for Both Sides to Get Sensible"; Bill McMurray, "High School Coaches Say NFL Player Strike Wrong," *HC*, July 29, 1974; Jerry Wizig, "Crowd Endorses Rookie Show," *HC*, August 4, 1974; Dick Gordon, "A Fan for Players," *Minnesota Star*, August 7, 1974.

80. "Sound Off," *Cleveland Plain Dealer*, July 10, 1974 (see also July 7); "Speaking the Public Mind" (letters to the editor), *Kansas City Star*, July 21, 1974; "Area Man Writes Curry," *Kansas City Times*, July 13, 1974.

81. "Fan Letters," *GBPG*, July 7, 1974. For the Hortonville massacre, see <http://www.weac.org/AboutWEA/1998-99/horton.htm>.

82. Joe Falls, "Why Not Televise NFL Picket Lines?," *Detroit Free Press*, July 5, 1974. See also Dick Young, "Independence Day and Players' Rights," *NYDN*, July 4, 1974; Jim Graham, "Players' Union Creates Bad Image," *DP*, July 7, 1974; Wells Twombly, "They Fight for Freedom Issues and $25,000 Per Year," *SFE*, July 21, 1974; Gordon Forbes, "Will Garvey's Stubbornness Endanger Some Careers?," *PI*, August 3, 1974; "NFL Strike: Fans Will Pay" (editorial), *Boston Evening Globe*, August 6, 1974.

83. "Fan Letters," *GBPG*, July 9, 1974; Chuck Heaton, "Luxury Ride for Rookies," *Cleveland Plain Dealer*, August 2, 1974; Chuck Heaton, "Love Letter," *Cleveland Plain Dealer*, August 30, 1974.

84. George Puscas, "Paging Mr. Kissinger . . . NFL 'War' Needs You," *Detroit Free Press*, July 25, 1974; Larry McMillen, "Williams Heads Cuts by Saints," *New Orleans Times-Picayune*, September 11, 1974; Bob Roesler, "Behind the Sports Scene," *New Orleans Times-Picayune*, September 15, 1974; Bob Oates, "No Pickets, No Veterans," *LAT*, July 22, 1974; John Hall, "The Middle Man," *LAT*, July 24, 1974; Bob Oates, "Hadl, Snow, Scibelli, Rentzel Quit Strike and Rejoin Rams," *LAT*, August 6, 1974; Hall, "Who's Boo Hoo?"

85. Tom Callahan, *Johnny U: The Life and Times of John Unitas* (New York: Viking, 2006), 360; Jerry Magee, "Unitas Zooms Past Pickets," *SDU*, July 13, 1974. In his celebration of Unitas as a 1950s-era player, Callahan does not mention the strike or the circumstances of Unitas's retirement.

86. Mark Kriegel, *Namath: A Biography* (New York: Viking, 2004), 360; Larry Felser, "O. J. Sympathizes with the Rookies," *Buffalo Evening News*, July 8, 1974.

87. Cliff Christl, "Will Offensive Linemen Protect Tagge?," *GBPG*, July 30, 1974.

88. Forbes, "Some Eagles Feel Gabriel Let Them Down"; Norm Miller, "3 Giants Cross Line to Cries of 'Stab in the Back,'" *NYDN*, July 27, 1974.

89. Cliff Christl, "Separate Paths for Two Fringe Veterans," *GBPG*, August 6, 1974; Larry Felser, "Bo Cornell Reports to Bills," *Buffalo Evening News*, August 5, 1974.

90. Tom LaMarre, "Raider Trio's Fast Visit," *Oakland Tribune*, July 19, 1974; Tom LaMarre, "Milan, Gaydos Report," *Oakland Tribune*, July 21, 1974; Gordon Forbes, "The Freedom Fighter," *PI*, July 31, 1974; Gordon Forbes, "Strike Got Luken Respect, Could Cost Him His Future," *PI*, August 15, 1974; Gordon Forbes, "Bouggess's September Days Are a Precious Few," *PI*, September 7, 1974.

91. Joe McGuff, "Sporting Comment," *Kansas City Star*, August 1, 1974.

92. Bob St. John, "Neely Quits NFLPA; Rookies Open Early," *DMN*, July 7, 1974; Dick Forbes, "Bengal Veterans Speak," *CE*, July 14, 1974; Jeff Meyers, "Stallings Defies Union," *St. Louis Post-Dispatch*, July 15, 1974.

93. Tom LaMarre, "Three Raider Veterans Report, Three Coming?," *Oakland Tribune*, July 24, 1974; Will McDonough, "Hannah Won't Strike: 'I Have No Complaints,'" *Boston Globe*, July 3, 1974.

94. Bill Braucher, "Langer, Matheson Won't Honor Strike," *MH*, July 7, 1974; Bob St. John, "Neely Says He Will Cross Picket Line," *DMN*, July 9, 1974; "Agile, Quick Patton Slips Bird Pickets," *PI*, July 29, 1974; Gary Long, "Yepremian, 3 Others Report," *MH*, August 1, 1974; Ron Hudspeth, "Falcons' Comments Sting Nobis," *AJ*, August 13, 1974.

95. Ron Hudspeth, "Falcons' Ray Ready to Play," *AJ*, July 15, 1974; Ron Hudspeth, "Two with a Calling," *Atlanta Journal and Atlanta Constitution*, July 21, 1974; Larry Fox, "'Free' Thompson Bucks Line," *NYDN*, July 10, 1974; "Ehrmann, 4 Other Vets Cross Picket Line," *BS*, July 25, 1974; Jack Saylor, "Landry's Out," *Detroit Free Press*, August 3, 1974; Bob St. John, "More Cowboy Vets Report," *DMN*, August 7, 1974; Jim Dent, "Breakdown Is Disturbing," *DMN*, August 2, 1974.

96. Don Pierson, "First Bears' Vet Crosses Line," *CT*, July 31, 1974; Will McDonough, "While Others Strike, Dorsey Becomes a Patriot," *Boston Globe*, July 23, 1974; Dick Forbes, "Walters Needs Camp, Not Strike," *CE*, July 16, 1974.

97. David DuPree, "Hancock Joins Carlisle Drills," *WP*, July 23, 1974; Pope, "Strike May Become Dolphin Triumph."

98. Bob Roesler, "Butler Gives Honest Opinion of Striking Vets," *New Orleans Times-Picayune*, July 16, 1974; Norm Miller, "Hilton Deserts Strike Ranks, Reports to Giants," *NYDN*, July 24, 1974; Larry Fox, "Little Crosses Line and Jets Get a Big Lift," *NYDN*, August 1, 1974; Norm Miller, "Young and Kelley Cross the Giants' Picket Line," *NYDN*, August 2, 1974; "Korver, Seiler Bring Raider Vet Total to 13," *Oakland Tribune*, July 29, 1974; "Griese, Bradshaw, Hadl Report," *WP*, August 6, 1974.

99. McDonough, "Hannah Won't Strike"; also "Garrison Says He Will Report Today," *DMN*, August 2, 1974; Bob St. John, "Jolly Roger Checking In," *DMN*, August 4, 1974; Bob St. John, "Cowboy Leaders Report," *DMN*, August 5, 1974; and Bob St. John, "Pearson in Camp Parade," *DMN*, August 8, 1974.

100. Cliff Christl, "Al Matthews Not Defying Strikers," *GBPG*, August 2, 1974; Dick Forbes, "In-Camp Bengals React Angrily to Matson's Remarks," *CE*, August 1, 1974; Dick Connor, "Cool Heads Needed for Settling Strike," *DP*, August 11, 1974; Bob St. John, "Sounds of Silence," *DMN*, August 8, 1974.

101. Chuck Heaton, "Independence Day for NFL Rookies?," *Cleveland Plain Dealer*, July 4, 1974; Cliff Christl, "Christl Ball," *GBPG*, July 17, 1974.

102. Bob St. John, "Richards Now Heading West," *DMN*, July 28, 1974; Bob St. John, "Cowboy Leaders Report," *DMN*, August 5, 1974; Hal Lundgren, "Oiler Eaglin Crosses Picket Line to 'Protect Job,'" *HC*, July 8, 1974; Marino Parascenzo, "Economic Talk Festers in NFL," *Pittsburgh Post-Gazette*, July 31, 1974; Young, "What's Going on Here?"

103. Bill Braucher, "Truce Good News to Shula, Csonka," *MH*, August 12, 1974; Dick Forbes, "Pritchard Striking for One Reason: Matson," *CE*, August 8, 1974.

104. Caffrey, "10 Colt Veterans Cross Picket Line at McDonogh Camp"; Chuck Heaton, "Browns' Adam Believes in 'Freedom Issues,'" *Cleveland Plain Dealer*, July 26, 1974; Bill Braucher, "Dolphin Picket Line Small but Orderly," *MH*, July 8, 1974.

105. Frank Dolson, "And after Scabs, Are There Scars?," *PI*, August 5, 1974; Forbes, "Strike Got Luken Respect"; Forbes, "The Freedom Fighter."

106. Edwin Pope, "Time for Garvey to Go," *MH*, August 9, 1974; Bob Oates, "Mack Turns on Garvey for Slap at Staubach," *LAT*, August 8, 1974. See also Bob St. John, "Garvey Angers Staubach," *DMN*, August 6, 1974; Dick Young, "What's Going on Here?"; Roesler, "Behind the Sports Scene" (Roesler returned to the incident in columns on August 22 and August 24); Bob Maisel, "The Morning After," *BS*, August 10, 1974.

107. Chuck Heaton, "Sad Lesson for Modell," *Cleveland Plain Dealer*, August 11, 1974; Chuck Heaton, "Player Pressure Brings Break," *Cleveland Plain Dealer*, August 12, 1974.

108. "Gillman: Strike Suspension 'Dumb,'" *HC*, August 12, 1974; "Have to Let Veterans in, Says Adams," *HC*, August 13, 1974; Hal Lundgren, "Oilers Cut Seven Vets," *HC*, August 14, 1974; John Wilson, "Sowing Bitter Seeds," *HC*, August 15, 1974.

109. Clint Roswell, "Giants Have Punch—at Each Other," *NYDN*, August 16, 1974.

110. Steve Jacobson, "Open Hostility to Gillman in Oiler Camp," *HC*, August 28, 1974.

111. Bill Free, "Colt Coach Turns Away 18 Reporting Veterans," *BS*, August 14, 1974; Alan Goldstein, "Colt Veterans Turned Away, Told to Come Back Sunday," *BS*, August 15, 1974; Bob Maisel, "The Morning After," *BS*, August 15, 1974; Alan Goldstein, "Thomas and 19 'Left Out' Colt Vets Met Secretly, Reached an Understanding," *BS*, August 16, 1974.

112. Ron Hudspeth, "Ready or Not . . .," *AJ*, August 12, 1974; Norman Arrey, "Sending Falcon Vets into Battle Like Custer Appointing Troops," *AJ*, August 15, 1974; Al Thomy, "Bengals Stop Falcons 13–7 in Overtime," *Atlanta Journal and Atlanta Constitution*, August 18, 1974.

113. "Owners Warned by House," *NYT*, August 14, 1974.

114. David DuPree, "Redskin Majority Prone to Walk-Out," *WP*, August 23, 1974; Klobuchar, "Page Accuses NFL Owners of 'Reprisals.'"

115. "NFL Players Ease Contract Demands in Settlement Bid," *WP*, August 19, 1974; "NFL Owners Nix 5-Month Contract," *WP*, August 20, 1974; William Barry Furlong, "NFL Players Vote to Stay in Camp," *WP*, August 28, 1974.

116. The term was used in Cleveland, New York (Giants), and Baltimore. See Chuck Heaton, "14 New Browns on Final Squad," *Cleveland Plain Dealer*, September 12, 1974; Norm Miller, "Giants Clean House; Randy, Evans, Rocky Evicted," *NYDN*, September 11, 1974; Alan Goldstein, "Colts Go with Youth after Cuts," *BS*, September 11, 1974.

117. Wellington Mara, "How Player Representatives Do," *NYT*, September 29, 1974. Mara also claimed that 267 rookies made their clubs, not the 272 claimed earlier by the Associated Press, a small discrepancy perhaps due to further roster shuffling.

118. Gwilym Brown, "Owners Can Be Tackled, Too," *SI*, March 22, 1971.

119. Hal Lundgren, "Player President Curry Put on Waivers," *HC*, August 31, 1974; Skip Myslenski, "Alexander to Be Released by Eagles," *PI*, August 21, 1974; Leonard Shapiro, "Wilbur, Rock, Pottios Waived by Redskins," *WP*, September 11, 1974; David Fink, "Steelers Waive Union Exec Keating," *Pittsburgh Post-Gazette*, September 5, 1974; Cliff Christl, "Packers or 'Brokers'?," *GBPG*, September 11, 1974; Alan Goldstein, "Five Colt Veterans Are Cut," *BS*, September 10, 1974; Chuck Heaton, "Browns Trade Pitts; Scott, Jones, McKay in Jeopardy," *Cleveland Plain Dealer*, September 4, 1974; Don Pierson, "'Great Day for Bears': 4 Go for Picks," *CT*, September 11, 1974; Miller, "Giants Clean House"; Larry McMillen, "Williams Heads Cuts by Saints," *New Orleans Times-Picayune*, September 11, 1974. On the previous trades of Alexander and Wilbur, see Brown, "Owners Can Be Tackled, Too."

120. Pierson, "'Great Day for Bears.'"

121. Bill Richardson, "Chiefs Infuse New Blood of 12," *Kansas City Times*, September 11, 1974; Gerald B. Jordan, "Some Ex-Chiefs Leave with Hope . . . Others Just Leave," *Kansas City Star*, September 11, 1974.

122. Alan Goldstein, "Five Colt Veterans Are Cut," *BS*, September 10, 1974; Ron Hudspeth, "Dropping of Falcons' Ax Brings Mixed Emotions," *AJ*, August 30, 1974.

123. "People in Sports," *NYT*, December 20, 1974.

Chapter Three

1. "Bullet Bob v. Roger the Dodger," *Time*, January 17, 1972; "Scouting Reports: The Pros Rate the Two Teams," *Life*, January 14, 1972; Don Weiss with Chuck Day, *The Making of the Super Bowl: The Inside Story of the World's Greatest Sporting Event* (Chicago: Contemporary Books, 2002), 190.

2. "The Super Show," *Time*, January 10, 1977.

3. Weiss, *The Making of the Super Bowl*, 187.

4. Ira Berkow, "And Now in Michigan, Return to Reality," *NYT*, January 25, 1982; Weiss, *The Making of the Super Bowl*, 115.

5. David Harris, *The League: The Rise and Decline of the NFL* (New York: Bantam, 1986), 239–44.

6. Michael MacCambridge, *America's Game: The Epic Story of How Pro Football Captured a Nation* (New York: Random House, 2004) 219–28; Harris, *The League*, 80, 239–44, 707.

7. William N. Wallace, "Davis in Multifront Battle to Move Raiders," *NYT*, February 3, 1980; AP, "Judge Declares a Mistrial in Raider Case," *NYT*, August 14, 1981; AP, "Raiders Trial Opens," March 30, 1982.

8. Edwin Pope, "Don't Pin Whole Rap on Players' Union," *MH*, July 12, 1974; Edwin Pope, "Time for Garvey to Go," *MH*, August 9, 1974.

9. Skip Myslenski, "What Next?," *PI*, September 1, 1974.

10. Harris, *The League*, 218.

11. "Vote on Strike Looms in N.F.L.," *NYT*, September 11, 1975; "Pro Football Dispute," *NYT*, September 15, 1975; Red Smith, "Football and Union-Busters," *NYT*, September 14, 1975; Dave Anderson, "Pro Football's Stubborn Quarterback," *NYT*, September 16, 1975; "Vikings Demand Garvey Resign," *NYT*, August 23, 1975; "Patriots Vote to Strike and Refuse to Play Today," *NYT*, September 14, 1975; Neil Amdur, "Giants Drop Strike Gesture and 31–13 Game to Dolphins," *NYT*, September 14, 1975; William N. Wallace, "Jets and Redskins Join Patriots' Strike," *NYT*, September 17, 1975; Wallace, "Football Teams End Their Strike," *NYT*, September 19, 1975; "N.F.L. Offers New Contract; No Progress Is Made in Talks," *NYT*, September 23, 1975; "N.F.L. Talks Collapse," *NYT*, September 24, 1975; "New Pact in N.F.L. Is Failing," *NYT*, September 26, 1975; Mark Kriegel, *Namath: A Biography* (New York: Viking, 2004), 372.

12. Henry Weinstein, "Pro Football Reserve Rule Held Illegal by U.S. Judge," *NYT*, December 21, 1974; William N. Wallace, "Rozelle Rule Found in Antitrust Violation," *NYT*, December 31, 1975.

13. Leonard Koppett, "Jury Rules Kapp Not Entitled to Damages," *NYT*, April 3, 1976; Leonard Koppett, "For Kapp, Defeat; for League, Limited Victory," *NYT*, April 4, 1976; "N.F.L. Held in Labor Code Violation," *NYT*, July 2, 1976; "Rozelle Speaks of Options in Light of Draft Ruling," *NYT*, September 28, 1976; "Rozelle Rule Again Is Held to Be Invalid," *NYT*, October 19, 1976; Harris, *The League*, 302.

14. William N. Wallace, "Pro Football Pact Talks Relieve Anxiety Slightly," *NYT*, January 30, 1977; "Player Unit and Owners Ratify Pact," *NYT*, February 26, 1977.

15. William N. Wallace, "Football Free Agents: Grass Isn't Greener," *NYT*, April 23, 1978; William N. Wallace, "N.F.L. Players Ask Free-Agent Review," *NYT*, May 14, 1978; William N. Wallace, "Free-Agent System Still an N.F.L. Issue," *NYT*, October 21, 1979; William N. Wallace, "Few N.F.L. Free-Agent Stars," *NYT*, February 10, 1980; Dave Anderson, "Payton Free, Owners Not," *NYT*, February 16, 1981; William N. Wallace, "N.F.L. Faces Labor Problems, Too, but Not on Free Agency," *NYT*, July 19, 1981.

16. "A Windfall for Players," *NYT*, March 31, 1977; "Pro Football Settlement Given Final Approval," *NYT*, August 2, 1977; Red Smith, "Conscience Money," *NYT*, August 7, 1977.

17. Red Smith, "Sins, Mortal and Venial," *NYT*, May 14, 1980.

18. Frank Deford, "Long Live the King!," *SI*, January 21, 1980.

19. Pete Rozelle, "Is It 'Parity'? 'Mediocrity'? Pete Rozelle Says No," *NYT*, January 3, 1982; "Record TV Rating," *NYT*, January 29, 1982; Tom Callahan, "Super Timing, Joe" (cover story), *Time*, January 25, 1982; Pete Axthelm, "Super Bowl: Duel of Wits" (cover story), *Newsweek*, January 25, 1982; Gerald Eskenazi, "N.F.L. TV Pact $2 Billion," *NYT*, March 23, 1982.

20. Gerald Eskenazi, "The State of the N.F.L.: It's Still Winning More Than It Loses," *NYT*, May 2, 1982.

21. AP, "N.F.L. Violated Law in Forbidding Team to Move, Jury Finds," *NYT*, May 8, 1982.

22. John Hogrogian, "The United States Football League," in *Total Football II: The Official Encyclopedia of the National Football League*, ed. Bob Carroll et al. (New York: HarperCollins, 1999), 534–37.

23. Don Reese with John Underwood, "I'm Not Worth a Damn," *SI*, June 14, 1982.

24. Ira Berkow, "When Johnny Blood Rode," *NYT*, July 11, 1982; Bil Gilbert, "Problems in a Turned-on World," *SI*, June 23, 1969. Subsequent installments appeared in the June 30 and July 7 issues.

25. Tom Callahan, *Johnny U: The Life and Times of John Unitas* (New York: Viking, 2006), 235–36; Arnold J. Mandell, "Pro Football Fumbles the Drug Scandal," *Psychology Today*, June 1975; Arnold J. Mandell, *The Nightmare Season* (New York: Random House, 1976), 172–216; John Underwood, "Speed Is All the Rage," *SI*, August 28, 1978.

26. Underwood, "Speed Is All the Rage"; Robert H. Boyle, "The Brutal Trip Down," *SI*, November 5, 1979; Frank Litsky, "Player Tells of Wide Drug Use in N.F.L.," *NYT*, June 10, 1982; "Henderson Hospitalized to Cure Drug Habit," *NYT*, February 14, 1981.

27. "Broncos Testing for Drug Use Angers N.F.L. Players Union," *NYT*, June 12, 1982; "Problems with Drugs Conceded by Browns," *NYT*, June 13, 1982; "Concession by Mecom," *NYT*, June 15, 1982; Philip Taubman, "Rogers of Saints Said to Admit Use of Cocaine," *NYT*, June 25, 1982; Michael Katz, "Ex-Saint Is Indicted Again in Drug Case," *NYT*, June 26, 1982.

28. Ronald Sullivan, "N.F.L. Says Players' Cocaine Use Could Threaten Integrity of Game," *NYT*, June 27, 1982; "Help on the Way," *NYT*, June 30, 1982; "Drug Tests Planned for Saints Players," *NYT*, July 4, 1982; Frank Litsky, "N.F.L. Teams Split on Tests for Drugs," *NYT*, July 18, 1982.

29. "N.F.L. Players Angry at Drug-Abuse Stigma," *NYT*, June 27, 1982; Taubman, "Rogers of Saints Said to Admit Use of Cocaine"; Michael Katz, "Ex-Saint Is Indicted Again in Drug Case," *NYT*, June 26, 1982; "White Reported in Drug Clinic," *NYT*, July 17, 1982; Frank Litsky, "Muncie Reported Warned," *NYT*, July 21, 1982; "Atlanta Pros Admit Drug Use," *NYT*, July 28, 1982; "Morris Arrested in Cocaine Raid," *NYT*, August 19, 1982; "Drug Selling by Morris Denied," *NYT*, August 21, 1982; "Card Linebacker Pleads Not Guilty," *NYT*, August 24, 1982; "Strachan Pleads Guilty," *NYT*, August 26, 1982; Jane Gross, "Mercury Morris's Other Identity," *NYT*, September 2, 1982.

30. Paul Zimmerman, "An Overdose of Problems," *SI*, September 5, 1983.

31. John M. Donlan, "Why Owners Must Maintain Their Control," *NYT*, February 14, 1982. On Dutton, see William N. Wallace, "Free-Agent System Still an N.F.L. Issue," *NYT*, October 21, 1979; and Timothy W. Smith, "N.F.L. Is Dusting Off Its Shield for Another Free Agency Battle," *NYT*, June 14, 1992.

32. Harris, *The League*, 591–92; Smith, "Sins, Mortal and Venial"; "Fouts and Two Raiders Threatened with Ban," *NYT*, December 16, 1981.

33. Harris, *The League*, 302–5.

34. AP, "League Earnings," *Portland Oregonian*, September 23, 1982.

35. Gerald Eskenazi, "N.F.L. Pay Average of $150,000 Is Proposed," *NYT*, June 8, 1982; Harris, *The League*, 643.

36. Harris, *The League*, 590–91, 643; Ed Garvey, "Why Players Want Altered Salary Plan," *NYT*, February 14, 1982; Donlan, "Why Owners Must Maintain Their Control."

37. William N. Wallace, "N.F.L. Players Say They Would Strike," *NYT*, April 18, 1982; "Difference of Opinion," *NYT*, April 20, 1982; "Bradshaw to Lead," *NYT*, May 20, 1982; "Montana Rejects Strike," *NYT*, May 22, 1982.

38. AP, "Strike Chronology," *NYT*, November 17, 1982; Eskenazi, "N.F.L. Pay Average of $150,000 Is Proposed"; "Players Defying N.F.L.," *NYT*, August 15, 1982; "N.F.L. Proposal Rejected," *NYT*, September 9, 1982; Michael Janofsky, "N.F.L. Talks Break Off; Owners Reject New Offer," *NYT*, September 18, 1982; "Stop-Action in the N.F.L.," *Time*, October 4, 1982; Michael Janofsky, "N.F.L. Players Start a Strike as Contract Impasse Holds," *NYT*, September 21, 1982.

39. AP, "Support by Players Is Strong, Not Total," *NYT*, September 21, 1982; AP, "Only a Few Players Are Defying Strike," *NYT*, September 22, 1982; Paul Zimmerman, "This Was the Week That Wasn't," *SI*, October 4, 1982.

40. "And the Strike Goes On," *Time*, November 8, 1982; Frank Litsky, "Football Returns for 80 on Strike," *NYT*, October 18, 1982; AP, "American Conference Wins by 31–27," *NYT*, October 19, 1982; Michael Janofsky, "N.F.L. Wins on Right to Sue," *NYT*, October 21, 1982; Harris, *The League*, 647.

41. Gerald Eskenazi, "N.F.L. Owners Make New Offer," *NYT*, November 1, 1982; Michael Janofsky, "Players Ease Demands," *NYT*, November 3, 1982; Michael Janofsky, "Players Offered Bonuses," *NYT*, November 4, 1982; Frank Litsky, "Five Teams Now Support N.F.L. Offer," *NYT*, November 11, 1982; Janofsky, "Strike Is Ended in Pro Football; Games Sunday," *NYT*, November 17, 1982.

42. Paul Zimmerman, "The Strike: The Winners, the Losers, And Who Did What to Whom," *SI*, November 29, 1982; AP, "Representatives Back NFL Pact, 19–9," *NYT*, December 7, 1982; AP, "Players Ratify N.F.L. Contract," *NYT*, December 9, 1982; "Players, N.F.L. Sign Contract," *NYT*, December 12, 1982.

43. Harris, *The League*, 651–52.

44. Gerald Eskenazi, "Rozelle Reviews '82 Season," *NYT*, January 29, 1983.

45. Zimmerman, "An Overdose of Problems."

46. Richard Demak and Jerry Kirshenbaum, "The NFL Fails Its Drug Test," *SI*, July 10, 1989.

47. "Reese Gets Prison Term in Probation Violation," *NYT*, October 29, 1982; "Morris Convicted in Drug Trial," *NYT*, November 6, 1982; "Morris Is Sentenced to 20 Years in Jail," *NYT*, January 21, 1983; Les Carpenter, "Long after His Retirement, Morris Still Making Claims," *WP*, January 28, 2007.

48. "Rozelle Suspends Four for Cocaine Use," *NYT*, July 26, 1983; Michael Janofsky, "Rozelle Backed on Cocaine Suspensions," *NYT*, July 27, 1983; "Peters of Redskins Seized in Drug Case," *NYT*, August 4, 1983; "Peters Pleads Guilty; N.F.L. Suspends Him," *NYT*, September 3, 1983. See also "Clack Indicted on Drug Charges," *NYT*, January 6, 1982; "E. J. Joiner Admits Having Cocaine," *NYT*, February 5, 1983; "Strachan Asks Freedom," *NYT*, February 12, 1983 (for Stemrick); "Oiler Arrested," *NYT*, April 5, 1983; "Niland Arrested Again," *NYT*, April 7, 1983; "Drug Indictment," *NYT*, June 15, 1983; Michael Janovsky, "Oilers React to Drug Problem," *NYT*, July 6, 1983.

49. Bryan Burwell, "50 Percent of NFL on Coke," *NYDN*, July 14, 1983; Bryan Burwell, "Rozelle: NFL Stepping Up Its War on Drug Abuse," *NYDN*, August 18, 1983. The entire series ran from August 15 through August 18.

50. "Martin Traced by Drug Agency," *NYT*, January 19, 1983; Jane Gross, "4 Cowboys Named as Cocaine Users," *NYT*, July 9, 1983; "5 Cowboys Face Charge, Paper Says," *NYT*, July 11, 1983; Michael Janofsky, "Cowboys Unsettled by Cocaine Inquiries," *NYT*, August 3, 1983; Zimmerman, "An Overdose of Problems"; Bruce Newman, "Where Have You Gone, Roger Staubach?," *SI*, August 29, 1983; Gary Smith, "A Shining Knight No More," *SI*, September 12, 1983; Sam Howe Verhovek, "America's Most Notorious Team," *NYT*, April 28, 1996.

51. Terry Todd, "The Steroid Predicament," *SI*, August 1, 1983; Michael Janofsky, "Adviser Suspects N.F.L. Steroid Use," *NYT*, August 28, 1983; "Steroid Use Said to Grow," *NYT*, August 29, 1983; Peter Alfano, "A League Wonders If It Is at Its Peak," *NYT*, January 17, 1984.

52. William Oscar Johnson, "Steroids: A Problem of Huge Dimensions" and "Getting Physical—And Chemical," *SI*, May 13, 1985.

53. "Survey Finds Split on Drug Problem," *NYT*, January 24, 1986; "Berry Says Team Has Drug Problem," *NYT*, January 28, 1986; Michael Janofsky, "Berry Admits Drug Problem on Patriots," *NYT*, January 29, 1986; Peter Alfano, "Putting Games Back into Perspective," *NYT*, February 1, 1986.

54. Michael Janofsky, "N.F.L. Drafted 26 Players on Drug List," *NYT*, May 1, 1986; "Bell Brothers Convicted," *NYT*, June 14, 1986; Judith Cummings, "Drugs Tied to Rogers's Death," *NYT*, June 29, 1986; Michael Goodwin, "N.F.L. Plans Random Drug Tests; Players Face Risk of Suspension," *NYT*, July 8, 1986; Michael Goodwin, "Union Seeks Drug-Plan Delay," *NYT*, July 10, 1986; "Rozelle's Plan for Unscheduled Drug Testing Is Overturned," *NYT*, October 28, 1986.

55. "Manley Gets Treatment," *NYT*, March 14, 1987; "Wilson Denies Report," *NYT*, July 4, 1987; "Raider Arrested," *NYT*, July 17, 1987; "Raider End Arrested," *NYT*, July

22, 1987; "A Little Incident," *NYT*, August 23, 1987; Lawrence Taylor and David Falkner, *LT: Living on the Edge* (New York: Times Books, 1987), 155–56; Thomas "Hollywood" Henderson and Peter Knobler, *Out of Control: Confessions of an NFL Casualty* (New York: Putnam, 1987), 11–14; Richard Demak and Jerry Kirshenbaum, "NFL Fails Its Drug Test," *SI*, July 10, 1989; Charles E. Yesalis, ed., *Anabolic Steroids in Sport and Exercise*, 2nd ed. (Champaign, Ill.: Human Kinetics, 2002), 59–62.

56. Michael Janofsky et al., "Steroids in Sports" (five-part series), *NYT*, November 17–21, 1988; Demak and Kirshenbaum, "NFL Fails Its Drug Test"; Timothy W. Smith, "N.F.L.'s Steroid Policy Too Lax, Doctor Warns," *NYT*, July 3, 1991; Steve Courson and Lee R. Schreiber, *False Glory: Steelers and Steroids, the Steve Courson Story* (Stamford, Conn.: Longmeadow Press, 1991), 183–84; Yesalis, *Anabolic Steroids in Sport and Exercise*, 59–62.

57. Thomas George, "Manley Is Out for 30 Days," *NYT*, July 28, 1988; "N.F.L. Suspends Four," August 6, 1988; "Collins Suspended," *NYT*, August 13, 1988; William N. Wallace, "Giants' Taylor Gets 30-Day Suspension for the Use of Drugs," *NYT*, August 30, 1988; "3 N.F.L. Players Are Banned," *NYT*, September 8, 1988; "2 Suspended by N.F.L.," *NYT*, September 14, 1988; Rick Reilly, "A Visit to Hell," *SI*, August 29, 1988; "Clearly an Overdose," *NYT*, October 13, 1988; "Waymer's Death Is Linked to Cocaine," *NYT*, May 19, 1993.

58. "Drug Charges for Banks," *NYT*, October 15, 1988; "Mike Bell Suspended," *NYT*, October 22, 1988; "Lions' Rogers Charged," *NYT*, October 22, 1988; "N.F.L. Bans 2 More for Drug Violations," *NYT*, December 1, 1988; Dave Anderson, "Suspended 5 'Down Here on Business,'" *NYT*, January 19, 1989; Gerald Eskenazi, "Wilson Suspended for Substance Use," *NYT*, January 23, 1989; "N.F.L. Bans Wilson," May 16, 1989; Robert McG. Thomas Jr., "Manley Barred Indefinitely by N.F.L.," *NYT*, November 19, 1989; "Lions' Cornerback Banned for Life," September 21, 1990; "Muncie Indicted on Cocaine Charges," *NYT*, October 27, 1988; "Muncie Jailed," *NYT*, January 27, 1989; "Muncie Is Sentenced," *NYT*, February 25, 1989.

59. Jane Gross, "Drug Addiction: The Threat to Sports Keeps Growing," *NYT*, July 25, 1983.

60. Dave Anderson, "The Sports Blotter," *NYT*, July 14, 1983.

61. Michael Janofsky, "For Armstrong, Pains Are Lingering," *NYT*, August 19, 1984; "Comings and Goings," *NYT*, December 1, 1984; Bob Glauber, "Cheering Stops, Trouble Starts," *Newsday*, January 14, 1997; Bob Glauber, "Temporary Relief," *Newsday*, January 14, 1997.

62. For Tatum's comments on hurting opponents, see Tatum and Bill Kushner, *Final Confessions of NFL Assassin Jack Tatum* (Coal Valley, Ill.: Quality Sports Publications, 1996), 17. *Final Confessions* includes the full text of *They Call Me Assassin* (1979), in which the contest with Atkinson was first reported, together with *They Still Call Me Assassin—Here We Go Again* (1989).

63. Paul Zimmerman, "The Agony Must End," *SI*, November 10, 1986; Gene Wojciechowski and Chris Dufresne, "Football Career Is Taking Its Toll on NFL's Players," *LAT*, June 26, 1988; Bill Utterback, "NFL Life, Early Death Linked," *CT*, March 4, 1988.

64. Bob Glauber, "Sudden Death," *Newsday*, January 15, 1997; Chuck Finder, "What Drove Justin Strzelczyk to His Death?," *Pittsburgh Post-Gazette*, October 31, 2004; "Document Says Former Steeler Drank Antifreeze in Suicide," *NYT*, January 27, 2006; Alan Schwarz, "Expert Ties Ex-Player's Suicide to Brain Damage," *NYT*, January 18, 2007; Wojciechowski and Dufresne, "Football Career Is Taking Its Toll on NFL's Players."

65. Dan Bickley, "You Play, You Pay," *Arizona Republic*, January 16, 2003 (on the NIOSH study); Mark Maske, "Retired Linemen at Risk," *WP*, June 2, 2006 (on the Living Heart Foundation's studies). On the Scripps Howard study, see Thomas Hargrove, "Supersized in the NFL: Many Ex-players Dying Young," Scripps Howard News Service, <http://www.shns.com> (January 31, 2006); also under the title "Super Sized," in *Chicago Sun-Times*, February 3, 2006. For the study of football players' BMI index, see Joyce B. Harp, "Obesity in the National Football League," *JAMA: The Journal of the American Medical Association* (online), March 2, 2005; and Lindsey Tanner (AP), "League Disputes Report That Many Players Obese," *Portland Oregonian*, March 2, 2005.

66. Bill Fay, "Bingo Bingaman—Pro Football's Immovable Object," *Collier's*, October 29, 1954; David Noonan, "Really Big Football Players," *New York Times Magazine*, December 14, 1997; Steve Rushin, "Big," *SI*, September 4, 1995; Dan Bickley, "Bigger Men, Bigger Pain," *Arizona Republic*, January 27, 2003.

67. Kevin Lamb, "The Evolution of Strategy," in *Total Football II*, 468.

68. John Underwood, "An Unfolding Tragedy," *SI*, August 14, 1978; and "Punishment Is a Crime," *SI*, August 21, 1978; Harris, *The League*, 294–97.

69. Noonan, "Really Big Football Players"; Peter King, "Painful Reality," *SI*, October 11, 2004.

70. Les Krantz, *Jobs Rated Almanac*, 6th ed. (Fort Lee, N.J.: Barricade Books, 2002). Previous editions were in 1988, 1992, 1995, 1999, and 2000.

71. Lamb, "The Evolution of Strategy," 468–69.

72. Ibid., 459–73; Ted Brock, "The West Coast Offense," in *Total Football II*, 491–94.

73. Lamb, "Evolution of Strategy"; Judy Battista, "Hold That Line, but Don't Hesitate to Supersize the Coaching Staff," *NYT*, July 12, 2006.

74. Tom Callahan, " 'Sweetness' and Might," *Time*, January 27, 1986; "Success for Bears off the Field Too," *NYT*, December 21, 1985.

75. Bernice Kanner, *The Super Bowl of Advertising: How the Commercials Won the Game* (Princeton, N.J.: Bloomberg, 2004); Andy Bernstein, "Word on the Street: 'Jimmy's Hanging Tough," *SBJ*, January 31–February 6, 2005; Kris Johnson, "Ad Meter More about Bragging Rights Than Gauge of an Ad's Effectiveness," *SBJ*, January 31–February 6, 2005.

76. The Harris Poll No. 77, <http://www.harrisinteractive.com/harris_poll/index .asp?PID=506> (October 13, 2004) includes a table of Harris polls on Americans' favorite sports from 1985 through 2004; N. R. Kleinfield, "Football's TV Ratings Lag," *NYT*, November 23, 1983; Alfano, "A League Wonders If It Is at Its Peak"; Peter Alfano, "N.F.L. Sees Problems, Argues Solutions," *NYT*, January 18, 1984; "N.F.L. Ratings Fall on Networks," *NYT*, October 19, 1984; "Attendance is up at N.F.L. Games," *NYT*,

December 19, 1984; "N.F.L. Drew 59,568 a Game," *NYT*, December 25, 1985; Michael Goodwin, "Deflated State of Football," *NYT*, November 26, 1986; Michael Janofsky, "Pro Football Fans Like Game as It Is," *NYT*, December 9, 1984.

77. Michael Goodwin, "Networks and N.F.L. Are Drawing the Battle Lines," *NYT*, January 18, 1987; Michael Janofsky, "$1.4 Billion Deal Adds Cable to N.F.L. Picture," *NYT*, March 16, 1987.

78. Thomas George, "Raiders Planning Return to Oakland," *NYT*, March 13, 1990; Dave Anderson, "Civic Sense Saves Dollars in Oakland," *NYT*, April 19, 1980.

79. Robert McG. Thomas Jr., "Colts' Move to Indianapolis Is Announced," *NYT*, March 30, 1984.

80. Gerald Eskenazi, "N.F.L. Approves Team Shift," *NYT*, March 16, 1988.

81. Gerald Eskenazi, "Players Miss U.S.F.L. Option," *NYT*, September 24, 1987; M. J. Duberstein, "NFL Economics Primer 2002," NFLPA, April 2002 (the *Times*'s figures were lower than the Players Association's); "Bosworth Signs," *NYT*, August 15, 1987.

82. Michael Janofsky, "Owners Oppose Free Agency," *NYT*, March 19, 1987; Smith, "N.F.L. Is Dusting Off Its Shield for Another Free Agency Battle."

83. Glenn Dickey, "Don't Blame NFL Players If They Strike," *San Francisco Chronicle*, September 21, 1987.

84. Janofsky, "Owners Oppose Free Agency"; Michael Janofsky, "Bargaining Proposals Reflect Wide Gap on Key Issues," *NYT*, May 3, 1987; Alex Yannis, "N.F.L. Owners Submit Offer," *NYT*, September 8, 1987; Gerald Eskenazi, "N.F.L. Union Offers to Soften Demands," *NYT*, September 16, 1987; "Where They Stand: N.F.L. Issues," *NYT*, September 18, 1987; Dickey, "Don't Blame NFL Players If They Strike."

85. Bill Livingston, "Players Take It on the Chin," *Cleveland Plain Dealer*, October 4, 1987.

86. Tony Kornheiser, "Alignment of the Stars, and How Many Cross, Crucial to Direction of Football Strike," *WP*, October 4, 1987.

87. AP, "15 More Regulars Cross the Picket Lines," *NYT*, October 1, 1987; "Sunday's Plans for Fans, Players," *NYT*, October 2, 1987; "38 Strikers Return before Deadline," *NYT*, October 3, 1987; Gerald Eskenazi, "35 More Players Cross Picket Lines," *NYT*, October 8, 1987; Frank Litsky, "Taylor, Rutledge Return to Work," *NYT*, October 15, 1987; Michael Janofsky, "N.F.L. Players End Strike but Can't Play Sunday," *NYT*, October 16, 1987. For a list of strikebreakers, see "Players Who Crossed Picket Lines," *MH*, October 15, 1987.

88. Bill Brenner, "Sun Was Out on Monday Despite Strike," *Indianapolis Star*, September 29, 1987; David Casstevens, "Randy White's Only Guilt: Taking Care of No. 54," *DMN*, September 24, 1987.

89. George Vecsey, "Brand X Football," *NYT*, September 23, 1987.

90. Fran Blinebury, "Sham Is Over, So Let the Real Games Begin," *HC*, October 19, 1987. See also Bernie Lincicome, "NFL's Irregulars Truly Suit Flutie," *CT*, October 14, 1987; Bud Collins, "By Any Name, It's Fraudball," *Boston Globe*, October 16, 1987.

91. Glenn Dickey, "49ers a Study in Group Psychology," *San Francisco Chronicle*,

October 5, 1987; Glenn Dickey, "Strike Causing Gap to Widen among 49ers," *San Francisco Chronicle*, October 8, 1987; Dave Kindred, "Montana Sneaks Out, Betrayal Unexplained," *Atlanta Constitution*, October 12, 1987. The *Pittsburgh Post-Gazette* noted the poignancy of Mike Webster's case. See Ed Bouchette, "Webster May End Career on Sour Note," *Pittsburgh Post-Gazette*, October 5, 1987.

92. Harris, *The League*, 719; and see Harris for detailed accounts of NFL owners' business in the 1980s. Also see Bill Livingston, " 'Poor' NFL Can't Afford Pensions," *Cleveland Plain Dealer*, September 23, 1987; and Bob Gretz, "Hunt Throws Fuel on Player Unrest with Ill-Timed Rhetoric," *Kansas City Star*, September 22, 1987.

93. In one of the strike's great columns, the *Plain Dealer*'s Bill Livingston described growing up during the Depression with a mother who had worked in a garment factory and a father who had been an "Okie" out of *The Grapes of Wrath*. Livingston told readers how he had started on a nonunion daily newspaper in Texas owned by a "paternalistic company" that paid about a third of what union journalists in the East and Midwest made. With professional freedom such as that sought by NFL players, he had moved on to Philadelphia, then to Cleveland. For Livingston, the striking players were "direct heirs to the union legacy." See "Players Aren't Offside," *Cleveland Plain Dealer*, September 27, 1987.

94. AP, "Upshaw Says His Race Is Becoming an Issue in NFL Talks," *Kansas City Times*, October 2, 1987; Michael Katz, "Is Strike Colored by Racism?," *NYDN*, October 1, 1987. For reactions (besides Katz's), see Ken Denlinger, "Owners Have Dug in Heels from Start," *WP*, October 3, 1987; Kornheiser, "Alignment of the Stars"; Bruce Keidan, "Quick Settlement Might Hurt Steelers," *Pittsburgh Post-Gazette*, October 6, 1987.

95. Joan Ryan, "Bonzo Football," *SFE*, October 6, 1987.

96. Howard Cosell, "An Open Letter to Those Who Would Cross the Picket Lines and Play Pro Football," *NYDN*, September 27, 1987. See also Bob Rubin, "These Guys Are a Joke," *MH*, September 30, 1987; and Bill Livingston, "Players Take It on the Chin," *Cleveland Plain Dealer*, October 4, 1987.

97. Bernie Lincicome, "Can Football Get Worse Than This?," *CT*, October 12, 1987. See also Bernie Lincicome, "Optimism Faces a 4th and Long," *CT*, October 4, 1987; and Tim Sullivan, "Well, Maybe Pestilence Will Show Up," *CE*, October 4, 1987.

98. Ira Berkow attributed the " 'Walter Mitty' Gimmick" to Schramm. See "Secret Life of a New Mitty," *NYT*, October 2, 1987.

99. AP, "Replacements Seek Another Sunday," *NYT*, October 6, 1987. Some dream, snorted Ira Berkow in the *New York Times*, "to take another man's job." See Berkow, "Secret Life of a New Mitty." The Dallas Cowboys and *Dallas Morning News* did everything possible to sell the dream as real. The Cowboys took an official team photograph with their replacement players, which the *Morning News* published on October 2—a memento for every faux Cowboy—along with thumbnail profiles of each player on October 4, the day of their debut, and several longer features over the course of the strike.

100. "Yesterday's NFL Crowds," *Seattle Post-Intelligencer*, October 12, 1987.

101. "Events Highlighting NFL Players' Strike," *Boston Globe*, October 16, 1987;

"Poll: Fans Will Watch Scabs," *MH*, September 22, 1987; Larry Dorman, "Fans Believe Players More at Fault in Strike," *MH*, October 3, 1987; Adam Clymer, "Poll Finds Support for Owners," *NYT*, October 25, 1987.

102. "N.F.L. TV Ratings Drop," *NYT*, October 9, 1987; Michael Goodwin, "Ratings Still Losing Yardage," *NYT*, October 14, 1987; "TV Audiences Increase a Bit," *NYT*, October 20, 1987. Attendance was down about 20 percent the first week, another 7 to 24 percent the second week, then bounced back in the third week without returning to prestrike levels.

103. Because of no-shows—fans who bought tickets but did not attend the games—average paid attendance was about 30,000 the first week, or roughly half of normal. Will McDonough of the *Boston Globe* pointed out that, at $20 a ticket, gross gate receipts averaged about $600,000 per club. Player payroll, on the other hand, dropped from about $1 million per club to $200,000 for minimally paid scabs. Dave Lagarde of the *New Orleans Times-Picayune* calculated a total weekly profit of about $1.25 million for each club during the strike. The *Miami Herald* offered a more precise calculation of Joe Robbie's profits, concluding that Robbie made $993,288 in profit over the three weeks of the strike, down from what would have been $2.2 million for the three games. See Will McDonough, "Owners Were the Winners," *Boston Globe*, October 7, 1987; Dave Lagarde, "Owners Laughing All Way to Bank," *New Orleans Times-Picayune*, October 9, 1987; and Reinaldo Ramos, "Robbie Still Made Money during Replacement Games," *MH*, October 25, 1987.

104. Mike Lupica, "NFL Goes into Oldest Profession," *NYDN*, October 1, 1987.

105. "Sports and TV" columnists in several newspapers noted that the pregame studio shows offered serious commentary on the strike. Bob Costas, for example, declared on *NFL Live!* before the first scab games, "I believe these games are a significant blow to the integrity of the National Football League. Nevertheless we are obliged to bring them to you." But the telecasts of the games themselves all but ignored it. Tim Ryan and Joe Theismann treated the Washington–St. Louis game "pretty much . . . like any other game," with Ryan at one point mentioning "the semi-capacity crowd" of 27,728. Don Criqui and Bob Trumpy (one of the first Bengal veterans to cross the picket lines in 1974) praised the substitute Browns' and Patriots' performance. Dick Enberg called Seattle's victory over Miami "as big an upset as I've ever seen." Brent Mussburger of CBS, at least in Mike Lupica's view, was the owners' "head cheerleader." See Shelley Smith, "On the Air," *SFE*, October 5, 1987; Dave Hyde, "Sports on the Air," *MH*, October 5, 1987; Norman Chad, "CBS Makes Best of NFL's Bad Situation," *WP*, October 5, 1987; Bob Dolgan, "On TV/Radio," *Cleveland Plain Dealer*, October 5, 1987; and Mike Lupica, "Victors a Truly Owner-ous Lot," *NYDN*, October 16, 1987.

106. Mike Lupica blamed "every hick fan who attended a scab game or watched a scab game" for helping the owners crush the union. Bernie Lincicome declared that "the public won this thing for the owners by accepting the Sunday swill as close enough to the real thing not to scare off television." According to Glenn Dickey, the strike proved that "owners and players alike know that fans are sheep." See Lupica, "Victors a Truly

Owner-ous Lot"; Bernie Lincicome, "Strike Lessons Sickening, Sad," *CT*, October 16, 1987; Glenn Dickey, "The Real Lesson of the Strike," *San Francisco Chronicle*, October 19, 1987.

107. AP, "Judgment Delayed in Free-Agency Bid," *NYT*, January 30, 1988; AP, "N.F.L. Impasse Declared," *NYT*, April 29, 1988; Thomas George, "Judge Declares Labor Impasse," *NYT*, June 18, 1988; Thomas George, "Court Backs the N.F.L. in Antitrust Challenge," *NYT*, November 2, 1989; "N.F.L. Players Union Seeks Decertification," *NYT*, November 8, 1989; MacCambridge, *America's Game*, 384.

108. Thomas George, "Stunning Owners, Rozelle Says He's Retiring," *NYT*, March 23, 1989; Paul Zimmerman, "He Quit, for Pete's Sake," *SI*, April 3, 1989.

109. Michael Janofsky, "Owners Contend Rozelle Is Slowing Down," *NYT*, January 22, 1989.

110. Thomas C. Hayes, "The N.F.L.'s Painful Profit Crunch," *NYT*, October 29, 1989.

111. Karl Taro Greenfeld, "The Big Man," *SI*, January 23, 2006.

112. Deford, "Long Live the King!"

113. Janofsky, "Pro Football Fans Like Game as It Is."

114. Michael Janofsky, "Rozelle Optimistic on Club Finances," *NYT*, March 12, 1985.

115. Rick Telander, "The Face of Sweeping Change," *SI*, September 10, 1990; "Inside the NFL: The Hard-Hat Commissioner," *SI*, October 10, 2005.

116. Janofsky, "Owners Contend Rozelle Is Slowing Down."

Chapter Four

1. Karl Taro Greenfeld, "The Big Man," *SI*, January 23, 2006; "Team Valuations," *Forbes*, September 18, 2006; Kurt Badenhausen, Michael K. Ozanian, and Maya Roney, "The Tape on Tagliabue," *Forbes* (online), August 31, 2006. (The online edition breaks down the team valuations from the print edition and includes this article, as well.)

2. Thomas George, "Owners Set on Free Agency," *NYT*, January 30, 1989; AP, "Free-Agent Plan to Stay," *NYT*, March 28, 1989; Frank Litsky, "As Plan B Deadline Passes, N.F.L. Has a New, Albeit Indistinct, Look," *NYT*, April 3, 1990; Thomas George, "N.F.L. Veterans Jump at Plan B," *NYT*, April 3, 1991; Timothy W. Smith, "N.F.L. Is Dusting Off Its Shield for Another Free Agency Battle," *NYT*, June 14, 1992.

3. Thomas George, "Tagliabue Testifies About the Virtue of Plan B," *NYT*, August 4, 1992.

4. "Eight Players Sue N.F.L.," *NYT*, April 11, 1990; Timothy W. Smith, "It's Players vs. Owners over Plan B," *NYT*, June 9, 1992.

5. NFLPA, "About Us," <http://www.nflpa.org>.

6. Thomas George, "N.F.L.'s Free-Agency System Is Found Unfair by U.S. Jury," *NYT*, September 11, 1992; Richard Sandomir, "A Better Bargaining Hand for N.F.L. Players," *NYT*, September 11, 1992; Michael Martinez, "N.F.L. Is Loser Again in 2 More Labor Cases," *NYT*, October 6, 1992; Thomas George, "Tentative Agreement on N.F.L. Labor Contract," *NYT*, December 23, 1992; Gerald Eskenazi, "N.F.L. Labor Accord Is

Reached, Allowing Free Agency for Players," *NYT*, January 7, 1993; Gerald Eskenazi, "N.F.L.-Players Agreement Alters Free Agent Rules," *NYT*, May 7, 1993.

7. Eskenazi, "N.F.L. Labor Accord Is Reached"; Thomas Boswell, "After Being Bounced Around Like a Football, Union Needs a Lesson in Hardball," *WP*, September 24, 1987; Skip Myslenski, "What Next?," *PI*, September 1, 1974.

8. Frank Litsky, "Free Agency Inflates Salaries," *NYT*, July 15, 1993.

9. Daniel Fisher, "Value Player," *Forbes*, September 2, 2002.

10. Michael K. Ozanian et al., "Sports Franchise Valuations," *Financial World*, May 25, 1993; Kurt Badenhausen et al., "The Business of Football," *Forbes*, September 18, 2006; Mike Freeman, "N.F.L. Finds Labor Peace that Eluded Others," *NYT*, November 8, 1998; Judy Battista, "Contract Makes N.F.L. Oasis of Labor Peace," *NYT*, July 5, 2001; Peter Richman, "My Team Left Town and All I Got Was This Lousy Helmet," *GQ*, September 1999.

11. NFLPA, "A New Look at Guaranteed Contracts in the NFL," <http://www.nflpa .org>.

12. Mike Freeman, "N.F.L. and Players Extend Pact in Principle into 2003," *NYT*, February 27, 1998; Freeman, "N.F.L. Finds Labor Peace That Eluded Others."

13. Allen Barra, "How the 49ers Beat the Salary Cap," *NYT Magazine*, January 8, 1995; Mike Freeman, "N.F.L.'s Elite Are Caught in the Cap," *NYT*, September 14, 2000; Mike Freeman, "Parcells-Era Free Agents Costly for Jets," *NYT*, February 25, 2001; Mike Freeman, "Walsh Sees Dark Side of Salary Cap's Impact," *NYT*, November 4, 2001; Dave Anderson, "Nobody Is Rooting for the Cap," *NYT*, March 1, 2002.

14. Ed Garvey, "Pro Football Needs a Real Labor Union," *NYT*, June 14, 1992. See also Garvey's earlier "Foreword to *The Scope of the Labor Exemption in Professional Sports*: A Perspective on Collective Bargaining in the NFL," *Duke Law Journal* (1989): 328–38.

15. Bruce Schoenfeld, "NFL Peace Guaranteed, Salaries Aren't," *SBJ*, August 12–18, 2002.

16. David Meggysey provided this estimate.

17. M. J. Duberstein, "NFL Economics Primer 2002," NFLPA, April 2002; NFLPA, "2005 Mid-season Salary Averages and Signing Trends," <http://www.nflpa.org> (November 2005). See also Mark Yost, *Tailgaiting, Sacks, and Salary Caps: How the NFL Became the Most Successful Sports League in History* (Chicago: Kaplan, 2006), 39.

18. NFLPA, "CBA Amended 2006," <http://www.nflpa.org/CBA/CBA_Complete .aspx; John Clayton, "Upshaw Saw Need to Aid Vets," <http://espn.go.com/nfl/colu mns/clayton_john/1210115.html>; " 'Performance Based Pay' Doubles," <http://www .nfl.xom/news/story/7219017> (March 29, 2004). For details on the convoluted economics of salary caps, free agency, and players' contracts under the latest collective bargaining agreement, see Yost, *Tailgating, Sacks, and Salary Caps*, 24–40.

19. M. J. Duberstein, "It Happens Every February: Media Misperceptions of the Current NFL System," NFLPA, March 2002. The NFLPA's "Economic Primer 2002" constantly insists on how much better off the players are under the 1993 agreement than before, an insistence that can only point to a perceived need to counter criticism.

20. "League Earnings," *Portland Oregonian*, September 23, 1982 (figures from NFL Management Council); "NFL Economics Primer 2001" (figures from NFLPA).

21. Michael Lewis, *The Blind Side: Evolution of a Game* (New York: W. W. Norton, 2006).

22. "The 50 Most Influential People in Sports Business: 17, Gene Upshaw," *SBJ*, December 19–25, 2005.

23. Michael Wilbon, "Gumbel Has the Right to Say What He Feels," *WP*, August 24, 2006.

24. Bill Saporito, "The American Money Machine," *Time*, December 6, 2004.

25. Stefan Fatsis, "Can Socialism Survive?," *Wall Street Journal*, September 20, 2004; Daniel Kaplan, "NFL's Next Battle: Revenue Sharing," *SBJ*, April 5–11, 2004; Liz Mullen and Daniel Kaplan, "NFLPA Seeks to Shake Up Revenue Model," *SBJ*, September 6–12, 2004; Daniel Kaplan, "NFL Open to Sharing All Local Revenue," *SBJ*, February 14–20, 2005; Daniel Kaplan, "Revenue-Disparity Split Deepens as Owners Meet," *SBJ*, March 28–April 3, 2005; Leonard Shapiro, "Union Chief Warns NFL Owners," *WP*, May 24, 2005; Liz Mullen and Daniel Kaplan, "NFL Sides Agree: Deal Must Be Done by March 1," *SBJ*, January 16–22, 2006; Daniel Kaplan, "On the Brink," *SBJ*, January 30–February 5, 2006; Daniel Kaplan, "NFL Labor Showdown Goes into OT," *SBJ*, March 6–12, 2006; Daniel Kaplan, "Chaos and Compromise in Dallas," *SBJ*, March 13–19, 2006; Clifton Brown, "N.F.L. Owners Accept Labor Deal," *NYT*, March 9, 2006.

26. Mike Lupica, "The Raid-uh Rules," *Esquire*, January 1996.

27. This is Mike Lupica's description of Bill Bidwell, owner of the Arizona Cardinals, in "The Raid-uh Rules."

28. Gerald Eskenazi, "Sale of Cowboys Expected Today, and Landry Might Be Out," *NYT*, February 25, 1989; AP, "Cowboys' Buyer Hires a New Coach," *NYT*, February 26, 1989.

29. Daniel Fisher and Mike K. Ozanian, "Cowboy Capitalism," *Forbes*, September 20, 1999; Mike K. Ozanian et al., "Foul Ball," *Financial World*, May 25, 1993; Mike K. Ozanian et al., "The $11 Billion Pastime," *Financial World*, May 10, 1994.

30. David Harris, *The League: The Rise and Decline of the NFL* (New York: Bantam, 1986), 36–37; E. M. Swift, "Another Gusher for Jones," *SI*, December 12, 1994; Peter King, "Jones Versus the NFL," *SI*, September 4, 1995; Richard Sandomir, "Dollars and Dallas: League of Their Own?," *NYT*, September 24, 1995.

31. Richard Hoffer, "Cowboys for Sale," *SI*, September 18, 1995; David Barboza, "Advertising," *NYT*, August 7, 1995; Richard Sandomir, "Cowboys' Jones Issues (Pepsi) Challenge to the N.F.L.," *NYT*, August 15, 1995; Richard Sandomir, "N.F.L. Sues Jones to Stop 'Ambush' Deals," *NYT*, September 19, 1995; Timothy W. Smith, "Cowboy Owner Fires Back with Suit Against N.F.L." *NYT*, November 7, 1995; "N.F.L. Settles with Cowboys," *NYT*, December 14, 1996.

32. Richard Alm, "Jerry Jones, NFL Now at Peace after Marketing Compromise," *DMN* (online), June 30, 1998; Daniel Kaplan, "Tagliabue: NFL Trust Survival 'a Done Deal,'" *SBJ*, March 29–April 4, 2004; Kaplan, "NFL's Next Battle: Revenue Sharing."

33. Daniel Kaplan, "Cowboys Indicate the Plug Hasn't Been Pulled on RSN," *SBJ*, May 30–June 4, 2005; "The 50 Most Influential People in Sports Business: 24, Jerry Jones," *SBJ*, December 19–25, 2005.

34. Fisher and Ozanian, "Cowboy Capitalism."

35. Robert Kraft bought the New England Patriots for $160 million from James Orthwein (who had paid $106 million just two years earlier when he bailed out Victor Kiam and his partner, who had paid $80 million in 1988 to cash-strapped Billy Sullivan). That same year, Jeffrey Lurie purchased the Philadelphia Eagles from Norman Braman for $173 million (Braman had bought the club in 1985 for $65 million) and H. Wayne Huizenga acquired 85 percent of the Miami Dolphins for $140 million (he already owned the other 15 percent). See Robert McG. Thomas Jr., "Sold! Time to Call Them the New England Permanents," *NYT*, January 22, 1994; Dave Anderson, "The Patriots' Cleanup Man," *NYT*, November 13, 1988; Richard Sandomir, "Eagles Purchased for Record Amount," *NYT*, April 7, 1994; Thomas George, "Miami Gets Interim Owner," *NYT*, March 24, 1994.

36. "Buccaneers Sold to Glazer," *NYT*, January 17, 1995; AP, "St. Louis's Generosity Overwhelms Rams," *NYT*, January 18, 1995; Thomas George, "Rams Given Green Light for St. Louis Move," *NYT*, April 13, 1995; Timothy W. Smith, "Raiders Run a Reverse Play Back to Oakland," *NYT*, June 24, 1995; Sandomir, "Cowboys Jones Issues (Pepsi) Challenge to the N.F.L."; Michael Janofsky, "The Browns Put N.F.L. Back in Baltimore," *NYT*, November 7, 1995; AP, "Nashville Expecting Oilers," *NYT*, November 16, 1995.

37. Peter King, "Down and Out," *SI*, November 13, 1995; Steve Rushin and Richard Deutsch, "The Heart of a City," *SI*, December 4, 1995; Susan Faludi, *Stiffed: The Betrayal of the American Man* (New York: Morrow, 1999), 153–223.

38. Thomas George, "Rams Given Green Light for St. Louis Move," *NYT*, April 13, 1995; Damon Hack, "Raiders Win $34 Million in Oakland Coliseum Case," *NYT*, August 27, 2003; Richard Sandomir, "Lerner Wins Browns for $530 Million," *NYT*, September 9, 1998; Thomas George, "N.F.L. Picks Los Angeles with Conditions," *NYT*, March 17, 1999; Todd S. Purdum, "Los Angeles's Chance to Recover Its Fumbles," *NYT*, April 14, 1999; Richard Sandomir, "N.F.L. Goes Back to Houston for $700 Million," *NYT*, October 7, 1999; Mike Allen, "Handshake on Deal to Move Patriots to Hartford," *NYT*, November 20, 1998; Richard Sandomir, "Tagliabue Fakes Out the Patriots," *NYT*, April 27, 1999; Mike Allen, "Massachusetts Unveils New Bid to Keep Patriots out of Hartford," *NYT*, April 28, 1999; Mike Allen, "As Deadline Closes In, Patriots Reject Lucrative Hartford Offer," *NYT*, May 1, 1999; Richard Sandomir, "Stadium Financing? New Twist for N.F.L.," *NYT*, May 6, 1999.

39. TV revenues from Tom Barnidge, "The NFL on TV," in *Total Football: The Official Encyclopedia of the National Football League*, ed. Bob Carroll et al. (New York: HarperCollins, 1999), 513; and "NFL TV Rights through the Years" (table), *SBJ*, April 15–21, 2002. League revenues are from the annual reports in *Financial World* (for the years 1990–1996) and *Forbes* (1997–2005).

40. Alex Frangos, "Bigger and Better," *Wall Street Journal*, September 20, 2004;

Saporito, "The American Money Machine"; Charles V. Bagli, "Three Winners in Stadium Deal: Giants, Jets, and Governor," *NYT*, October 1, 2005; Don Muret, "Very Cool," *SBJ*, September 18–24, 2006; AP, "University of Phoenix Gets Naming Rights to Cardinals' Stadium," *WP*, September 26, 2006; Kevin Duchschere, "Vikings Plan Draws Cheers and Concern," *Minneapolis Star Tribune*, September 21, 2005. See also Yost, *Tailgating, Sacks, and Salary Caps*, 178–202.

41. "Suite Deals," *Forbes*, September 17, 2001; League of Fans, "Summary of Total Cost and Public Subsidy for NFL Stadiums Constructed or Significantly Renovated since 1990," <http://www.leagueoffans.org/nflstadiums1990.html> (updated September 9, 2003); Dennis Zimmerman, "Subsidizing Stadiums: Who Benefits, Who Pays?," and Roger G. Noll and Andrew Zimbalist, "Sports, Jobs, and Taxes: The Real Connection," both in *Sports, Jobs, and Taxes: The Economic Impact of Sports Teams and Stadiums*, ed. Roger G. Noll and Andrew Zimbalist (Washington, D.C.: Brookings Institution, 1997), 119–45, 500–501; Glenn M. Wong, *Essentials of Sports Law*, 3rd ed. (Westport, Conn.: Praeger, 2002), 718–22; "Public Financing Alive and Well," a table in "In-Depth: Facility Finance," *SBJ*, June 20–26, 2005. The League of Fans reported greater disparities between the public and private financial burdens than did *Forbes*.

42. See Kenneth L. Shropshire, *The Sports Franchise Game: Cities in Pursuit of Sports Franchises, Events, Stadiums, and Arenas* (Philadelphia: University of Pennsylvania Press, 1995); Mark S. Rosentraub, *Major League Losers: The Real Cost of Sports and Who's Paying for It* (New York: Basic Books, 1997); Joanna Cagan and Neil DeMause, *Field of Schemes: How the Great Stadium Swindle Turns Public Money into Private Profit* (Monroe, Maine: Common Courage Press, 1998); Noll and Zimbalist, eds., *Sports, Jobs, and Taxes*; and Yost, *Tailgating, Sacks, and Salary Caps*.

43. AP, "St. Louis's Generosity Overwhelms Rams"; Richard Sandomir, "Owners' New Strategy: Take the Team and Run," *NYT*, January 14, 1996; Kevin J. Delaney and Rick Eckstein, *Public Dollars, Private Stadiums: The Battle over Building Sports Stadiums* (New Brunswick, N.J.: Rutgers University Press, 2003), 4, 22; Kevin Sack, "Can Nashville Say No to N.F.L. Team? Maybe," *NYT*, May 3, 1996; AP, "Nashville Voters Want Oilers," *NYT*, May 8, 1996; Allen, "Handshake on Deal to Move Patriots to Hartford."

44. Delaney and Eckstein, *Public Dollars, Private Stadiums*, 22, 39, 62.

45. "Gauging Support for the NFL among Los Angeles Area Residents," *SBJ*, September 4–10, 2006; "Comparing NFL Fan Avidity Levels," *SBJ*, September 4–10, 2006; Purdum, "Los Angeles's Chance to Recover Its Fumbles"; Richard Sandomir, "Houston Franchise Could Set Mark," *NYT*, October 6, 1999; Sandomir, "N.F.L. Goes Back to Houston for $700 Million."

46. "In-Depth: Facility Finance," *SBJ*, June 20–26, 2005.

47. "Team Valuations," *Forbes*, September 19, 2005; "Stop the Stadium in Its Tracks," *NYT*, December 4, 2004, A30; Daniel Kaplan, "Jets Plan to Borrow More Than $1 Billion for Stadium," *SBJ*, May 9–15, 2005; Amy Shipley, "N.Y.'s Bid for 2012 Olympics Set Back," *WP*, June 7, 2005; Bagli, "Three Winners in Stadium Deal."

48. Daniel Kaplan and John Lombardo, "NFL Will Borrow Big for Stadium Loans,"

SBJ, May 22–28, 2000; John Lombardo, "NFL Stadium Loan Pool Drying Up," *SBJ*, December 4–10, 2000; Daniel Kaplan, "NFL Debt a Hit with Investors," *SBJ*, September 10–16, 2001; Daniel Kaplan, "Team Dues in NFL Jump 28 Percent," *SBJ*, February 17–23, 2003; Daniel Kaplan, "Benson to Lead NFL Panel Deciding Fate of G-3 Fund," *SBJ*, March 3–9, 2003; Daniel Kaplan, "Minnesota Afraid Jets Will Tap Out NFL's Stadium-Finance Fund," *SBJ*, April 5–11, 2004; Saporito, "The American Money Machine"; Daniel Kaplan, "Cowboys and Colts Score Stadium Grants," *SBJ*, June 27–July 3, 2005.

49. "In-Depth: Facility Finance"; Don Muret, "Cowboys Plan Unique Field-Level Suites," *SBJ*, December 18–24, 2006.

50. FCI from *Team Marketing Report* (online); Les Carpenter, "A Solution, or Merely a Cover?," *WP*, September 27, 2006.

51. Monte Burke, "A New Test for an Old Raider," *Forbes*, September 18, 2006.

52. Ibid.

53. Brett Pulley, "The $1 Billion Team," *Forbes*, September 20, 2004. *Financial World* published annual valuations from 1991 through 1997 (July 9, 1991; July 7, 1992; May 25, 1993; May 10, 1994; May 9, 1995; May 20, 1996; June 17, 1997), then was succeeded by *Forbes* (December 14, 1998; September 20, 1999; September 18, 2000; September 17, 2001; September 2, 2002; September 15, 2003; September 20, 2004).

54. Kurt Badenhausen, "Cardinal Red," *Forbes*, September 20, 2004.

55. In 1986, according to NFL figures, gross revenue for the league was $500 million from television, $275 from gate receipts, and just $50 million from "other," which included stadium revenue. By 1990—the figures are from *Financial World* and *Forbes*—total stadium revenue had more than tripled, to $156 million. By 1996 it was $228 million, and by 2002, $576 million. See "N.F.L. Income Sources," *NYT*, January 18, 1987; Anthony Baldo et al., "Secrets of the Front Office: What America's Pro Teams Are Worth," *Financial World*, July 9, 1991; Kurt Badenhausen et al., "Sports Valuations: More Than a Game," *Financial World*, June 17, 1997; Monte Burke, "Like Father, Unlike Son," *Forbes*, September 15, 2003.

56. Michael Duberstein, "NFL 2003 Franchise History and Values Stadium Data," <http://www.nflpa.org/PDFs/Shared/Franchise_Values_&_Stadium_Data_(Revised_October_2003).pdf>; Adam Brenner, "Welcome to the Club," *Forbes* (online), September 2, 2004.

57. "Stadium Naming Rights," <http://sports.espn.go.com/espn/sportsbusiness/news/story?page=stadiumnames> (January 14, 2002); supplemented by information on the Seattle Seahawks, New England Patriots, and Miami Dolphins.

58. Richard Sandomir, "How Green Is Your Gridiron?," *NYT*, March 13, 1999. See also Richard Sandomir, "Gauging Value on Seats and Suites," *NYT*, January 12, 1999; and "The NFL's Financial Standings," *Forbes*, September 20, 1999.

59. Michael K. Ozanian and Kurt Badenhausen, "Two Minute Drill," *Forbes*, September 18, 2000; Pulley, "The $1 Billion Team"; Tony Kornheiser, "Season Ticket: $2,350 . . . Redskins MasterCard: Priceless," *WP*, January 31, 2005; Thomas Heath, "Redskins Drop Payment Policy," *WP*, February 2, 2005.

60. Calculations from data in online edition of *Forbes*, August 31, 2006.

61. Fisher and Ozanian, "Cowboy Capitalism."

62. "Team Valuations," *Forbes* (online edition), September 1, 2006.

63. Fisher and Ozanian, "Cowboy Capitalism"; Ozanian and Badenhausen, "Two Minute Drill"; Daniel Kaplan, "NFL OKs Redskins' $700M Refinancing," *SBJ*, August 12–18, 2002.

64. Kurt Badenhausen, "Salary Cap? What Cap?," *Financial World*, May 20, 1996; Dave Anderson, "How Jones Bought the Super Bowl," *NYT*, January 29, 1996.

65. "Figures Show Redskins Spent Most," *NYT*, February 14, 2001.

66. Kimball Perry, "Losing Bengals Winners in Profits," *Cincinnati Post* (online), August 4, 2004; Joseph White (AP), "NFL Owners Approve Vikings Sale to Wilf," *WP*, May 25, 2005. On Hamilton County's so far unsuccessful lawsuit, see Tony Cook, "Bengals Win Antitrust Lawsuit," *Cincinnati Post* (online), February 9, 2006; Kimball Perry, "Commissioners Vote to Appeal Dismissed Bengals, NFL Suit," *CE* (online), March 9, 2006.

67. Daniel Kaplan, "NFL's Packers Count the Green $25M Net," *SBJ*, June 20–26, 2005; Daniel Kaplan, "Profit for Packers Down 29%," *SBJ*, June 19–25, 2006.

68. Daniel Kaplan, "Revenue-Disparity Split Deepens as Owners Meet," *SBJ*, March 28–April 3, 2005; Daniel Kaplan, "Revenue-Sharing Plan Going to Owners," *SBJ*, May 23–29, 2005; Daniel Kaplan, "NFL Execs Optimistic on Revenue Sharing," *SBJ*, August 1–7, 2005.

69. Daniel Kaplan, "Chaos and Compromise in Dallas," *SBJ*, March 13–19, 2006; Ross Nethery, "The End of His Era," *SBJ*, July 31–August 6, 2006; Ashley Fox, "League's New Boss Must Tackle the Tough Jobs," *PI* (online), August 13, 2006; Les Carpenter, "A Solution, or Merely a Cover?," *WP*, September 27, 2006.

70. Tom Lowry, "The NFL Machine," *Business Week*, January 27, 2003.

71. "Monday Night Inflation" (table), *NYT*, January 14, 1998; "Media Tracker," *SBJ*, January 10–16, 2005; "Media Tracker," *SBJ*, January 23–29, 2006; "Media Tracker," *SBJ*, January 16–22, 2006; Neil Best, "Sports Watch," *Newsday* (online), December 30, 2005.

72. William Taaffe, "Don't Let It Go Down the Tube, Pete," *SI*, November 12, 1984; Bill Carter, "Where the Boys Are," *NYT*, January 31, 1999; Joe Flint, "Air Games," *Wall Street Journal*, September 20, 2004; "Media Tracker," *SBJ*, December 26–January 1, 2005; "Media Tracker," *SBJ*, January 23–29, 2006; "NFL Averages and Prime-Time Ratings," a table accompanying Andrew Marchand, "Can the NFL Push NBC's Prime-Time Lineup from Worst to First?," *SBJ*, August 21–27, 2006.

73. Michael Goodwin, "Networks Save Cash, Gain a Competitor," *NYT*, March 17, 1987; Bill Carter, "New TV Contracts for N.F.L.'s Games Total $3.6 Billion," *NYT*, March 10, 1990; Richard Sandomir, "Free Agents and the Ratings Pie," *NYT*, January 8, 1993; Richard Sandomir, "Fox Network's Bid Beats CBS for Rights to N.F.C. Football," *NYT*, December 18, 1993; Bill Carter, "Stunned CBS Now Scrambling for A.F.C.," *NYT*, December 19, 1993; Richard Sandomir, "CBS Guarantees Billions to Get N.F.L. Back," *NYT*, January 13, 1998.

74. Richard Sandomir, "Monday Football Stays on ABC; NBC out of Game after 33 Years," *NYT*, January 14, 1998; Bill Carter, "N.F.L. Is Must-Have TV: NBC Is a Have-Not," *NYT*, January 14, 1998; Richard Sandomir, "How One Network's Urgency Spelled Riches for the N.F.L.," *NYT*, January 17, 1998.

75. Adam Bryant, "Beyond the Bottom Line: The New Math of TV Sports," *NYT*, January 18, 1998; Carter, "Where the Boys Are."

76. David Leonhardt, "The Real Super Bowl," *Business Week*, February 3, 1997; Carter, "Where the Boys Are"; Mark Hyman, "How to Lose Fans and Get Richer," *Business Week*, January 26, 1998.

77. Bryant, "Beyond the Bottom Line."

78. Leonhardt, "The Real Super Bowl"; Bill Carter, "CBS Affiliates to Share Costs for First Time," *NYT*, May 30, 1998; Jere Longman, "Pro Leagues' Ratings Drop; Nobody Is Quite Sure Why," *NYT*, July 29, 2001; Richard Sandomir, "Advertising," *NYT*, February 14, 2002; "Fox Official Derides Huge Rights Fees," *NYT*, May 15, 2002.

79. Seth Schiesel, "Football Fans with Cable Hope to Have Wider Choices," *NYT*, January 28, 2002; Daniel Kaplan, "NFL Goes on Offense with Network," *SBJ*, May 5–11, 2003; Richard Sandomir, "Giving N.F.L. Fans More, More, More," *NYT*, July 10, 2003; Ronald Grover, "Is This an End Run by the NFL?," *Business Week*, October 27, 2003; Joe Flint, "Air Games," *Wall Street Journal*, September 20, 2004; Bill King, "Reaching Today's Fans," *SBJ*, March 14–20, 2005.

80. Barry Wilner (AP), "NFL OKs 6-Year Extensions with Fox, CBS," *WP*, November 9, 2004; "Fox and CBS Deals Extended Six Years," *Portland Oregonian*, November 9, 2004; Andy Bernstein, "Big Ticket Item Highlights NFL TV Deals," *SBJ*, November 15–21, 2004.

81. Leonard Shapiro and Mark Maske, "'Monday Night Football' Changes the Channel," *WP*, April 19, 2005; Andy Bernstein, "NFL Restores NBC's Clout," *SBJ*, April 25–May 1, 2005; Daniel Kaplan, "Deal Sends Team Values Shooting Above $1B Mark," *SBJ*, April 25–May 1, 2005; Marchand, "Can the NFL Push NBC's Prime-Time Lineup from Worst to First?"

82. Richard Sandomir, "NFL Network Will Carry Eight Prime-Time Games," *NYT*, January 28, 2006; Richard Sandomir, "Wooed by Many, N.F.L. Chooses Itself," *NYT*, January 31, 2006; Andy Bernstein, "Television Package Raises Questions about NFL Network Distribution, Future of OLN," *SBJ*, February 6–12, 2006; Daniel Kaplan and Liz Mullen, "TV Plan Adds Labor Friction," *SBJ*, February 6–12, 2006.

83. Richard Sandomir, "ABC Sports Is Dead at 45; Stand By for ESPN," *NYT*, August 11, 2006; Marchand, "Can the NFL Push NBC's Prime-Time Lineup from Worst to First?"; Richard Sandomir, "Getting Back in the Game," *NYT*, September 7, 2006.

84. Richard Sandomir, "N.F.L. Learns Its Worth and Makes ESPN Pay," *NYT*, September 8, 2006.

85. John Ourand, "NFL Ad Sales a Bonanza for Networks," *SBJ*, September 4–10, 2006.

86. Marchand, "Can the NFL Push NBC's Prime-Time Lineup from Worst to First?";

John Ourand, "NFL Wants to Limit Overlap of Fox, NBC Shows on Sunday," *SBJ*, August 28–September 3, 2006; Judy Battista, "Deal Helps Free Agents and Top Draft Picks," *NYT*, March 10, 2006.

Chapter Five

1. John Steinbreder, "Hot Properties," *SI*, March 9, 1992; David Harris, *The League: The Rise and Decline of the NFL* (New York: Bantam, 1986), 80; Peter King et al., "The Path to Power," *SI*, August 30, 1999.

2. Gerald Eskenazi, "Harassment Charge Draws N.F.L.'s Attention," *NYT*, September 27, 1990; Gerald Eskenazi, "Investigator to Look Into Harassment," *NYT*, September 28, 1990; Thomas Rogers, "Patriot Shake-Up Promised," *NYT*, October 1, 1990.

3. Robin Finn, "Female Reporters See Renewed Resistance," *NYT*, October 3, 1990; Dave Anderson, "The Only Issue Is Human Decency," *NYT*, September 30, 1990; Russell Baker, "Boys Will Be Forever," *NYT*, October 2, 1990; George Vecsey, "Sam Wyche Needs Some Time Off," *NYT*, October 3, 1990; "The Right Place for Women" (editorial), *NYT*, October 4, 1990; Robert McG. Thomas Jr., "Wyche Fined by N.F.L. for Barring Female Writer," *NYT*, October 6, 1990; Frank Litsky, "A Sportswriter's Place Is in the Locker Room," *NYT*, October 6, 1990; Ira Berkow, "What Is She Doing Here?," *NYT*, October 7, 1990; Robert McG. Thomas Jr., "The Poll Story: Everybody Out," *NYT*, October 21, 1990; Thomas George, "Patriots and 3 Players Fined in Olson Incident," *NYT*, November 28, 1990; Thomas Rogers, "Kiam Apologizes after Joking about the Olson Incident," *NYT*, February 7, 1991; "Olson Sues Patriots," *NYT*, April 26, 1991; "Olson Settles Suit," *NYT*, February 25, 1992.

4. Sam Allis, "What Do Men Really Want?," *Time*, Fall 1990; Doug Stanton, "Inward, Ho!," *Esquire*, October 1991.

5. Steinbreder, "Hot Properties."

6. Ibid.; Richard Sandomir, "Dollars and Dallas: League of Their Own?," *NYT*, September 24, 1995.

7. Sandomir, "Dollars and Dallas."

8. Andy Bernstein, "Levinson Bolts NFLP for Internet," *SBJ*, March 20–26, 2000.

9. In a best-selling book with that title in 2000, the journalist Malcolm Gladwell borrowed the term "tipping point" from epidemiology to explain social and cultural changes.

10. Timothy W. Smith, "Cowboy Owner Fires Back with Suit against N.F.L.," *NYT*, November 7, 1995; Tom Lowry, "The NFL Machine," *Business Week*, January 27, 2003.

11. John Seabrook, "Tackling the Competition," *New Yorker*, August 18, 1997; Ruth Coxeter and Chris Roush, "Meet the NFL's Newest Quarterback," *Business Week*, November 7, 1994.

12. Coxeter and Roush, "Meet the NFL's Newest Quarterback"; Terry Lefton, "NFL Properties' New Signal Caller Maps a Mantra of Marketing Plays," *Brandweek*, April 24, 1995; Jeff Jensen, " 'Experiential Branding' Makes It to Big Leagues," *Advertising Age*,

April 14, 1997; Jeff Jensen, "NFL Ad Blitz Targets Next-Generation Fans," *Advertising Age*, August 24, 1998.

13. Stuart Elliott, "Advertising," *NYT*, August 28, 1996; Elliott, "Advertising," *NYT*, August 29, 1997; Elliott, "Advertising," *NYT*, July 14, 1998; Courtney Kane, "Advertising," *NYT*, September 24, 1999.

14. Seabrook, "Tackling the Competition."

15. Jeff Jensen, "Promotional Marketer of the Year: NFL," *Advertising Age*, March 4, 1996.

16. Andy Bernstein, "Levinson Bolts NFLP for Internet," *SBJ*, March 20–26, 2000; John Lombardo and Andy Bernstein, "Goodell to Oversee New-Look NFL Biz Side," *SBJ*, May 8–14, 2000; Andy Bernstein, "Sponsorship Sales Face Likely Overhaul; Team Needs Rise to Top," *SBJ*, April 23–29, 2001; Terry Lefton, "Marketing Integration Will Happen or Be Forced," *SBJ*, April 15–21, 2002.

17. Terry Lefton, "NFL Sacks 'Power' Ploy; MLB Aims for One Voice," *Brandweek*, July 31, 2000.

18. Stuart Elliott, "Advertising," *NYT*, September 7, 2001; Michael MacCambridge, *America's Game: The Epic Story of How Pro Football Captured a Nation* (New York: Random House, 2004), 427.

19. Andy Bernstein, "NFL Aims at Exclusive Licensees," *SBJ*, September 3–9, 2001; Terry Lefton, "League Deals Signal Change," *SBJ*, April 15–21, 2002; "2003 NFL Sponsors," *SBJ*, September 1–7, 2003; Mark Yost, *Tailgaiting, Sacks, and Salary Caps: How the NFL Became the Most Successful Sports League in History* (Chicago: Kaplan, 2006), 121–38.

20. James H. Harris, "NFL Again Shows It Knows How to Use Entertainment for a Big Kickoff," *SBJ*, September 15, 2003; "Sponsorship Report Cards: Experts Sound Off on Music Marketing," *SBJ*, January 19–25, 2004; "News in Brief," *SBJ*, August 16–22, 2004; "NFL Kicks Off with Concerts," *Portland Oregonian*, August 14, 2005; Terry Lefton, "NFL Mixes Monster Brands in Stones/Super Bowl Merchandise," *SBJ*, January 9–15, 2006.

21. Daniel Kaplan, "World of Uncertainty for NFL Europe," *SBJ*, June 9–15, 2003; "2006 TV Report: Global Football Tops U.S. Football," *SBJ*, January 15–21, 2007; John Lyons, "The NFL Asks Soccer-Mad Mexicans if They're Ready for Some Football," *Wall Street Journal*, November 30, 2006; Mark Maske, "Owners Give Approval for NFL Games Overseas," *WP*, October 25, 2006; Langdon Brockington, "NFL and Nickelodeon Have More Fun Planned, Fueled by PP&K Competition," *SBJ*, February 12–18, 2001; Langdon Brockington, "NFL Tries to Score with Nation's Largest Minority," *SBJ*, September 2–8, 2002; Terry Lefton, "NFL Gobbles Up Spot in Macy's Parade," *SBJ*, November 15–21, 2004; Bill King, "Reaching Today's Fans," *SBJ*, March 14–20, 2005; Terry Lefton and Daniel Kaplan, "Sprint, NFL Near $200M Deal," *SBJ*, June 20–26, 2005. See also Yost, *Tailgating, Sacks, and Salary Caps*.

22. Terry Lefton, "After Building Up Super Bowl and Kickoff, NFL Targets Draft," *SBJ*, February 13–19, 2006; Michael Wilbon, "A Strong Feeling about the NFL Draft,"

WP, April 27, 2006; Terry Lefton, "NFL Still Working Out Details on In-Game Ads," *SBJ*, May 1–7, 2006; "NFL Launching Season Platform in Mold of XL," *SBJ*, April 24–30, 2006; Terry Lefton, "NFL Adds to XL Success," *SBJ*, January 29–February 4, 2007.

23. Terry Lefton, "NFL Provides Teams Tips on Entertainment Options," *SBJ*, March 3–9, 2003.

24. Kane, "Advertising."

25. MacCambridge, *America's Game*, 212; Harris Poll No. 54, September 24, 2003; Harris Poll No. 77, October 13, 2004; Harris Poll No. 94, December 27, 2005 (all at <http://www.harrisinteractive.com>).

26. Langdon Brockington, "Under Blank, Falcons Give Fans What They Want," *SBJ*, September 2–8, 2002.

27. Michael Freeman, *ESPN: The Uncensored History* (Lanham, Md., and New York: Taylor Trade Publishing, 2001), 92–96, 103, 117, 121–22.

28. Freeman, *ESPN*, 232; Norman Chad, "To TV Sports Fans, ESPN Grows from Novelty to Necessity," *NYT*, October 18, 1987; William Oscar Johnson and John Walters, "Every Day Is Game Day," *SI*, December 21, 1992; Mark Lacter, "Fox and Mouse," *Forbes*, January 22, 2001; Dorothy Pomerantz, "Seventh-Inning Slump," *Forbes*, May 14, 2001; Brett Pulley, "Disney the Sequel," *Forbes*, December 9, 2002; Andy Bernstein, "New Twist in ESPN-Cable Fight," *SBJ*, February 16–22, 2004; Andy Bernstein, "ESPN Sees Its Television Viewership Reach All-Time High," *SBJ*, January 10–16, 2005.

29. Michael MacCambridge, *The Franchise: A History of Sports Illustrated Magazine* (New York: Hyperion, 1997), 358, 398, 403.

30. "Mario-elous: ESPN's NFL Draft Ratings Trend," *SBJ*, May 8–14, 2006.

31. Charles Hirshberg, *ESPN 25: 25 Mind-Bending, Eye-Popping, Culture-Morphing Years of Highlights* (New York: Hyperion, 2004), 89–90; Johnson and Walters, "Every Day Is Game Day."

32. Keith Olbermann and Dan Patrick, *The Big Show: Inside ESPN's SportsCenter* (New York: Pocket Books, 1997), 11, 23, 25–26.

33. Hirshberg, *ESPN 25*, 106; King, "Reaching Today's Fans."

34. Steven Levingston, "NFL Plays Smash-Mouth Ball When It Comes to Branding," *WP*, February 5, 2006; "The Light Side," *Portland Oregonian*, March 10, 2005.

35. Jeff Jensen, "NFL Plans Rush into Hollywood," *Advertising Age*, October 24, 1994; Jeff Jensen, "NFL Teams Up with TriStar to Tout 'Jerry McGuire,'" *Advertising Age*, September 2, 1996.

36. Craig Rosen, "Eminem Tackled by NFL," *Launch* (online at <http://launch.yahoo.com/read/news.asp?contentID=164550>), November 16, 1999.

37. Steinbreder, "Hot Properties."

38. Wayne Friedman, "CBS Drafts MTV to Create Super Bowl Programming," *Advertising Age*, July 3, 2000.

39. James Poniewozik et al., "The Hypocrisy Bowl," *Time*, February 16, 2004; Andy Bernstein, "Fiasco May Change NFL's Youth Strategy in a Flash," *SBJ*, February 9–15, 2004; MacCambridge, *America's Game*, 448.

40. Leonard Shapiro, "ABC Apologizes for 'Desperate' Football Intro," *WP*, November 17, 2004.

41. Jon Pareles, "ABC Avoids a Lyric Malfunction but Allows Mick's Midriff," *NYT*, February 6, 2006.

42. Bernice Kanner, *Super Bowl of Advertising: How the Commercials Won the Game* (Princeton, N.J.: Bloomberg, 2004), 1–3; Don Weiss with Chuck Day, *The Making of the Super Bowl: The Inside Story of the World's Greatest Sporting Event* (Chicago: Contemporary Books, 2003); Tony Perry, "Myth America: The Legend of Super Sunday," *LAT*, January 31, 1999; Leonard Koppitt, "Quarterbacking the Market," *NYT*, November 3, 1987.

43. The fullest account of the claim about violence on Super Bowl Sunday is in the antifeminist book by Christina Hoff Sommers, *Who Stole Feminism? How Women Have Betrayed Women* (New York: Simon & Schuster, 1994), 188–92.

44. A search of "domestic violence" and "NFL" in the newspaper database in LexisNexis turned up 13 references for 1993, 44 for 1994 (the year of Nicole Simpson's murder), 165 for 1995, and 174 for 1996, followed by a drop to 93 in 1997 and 106 in 1998.

45. Darren Rovell, "NFL Reaction to Series a Factor in Cancellation," ESPN.com, February 4, 2004.

46. Bill Brubaker, "Violence in Football Extends off Field," *WP*, November 13, 1994; William Nack and Lester Munson, "Sports' Dirty Secret," *SI*, July 31, 1995; Maryann Hudson, "From Box Scores to the Police Blotter," *LAT*, December 27, 1995. This edition has other stories by Hudson, Elliott Almond, Mike Downey, Julie Cart, Johnny White and Jason Reid, and George Dohrmann and Ara Najarian, along with a chronology of the year's incidents filling five full pages. Cart's "Sex and Violence" focuses specifically on domestic and sexual violence, with Houston quarterback Warren Moon, a former NFL Man of the Year now charged with abusing his wife, at the center of the story. See also Rachel Shuster, "Domestic Abuse No Stranger to Sports," *USA Today*, October 4, 1994; Bill Falk, "Bringing Home the Violence," *Newsday*, January 8, 1995; David Holmstrom, "Do Aggressive Sports Produce Violent Men?," *Christian Science Monitor*, October 16, 1995; Geoff Calkins, "Athletes and Domestic Violence," *Fort Lauderdale Sun-Sentinel*, October 17, 1995; Paul Levy, "Studies Find More Violence by Athletes," *Minneapolis Star Tribune*, January 9, 1996; and "Out of Bounds: Professional Sports Leagues and Domestic Violence," *Harvard Law Review* 109 (March 1996): 1048–65.

47. Laurie Nicole Robinson, "Professional Athletes Held to a Higher Standard and above the Law: A Comment on High-Profile Criminal Defendants and the Need for States to Establish High-Profile Courts," *Indiana Law Journal* 73 (Fall 1998): 1–33 (online through LexisNexis).

48. Brubaker, "Violence in Football Extends Off Field"; Hudson, "From Box Scores to the Police Blotter."

49. Todd W. Crossett, Jeffrey R. Benedict, and Mark A. McDonald, "Male Student-Athletes Reported for Sexual Assault: A Survey of Campus Police Departments and

Judicial Affairs Offices," *Journal of Sport and Social Issues* 19 (May 1995): 126–40; Todd Crossett, "Male Athletes' Violence against Women: A Critical Assessment of the Athletic Affiliation, Violence against Women Debate," *Quest* 51 (1999): 244–57. Jeff Benedict also published a book based on this data titled *Public Heroes, Private Felons: Athletes and Crimes Against Women* (Boston: Northeastern University Press, 1997).

50. Jeff Benedict and Don Yaeger, *Pros and Cons: The Criminals Who Play in the NFL* (New York: Warner, 1998). The studies on which Benedict collaborated were routinely cited in the newspaper reports on athletes' sexual violence.

51. Alfred Blumstein and Jeff Benedict, "Criminal Violence of NFL Players Compared to the General Population," *Chance* 12 (Summer 1999): 12–15.

52. Gary Smith, "Crime and Punishment," *SI*, June 24, 1996.

53. Michael Bamberger, "First-Degree Tragedy," *SI*, December 27, 1999; Mark Starr et al., "A Season of Shame," *Newsweek*, May 29, 2000; Grant Wahl and Jon L. Wertheim, "Paternity Ward," *SI*, May 4, 1998.

54. Brubaker, "Violence in Football Extends Off Field"; Mike Freeman, "Stains from the Police Blotter Leave N.F.L. Embarrassed," *NYT*, January 9, 2000; Mike Freeman, "N.F.L. Rookies Go to Class before Going to Camp," *NYT*, July 4, 2001; Stephen J. Dubner, "Life Is a Contact Sport," *New York Times Magazine*, August 16, 2002.

55. John Gibeaut, "When Pros Turn Cons" (cover story), *ABA Journal* 86 (July 2000): 38–46 (this is the official publication of the American Bar Association).

56. Forty-nine players or team employees in the NFL (with a total of 1,600 players) were charged with crimes, compared to 25 from Major League Baseball (roughly 700 players) and 21 from the NBA (around 325 players).

57. Mariah Burton Nelson, *The Stronger Women Get, the More Men Love Football: Sexism and the American Culture of Sports* (New York: Harcourt Brace, 1994). For a sampling of sociologists' view of sport and destructive masculinity, see Donald F. Sabo Jr. and Ross Runfolo, *Jock: Sports and Male Identity* (Englewood Cliffs, N.J.: Prentice-Hall, 1980); Michael A. Messner and Donald F. Sabo, eds., *Sport, Men, and the Gender Order: Critical Feminist Perspectives* (Champaign, Ill.: Human Kinetics, 1990); Michael A. Messner, *Power at Play: Sports and the Problem of Masculinity* (Boston: Beacon Press, 1992); Michael A. Messner and Donald F. Sabo, *Sex, Violence, and Power in Sports: Rethinking Masculinity* (Freedom, Calif.: Crossing Press, 1994); Varda Burstyn, *The Rites of Men: Manhood, Politics, and the Culture of Sport* (Toronto: University of Toronto Press, 1999); Jim McKay, Michael A. Messner, and Don Sabo, eds., *Masculinities, Gender Relations, and Sport* (Thousand Oaks, Calif.: Sage, 2000); Michael A. Messner, *Taking the Field: Women, Men, and Sports* (Minneapolis: University of Minnesota Press, 2002). Messner and Sabo are obviously the leading scholars on this subject.

58. Terrence Real, *I Don't Want to Talk About It: Overcoming the Secret Legacy of Male Depression* (New York: Simon & Schuster, 1997), 169, 176, 178, 183.

59. Bob Glauber, "Breaking Point," *Newsday*, January 15, 1997; Bob Glauber, "Surveying the Situation," *Newsday*, January 12, 1997. Glauber's "Special Report: Life after Football," a series of articles based on the survey, appeared in *Newsday* from January 12

through January 16, 1997. They are also posted on the website GamesOver.org, run by former Green Bay Packer player Ken Ruettgers to provide advice to retired players.

60. Shannon O'Toole, *Wedded to the Game: The Real Lives of NFL Women* (Lincoln: University of Nebraska Press, 2006), xvi, 150–68.

61. Jack McCallum and Richard O'Brien, "NFL Dads: The Sequel," *SI*, November 8, 1993; Peter King, "Doing the Right Thing," *SI*, December 14, 1998; Elizabeth Gilbert, "Losing Is Not an Option," *GQ*, September 1999.

62. Seabrook, "Tackling the Competition."

63. Sally Jenkins, "He Saw, She Saw," *WP*, January 29, 2005; Dale Russakoff, "Team Rice, Playing Away," *WP*, February 6, 2005.

64. John Rosengren et al., "Chicks Dig the Oblong Ball," *SI*, October 11, 1999; Kelley King et al., "Saturday Night Lights," *SI*, October 18, 1999; Paula Hunt, "Football Femmes," *Village Voice*, December 21, 1999; Kelley King, "Gridiron Girls," *SI for Women*, January–February 2001; Michael Weinreb, "Playing for Fun, and Little Else, on Football's Edge," *NYT*, July 18, 2006; "NFHS 2005–06 High School Athletics Participation Survey," National Federation of State High School Associations, 2006 (online). For women's football, also see the websites of the National Women's Football Association, Women's Professional Football League, and the Independent Women's Football League (my hometown Corvallis has a team), as well as "Queens of the Gridiron," <http://www.angelfire.com/sports/womenfootball/index.html>.

65. This is the subject of my *Reading Football: How the Popular Press Created an American Spectacle* (Chapel Hill: University of North Carolina Press, 1993).

66. *New York Journal*, November 22, 1896; quoted in *Reading Football*, 186.

67. I develop these ideas at length in *Reading Football*.

68. Again, I have developed these ideas more fully elsewhere, in this case in *King Football: Sport and Spectacle in the Golden Age of Radio and Newsreels, Movies and Magazines, the Weekly and the Daily Press* (Chapel Hill: University of North Carolina Press, 2001).

69. Harry Stein, "The Post-Sensitive Man Is Coming! The Post-Sensitive Man Is Coming!," *Esquire*, May 1994; Michael Segell, "The Second Coming of the Alpha Male," *Esquire*, October 1996; Geoffrey Cowley and Claudia Kalb, "Attention: Aging Men," *Newsweek*, September 16, 1996; Richard Lacayo, Lisa McLaughlin, and Alice Park, "Are You Man Enough?," *Time*, April 24, 2000. On drugs and the performance culture, see Kate Zerenike, "The Difference between Steroids and Ritalin Is . . .," *NYT*, March 20, 2005; Michael Bamberger and Don Yaeger, "Over the Edge," *SI*, April 14, 1997; E. M. Swift and Don Yaeger, "Unnatural Selection," *SI*, May 14, 2001; Michael Sokolove, "The Lab Animal," *New York Times Magazine*, January 18, 2004; John Hoberman, *Testosterone Dreams: Rejuvenation, Aphrodisia, Doping* (Berkeley and Los Angeles: University of California Press, 2005).

70. See Ken Fuson, "Guts and Glory," *Esquire*, October 1996; Curry Kirkpatrick, "Romo Cop," *ESPN The Magazine*, December 14, 1998; Charles P. Pierce, "Ain't I Pretty?," *Esquire*, September 2000; Michael Silver, "Belly Laughs," *SI*, January 29,

2001; Chris Smith, "Jeremy Shockey Is Living Large," *New York*, August 18, 2003. See also Charles P. Pierce, "Mike Alstott's Head," *Esquire*, October 1998; and Tom Chiarella, "The Nicest Mother F#@ker in the NFL," *Esquire*, November 2002.

71. Silver, "Belly Laughs"; and Michael Silver, "Livin' Large," *SI*, February 7, 2001 (special issue). These two pieces are essentially the same, published in the magazine's regular issue and then in a special on the Super Bowl.

72. Smith, "Jeremy Shockey Is Living Large."

73. Jeanne Marie Laske, "The Enlightened Man," *Esquire*, September 2001; Lyle Alzado, as told to Shelley Smith, "I'm Sick and I'm Scared," *SI*, July 8, 1991; Mark Maske and Leonard Shapiro, "49ers' Herrion Likely Died from Undetected Heart Ailment," *WP*, September 7, 2005.

74. David Brooks, "The Return of the Pig," *Atlantic Monthly*, April 2003; Matthew Grimm, "Gridiron Gladiators," *American Demographics*, April 2001; Mark Lacter, "Fox and Mouse," *Forbes*, January 22, 2001.

75. "Big Football Blowout!," *FHM*, September 2001.

76. Glauber, "Special Report: Life after Football"; Paul Gutierrez, "Pain Game" (part of a special report on NFL injuries), *LAT*, January 25, 2000; Dan Bickley, "Modern-Day Gladiators" (three parts), *Arizona Republic*, January 16–18, 2003. Glauber reported on the Ball State study in "Cheering Stops, Trouble Starts," *Newsday*, January 12, 1997. Bickley reported on the Harvard study in "You Play, You Pay," *Arizona Republic*, January 16, 2003; and in "Quality of Life, Early Deaths Haunt Linemen," *Arizona Republic*, January 17, 2003.

77. William Nack, "The Wrecking Yard," *SI*, May 7, 2001.

78. Chris Jones, "Vicodins for Breakfast," *Esquire*, October 2004; Glauber, "Cheering Stops, Trouble Starts"; and Glauber, "Temporary Relief," *Newsday*, January 14, 1997.

79. Leonard Shapiro, "NFL's Treatment of Retired Players Needs More Coverage," *WP*, January 23, 2007; Les Carpenter, "Long after His Retirement, Morris Still Making Claims," *WP*, January 28, 2007; Alan Schwarz, "Dark Days Follow Hard-Hitting Career in N.F.L.," *NYT*, February 2, 2007. Players were not even allowed to seek second medical opinions until the 1982 collective bargaining agreement established that right. The Bears' Dick Butkus and 49ers' Charlie Krueger successfully sued; Houston Ridge, in another well-documented case, is among those who settled out of court. See Dan Bickley, "Bigger Men, Bigger Pain," *Arizona Republic*, January 17, 2003; Joseph Nocera, "Bitter Medicine," *SI*, November 6, 1995; Sandy Padwe, "When Trust Is Betrayed," *SI*, June 27, 1988; Gene Wojchiechowski and Chris Dufresne, "Football Career Is Taking Its Toll on NFL's Players," *LAT*, June 26, 1988.

80. Glauber, "Cheering Stops, Trouble Starts," "Surveying the Situation," and "Breaking Point"; Bob Glauber, "The Big Hurt," *Newsday*, January 14, 1997.

81. Don Muret, "Cowboys Plan Unique Field-Level Suites," *SBJ*, December 18–24, 2006.

Chapter Six

1. Michael MacCambridge, *America's Game: The Epic Story of How Pro Football Captured a Nation* (New York: Random House, 2004), 165; Jay J. Coakley, *Sport in Society: Issues and Controversies*, 4th ed. (St. Louis, Boston, and Los Altos, Calif.: Times Mirror/Mosby College Publishing, 1990), 208; Richard Lapchick, *The 2005 Racial and Gender Report Card: National Football League*, Institute for Diversity and Ethics in Sports, University of Central Florida (2005).

2. Charles K. Ross, *Outside the Lines: African Americans and the Integration of the National Football League* (New York: New York University Press, 1999); Alan H. Levy, *Tackling Jim Crow: Racial Segregation in Professional Football* (Jefferson, N.C.: McFarland, 2003).

3. William C. Rhoden, *Forty Million Dollar Slaves: The Rise, Fall, and Redemption of the Black Athlete* (New York: Crown, 2006), 127.

4. Jack Olsen, "The Anguish of a Team Divided," *SI*, July 29, 1968. The series ran from July 1 to July 29. For a rare sports biography that fully addresses race and the racism of this era, see Mike Freeman, *Jim Brown: The Fierce Life of an American Hero* (New York: William Morrow, 2006).

5. Jim Brown with Myron Cope, *Off My Chest* (Garden City, N.Y.: Doubleday, 1964), 159–73; "Look at Me, Man!," *Time*, November 26, 1965; Jim Brown, as told to Herman Weiskopf, "How I Play Fullback," *SI*, September 26, 1960; Freeman, *Jim Brown*, 134. See also Jim Brown with Steve Delsohn, *Out of Bounds* (New York: Zebra Books, 1989), 45–67.

6. Levy, *Tackling Jim Crow*, 138–47; Jeff Miller, *Long Gone: The Wild 10-Year Saga of the Renegade American Football League in the Words of Those Who Lived It* (Chicago: Contemporary Books, 2003), 155–61.

7. Ellis Cose, *The Rage of a Privileged Class* (New York: HarperCollins, 1993); Deion Sanders with Jim Nelson Black, *Power, Money, and Sex: How Success Almost Ruined My Life* (Nashville, Tenn.: Word Publishing, 1998), 54–61. On post-football prospects, see Bob Glauber, "A Whole New Ballgame," *Newsday*, July 14, 2002.

8. Jack Olsen, "In the Back of the Bus," *SI*, July 22, 1968.

9. See, for example, Stanley D. Eitzen and David C. Sanford, "The Segregation of Blacks by Playing Position in Football: Accident or Design?," *Social Science Quarterly* 55 (March 1975): 948–59; and John J. Schneider, "Racial Segregation by Professional Football Positions, 1960–1985," *Sociology and Social Research* 70 (July 1986): 259–62.

10. Lapchick, *2005 Racial Report Card*. In 2005, 24 percent of centers, 39 percent of guards, and 55 percent of offensive tackles were African American.

11. Lapchick, *2005 Racial Report Card*.

12. On black quarterbacks, see William C. Rhoden, *Third and a Mile: The Trials and Triumphs of the Black Quarterback* (New York: ESPN Books, 2007); Phillip M. Hoose, *Necessities: Racial Barriers in American Sports* (New York: Random House, 1989), 51–69; and Roy S. Johnson, "Black Quarterbacks Find a Smoother Path to the Pros," *NYT*, November 8, 1987. On Gilliam, see Rhoden, *Third and a Mile*, 27–42; on Briscoe, 87–98; on Harris, 101–25; on Williams, 145–63.

13. Daniel Buffington, "Contesting Race on Sundays: Making Meaning out of the Rise in the Number of Black Quarterbacks," *Sociology of Sport Journal* 22, no. 1 (2005): 21.

14. Craig Marine and Lynn Ludlow, "Rice Says He Feels Slighted by Media," *SFE*, January 26, 1989; David Armstrong, "Editors Re-examine Coverage of Rice," *SFE*, January 27, 1989; "How Super Bowl Played in Papers," *SFE*, January 27, 1989.

15. "Rice Seeks Attention but Softens Remarks," *NYT*, January 31, 1989; Ron Fimrite, "The Hero as Huckster," *SI*, February 13, 1989. For a response from the black press, see Howie Evans, "Rice Questions No Endorsements," *New York Amsterdam News*, February 4, 1989.

16. William Oscar Johnson, "How Far Have We Come?" and "A Matter of Black and White," *SI*, August 5, 1991.

17. Charlie Nobles, "Dolphin Suing N.F.L. Over Civil Rights," *NYT*, July 27, 1994; Thomas George, "For Reggie White, Racism Is Hardest Foe," *NYT*, January 12, 1996; Mike Freeman, "Panthers' Collins Finds Himself Tangled Up in Racial Barbs," *NYT*, August 24, 1997.

18. Buffington, "Contesting Race on Sundays," 24–28.

19. Lapchick, *2005 Racial and Gender Report Card.*

20. Ibid. (and *2004 Racial and Gender Report Card* for blacks in NFLPA positions); Kenneth L. Shropshire, "Merit, Ol' Boy Networks, and the Black-Bottomed Pyramid," *Hastings Law Journal* 47 (January 1996): 455–72; William C. Rhoden, "N.F.L.'s Silent Majority Afraid to Force Change," *NYT*, January 29, 1999; Rhoden, *Forty Million Dollar Slaves*, x, 142; Kenneth L. Shropshire (quoting Rob Parker in *Newsday*), "Sports Agents, Role Models, and Race-Consciousness," *Marquette Sports Law Journal* 6 (Spring 1996): 267.

21. "N.F.L. Is Prodded [by Jesse Jackson] on Minority Plan," *NYT*, January 31, 1993; William C. Rhoden, "In the End, Where Will Power Lie?," *NYT*, January 25, 1997; Jack McCallum and Richard O'Brien, "The NFL's Numbers Problem," *SI*, March 31, 1997; William C. Rhoden, "In the N.F.L., Justice Is Still Denied," *NYT*, January 31, 1998; Rhoden, "N.F.L.'s Silent Majority Afraid to Force Change"; "Minorities Can't Even Get a Call," *SI*, November 27, 2000; Selena Roberts, "For Progress, Perceptions Must Change," *NYT*, January 8, 2003; Leonard Shapiro and Mark Maske, "NFL Improves in Minority Hiring," *WP*, January 29, 2005.

22. Patrick Miller, "The Anatomy of Scientific Racism: Racialist Responses to Black Athletic Achievement," *Journal of Sport History* 25 (Spring 1989): 119–51.

23. See, for example, Montague Cobb, "Race and Runners," *Journal of Health and Physical Education* 7 (January 1936): 3–7, 52–56.

24. Martin Kane, "An Assessment of 'Black Is Best,' " *SI*, January 18, 1971.

25. See the published letters to the editor ("19th Hole: The Readers Take Over") in the February 1 and February 15 issues.

26. Harry Edwards, "The Sources of the Black Athlete's Superiority," *Black Scholar*, November 1971.

27. See David K. Wiggins, " 'Great Speed but Little Stamina': The Historical Debate over Black Athletic Superiority," *Journal of Sport History* 16 (Summer 1989): 158–85; Gary A. Sailes, "The Myth of Black Sports Supremacy," *Journal of Black Studies* 21 (June 1991): 480–87; John M. Hoberman, *Darwin's Athletes: How Sport Has Damaged Black America and Preserved the Myth of Race* (Boston: Houghton Mifflin, 1997); Miller, "The Anatomy of Scientific Racism"; and David W. Hunter, "Race and Athletic Performance: A Physiological Review," in *African Americans in Sport*, ed. Gary A. Sailes (New Brunswick, N.J.: Transaction Publishers, 1998), 85–101.

28. "The Black Dominance," *Time*, May 9, 1977.

29. Derrick Z. Jackson, "Calling the Plays in Black and White," *Boston Globe*, January 22, 1989; Richard E. Lapchick, *Five Minutes to Midnight: Race and Sport in the 1990s* (Lanham, Md., and New York: Madison Books, 1991), 249. See also Laurel R. Davis and Othello Harris, "Race and Ethnicity in U.S. Sports Media," in *MediaSport*, ed. Lawrence A. Wenner (New York: Routledge, 1998), 154–69; Hoose, *Necessities*, 12.

30. The Brokaw show was broadcast on April 25, 1989, and is discussed in Laurel R. Davis, "The Articulation of Difference: White Preoccupation with the Question of Racially Linked Genetic Differences among Athletes," *Sociology of Sport Journal* 7, no. 2 (1990): 179–87.

31. Jim Myers et al., "Race and Sports: Myth and Reality," *USA Today*, December 16–19, 1991; S. L. Price, "Is It in the Genes?," *SI*, December 8, 1997; Hoberman, *Darwin's Athletes*; S. L. Price and Grace Cornelius, "What Ever Happened to the White Athlete?," *SI*, December 8, 1997.

32. A study published in 1994 claimed that print coverage of three black quarterbacks continued to emphasize natural ability, while coverage of three white quarterbacks emphasized hard work; yet the data themselves revealed only marginal differences, a possible sign that broadcasters had indeed become more racially conscious. See Audrey J. Murrell and Edward M. Curtis, "Causal Attributions of Performance for Black and White Quarterbacks in the NFL: A Look at the Sports Pages," *Journal of Sport and Social Issues* 18 (August 1994): 224–33. In recent years, I have been repeatedly struck by an apparent self-consciousness in commentators' marveling at the speed or athletic move of a white receiver, or praising the field vision or good decisions of a black quarterback.

33. Dawkins's hugely influential *The Selfish Gene* (1976) appeared in a new edition in 1989, to be followed by his controversial assault on religion, *The God Delusion*, in 2006. Dennett generated considerable controversy by debunking religion and the spiritual in *Darwin's Dangerous Idea: Evolution and the Meaning of Life* (1995) and later *Breaking the Spell: Religion as a Natural Phenomenon* (2006).

34. Steven Pinker, *How the Mind Works* (New York: W. W. Norton, 1997), 525; Terry Burnham and Jay Phelan, *Mean Genes: From Sex to Money to Food, Taming Our Primal Instincts* (Cambridge, Mass.: Perseus Publishing, 2000); Martin Daly and Margo Wilson, *The Truth about Cinderella: A Darwinian View of Parental Love* (New Haven, Conn.: Yale University Press, 1998); Mary Batten, *Sexual Strategies: How Females Choose Their*

Mates (New York: G. P. Putnam's Sons, 1992); David M. Bruss, *The Evolution of Desire: Strategies of Human Mating* (New York: Basic Books, 1994); Meredith M. Small, *What's Love Got to Do with It? The Evolution of Human Mating* (New York: Anchor Books, 1995); David P. Barash and Judith Eve Lipton, *The Myth of Monogamy: Fidelity and Infidelity in Animals and People* (New York: W. H. Freeman, 2001); Nigel Barber, *The Science of Romance: Secrets of the Sexual Brain* (Amherst, N.Y.: Prometheus Books, 2002).

35. Richard J. Herrnstein and Charles Murray, *The Bell Curve: Intelligence and Class Structure in American Life* (New York: Free Press, 1994).

36. Stephen J. Gould, *The Mismeasure of Man*, revised ed. (New York: Norton, 1996), 399.

37. Jon Entine, *Taboo: Why Black Athletes Dominate Sports and Why We Are Afraid to Talk about It* (New York: Public Affairs, 2000), 10.

38. For recent challenges to "racial" ideas, see Jonathan Marks, *Human Biodiversity: Genes, Race, and History* (New York: Aldine de Gruyter, 1995), and *What It Means to Be 98% Chimpanzee: Apes, People, and Their Genes* (Berkeley and Los Angeles: University of California Press, 2002); and particularly Joseph L. Graves Jr., *The Race Myth: Why We Pretend Race Exists in America* (New York: Dutton, 2004). Graves includes a chapter on "The Social Construction of Race and Sports," which expands on a brief discussion in his "academic" study, *The Emperor's New Clothes: Biological Theories of Race at the Millennium* (New Brunswick, N.J.: Rutgers University Press, 2001). Graves, an evolutionary biologist and an African American, begins his chapter on race and sports with the statement: "One of the most pernicious of all the racial beliefs is the idea that blacks are innately superior athletes" (137).

39. Entine, *Taboo*, 5, 8–10, 336.

40. Ibid., 34.

41. Malcolm Gladwell, "The Sports Taboo," *New Yorker*, May 19, 1997.

42. Jim Myers, "Race Still a Player," *USA Today*, December 16, 1991 (the series ran from December 16 through December 19); Price and Cornelius, "What Ever Happened to the White Athlete?"

43. Elmer Mitchell, "Racial Traits in Athletics," *American Physical Education Review* 27 (April 1922): 151–52; William G. Nunn, "WGN Broadcasts," *Pittsburgh Courier*, November 19, 1932. I explore this issue in *King Football: Sport and Spectacle in the Golden Age of Radio and Newsreels, Movies and Magazines, the Weekly and the Daily Press* (Chapel Hill: University of North Carolina Press, 2001), 319–27.

44. George Frazier, "A Sense of Style," *Esquire*, November 1967; Clayton Riley, "Did O. J. Dance?," *Ms.*, March 1974.

45. Mark Kriegel, *Namath: A Biography* (New York: Viking, 2004), 36.

46. Curry Kirkpatrick, "No Fun League," *SI*, September 2, 1991.

47. Mark Newman, "No! No! No! Gastineau," *SI*, September 5, 1984; Kirkpatrick, "No Fun League"; George Vecsey, "Free Mark Gastineau," *NYT*, March 28, 1984.

48. Kirkpatrick, "No Fun League."

49. "N.F.L. Will Allow the Ickey Shuffle," *NYT*, August 9, 1989; Ira Berkow, "Ickey

and Gizmo and Other Extravaganzas," *NYT*, August 13, 1989; Kirkpatrick, "No Fun League."

50. Newman, "No! No! No! Gastineau"; Kirkpatrick, "No Fun League."

51. Eddie Jefferies, "Sports Spectrum," *New Pittsburgh Courier*, September 22, 1984.

52. "Ethnic Identity and the Ickey Shuffle," *Harper's*, January 1993. See also Thomas Kochman, *Black and White Styles in Conflict* (Chicago: University of Chicago Press, 1981), 130–52; Richard Majors, "Cool Pose: Black Masculinity and Sports," in *Sport, Men, and the Gender Order: Critical Feminist Perspectives*, ed. Michael A. Messner and Donald F. Sabo (Champaign, Ill.: Human Kinetics, 1990), 109–14; Shane White and Graham White, *Stylin': African American Expressive Culture from Its Beginnings to the Zoot Suit* (Ithaca, N.Y.: Cornell University Press, 1998); and Gena Dagel Caponi, ed., *Signifyin(g), Sanctifyin' and Slam Dunking: A Reader in African American Expressive Culture* (Amherst: University of Massachusetts Press, 1999).

53. I discuss this topic, as well as "gamesmanship," in *Sporting with the Gods: The Rhetoric of Play and Game in American Culture* (New York: Cambridge University Press, 1991).

54. Rhoden, *Forty Million Dollar Slaves*, 135.

55. See H. Munro Chadwick, *The Heroic Age* (Cambridge, England: Cambridge University Press, 1912); Dwight Conquergood, "Boasting in Anglo-Saxon England: Performance and the Heroic Ethos," *Literature in Performance* 1 (April 1981): 24–35; Alta Cools Halama, "Flytes of Fancy: Boasting and Boasters from *Beowulf* to Gangsta Rap," *Essays in Medieval Studies* 13 (1996): 81–96; and Marie Nelson, "*Beowulf*'s Boast Words," *Neophilologus* 89 (April 2005): 299–310.

56. Ward Parks, *Verbal Dueling in Heroic Narrative: The Homeric and Old English Traditions* (Princeton, N.J.: Princeton University Press, 1990).

57. Elliott J. Gorn, *The Manly Art: Bare-Knuckle Prize Fighting in America* (Ithaca, N.Y.: Cornell University Press, 1986); Michael T. Isenberg, *John L. Sullivan and His America* (Urbana and Chicago: University of Illinois Press, 1988).

58. Kochman, *Black and White Styles in Conflict*, 63–73.

59. See Jeffrey C. Ward, *Unforgivable Blackness: The Rise and Fall of Jack Johnson* (New York: Knopf, 2004); Chris Mead, *Champion—Joe Louis, Black Hero in White America* (New York: Scribner's, 1985); and Dave Zirin, *What's My Name, Fool? Sports and Resistance in the United States* (Chicago: Haymarket Books, 2005).

60. Gerald Early, "Why Baseball *Was* the Black National Pastime," in *Basketball Jones: America above the Rim*, ed. Todd Boyd and Kenneth L. Shropshire (New York: New York University Press, 2000), 35–36.

61. Rhoden, *Forty Million Dollar Slaves*, 162.

62. Thomas Hauser, *Muhammad Ali: His Life and Times* (New York: Simon & Schuster, 1991), 39. For other descriptions of the encounter, see Muhammad Ali with Richard Durham, *The Greatest: My Own Story* (New York: Random House, 1975), 106; David Remnick, *King of the World: Muhammad Ali and the Rise of an American Hero* (New York: Random House, 1998), 119–20; and Muhammad Ali and Hana Yasmeen Ali, *The Soul of a Butterfly: Reflections on a Life's Journey* (New York: Simon & Schuster, 2004), 71–72.

63. Newman, "No! No! No! Gastineau"; Curry Kirkpatrick, "Chicago's Easy Rider," *SI*, September 3, 1986; Rick Reilly, "The Boz," *SI*, September 3, 1986.

64. Paul Zimmerman, "Nickname," *SI*, November 4, 2002.

65. Thomas "Hollywood" Henderson and Peter Knobler, *Out of Control: Confessions of an NFL Casualty* (New York: G. P. Putnam's Sons, 1987), 145, 194, 202, 204, 205.

66. Kirkpatrick, "No Fun League."

67. Sanders with Black, *Power, Money, and Sex*, 43–46; Curry Kirkpatrick, " 'They Don't Pay Nobody to Be Humble,' " *SI*, November 13, 1989.

68. Bruce Schoenfeld, "How They Make It Now," *New York Times Magazine*, October 19, 1995.

69. Kirkpatrick, "No Fun League"; Rick Reilly, "Too Many Spoilsports," *SI*, January 11, 1993; Charles P. Pierce, "Ain't I Pretty?," *Esquire*, September 2000; Chick Ludwig, "Chad Johnson off to Shuffling Start for Bengals," *Dayton Daily News*, September 9, 2005; AP, "Chad Johnson Thinking Up More Celebrations," <http://www.tsn.ca/tools/print_story.asp?id=138014> (September 28, 2005).

70. Joe Freeman, "On Signing Day, Lomax Looks East," *Portland Oregonian*, February 2, 2005.

71. Sanders with Black, *Power, Money, and Sex*, 46; Steve Rushin, "Catch-21," *SI*, July 31, 1995.

72. "Talking Heads" (a sidebar), *USA Today*, November 11, 2005; Adam Duerson, "The Beat," *SI*, March 6, 2006. For receivers' and cornerbacks' salaries, see "League Earnings," *Portland Oregonian*, September 23, 1982 (these are NFL Management Council figures); NFLPA, "NFL Economics Primer 2002," <http://www.nflpa.org>; NFLPA, "NFL 2005 Mid-Season Salary Averages and Signing Trends November 2005," <http://www.nflpa.org>; Karl Taro Greenfield, "It's Good to Be Chad," *SI*, October 30, 2006; "Wild Man," *Maxim*, September 2006.

73. Geoffrey C. Arnold, "Now the NFL Got Its Groove On," *Portland Oregonian*, November 9, 2005.

74. Judy Battista, "Cost of Celebrations Rises in the N.F.L.," *NYT*, March 30, 2006; Mark Maske, "NFL's Dance Recital: Get Up, Don't Get Down," *WP*, March 30, 2006; Jim Litke, "NFL Really Is the 'No Fun League,' " *HC*, March 29, 2006; AP, Joe Kay, "Chad Johnson Markets Hairstyle," *Corvallis Gazette-Times*, September 10, 2006.

75. Richard Carter, "The Giants, the Super Bowl, and TV Football Showoffs," *New York Amsterdam News*, January 25, 2001; Jaime C. Harris, "Terrell Owens Is a Bona-Fide Star and Controversial Magnet," *New York Amsterdam News*, December 2, 2004; Michael Wilbon, "The Colts Are Entering a Perfect Storm," *WP*, December 8, 2005; Rhoden, *Forty Million Dollar Slaves*, 147–70. See also Richard Carter, "Television's Doofus Dozen: Dumb, Dumber, Dumbest," *New York Amsterdam News*, September 29, 2005.

76. Thomas George, "Blacks at Center Stage in Rancorous Debate on Headgear," *NYT*, April 4, 2001. On black ambivalence about the broader hip-hop culture, see Ellis Cose, *The Envy of the World: On Being a Black Man in America* (New York: Washington Square Press, 2002).

77. Vernon L. Andrews, "African American Player Codes on Celebration, Taunting, and Sportsmanlike Conduct," *Journal of African American Men* 2 (Fall 1996/Winter 1997): 57–92.

78. Buffington, "Contesting Race on Sundays," 28–30.

79. Michael Wilbon, "Sometimes, Similarities Are Only Skin-Deep," *WP*, January 19, 2005.

80. See, for example, Peter King, "A League of Their Own," *SI*, October 18, 2004; Peter King, "Pats' Blueprint for Success," *SI*, December 6, 2004; Leonard Shapiro, "Patriots' Dillon Has Shed Island Image," *WP*, February 1, 2005.

81. Jaime C. Harris, "Fox's Hyped Super Bowl XXXIX Broadcast Was Not So Super," *New York Amsterdam News*, February 10, 2005.

82. David Theo Goldberg, "Call and Response: Sports, Talk Radio, and the Death of Democracy," *Journal of Sport and Social Issues* 22 (May 1998): 217.

83. "Race Enters Dispute between McNabb, Owens," *Portland Oregonian*, February 2, 2006.

84. J. Whyatt Mondesire, "Donovan McNabb: Mediocre at Best," *Philadelphia Sun*, December 4, 2005. See also William Bunch, "Mondesire Blisters McNabb," *Philadelphia News*, December 6, 2005; and Thomas Fitzgerald, "Mondesire Disses McNabb as a 'Mediocre Talent,' " *PI*, December 7, 2005. Bunch and Fitzgerald reported that local talk shows were buzzing with the story.

85. Michael Wilbon, "This Color Scheme Works," *WP*, September 29, 2006.

86. Rob Maaddi (AP), "McNabb's Good Day Is Bad One for Favre," *Portland Oregonian*, October 3, 2006.

87. Rich Hofman, "McNabb Will Stomach More Criticism," *PI*, October 23, 2006.

88. William C. Rhoden, "Even the Toast of the Town Gets Burned Sometimes," *NYT*, January 1, 2007.

89. Michael Wilbon, "The Vick Dilemma," *WP*, November 28, 2006.

90. Selena Roberts, "Coach vs. Coach, Progressive vs. Dictator," *NYT*, January 21, 2007. Had a black quarterback played in the Super Bowl, William Rhoden's *Third and a Mile*, published just days before the game, would likely have provoked unprecedented attention on the position and its perils.

91. See my *King Football*, 146–52.

92. Michael Wilbon, "An Ultimate, and Hopefully Final, Precedent for Black Coaches," *WP*, January 18, 2007.

Conclusion

1. Judy Battista, "Deals Done, Tagliabue Will Retire This Summer," *NYT*, March 21, 2006; Daniel Kaplan, "Tagliabue Brought Media into Every Corner of the League," *SBJ*, March 27–April 2, 2006; Ross Nethery, "The End of His Era," *SBJ*, July 31–August 6, 2006.

2. Kurt Badenhausen, Michael K. Ozanian, and Maya Roney, "The Tape on Tagliabue," *Forbes* (online), September 18, 2006.

3. Kaplan, "Tagliabue Brought Media into Every Corner of the League."

4. Daniel Kaplan, "Who'll Follow Tagliabue?," *SBJ*, March 27–April 2, 2006.

5. Judy Battista, "Goodell Gets Enough Votes to Lead N.F.L.," *NYT*, August 9, 2006; Mark Maske, "Owners Pick Goodell as NFL Commissioner," *WP*, August 9, 2006; Daniel Kaplan, "Two Days in Chicago," *SBJ*, August 14–20, 2006; Peter King, "A Man Born for the Job," *SI*, August 21, 2006.

6. Various charts in "The Changing Dynamics of Sports Business," *SBJ*, March 27–April 2, 2006.

7. "Roger Goodell," in "The 50 Most Influential People in Sports Business," *SBJ*, December 18–24, 2006.

8. Daniel Kaplan and Liz Mullen, "NFL Faces High Costs of Jets-Giants Plan," *SBJ*, October 30–November 5, 2006; Daniel Kaplan and Liz Mullen, "NFL Union: We'll Cut Salary Cap," *SBJ*, December 4–10, 2006; Daniel Kaplan, "NFL Owners Give $300M for N.Y. Stadium," *SBJ*, December 11–17, 2006; AP, "Talks Re-open Amid 49ers Move Fallout," *NYT*, November 20, 2006.

9. Les Carpenter, "All a Part of Its Vision," *WP*, November 21, 2006; John Ourand, "Will NFL Fans Defect to Satellite?," *SBJ*, December 4–10, 2006; Richard Sandomir, "Cable Subscribers Aren't Saying, 'I Want My N.F.L.,'" *NYT*, November 28, 2006; AP, "Specter Wants to Revisit NFL's Antitrust Status," *WP*, December 8, 2006; John Ourand, "NFL's TV Changes Pay Off," *SBJ*, January 8–14, 2007.

10. Richard Sandomir, "NFL Network Is Counting on Fans to Pay a Lot for a Little," *NYT*, September 19, 2006; John Ourand, "Comcast Plan Is Setback for NFL Network," *SBJ*, September 18–24, 2006; Terry Lifton, "NFL Taking Internet In-house," *SBJ*, October 23–29, 2006; Eric Fisher and John Ourand, "Restricted Access," *SBJ*, November 13–19, 2006.

11. Ourand, "NFL's TV Changes Pay Off"; John Sonsoli, "Ebersol: SNF Key to NBC's Turnaround," <http:www.Mediaweek.com> (January 1, 2007); Andrew Marchand, "'SNF' Perks up the Peacock," *SBJ*, January 22–28, 2007.

12. Ourand, "NFL's TV Changes Pay Off"; John Ourand, "ESPN Ship Sails Smoothly Under Skipper," *SBJ*, October 9–15, 2006.

13. Mark Maske and Les Carpenter, "Player Arrests Put the NFL in a Defensive Mode," *WP*, December 16, 2006; Mark Maske, "Goodell Weighs in on Behavior, Drugs," *WP*, February 3, 2007; Leonard Shapiro, "NFL's Treatment of Retired Players Needs More Coverage," *WP*, January 23, 2007; Alan Schwarz, "Expert Ties Ex-Player's Suicide to Brain Damage," *NYT*, January 18, 2007; William C. Rhoden, "In the N.F.L., Violence Sells, but at What Cost?," *NYT*, January 20, 2007; Clifton Brown, "Ex-Players Dealing with Not-So-Glamorous Health Issues," *NYT*, February 1, 2007; Alan Schwarz, "Dark Days Follow Hard-Hitting Career in N.F.L.," *NYT*, February 2, 2007; John Branch and Alan Schwarz, "N.F.L. Culture Makes Issue of Head Injuries Even Murkier," *NYT*, February 3, 2007; Selena Roberts, "In Face of Injuries, N.F.L.'s Leader Doesn't Flinch," *NYT*, February 4, 2007.

14. Daniel Kaplan, "Revenue Issue Gets Personal for NFL Owners," *SBJ*, February 5–11, 2007.

15. Les Carpenter, "A Virtual Chalkboard for Budding NFL Fans," *WP*, December 5, 2006; Eric Fisher, "Fantasy Football Gets Early Jump on Season," *SBJ*, July 31–August 6, 2006; Matt Youmans, "Super Bowl Wagering Sets Record," *Las Vegas Review-Journal*, February 8, 2006; Richard O. Davies and Richard G. Abram, *Betting the Line: Sports Wagering in American Life* (Columbus: Ohio State University Press, 2001), 159; Dan E. Moldea, *Interference: How Organized Crime Influences Professional Football* (New York: William Morrow, 1989), 20.

16. "Go Big," *Outside*, January 2006.

17. "Commitment to the Brand," *SBJ*, September 1–7, 2003.

18. Battista, "Goodell Gets Enough Votes to Lead N.F.L."; Maske, "Owners Pick Goodell as NFL Commissioner."

Afterword

1. "NFL Attendance—2009," on ESPN.com.

2. "NFL Football Putting up huge Ratings," *Business Insider* (available on business insider.com), January 30, 2010. See also John Ourand, "NFL's TV Changes Pay Off," *SBJ*, January 8–14, 2007; "Fox Leads, NBC and ESPN Gain for NFL '08," *SBJ*, January 12–18, 2009.

3. Revenues and franchise values from the issues of *Forbes* on "The Business of Football" published on Forbes.com (and in the print edition) in September each year.

4. The income figures are from *Forbes*'s annual reports; salary information is from "USA Today Salaries Databases," on USATODAY.com.

5. From figures that have been reported, total payroll declined in 2009 more than attendance. Attendance declined 2.6 percent (ESPN.com); total salary declined 9 percent, from $3.62 billion to $3.28 billion ("USA Today Salaries Databases"). One of the closest observers of NFL finances, *SportsBusiness Journal*'s Daniel Kaplan, addressed the competing claims from the two sides without in any way confirming the owners' supposed loss of $200 million since 2006. See Daniel Kaplan, "Making Sense of Claims in NFL Labor Talks," *SBJ*, March 22–28, 2010.

6. Revenues from "NFL Team Valuations" on Forbes.com, September 2, 2009; payroll from "USA Today Salaries Databases."

7. The Green Bay Packers, as the NFL's only publicly owned franchise, are the exception in having to report their finances. Since the extension of the collective bargaining agreement in 2006, Green Bay's player costs have risen 25 percent, while operating income increased 14 percent. See Liz Mullen, "Union Economist: NFL Numbers Don't Add Up," *SBJ*, January 11–17, 2010.

8. Judy Battista, "TV Deal Bolsters League's War Chest in Event of Lockout," *NYT*, May 20, 2009; Liz Mullen, "NFL Labor Fears Affect Deals for Execs, Coaches," *SBJ*, September 21–27, 2009; Ken Elson and Alan Schwarz, "Antitrust Case Has Implica-

tions Far Beyond N.F.L.," *NYT*, January 7, 2010; John Ourand, Terry Lefton, and Daniel Kaplan, "ESPN to Land More NFL Rights," *SBJ*, March 29–April 4, 2010.

9. See Alan Schwarz, "Dementia Risk Seen in Players in N.F.L. Study," *NYT*, September 30, 2009; Jeanne Marie Laskas, "Game Brain," *GQ*, October 2009; Malcolm Gladwell, "Offensive Play," *New Yorker*, October 19, 2009. Schwarz contributed more than thirty articles on concussions over the course of the 2009 season and postseason. The Michigan "Study of Retired NFL Players," September 10, 2009, is available online on the University of Michigan's website, <umich.edu/news/Releases/2009/Sep09/FinalReport.pdf>. Among the numerous other online and print contributions to the discussion, *Time* magazine added a cover story, "The Most Dangerous Game," on February 8, 2010. *Outside the Lines* even addressed concussions on Super Bowl Sunday.

10. Alan Schwarz, "N.F.L. Scolded Over Injuries to Its Players," *NYT*, October 29, 2009; Alan Schwarz, "N.F.L.'s Moves Signal a Truce on Concussions," *NYT*, November 26, 2009; Alan Schwarz, "N.F.L. Issues New Guidelines on Concussions," *NYT*, December 3, 2009; Alan Schwarz, "N.F.L. Acknowledges Long-Term Concussion Effects," *NYT*, December 21, 2009; Alan Schwarz, "Helmet Standards Are Latest N.F.L. Battleground," *NYT*, December 24, 2009; Alan Schwarz, "N.F.L. Picks New Chairmen for Panel on Concussions," *NYT*, March 17, 2010.

11. Sean Gregory, "The Problem with Football," *Time*, February 8, 2010. Turley's testimony before the House Judiciary Committee in Detroit on January 4, 2010, can be found online at <judiciary.house.gov/hearings/pdf/Turley100104.pdf>.

12. Gladwell, "Offensive Play."

ACKNOWLEDGMENTS

I owe thanks to John Wright for suggesting that I split a book on college and pro football in two, fleshing out a narrative about the NFL alone. I am also grateful for the various suggestions provided by the two anonymous scholars who read my manuscript as part of the editorial process, particularly for their endorsement of my decision to wed a personal perspective to my interpretation of the NFL's recent history.

Producer Steve Seidman and archivist Chris Willis at NFL Films were generous with videos and print materials to help me understand the company's history. And from a serendipitous meeting with Dave Meggyesy—for 25 years the western regional director of the National Football League Players Association, after having been pro football's original radical critic—came his agreeing to read my discussion of the NFL's labor wars. Dave is blameless for my own take on the subject but fully responsible for clarifying some issues.

I also thank the former chair of my department at Oregon State University, Bob Schwartz, and my current boss, Dean Kay Schaffer, for many kinds of support. Most particularly, I thank Kay for allowing me the time to continue writing as I have taken on my responsibilities as her associate dean. In the early stages of my research, a number of my undergraduate students photocopied newspaper and magazine articles for me. To Rimi Arrell, Travis Huntington, Courtney Bowman, Brad Canfield, and Molly Ostrem: thank you all. As always, my manuscript benefited from superb editing and production at the University of North Carolina Press. Much thanks to David Perry, Jay Mazzocchi, Richard Hendel, and their staffs. A book about football during my own lifetime is inevitably informed by innumerable interactions with friends, family members, teammates (and opponents), and colleagues both at Oregon State and around the country. I cannot name them all, and I will not attempt to single out the most important ones because I would regret my egregious omissions. Instead, if you are reading my book, I hope that you know who you are.

In attempting to understand the great public spectacle and drama of football, I have never forgotten that individuals always experience it as human beings. My own sense of football over the past 40-odd years, as well as my attempts to grasp its larger meanings, have been inextricably linked to my wife and sons. To them, my secret sharers, I dedicate this book.

INDEX

Adams, Bud, 19, 90, 132, 152

Adams, Pete, 89

Adderley, Herb, 10

Advertising Age, 182

African Americans in the NFL: dominance of, 210; percentages of, 210; as quarterbacks, 211n, 215–16, 223–24, 244, 245–46, 247–48; integration by, 211–12; discrimination against, 211–20; "stacking" of, 214–15; accusations of racism by, 216; as coaches, 218–19, 244, 248–49; as executives and owners, 219–20, 244–45; stereotypes of, 220, 221–22, 223–24, 227–29; athletic superiority of, 220–30; and style, 230–44. *See also* Black style in football

Aikman, Troy, 120, 142

Alexander, Kermit, 67, 92, 93, 103

Alexander, Shaun, 242

Ali, Muhammad, 27, 51, 211, 220, 237–38, 239

All-America Football Conference, 56, 211

Allen, George, 74

Allen, Marcus, 125, 131, 183, 210

Allen, Paul, 164

Alworth, Lance, 52

Alzado, Lyle, 203

American Broadcasting Company (ABC), 19, 20, 25, 26, 104, 167, 169; NFL rights fees paid by, 19, 20, 169, 170; losses on NFL for, 167, 172; NFL ratings for, 168, 253; purchase of by Disney, 187; purchase of ESPN by, 187. *See also Monday Night Football*; Television

American Football League (1926), 56

American Football League (1936–37), 56

American Football League (1940–41), 56

American Football League (1960–69), 4, 6, 12, 13, 26; history of, 19–21; television revenue for, 20; integration of, 211; black boycott of All-Star Game in, 212–13

Anderson, Dave, 59, 79, 80, 119, 128

Anderson, Donny, 20

Anderson, Jack, 108

Anderson, Ken, 71, 86n, 104

Andruzzi, Jimmy, 24

Andruzzi, Joe, 23

Any Given Sunday (film), 7, 190

Araton, Harvey, 133

Arizona Cardinals, 24, 128, 153, 158, 163, 252. *See also* St. Louis Cardinals

Arizona Republic, 207

Arledge, Roone, 25–28; and *Monday Night Football*, 25, 26–28; on football as show business, 25–26; and storytelling, 26–27; influence of, 26, 27, 28

Armstrong, Otis, 119

Arnold, Tom, 190

Arrington, Rick, 76

Atkinson, George, 120n, 123

Atlanta Constitution, 131

Atlanta Falcons, 20, 72, 75, 91, 132, 186, 248

Atlanta Journal, 79

Axthelm, Pete, 49

Babinecz, John, 94

Bahr, Chris, 110

Baker, Howard, 105

Baltimore Colts, 2, 5, 8, 24, 40, 54, 62, 72, 73, 91, 93, 94, 95, 128, 153. *See also* Indianapolis Colts

Baltimore Ravens, 153. *See also* Cleveland Browns

Baltimore Sun, 93

Baugh, Sammy, 76

Beathard, Pete, 83, 93

Belichick, Bill, 246, 249

Bell, Bert, 2, 19, 57, 175

Bell Curve, The (Herrnstein and Murray), 226, 227

Benedict, Jeff, 194

Berkow, Ira, 97–98

Berman, Chris, 188, 189

Berry, Raymond, 10, 117

Berry, Royce, 71

Best Damned Sports Show, Period, 204

Bethea, Elvin, 90

Bethea, Larry, 121

Bidwell, Bill, 128–29, 132

Biletnikoff, Fred, 85

Billick, Brian, 243

Bingaman, Les ("Bingo"), 122, 202

Bisher, Furman, 79

Black style in football, 230–44; early history of, 231–32; in end zone celebrations, 232–34, 240–41, 242–44; in sack dances, 233, 241; NFL rules to restrict, 233–34, 242, 243–44; in relation to economic and social class, 234–36; in relation to heroic boasts and taunts, 236–38; in relation to self-marketing, 238–44

Blaik, Earl ("Red"), 30, 32

Blanda, George, 85

Blank, Arthur, 186

Bleier, Rocky, 24, 96, 125

Blood, Johnny, 30, 41, 107

Bly, Robert, 177

Boggs, Hale, 20, 57, 105

Boston Globe, 223

Boston Herald, 176

Boston Patriots, 19, 24, 63, 72, 74, 99. *See also* New England Patriots

Bosworth, Brian, 29, 129, 238, 239

Bouggess, Lee, 86

Bowlen, Pat, 158

Bowman, Ken, 75, 83, 92, 93

Boyle, Robert, 42

Bradshaw, Terry, 50n, 77, 86n, 89, 111, 216, 223–24, 239

Brady, Tom, 244, 245, 246

Branch, Deion, 246

Brandt, Gil, 150

Braucher, Bill, 72, 80, 81

Brenner, Bill, 131, 133n

Brezina, Greg, 87

Briscoe, Marlin, 211n, 215

Brister, Bubby, 142

Brokaw, Tom, 224, 226, 228

Bronstein, Steve, 172

Brooks, Aaron, 218

Brooks, David, 204

Brown, Gwilym, 92

Brown, Jim, 5, 10, 125, 126, 231; outspokenness of, 10, 212, 214.

Brown, Mike, 159, 166–67

Brown, Paul, 30, 71

Brown, Willie, 67, 69

Browner, Ross, 115

Brubaker, Bill, 193

Brunell, Mark, 248

Bryant, Cullen, 101n

Bryant, Warrant, 109

Bryant, William B., 101

Buchanan, Buck, 84, 211n

Buckley, William F., Jr., 47–48, 49

Budde, Ed, 84

Buffalo Bills, 5, 19, 72, 74, 76, 86, 91, 101, 161, 167, 176, 177–78

Buffalo News, 133n

Bunting, John, 86, 89

Bunz, Dan, 104

Burnam, George, 77
Business Week, 180
Butkus, Dick, 10, 215
Butler, Billy, 38
Byrd, Dennis, 120

Callahan, Tom, 79, 80
Campanis, Al, 220, 223
Campbell, Earl, 208, 210
Campbell, Jason, 248
Carmichael, Harold, 210
Carolina Panthers, 144, 152
Caroline, J. C., 231
Carruthers, Rae, 195
Carson, Harry, 208
Carter, Jim, 85
Casanova, Tommy, 93
Casstevens, David, 131
Charles, Mike, 233
Chernin, Peter, 172
Chester, Ray, 89
Chicago Bears, 12, 72, 73, 75, 92, 126, 131, 151, 203
Chicago Tribune, 73, 121, 134
Chmura, Mark, 194n, 195
Cincinnati Bengals, 70, 71, 72, 80, 91, 118, 153, 159, 165, 167, 176, 254
Cincinnati Enquirer, 69, 71, 79, 82
Clark, Dwight, 104, 131
Cleveland Browns, 10–11n, 53, 72, 80, 84, 90, 94, 108, 152, 211. *See also* Baltimore Ravens
Cleveland Browns (1998), 144
Cleveland Plain Dealer, 80, 82, 90, 130, 133
Cobb, Montague, 221
Cohane, Tim, 32
College All-Star Game, 58–59, 60, 68, 70, 76
Collins, Kerry, 218n
Columbia Broadcasting System (CBS), 2, 25, 26, 27, 104, 138, 167, 169, 170, 174, 177, 203; losses on NFL for, 167; ratings on NFL for, 168, 254; NFL rights fees paid by, 169, 172. *See also* Television
Connor, Dick, 88
Cook, Greg, 52
Cosell, Howard, 27–28, 133, 134, 220, 223; and *Monday Night Football*, 27–28
Costas, Bob, 289 (n. 105)
Courson, Steve, 117
Cox, Bryan, 218
Craig, Neal, 80
Craig, Roger, 131
Criqui, Don, 289 (n. 105)
Croudip, David, 118
Crowder, Randy, 106
Csonka, Larry, 55, 56, 69, 115, 125, 210
Culpepper, Daunte, 218, 244, 245, 246, 247, 248
Cunningham, Randall, 142, 216, 223–24
Curry, Bill, 66, 74, 92
Curtis, Mike, 59, 67, 84

Dallas Cowboys, 5, 19, 20, 24, 31, 35, 59, 69, 70, 72, 85, 88, 96, 99, 104, 150–52, 153, 160, 161, 163, 165, 175, 209; as "America's Team," 96; as "South America's Team," 116
Dallas Morning News, 87, 88, 131
Dallas Texans, 19. *See also* Kansas City Chiefs
Danahy, Jack, 107
Daney, George, 54n, 84
Davis, Al, 5, 8, 20, 28, 62, 67, 95, 98–99, 105, 110, 128, 130, 132, 136, 140, 144, 149, 158n, 159, 161–62, 175, 250; as Rozelle's nemesis, 21, 98, 99
Davis, Willie, 10, 34, 38
Dawson, Len, 84, 85
DeBartolo, Eddie, Jr., 158n
Deford, Frank, 104
Delaney, Kevin, 159

Delhomme, Jake, 245
Dempsey, Tom, 76
Dent, Richard, 118
Denver Broncos, 19, 72, 74–75, 96, 108
Denver Post, 75, 76, 88
Desperate Housewives, 191
Detroit Lions, 72, 76, 83, 99, 101
Devine, Dan, 75
Dickerson, Eric, 125, 210
Dickey, Curtis, 125
Dickey, Eldridge, 216
Dickey, Glenn, 131
Dillon, Corey, 246
DirecTV, 172; Sunday Ticket on, 172, 184
Ditka, Mike, 126
Domres, Marty, 52, 86n
Donlan, Jack, 111, 142
Dorsett, Tony, 125, 131, 210
Doty, David, 136, 141, 142
Douglass, Bobby, 86n
Dowler, Boyd, 10
Drougas, Tom, 73
Drugs. *See* NFL players: and drug
    problems
Dungy, Tony, 243, 244, 248–49, 254
Dutton, John, 110, 130

Early, Gerald, 238
Easterling, Ray, 87
Ebersol, Dick, 171, 253
Eckstein, Rick, 159
Edwards, Harry, 216, 222, 224, 225, 230
Edwards, Herman, 243
"Electric Company" (Buffalo Bills offen-
    sive line), 202
Eller, Carl, 109
Elway, John, 130, 142
Eminem, 190
Emtman, Steve, 142
Enberg, Dick, 289 (n. 105)
Entine, Jon, 224, 227–28, 229
Esaison, Boomer, 130

Eskenazi, Gerald, 104
ESPN, 6, 28, 141, 169–70, 174, 186, 187–
    89, 190, 192, 246, 253; and televising
    the NFL, 127–28; NFL rights fees paid
    by, 170; acquires *Monday Night Foot-
    ball*, 173; and celebrity culture, 188,
    243; and irony, 189, 205. See also
    SportsCenter; *Sunday Night Football*
ESPN The Magazine, 188, 205, 253
Esquire, 2, 28, 30, 36, 46, 50, 52, 177, 201,
    202, 241
Evans, Charlie, 92
Everett, Jim, 142
Ewbank, Weeb, 45
Extreme Football League (XFL), 200–
    201, 204

Facenda, John, 17
"Fan Cost Index," 161
Favre, Brett, 119
"Fearsome Foursome" (Los Angeles
    Rams defensive line), 202
Felser, Larry, 133n
Ferguson, Joe, 86n
Fernandez, Manny, 70, 71
FHM, 204, 205
Fiedler, Leslie, 42
Fimrite, Ron, 216
Financial World, 6, 144, 158n
Finks, Jim, 137
Finney, Peter, 132n
Fisher, Pat, 62
Flanagan, Ed, 83
Flutie, Doug, 131
Forbes, 5, 6, 140, 144, 152, 158n, 163, 164,
    167, 173n, 250
Ford, Gerald, 90
Forte, Chet, 27, 28
Fortune, 4
Foss, Joe, 20, 213
Fouts, Dan, 86n, 110, 124
Fowler, Reggie, 244–45

Fox Broadcasting Company, 23, 141, 167, 173, 174, 188, 190, 203, 205; losses on NFL for, 167, 172; NFL ratings for, 168n, 169, 254; NFL rights fees paid by, 169, 170, 172; "legitimacy" of through NFL, 170. *See also* Television
Frazier, George, 231, 234
Free agency. *See* National Football League Players Association: and free agency
Freitas, Jesse, 69
Frontiere, Georgia, 132
"Fun Bunch" (Washington Redskins receivers), 233

Gabriel, Roman, 75, 85
Gambling: on NFL football, 13, 113, 117n, 255–56n
Garcia, Jeff, 248
Garrard, David, 248
Garrett, Alvin, 220
Garrison, Walt, 85
Garvey, Ed, 60, 66, 67, 68, 69, 70, 78, 80, 85, 88, 89, 99–100, 101, 102, 103, 105, 109, 110–11, 112, 113, 135, 143, 146; resignation of, 113, 129
Gastineau, Mark, 131, 233, 234, 238, 239
Gay, Randall, 190
Gaydos, Kent, 86
George, Bill, 77
Gifford, Frank, 28
Gilbert, Bil, 106
Gilliam, Joe, 107, 216
Gillman, Sid, 73–74, 90–91, 94, 123
Gilman, Kay, 52
Givens, Ernest, 232
Gladwell, Malcolm, 229
Glory Road (film), 217n
Goode, Don, 69, 70
Goodell, Roger, 8, 23, 167, 182, 183, 206; as commissioner, 251, 252, 254, 256
Gorgeous George, 238–39
Gould, Stephen Jay, 223, 226, 228

Grabowski, Jim, 20
Graham, Jim, 75, 76
Grange, Red, 56
Grant, Rebecca, 205
Green Bay Packers, 6, 10–11, 12, 15, 20, 21, 24, 31–34, 72, 75, 76, 82, 83, 86, 92, 114, 158, 160, 166, 203
Green Bay Press-Gazette, 81
Green, Cornell, 85
Green, Dennis, 243, 244
Greene, Joe ("Mean Joe"), 96
Greenwood, L. C., 96
Gregg, Forrest, 10
Griese, Bob, 77, 85, 89
Gruden, Jon, 162
Guidry, Paul, 90
Gumbel, Bryant, 148
Gunsel, Austin, 11

Hadl, John, 77, 85, 89
Halas, George, 12, 72, 92
Hall, John, 80
Handler, Howard, 181
Hannah, John, 85
Hardy, Kevin, 61
Harper's Monthly, 234
Harris, Cliff, 85, 88
Harris, David, 12, 95, 98
Harris, Franco, 24, 96, 125
Harris, James, 211n, 216, 247–48, 249
Harrison, Marvin, 257
Harrison, Rodney, 246
Harris polls. *See* Polls
Hart, Jim, 85
Hart, Leon, 76
Hearst, William Randolph, 199
Heaton, Chuck, 82, 90
Heffelfinger, Pudge, 202
Henderson, Thomas ("Hollywood"), 108, 118, 232–33, 237, 239
Hendricks, Ted, 73, 110
Herrion, Thomas, 203

Hess, Leon, 132

Hill, Calvin, 223

Hill, Dave, 84

Hirshberg, Al, 46

Hoberman, John, 201n, 224

Hofman, Rich, 248

Hogeboom, Gary, 131

"Hogs" (Washington Redskins offensive line), 202

Holmes, Ernie, 96

Holmes, Pat, 93

Holmgren, Mike, 243

Holub, E. J., 214

Home Box Office (HBO), 188

Hoover, J. Edgar, 51

Horn, Joe, 242

Hornung, Paul, 10, 13, 32, 34, 35, 36, 37, 41, 42, 44, 48, 76–77, 107, 110, 125, 138, 176

Houston Astrodome, 150

Houston Chronicle, 80, 90

Houston Oilers, 9, 19, 73–74, 90–91, 152, 159. See also Tennessee Titans

Houston Texans, 144, 153, 160, 163, 164

Huarte, John, 39

Hudson, Maryann, 193

Huff, Sam, 2, 215

Hughes, Howard, 25

Hunt, H. L., 19

Hunt, Lamar, 19, 20, 132

Indianapolis Colts, 8, 95, 128, 132, 153, 159, 246. See also Baltimore Colts

Indianapolis Star, 131, 133n

Instant Replay (Kramer), 35, 37

Invincible (film), 190

Iron John (Bly), 177

Irsay, Robert, 73, 94, 95, 128, 132

Irvin, Michael, 29, 142, 210, 238

Iselin, Philip, 47

Jackson, Bo, 125

Jackson, Derrick, 223

Jackson, Janet, 183; and "wardrobe malfunction," 190, 191

Jacksonville Jaguars, 144, 152, 163, 167

Jacoby, Joe, 208

James, Edgerrin, 210

Janofsky, Michael, 119

Jenkins, Dan, 43, 44

Jenkins, Sally, 198

Jerry McGuire (film), 190

Jessie, Ron, 101n

Jobs Rated Almanac, 124

Jock New York, 40

John Madden NFL Football (video game), 185, 241, 255

Johnson, Billy ("White Shoes"), 232, 238, 239

Johnson, Bob, 71

Johnson, Butch, 232, 239

Johnson, Chad, 232, 237, 238, 241, 242–43

Johnson, Charley, 85, 93

Johnson, Jack, 221, 237

Johnson, Pete, 115

Johnson, Randy, 85

Johnson, Ted, 254

Johnson, William Oscar, 217

Jones, Deacon, 10

Jones, Jerry, 5, 29, 137, 140, 149, 150–52, 159, 161, 165, 175, 186, 250

Jones, Matt, 247, 248

Jones, Sean, 142

Jones, Thomas, 254

Jordan, Henry, 10, 34

Jordan, Lee Roy, 85, 88

Junior, E. J., 109, 115

Jurgensen, Sonny, 10, 42

Kahn, Roger, 28

Kalsu, Bob, 23, 24

Kane, Martin, 221–22, 223, 224, 225, 228

Kansas City Chiefs, 7, 21, 49, 53, 55, 58, 59, 64, 65, 71, 72, 83–84, 92, 93, 97, 121, 131

Kansas City Star, 93

Kansas City Times, 92

Kaplan, Daniel, 251

Kapp, Joe, 100, 101

Karras, Alex, 13, 48, 107, 110, 138, 176

Kearney, Jim, 83

Keating, Tom, 67, 92

Kelly, Jim, 130, 142

Kempton, Murray, 50

Kent, Larry, 3

Kern, Rex, 92, 93

Kiam, Victor, 137, 176, 177

Kiick, Jim, 55, 56, 69, 115, 125, 210

Kilmer, Billy, 42, 85

Kimmel, Jimmy, 190, 206

Kindred, Dave, 131–32

Kiner, Steve, 74, 90–91

Kishi, Yoshio, 17

Klecko, Joe, 131

Klein, Eugene, 69, 72

Koppitt, Leonard, 60, 192n

Kornheiser, Tony, 163

Kraft, Robert, 151, 164

Krakau, Merv, 86

Kramer, Jerry, 10, 35, 36, 37

Kramer, Ron, 10

Kramer, Tommy, 108

Kratzer, Danny, 84

Krause, Larry, 86

Labor conflict, 4, 6, 7, 8, 55–94, 95, 98, 99–103, 109–13, 129–36; early history of, 56–57; and "freedom" issues in 1974, 61–66; in 1975, 100–101; resolution of, 56, 140, 141–42. *See also* National Football League Players Association; Strikes

Lambeau, Curly, 33

Landry, Greg, 86n

Landry, Tom, 31, 137, 215

Lane, Dick ("Night Train"), 77

Langer, Jim, 68, 70

Lanier, Willie, 50, 84, 211n, 215

Largent, Steve, 131, 210, 233

Larson, Earl R., 101, 135

Layne, Bobby, 2, 41, 42, 107, 121

League of Fans, 158

"League Think," 12, 98, 149

Leahy, Marshall, 11

Lebovitz, Hal, 80

Lee, Bob, 86n

Leftwich, Byron, 218, 245, 247, 248

Lerner, Alfred, 144, 153

Levinson, Sara, 175, 179–82, 183, 197–98, 206, 251; hiring of, 175; as "Promotional Marketer of the Year," 182; resignation of, 182. *See also* NFL Properties

Levy, Gregg, 251

Lewis, Albert, 241

Lewis, Marvin, 243, 244

Lewis, Ray, 195

Life, 2, 24, 42, 45, 47, 51; cover stories in, 97

Lillard, Joe, 231

Lilly, Bob, 85

Limbaugh, Rush, 190, 245

Lincicome, Bernie, 134

Lipscomb, Eugene ("Big Daddy"), 42, 231

Lipsyte, Robert, 36, 37, 39

Litke, Jim, 242

Little Giants (film), 190

Little, Larry, 70, 71, 88

Living Heart Foundation, 122

Lomax, Michael, 57

Lombardi, Marie, 28, 34

Lombardi, Vince, 6, 11, 28–38, 39, 53, 54, 203; death of, 28–29; as defender of "traditional values," 28–29, 30, 53–54; as savior of the Packers, 31, 33; legend of, 32–34; as "father," 37;

Long, Barbara, 50
Long, Howie, 131
Long, Russell, 20, 57, 105
Look, 2, 32, 35
Looney, Joe Don, 42
Los Angeles Chargers, 19, 73. *See also* San Diego Chargers
Los Angeles Memorial Coliseum Commission (LAMCC), 98, 99, 105
Los Angeles Raiders, 8, 98, 128, 131, 152, 208. *See also* Oakland Raiders
Los Angeles Rams, 9, 11, 12, 63, 72, 73, 83, 85, 92, 101n, 152, 153, 210. *See also* St. Louis Rams
Los Angeles Times, 80, 121, 207; front-page stories in, 193, 196
Lott, Ronnie, 142
Louis, Joe, 221, 237
Luken, Tom, 86, 89
Lupica, Mike, 133, 135, 149
Lyons, Marty, 131

Mack, Tom, 80, 83, 89, 93
Mackey, John, 10, 59, 60, 67, 138, 223
Mackey v. NFL. See National Football League Players Association: and *Mackey* decision
Madden, John, 178, 203
Major League Baseball, 7, 196, 217
Mandell, Arnold, 107
Mandich, Jim, 70
Manley, Dexter, 117, 118
Manning, Archie, 85
Manning, Peyton, 244, 245, 246, 254, 257
Mara, Wellington, 12, 41, 66, 72, 91–92, 136
Maraniss, David, 28, 29, 31–32
Marino, Dan, 125, 142
Marsh, Curt, 208
Marshall, George Preston, 211
Marshall, Larry, 93
Marshall, Wilbur, 130

Martin, Harvey, 116
Mathis, Bill, 46
Matson, Ollie, 231
Matson, Pat, 71, 89
Maule, Tex, 13 46
Maxim, 204, 205, 242
Mayhem on a Sunday Afternoon (television special), 2
McBride, Mickey, 84
McCafferty, Don, 76
McCombs, Red, 144, 165–66
McCormack, Mike, 75
McCullum, Sam, 111
McDaniel, Mike, 86, 92
McDermott, John, 45
McDonald, Tommy, 212
McGee, Max, 10, 42
McGinest, Willie, 246
McKay, Rich, 251
McMahon, Jim, 126, 238, 239, 243
McNabb, Donovan, 190, 244, 245, 246, 247, 248
McNair, Robert, 153, 160, 164
McNair, Steve, 218, 247
McNeil, Freeman, 141
McNeil v. NFL. See National Football League Players Association: and *McNeil* decision
Medlin, Dan, 86
Meggysey, Dave, 51, 106
Merchant, Larry, 36, 37, 39
Meredith, Don, 27, 28
Metcalf, Terry, 108
Meyers, Jeff, 64
Miami Dolphins, 6, 55, 69, 70–71, 71–72, 78, 80, 85, 88, 106, 151, 152
Miami Herald, 70, 72, 77, 79, 80, 88, 133
Milan, Don, 86
Miller, Alan, 60
Miller, Creighton, 57
Miller, Dennis, 190
Million Man March, 201

Milwaukee Journal, 81

Minnesota Vikings, 19, 49, 72, 74, 91, 97, 101, 158, 163, 166

Mismeasure of Man, The (Gould), 223, 226, 228

Mix, Ron, 121

Modell, Art, 29, 75, 80, 82, 89, 128, 130, 132, 152, 158n

Moldea, Dan, 13n, 113n

Monday Night Football, 18, 25–28, 53, 54, 120, 127, 151, 170, 186, 190, 191, 220; ratings for, 28, 168, 170, 253; rights fees for, 168, 169, 170; losses on, 167, 172; on ESPN, 173

Mondesire, J. Whyatt, 247

Monk, Art, 125, 210

Montana, Joe, 50n, 104, 110, 124, 129, 131, 132, 216

Moon, Warren, 130, 142, 216, 247

Moonves, Leslie, 172

Moore, Lenny, 10

Morgan, Thomas, 30

Morrall, Earl, 40, 46

Morris, Mercury, 70, 115, 210

Morton, Craig, 59, 85

Motley, Marion, 211

Mowatt, Zeke, 177

Muncie, Chuck, 109

Munson, Lester, 193

Murdoch, Rupert, 169

Murphy, Jack, 69

Murray, Albert, 231, 234

Musburger, Brent, 289 (n. 105)

Myslenski, Skip, 66

Nack, William, 193

Nader, Ralph, 158

Namath, Joe, 4, 6, 28–29, 38–54, 64, 85, 94, 101; signing of, 20; as Bad Boy, 30, 41, 42; and Super Bowl III, 38, 39, 40, 42, 46–47; as anti-Establishment figure, 39–40; as celebrity, 41, 44, 48–

49; as playboy, 41, 44, 52; as "Broadway Joe," 42; as "jerk," 42, 44–45; and military draft, 43; as countercultural figure, 43, 47, 52, 53; as transformer of football style, 44, 46, 52, 53, 54, 232, 237, 238, 239; and sportswriters, 45; as quarterback, 45–46, 50; as "political" figure, 47–48, 51–52; and Bachelors III, 47–48, 138, 176; as wounded hero, 49–51; as advertisement for a lifestyle, 52–53

NASCAR, 253, 256

National Basketball Association (NBA), 179, 180, 196, 210, 217, 232, 253

National Broadcasting Company (NBC), 2, 20, 26, 27, 104, 169, 174, 203, 224; NFL ratings for, 168, 253; NFL rights fees paid by, 20, 169, 170. See also Sunday Night Football; Television.

National Football League (NFL): early history of, 1–3; revenues of, 4–5, 61, 77, 140, 153, 170; and war with American Football League, 6, 19–21; marketing of, 8; as "modern NFL," 8, 139; as "new NFL," 8, 96, 137–38, 139, 140–74; and rule changes, 120, 122–23, 124, 176, 233–34, 242–43; and salary cap, 142, 145–46, 165; and brand management, 186, 189–92, 197; racial issues in, 210–49; as media company, 253. See also African Americans in the NFL; Labor conflict; NFL Charities; NFL.com; NFL Films; NFL football; NFL franchises; NFL Management Council; NFL Network; NFL players; NFL Properties; NFL Trust; Stadiums; Strikes; Super Bowl; Television

National Football League Players Association (NFLPA), 56, 98, 115, 174, 207; beginnings of, 57; and Mackey decision, 100, 101, 113; and collective bargaining agreements, 102–3 (1977),

112–13 (1982), 115 (1982), 142 (1993), 143, 145–48; and free agency, 110, 129, 141, 143–45; and *Powell* decision, 136, 141; decertification of, 136, 141; and *McNeil* decision, 141–42; as partner with NFL, 143, 147–48; and extensions of 1993 labor agreement, 145, 147, 148–49, 167, 250; black executives in, 219. *See also* Labor conflict; NFL Alumni; Strikes

National Labor Relations Board, 60, 69, 79, 101

National Organization of Women, 176

National Review, 47

Neely, Ralph, 84–85

Nelson, Al, 76

Nelson, Mariah Burton, 196, 204

New England Patriots, 6, 23, 99, 117, 145, 151, 153, 159, 160, 161, 163, 164, 176, 177, 245–46; and "strike" in 1975, 100–101. *See also* Boston Patriots

New Orleans Saints, 21, 61, 62, 72, 74, 83, 92, 106, 108, 158, 163, 254

New Orleans Times-Picayune, 132nn

New York Amsterdam News, 246

New York Daily News, 52, 78, 80, 116, 133, 135

New York Giants, 2, 5, 12, 15, 73, 76, 85, 90, 92, 99, 101, 116, 132, 134, 153, 160, 252

New York Jets, 39, 40, 41, 45, 46, 48, 49–50, 52, 53, 101, 116, 132, 153, 160, 164, 252. *See also* New York Titans

New York Post, 36

New York Times, 17, 36, 43, 58, 59, 60, 67, 69, 79–80, 94, 97, 104, 105, 108, 116, 117, 119, 128, 131, 133, 137, 138, 139, 170, 171, 177, 185, 192n, 219, 243, 248, 249, 254; front page stories in, 108, 118

New York Titans, 19, 41. *See also* New York Jets

New Yorker, 34, 180, 229

Newsday, 91, 119n, 197, 207

Newsome, Ozzie, 125, 131, 243

Newsweek, 48, 49; cover stories in, 97, 201, 239

NFL Alumni, 76

NFL Charities, 98, 151, 176

NFL Films, 12, 14–18, 26, 28, 96, 176, 177, 187, 189; history of, 14–15; and storytelling, 16; style of, 16–17; music in, 17; influence of, 18, 26

NFL football: image of, 1–2, 14, 22, 24, 31, 38, 43, 54, 115, 124, 138–39, 175–79, 186, 189, 208, 234; as "product" or "brand," 8, 9, 141, 175, 179–86, 189–92, 197–98, 256; cultural power of, 9, 14, 18, 27, 29, 141, 170–71, 174, 180, 189, 191, 199–200, 209, 255–57; as entertainment, 25, 28, 41, 53, 180, 200, 238–41; as work, 65–66; "dark side" of, 113–24, 192–97; development of strategy in, 124–26; as "morality play," 195, 255; appeal of to women, 197–99; and "Guy Culture," 204–6. *See also* African Americans in the NFL; National Football League; NFL players

NFL franchises: revenues of, 4–5, 140, 144, 154–57, 162–64; values of, 6, 140, 144, 152, 154–57, 162, 163–64, 173n; shifts of ("free agency"), 95, 98, 128–29, 132, 140, 149, 152; revenue disparity among, 148–49, 162–63, 164, 166–67, 254–55; for Los Angeles, 153, 159–60, 250, 252; indebtedness of, 164; and signing free agents, 164, 165

NFL Management Council, 60, 61, 66, 67, 77, 78, 90, 110, 111, 113, 129, 133, 136, 138, 142, 143

NFL Network, 172, 173–74, 252–53; ratings for, 252

NFL players: image of, 2, 4, 52, 66, 81–83, 109, 132–33, 178–79, 202–4; as celebrities, 4, 188, 238–43; salaries of, 4–5, 8, 61, 64, 65, 110, 129–30, 131, 143–44, 144–45, 146, 147, 148, 174, 242n; and drug problems, 6, 73, 95, 105–9, 115–19, 254; and domestic or sexual violence, 6, 192–96; and war, 24; relations of with media, 76–80, 108–9, 114, 131–33; and pain and injuries, 119–21, 206–9, 254; suicides of, 121; and life expectancy, 121–22; size of, 122–24; and media "morality plays," 195; and marriage, 197; as "livin' large," 202–4. *See also* African Americans in the NFL

NFL Properties, 3, 12–13, 14, 98, 142, 150–51, 152, 179–86, 197–98, 206, 251; revenues from, 151, 179; and marketing to children, 175, 181, 184; and marketing to women, 175, 181; and marketing themes, 181–82; and fan development, 181–82, 184, 185; and "Game Plan 1997," 182; and "NFL Kickoff," 183, 184, 255; and marketing overseas, 184; and taglines for season, 184–85. *See also* Levinson, Sara

NFL Trust, 152

NFL.com, 252, 253

Nike, 179, 243

Niland, John, 85, 87

Nitschke, Ray, 2, 36

Nixon, Richard, 7, 23, 51, 90

Nobis, Tommy, 20, 54, 85

Nolan, Dick, 53

Noll, Chuck, 74, 123

Oakland Raiders, 8, 19, 21, 72, 73, 76, 85, 98, 99, 128, 151, 152, 153, 203. *See also* Los Angeles Raiders

Oakland Tribune, 79, 86

Olbermann, Keith, 188, 189

Oliver, Chip, 51, 106

Olsen, Jack, 212, 214, 221

Olsen, Phil, 62, 64

Olson, James, 26

Olson, Lisa, 176, 177, 192, 195

Orange Bowl, 22

Orduna, Joe, 87

Oregon Statesman, 47

Orlando Sentinel, 108

Orwell, George, 104

Otto, Jim, 85

Outside the Lines, 188

Ovitz, Michael, 160

Owens, Jesse, 221, 231

Owens, R. C., 61

Owens, Terrell ("T. O."), 191, 210, 238, 242, 246–47; as author, 247

Page, Alan, 67, 74, 83, 91, 94, 101

Palmer, Carson, 241

Parcells, Bill, 249

Parks, Dave, 61

Parrish, Bernie, 57, 106

Pastorini, Dan, 86n

Patrick, Dan, 188, 189

Payton, Sean, 249

Payton, Walter, 102, 125, 126, 131, 210, 244

Peebles, Dick, 80

Pepe, Phil, 80

Percival, Mac, 92

Perry, William ("the Refrigerator"), 122, 126, 202, 241

Peters, Tony, 116

Philadelphia Eagles, 24, 31, 72, 73, 75–76, 152, 248

Philadelphia Inquirer, 75, 79, 86, 167, 245, 248

Philadelphia Sun, 247

Philbin, Gerry, 45

Phipps, Gerald, 75

Phipps, Mike, 86n

Pierce, Charles, 30

Pitts, Frank, 92

Pittsburgh Steelers, 40, 72, 74, 96

Playboy, 49, 53

Playmakers, 192

Plunkett, Jim, 86n

Plunkett, Sherman, 42

Podolak, Ed, 67, 84

Polls, 7, 81, 82–83, 127, 134, 138, 177, 185–86, 251

Pope, Edwin, 70, 72, 77, 79, 80, 89, 100

Portland Oregonian, 173

Powell v. NFL. See National Football League Players Association: and *Powell* decision

Pritchard, Ron, 89

Promise Keepers, 201

Pros and Cons (Benedict and Yaeger), 194

Prothro, Tommy, 68

"Purple People Eaters" (Minnesota Vikings defensive line), 109, 202

Radovich v. NFL, 57

Ralston, John, 74, 75

Randle, John, 237n

Rather, Bo, 89

Reaves, Ken, 75, 92

Reed, Rex, 49

Reese, Don, 106, 107–8, 115, 192, 195

Reeves, Dan, 12

Reid, Mike, 71

Reilly, Kevin, 89

Renfro, Mel, 85

Rentzel, Lance, 85, 107

Replacements, The (film), 134n

Reston, James, 51

Retzlaff, Pete, 57

Rhoden, William, 219, 236, 238, 248

Rice, Condoleezza, 199

Rice, Grantland, 199

Rice, Jerry, 124, 210, 216–17

Richardson, Jack, 49

Ridge, Houston, 106–7

Riggins, John, 125

Riley, Clayton, 231, 236

Riley, Ken, 93

Ringo, Jim, 10

Rison, Andre, 232

Rivers, Philip, 254

Robbie, Joe, 56, 81, 132

Roberts, Archie, 122n

Roberts, Randy, 26

Roberts, Selena, 249

Robinson, Eddie, 212

Robinson, Jackie, 231

Roesler, Bob, 132n

Rogers, Don, 117

Rogers, George, 109

Romanowski, Bill, 202, 206

Romo, Tony, 254

Rooney, Art, 72, 96

Rooney, Dan, 219, 244

Rosenbloom, Carroll, 73, 75, 98, 132; as gambler, 13, 47

Roussel, Tom, 76

Roy Rogers Enterprises, 3, 150, 175

Rozelle, Pete, 3, 7, 8, 11–28, 104, 110, 129, 140, 142, 162, 175, 176, 179, 239, 250, 251; and television, 3, 12, 25; election of, 11; and "modern NFL," 11, 12–13; and public relations, 11, 14, 48, 116, 137, 139; and NFL Films, 12, 14, 15; and Congress, 12, 20–21, 57, 105; and NFL Properties, 12–13; and war with American Football League, 13, 19–21; and Super Bowl, 13, 21–22; and fining or suspension of players, 13, 47–48, 73, 95–96, 106–7, 115–16, 118, 243; and concern for the game's image, 13–14, 107, 116, 139, 176; and Al Davis, 21, 98, 99; and football as entertainment, 28; and labor conflict, 59, 62, 64, 109–10, 113, 136; resignation of, 96, 136; legacy of, 136–39

Rozelle Rule, 61, 62, 63, 64, 65, 100, 101, 102, 103

Rudnay, Jack, 84, 92, 93

Russell, Bill, 212

Ryan, Buddy, 95, 125

Ryan, Tim, 289 (n. 105)

Saban, Lou, 94

Sabol, Ed, 14–15, 17

Sabol, Steve, 15–16, 17, 26, 187; artistic influences on, 15–16;

St. John, Bob, 88

St. Louis Cardinals, 40, 62, 72, 74, 76, 128, 131, 153; racial prejudice on, 212. *See also* Arizona Cardinals

St. Louis Post-Dispatch, 64

St. Louis Rams, 9, 23, 152, 159. *See also* Los Angeles Rams

Salary cap. *See* National Football League: and salary cap

Sample, Johnny, 106

San Diego Chargers, 68–69, 70, 73, 85, 106, 158, 176, 203. *See also* Los Angeles Chargers

San Diego Union, 69

San Francisco Chronicle, 131, 216

San Francisco Examiner, 53, 80, 131, 216

San Francisco 49ers, 11, 62, 72, 95, 104, 113, 116, 118, 151, 158, 163, 203

Sanders, Barry, 210, 244

Sanders, Deion, 6, 29, 53, 165, 238; and racial prejudice, 213; and "Prime Time," 240, 241

Sapp, Warren, 202, 241

Saturday Evening Post, 2, 42

Sayers, Gayle, 10, 77, 125

Schaap, Dick, 35, 37

Schickel, Richard, 37

Schmidt, Joe, 2, 215

Schnellenberger, Howard, 94

Schottenheimer, Marty, 243

Schramm, Tex, 20, 134, 137, 138, 150, 151

Scibelli, Joe, 83, 85

Scott, Jake, 70, 78–79

Scripps Howard News Service, 122

Seabrook, John, 180, 181, 182, 197, 198, 199, 206, 207

Seattle Seahawks, 99, 129, 152, 153

Seiler, Earnie, 22

Senior Scholastic, 52

Sexual violence. *See* NFL players: and domestic or sexual violence

Seymour, Richard, 246

Shecter, Leonard, 36

Shell, Art, 218, 244

Shockey, Jeremy, 202, 238

Shropshire, Kenneth, 219

Shula, Don, 72

Silver, Michael, 202

Simmons, Chet, 105

Simmons, Oze, 231

Simms, Phil, 142

Simpson, O. J., 55, 64, 85, 125, 192, 195, 216, 223, 231

Singletary, Mike, 126, 215

Siragusa, Tony, 202–3, 205

Skorich, Nick, 94

Slater, Jackie, 233

Small, John, 87

Smith, Bruce, 210, 233, 238

Smith, Dave, 93

Smith, Emmitt, 210

Smith, Gary, 116

Smith, Jim ("Yazoo"), 101

Smith, Lovie, 244, 248–49, 254

Smith, Red, 67, 69, 77, 79, 80

Smith, Sandy, 47

Smith, Sid, 74

Smith, Steve, 242

Snead, Norm, 85

Snell, Matt, 45

Snow, Jack, 85

Snyder, Daniel, 163, 164, 165, 186

Snyder, Jimmy ("the Greek"), 220, 223

Spence, Sam, 17

Spielman, Chris, 197

Sport, 37

SportsBusiness Journal, 6, 23, 149, 152, 158, 160, 164, 166, 167, 173, 182, 251, 253

SportsCenter, 28, 187–89, 210; and storytelling, 188; and celebrity, 188, 241, 242, 243; and irony, 189, 205. *See also* ESPN

Sports Illustrated, 6, 13, 15, 32, 33, 40, 41, 43, 44, 45, 46, 92, 104, 106, 114–15, 136, 151, 179, 187, 188, 194, 195, 202, 205, 216, 222, 228, 230, 234, 239, 242; cover stories in, 24, 105, 107, 193, 208, 212, 221; on drugs, 105–6, 108, 116, 117, 118; on violence and injuries in football, 107, 121, 123, 208; on domestic and sexual violence, 193; on race and racism, 212, 217, 221, 223, 224, 225, 226

Sports talk radio, 201, 246

Spurrier, Steve, 86n

Stabler, Kenny, 85

Stadiums, 4, 149–62, 252; revenue from, 140, 149, 150, 153, 158; luxury suites in, 150, 158, 163; naming rights for, 158, 163; public funding of, 158–60; for New York, 160, 252; G-3 program for funding of, 160–61, 166, 250, 252; debts on, 164

Stallings, Larry, 85

Stallworth, John, 96

Stanfill, Bill, 70, 71

Starr, Bart, 10, 32, 34, 35, 36, 53

Staubach, Roger, 85, 88, 89

Stecher, Chris, 93

"Steel Curtain" (Pittsburgh Steelers defensive line), 202

Stemrick, Greg, 115

Stephenson, Dwight, 215

Stingley, Daryl, 120

Stone, Oliver, 7, 190

Strachan, Mike, 109

Stram, Hank, 53, 65, 86, 87, 92, 94

Strikes: in 1968, 53, 58; in 1970, 55, 58–59; in 1974, 4, 7, 8, 56, 60–94; in 1982, 4, 7, 8, 109–13; in 1987, 4, 7, 8, 95, 129–36. *See also* Labor conflict; National Football League Players Association

Stringer, Korey, 203

Strode, Woody, 211

Stronger Women Get, the More Men Love Football, The (Nelson), 196, 204

Sullivan, John L., 236

Sullivan, Prescott, 53

Summerall, Pat, 178

Sunday Night Football, 173, 187, 253. *See also* ESPN; National Broadcasting Company

Super Bowl, 6, 21–24; beginnings of, 21; television audiences for, 21, 96–97, 104; halftime shows at, 22, 97, 190–91, 255; and superpatriotism, 22–24; full emergence of, 95, 96–98; as advertisement for NFL, 98, 191; advertising in, 127–28; and "wardrobe malfunction," 190–91; mythology of, 192; in 1967 (I), 21, 22, 97; in 1968 (II), 21, 22; in 1969 (III), 21, 22, 38, 39, 40, 46–47; in 1970 (IV), 21, 22, 49, 97; in 1971 (V), 22; in 1972 (VI), 55, 97; in 1973 (VII), 22, 55; in 1976 (X), 97; in 1977 (XI), 28, 97; in 1978 (XII), 96, 98; in 1979 (XIII), 98, 232, 239; in 1981 (XV), 99; in 1982 (XVI), 96, 97, 104; in 1985 (XIX), 126; in 1986 (XX), 117, 126; in 1988 (XXII), 134, 216; in 1989 (XXIII), 118, 126, 216, 223; in 1990 (XXIV), 126; in 1992 (XXVI), 176, 178, 201; in 1993 (XXVII), 150; in 1994 (XXVIII), 150; in 1996 (XXX), 150, 216, 218; in 2002 (XXXVI), 23–24; in 2003 (XXXVII), 162, 206;

in 2004 (XXXVIII), 183; in 2005
(XXXIX), 245; in 2006 (XL), 184, 246;
in 2007 (XLI), 248–49.
Swann, Lynn, 96, 111
Sweeney, Walt, 73
Sweigert, William T., 101
Swift, Doug, 71, 72, 81, 89, 93

*Taboo: Why Black Athletes Dominate Sports
and Why We're Afraid to Talk about It*
(Entine), 224, 227
Tagge, Jerry, 86n
Tagliabue, Paul, 8, 23, 139, 140–41, 142,
153, 176, 177, 179, 180, 182, 195, 206,
250, 252, 256; election of, 137; retire-
ment of, 250; achievements of, 250–
51
Tampa Bay Buccaneers, 99, 152, 153
Tarkenton, Fran, 39–40, 85, 247
Tatum, Jack, 120
Taylor, Marshall ("Major"), 221
Taylor, Jason, 257
Taylor, Jim, 10, 125
Taylor, Lawrence, 95, 118, 120, 125–26,
129, 131, 203, 210
Taylor, Otis, 84
Teeuws, Len, 121, 124
Television, 2–3, 8, 135, 161, 167–74; NFL
revenues from, 4, 5, 111, 127, 134, 140,
152, 153, 173; NFL rights fees for, 12, 20
(AFL), 104, 168, 169, 170, 172–74;
NFL ratings for, 28, 124, 127, 134, 168,
174, 252–53, 253–54; network losses
on NFL for, 167, 172; male viewers of,
169, 170; and "intangibles," 171–72,
174. *See also* American Broadcasting
Company; Columbia Broadcasting
System; ESPN; Fox Broadcasting
Company; National Broadcasting
Company
Tennessee Titans, 9. *See also* Houston
Oilers

Theismann, Joe, 120, 289 (n. 105)
They Call It Pro Football (film), 16
Thomas, Duane, 107
Thomas, Joe, 73, 91, 94
Thompson, Norm, 110
Thompson, Steve, 87
Thrower, Willie, 215
Thurston, Fuzzy, 10
Tillman, Pat, 24–25n
Time, 2, 11, 32, 33, 37, 45, 112, 148, 177,
212, 224; cover stories in, 34, 97, 126,
202
Tittle, Y. A., 2, 50n
Tomczak, Mike, 224
Tomlin, Mike, 244
Tomlinson, LaDainian, 210, 244, 254
Tose, Leonard, 75
Twombly, Wells, 80
Trope, Mike, 110
True, 49
Trumpy, Bob, 71, 289 (n. 105)
Tucker, Bob, 85
Turner, Jim, 75, 76
Turner Network Television (TNT), 170;
rights fees paid by, 169
Tyrer, Jim, 84, 93; suicide of, 121

Underwood, John, 40, 106, 107, 123
Unitas, John, 2, 5, 10, 40, 50n, 64, 73,
208
United States Football League (USFL),
105, 129, 130, 136
Upshaw, Gene, 116, 129, 133, 135–36, 139,
143, 146, 148, 250, 252, 254
Urlacher, Brian, 257
USA Today, 127, 224, 225, 226, 229–30
Utley, Mike, 120

Valley, Wayne, 98
Van Brocklin, Norm, 54, 68n, 75, 91, 94,
121
Van Buren, Steve, 77

Vecsey, George, 131, 133
Verdin, Clarence, 240–41
Vick, Michael, 218, 244, 245, 247, 248
Violent World of Sam Huff, The (television special), 2
Vogue, 50

Walker, Herschel, 104
Wall Street Journal, 172
Wallace, Bob, 243
Wallace, William, 58
Walsh, Bill, 30, 95, 104, 125, 131, 216, 243
Walt Disney Company, 97, 187
Walton, Wayne, 84, 93
Ward, Hines, 254
Warfield, Paul, 56, 69, 223
Warner, Curt, 125
Washington, Chris, 208
Washington, Kenny, 211
Washington, Vic, 53, 85
Washington Post, 79, 130, 148, 161, 163, 184, 198, 243, 245; front-page stories in, 192, 193
Washington Redskins, 5, 24, 31, 38, 62, 72, 74, 101, 131, 134, 152, 160, 162, 163–64, 165, 176, 177–78, 211
Waters, Charlie, 85, 88
Waymer, David, 118
Webster, Mike, 96, 131, 206–7, 209
Werblin, David A. ("Sonny"), 20, 41, 44
Werner, Clyde, 84
White, Charles, 109, 117, 118
White, Danny, 131
White, Dwight, 96

White, Randy, 131
White, Reggie, 143, 218
Wilbon, Michael, 148, 184, 243, 245, 247, 248
Wilbur, John, 76, 92
Williams, Del, 83, 92
Williams, Doug, 216
Willis, Bill, 211
Wilson, John, 90
Wilson, Stanley, 118
Wind, Herbert Warren, 34
Winslow, Kellen, 124, 125
Winter, Max, 72
Wood, Willie, 10, 34
Woods, Elbert ("Ickey"), 232, 233, 238, 239–40
World Football League (WFL), 56, 69, 70, 73
World Wrestling Entertainment (WWE), 200, 239, 256
Wright, Elmo, 232, 233, 234, 238
Wyche, Sam, 176–77

Yaeger, Don, 194
Young, Buddy, 231
Young, Dick, 78, 80
Young, Steve, 50n, 120, 247
Young, Vince, 247, 248
Young, Wilbur, 83
Younger, Tank, 211

Zeno, Coleman, 69
Zimmerman, Paul, 114